**Institutional Economics and the Theory of Social Value: Essays in Honor of Marc R. Tool**

# Institutional Economics and the Theory of Social Value: Essays in Honor of Marc R. Tool

edited by
**Charles Michael Andres Clark**
Associate Professor of Economics
St. John's University
Jamaica, New York
USA

**Kluwer Academic Publishers**
Boston/Dordrecht/London

**Distributors for North America:**
Kluwer Academic Publishers
101 Philip Drive
Assinippi Park
Norwell, Massachusetts 02061 USA

**Distributors for all other countries:**
Kluwer Academic Publishers Group
Distribution Centre
Post Office Box 322
3300 AH Dordrecht, THE NETHERLANDS

---

**Library of Congress Cataloging-in-Publication Data**
Institutional economics and the theory of social value : essays in
honor of Marc R. Tool / edited by Charles Michael Andres Clark.
p. cm.
Includes bibliographical references and index.
ISBN 0-7923-9606-5
1. Institutional economics. 2. Economics--Sociological aspects.
3. Social values. 4. Value. 5. Social choice. 6. Tool, Marc R.
I. Tool, Marc R. II. Clark, Charles Michael Andres.
HB99.5.I564 1995
306.3--dc20 95-20398
CIP


---



*Printed on acid-free paper.*

Printed in the United States of America

## Contents

# Contributing Authors


Glen Atkinson
Department of Economics
University of Nevada-Reno
Reno, Nevada 89557-0016

Doug Brown
Department of Economics
Northern Arizona University
P.O. Box 15066
Flagstaff, Arizona 86011-5066

Paul D. Bush
Department of Economics
California State University
Fresno, CA 93740-0020

Charles M. A. Clark
Department of Economics
St. John's University
Jamaica, New York 11439

William M. Dugger
Economics Department
University of Tulsa
Tulsa, Oklahoma 74104-3189

Gladys Parker Foster
6468 S. Hudson St.
Littleton, Colorado 80121

Lewis Hill
Economics Department
Texas Tech
Box 41014
Lubbock, Texas 79409-1014

Philip A. Klein
Department of Economics
Pennsylvania State University
University Park, PA 16802

Edythe S. Miller
580 Front Range Road
Littleton, Colorado 80120

Warren J. Samuels
Department of Economics
Michigan State University
East Lansing, Michigan 48824

Jacqueline B. Stanfield
Department of Sociology
University of Northern Colorado
Greeley, Colorado 80639

J. R. Stanfield
Department of Economics
Colorado State University
Fort Collins, Colorado 80523

Rick Tilman
Department of Public
Administration
University of Nevada-Las Vegas
4505 Maryland Parkway
Box 456026
Las Vegas, Nevada 89154-6026

Roger Traub
Department of Economics
Texas Tech
Lubbock, Texas 79409-1014

Harry Trebing
Department of Economics
Michigan State University
East Lansing, Michigan 48824

William T. Waller
Department of Economics
Hobart & William Smith Colleges
Geneva, New York 14456

Charles J. Whalen
Jerome Levy Economics Institute
Bard College
Annandale-on-Hudson, New York
12504-50000

# Preface

Marc R. Tool, both through his writings and his editorship of the *Journal of Economic Issues*, has had a profound influence on institutional economics. Tool's efforts, in his own words, "has been to keep values on the agenda of economic inquiry," which is another way of saying "keep economic inquiry relevant." Tool's work on the theory of social value and instrumental valuation has helped to keep institutional economics focused on the core economic and social issues facing society, providing both a perspective from which to analyze the economy and a criteria for evaluating outcomes. This collection of essays is a testament to this legacy. Although these 15 chapters cover a wide and diverse range of topics, it is the common themes which are most striking: the inescapable necessity of values in economic discourse; the central role of valuation in economic activity; and most importantly, the requirement of democratic participation to achieve "efficient" solutions to the economic problem.

These essays are offered to honor a body of work, a set of ideas, but mostly a man who, by directing economic inquiry to these core issues, has promoted "the continuity of human life and the noninvidious recreation of community through the instrumental use of knowledge."

The editor would like to thank all the participating authors for their contributions, and the numerous AFEE members who gave suggestions which helped to improve this volume, especially Warren Samuels, without whose early encouragement this book would not have been started, muchless completed, and Paul Bush, who undertook the enormous task of summarizing Tool's career and ideas, and who also gave considerable encouragement through out this project.

The staffs at St. John's University, New York, and University College Cork, Cork, Ireland, both provided the author with considerable assistance and technical support, and thus deserve recognition.

# 1. MARC R. TOOL'S CONTRIBUTIONS TO INSTITUTIONAL ECONOMICS

Paul D. Bush[1]

After a period of over twenty years in which institutionalists found it virtually impossible to get their books published or their articles accepted by professional journals, the literature of institutional economics began to expand dramatically in the mid-1970s.[2] The establishment in 1966 of the Association for Evolutionary Economics (AFEE) finally made it possible for institutionalists to meet on an annual basis to encourage institutionalist research and to provide a forum for its critique. The papers presented at the annual meetings of AFEE began to appear regularly in AFEE's *Journal of Economic Issues*, which was launched in 1967. In 1979, the Association for Institutional Thought (AFIT) was organized, creating a second professional forum for institutional thought.[3]

Marc R. Tool was a founding member and the first president of AFIT. In his presidential address, "The Compulsive Shift to Institutional Analysis," he set forth his optimistic belief that

> [t]he economist's abiding commitment to develop and apply theory which is relevant, directly or indirectly, to the great issues and problems of the day, is driving economists out of orthodoxy to positions similar to or compatible with the positions institutional economists have been evolving over this century.[4]

Whether or not the compulsive shift to institutional analysis as he conceives it is underway among orthodox economists, there can be no question of Marc Tool's commitment to the expansion of the institutionalist literature. His contributions to institutional economics have been fundamental. Through his writings—particularly *The Discretionary Economy* (Tool 1979)—and through his ten-year editorship of the *Journal of Economic Issues* (1981-1991), Tool has offered both a programmatic agenda for the development of institutional thought and the editorial leadership necessary to encourage and refine the institutionalist research program in the United States and abroad. Any assessment of his contributions to institutional economics must consider both of these dimensions of his professional endeavors.

## Beginnings: The University of Denver and J. Fagg Foster

In his remarks upon receipt of the Veblen-Commons Award, Tool made the following observation:

> Unlike the career of Gardner C. Means, among others, whose intellectual commitment to an institutionalist perspective was a gradual transformation extending over some years, my own self-identification as an institutionalist was more in the nature of a "conversion" following exposure after just a few months, as a very young graduate student, to the ideas of John Fagg Foster at the University of Denver.[5]

Tool was one of many students whose career was influenced by Foster's teaching.[6] Beginning with his doctoral dissertation, Tool's scholarly contributions present a systematic documentation and extension of Foster's ideas. Since Foster wrote very little, much of what the profession at large knows of Foster's views is derived from Tool's interpretation of his work.[7] But while Foster's ideas constitute the intellectual foundation upon which Tool bases his own work, due recognition must be given to the fact that Tool's writings incorporate creative contributions that move the institutionalist agenda beyond the point that Foster had taken it by the time of his death.

Marcus Reed Tool, the third son in a family of four children, was born on August 3, 1921, in Murdock, Nebraska. His father was a retail lumber dealer. Hard times in rural Nebraska during the Great Depression forced the Tool family in 1935 to resettle in Denver, Colorado. Tool entered the University of Nebraska in 1939, but in 1941 he transferred to the University of Denver, where he pursued an undergraduate degree in economics and finance. The coursework for the B.S. degree was essentially finished in early 1943 when he was called to active duty in the armed forces.[8]

He volunteered for the U.S. 10th Mountain Division (infantry) and underwent mountain and ski combat training at Camp Hale, Colorado. In 1945 he served as a combat platoon leader in the 10th Mountain's Apennine and Po Valley campaigns in Northern Italy during the last three months of the war. In those campaigns the 10th Mountain Division suffered heavy losses in some of the bloodiest battles of the war. He has remarked that his combat experience in Northern Italy forced him come to terms with his own mortality. His military experience may also have predisposed him to a life-long opposition to the use of invidious distinctions in human affairs. The words he wrote many years later in a eulogy for his dear friend and colleague, John C. (Jack) Livingston, would appear to capture his own emerging views precisely: "As a battlefield-commissioned infantryman in World War II, he came early to distinguish between military pomp (quest for status and rank) and actual circumstances (the leveling realities of combat)" (Tool 1981c).

In 1946 Tool reentered the University of Denver to pursue a masters degree in political economy and education. His undergraduate and graduate training in economics was rigorously neoclassical in every respect. It was not until he had nearly finished his master's degree that he met J. Fagg Foster and received his first exposure to institutional economics. From 1948 through 1951, Tool took courses (by audit and for credit) taught by Foster, and he worked with him as a teaching colleague in the interdisciplinary undergraduate course entitled the "Problems of Modern Society." By the time he began working on his doctorate at the University of Colorado, he was a committed institutionalist.

Tool began working with Foster during a propitious moment in the history of the University of Denver. From the late 1940s through the late 1950s, the University of Denver had in its social sciences and philosophy faculty a group of unusually dedicated and talented teachers. J. Fagg Foster was the senior member of this group. In addition to Tool, the group included Francis M. Myers in philosophy,[9] Fritz Freitag and Jack Livingston in political science, and Charles Merrifield in social science. They came together in the formulation and teaching of the "Problems of Modern Society."[10] The members of this group shared an interest in working out Dewey's pragmatic instrumentalist philosophy in the field of political economy. Under Foster's guidance, the Deweyan perspective was integrated with the Veblen-Ayres's version of institutional analysis. This was a heady intellectual brew to pour into the undergraduate curriculum, but given the unusual teaching abilities of the members of the group, the "Problems of Modern Society" was one of the most successful interdisciplinary general education courses undertaken at the University of Denver in the immediate post-World War II period.

A critical dimension of their pedagogy was the desire to help students emancipate themselves from ideological preconceptions, absolutisms, and other forms of dysfunctional thinking. While they were intent on demonstrating that ideas have consequences, they tried to teach their students not to be fearful when confronting new ideas, no matter how threatening they might appear to be. Equally important, they taught their students to respect dissent from their own views and to refrain from drawing invidious distinctions of the "us" versus "them" variety. Given the poisoned ideological climate of the times, this was courageous teaching.

## Launching an Academic Career in the Age of McCarthyism

The decade in which Marc Tool pursued his advanced degrees and began his career as a teacher and scholar was also the age of McCarthyism. The ideological vigilantism that was the *modus operandi* of McCarthyism had a devastating impact on institutions of higher learning throughout the United States. Mandatory loyalty oaths and political purges of the faculties became all too common in universities across the nation. And even on those campuses that were spared the most egregious academic atrocities, the insidious influence of McCarthyism caused administrators to become timid in their defense of academic freedom and the faculty to engage in self-censorship as a mode of survival.

By the mid-1950s most of the Marxians had gone underground, and they were no longer easily identified on university faculties. Many who did remain in academia took on the protective coloration of the mainstream in order to ride out the storm. Institutionalists were among the few visible economists remaining on the campuses who openly challenged the conventional wisdom of the American Business Creed. By virtue of such self-confessed subversive ideas they became targets of opportunity for witch-hunters bent on purging higher education of ideological impurities.

J. Fagg Foster had always been a vigorous advocate of the view that intellectual freedom is the indispensable foundation of democracy and that academic freedom is the foundation of the process of inquiry in institutions of higher learning. He believed that it was the obligation of the university to recognize these fundamental truths and to assume the responsibilities they entailed. One of those responsibilities was the open recognition that the university's mission in a free society was to probe the values of the existing institutional structure and hold them up to critical scrutiny. As Tool (1989, p. 327) put the matter in 1989,

> [t]here is a very real sense in which the university must be a threat to received doctrines and to the institutional power systems these doctrines sanction. That critical role cannot be provided unless free inquiry exists. Support for ideas and belief systems cannot be commanded by coercive authority; it must be sought through deliberative means in an appeal to reason. . . . . That some sacred tenet, conventional wisdom, or invidiously grounded power complex will be questioned or eroded is . . . a high probability. A university that does not promote heterodoxy has abandoned one of its primary instrumental functions.

Such ideas were, and continue to be, anathema to those, like the McCarthyites, who find it impossible to countenance dissent from their own ideological preconceptions and who will tolerate only that teaching which is consonant with them.

Most institutionalists would agree with the view expressed by Tool in the above passage. Accordingly, during the 1950s, they were often in the forefront of the struggles against the imposition of loyalty oaths and other academic tyrannies designed to suppress the teaching of unorthodox views in institutions of higher learning. For example, Clarence E. Ayres testified before the Texas legislature against the imposition of loyalty oaths on students and employees of the University of Texas. For this testimony and other public utterances critical of the ideology of free enterprise, Ayres became a target of the right-wing dominated Texas legislature. Breit and Culbertson (1976, p. 16) describe the incident as follows:

> By a vote of 130-to-1, the legislature announced that "we believe his presence [at UT] can contribute nothing to the culture and progress of this State." The sponsor of the bill labeled Ayres an "educational termite," and another member suggested that . . . Ayres should be expelled from the University faculty and action should be taken to deport him from the United States.

Ayres ultimately weathered the ideological storm and his job was saved in large part by the vigorous defense mounted in his behalf by faculty and administrators at the University of Texas.[11]

Foster's struggle against anti-intellectual purges of the university began while he was still a graduate student and teaching assistant at the University of Texas. In June 1942 he was fired from the University of Texas for antagonizing powerful right-wing interests. Baldwin Ranson describes the episode as follows:

> In 1938, the House of Representatives created the Special Committee on Un-American Activities, known by the name of its chairman, Martin Dies (D-Texas). It concentrated on exposing "subversive" left-wing activities and attacked legislation such as the Fair Labor Standards Act, which the committee claimed contributed to U.S. military defeats. When a mass meeting was called in Dallas to protest application of that statute, especially its forty-hour week and overtime pay provisions, Foster attended in the company of Nelson Peach and Wendell Gordon, fellow instructors, and Valdemar Carlson, a visiting professor. The three instructors subsequently wrote a letter to the *Dallas News* criticizing the meeting; it was for that letter that the Regents refused to renew the instructors' contracts.[12]

Foster refused to be intimidated by this experience, and he continued to struggle against repressive ideological forces throughout his professional career.

He fought one such battle in behalf of his young colleague Jack Livingston. While on leave from the University of Denver, Livingston taught part-time at the University of Colorado. He became a victim of the McCarthyites when he was named on the floor of the Senate by State Senator Morton G. Wyatt of Lamar, Colorado, as one of several "subversives" teaching on the university faculty. In a shameful act of cowardice, the University Board of Regents knuckled under to the McCarthyites and fired Livingston and several others. At grave risk to his own reputation and career, Foster made a vigorous public defense of Livingston and condemned those who would engage in such assaults on academic freedom.

In a dramatic confrontation with Senator Wyatt during a one-on-one public debate at the University of Colorado, Foster emphatically refuted the disingenuous claims of "patriotism" and "love of country" that Senator Wyatt and the McCarthyites used as their justification for character assassination. Toward the end of the debate, Senator Wyatt pointed with pride to the fact that Senator Joseph McCarthy had offered $10,000 to anyone who could prove that he had wrongly accused anyone of being a subversive. Jack Livingston, sitting in the audience, called out in an angry voice, "Would you make the same offer, Senator?" Visibly shaken by such a bold and direct challenge, Senator Wyatt attempted a bit of humor by saying that he was not a wealthy man and couldn't offer even ten dollars. And Livingston responded, "Have you got five, Senator?"

Judging from the overflow crowd's enthusiastic response to Foster's performance, it was clear that those in attendance believed Foster had won the debate and exonerated Livingston. Nevertheless, both he and Livingston knew that Senator Wyatt's scurrilous accusations could easily destroy Livingston's career, as similar accusations had done in so many other instances in those dark days. Livingston returned to his academic post at the University of Denver, but the continuing controversy over his firing at the University of Colorado was an ordeal that ultimately proved to be too much of a strain on his family, and the following year (1954) he accepted a position on the faculty of Sacramento State College (now California State University, Sacramento).[13]

Having finished his Ph.D. in 1953, Tool was teaching at San Diego State College (now San Diego State University) when the Livingston case erupted. He was devastated by the injustice done to his dear friend. McCarthyism was no longer a topic that could be merely debated at an intellectual distance. It had become a very personal, brooding menace in his life. The Livingston case was the second instance in which the academic freedom of a friend and colleague had been violated by the McCarthyites. While Tool was working on his Ph.D. at Boulder, one of his very able instructors in philosophy, Morris Judd, was hounded both on and off campus with wild and contrived charges of communist leanings and insidious behavior. Tool testified in support of Judd's scholarly competence and intellectual integrity during administrative hearing held on the campus in the Judd case; but all efforts made in Judd's behalf came to no avail, and he was dismissed from the faculty. He left academe never to return. Most distressing to Tool was the fact that neither the general faculty nor any of the faculty organizations on campus came to Judd's defense. In failing to defend Judd's academic freedom, they forfeited their own.

Unhappily for Tool, the city of San Diego was a bastion of right-wing political extremism. This repressive political climate in the community contributed to ideological intolerance on the campus. Tool belonged to a relatively small group of "liberals" who were coming under increasingly obtrusive scrutiny by those on the campus who took it upon themselves to take care of such matters. Tool's colleagues in the Department of Economics, with one significant exception, were supportive. But the pattern of rumors, innuendoes, and allegations was all too familiar; and Tool resolved to find a less threatening professional environment. In 1955 he left San Diego to join the economics faculty at Sacramento State College.

**Institution-building, Advocacy, and Teaching**

The change of venue proved to be the beginning of an ascendant career. At Sacramento Tool was reunited with Jack Livingston who taught in the Department of Government. Working with Livingston and a creative group of faculty ranging across the disciplines of the arts and sciences, Tool helped to establish a new social science curriculum, a system of democratic self-governance on the campus, and an annual Social Science Forum patterned on the Colorado University model.[14] In the mid-1960s, he became actively involved in statewide faculty affairs and was elected president of the Association of California State College Professors (ACSCP), which was one of several organizations representing the professional interests of the faculties on the (then) nineteen campuses of the California State University System (CSU).

Tool became well-known throughout the state for his vigorous advocacy of collegial self-governance of institutions of higher learning, the necessity of protecting academic freedom and due process, and the need for increasing access to higher education for students of all racial, ethnic, and economic backgrounds.[15] On behalf of ACSCP, he publicly challenged then newly-elected Governor Ronald Reagan's "multi-faceted assault on higher education" (Tool 1992, p. 587). His was one of only a few voices raised against the repressive educational policies of the immensely popular governor. Over the years, Tool supported faculty leaders who laid the foundation for a system of academic due process in the CSU that was ultimately enacted into law. Today the grievance and disciplinary action procedures available to CSU faculty—now reinforced by collective bargaining agreements—provide some of the strongest protections in the nation to faculty who become the targets of those who would deny them their academic freedom. In recognition of his academic leadership, the Statewide Academic Senate commissioned Tool to do a comprehensive study of the comparative support levels in California higher education. The book he produced, *The California State Colleges Under the Master Plan* (Tool 1966) became a standard reference for academics, politicians, and others interested in understanding the funding complexities of the system of higher education in the State of California.

In spite of all of the rough and tumble of the academic politics he was caught up in during his years of campus and statewide academic leadership, Tool was known to both ally and adversary as a person of uncommon civility and good humor who refused to carry personal grudges or to engage in drawing invidious distinctions between "us" and "them." Whether tending to small details or formulating broad agendas, Tool practiced the instrumentalist ethic he was later to elaborate as the "social value principle." The leadership skills he developed in this phase of his career served him well years later during his tenure as editor of the *Journal of Economic Issues.*

Except for those years in which he received released time to edit the *Journal of Economic Issues*, Tool carried the standard CSU teaching load of twelve units per semester. As burdensome as the teaching load was, he never lost his enthusiasm for working with students. Long before he began publishing, he mastered the "lecture method" of Fagg Foster, which Tool believed Foster had demonstrated "could be an exceedingly effective means of instruction" (Tool 1989, p. 329). Successive generations of students sang Tool's praise as a teacher, and in 1982 he was awarded the Phi Kappa Phi Outstanding Faculty Award at CSU, Sacramento. He retired from teaching in 1991, the same year in which he retired as editor of the *Journal of Economic Issues.*[16]

**The Emergent Scholar: The Importance of Tool's Doctoral Dissertation**

The fact that institutionalists were recognized both within the profession and without (particularly among college and university administrators) as being easy prey for the witch-hunters during the McCarthy period did not make them any easier to hire, retain, or promote. No matter how committed in principle the university might be to the cause of academic freedom, hiring such people exposed the institution to a public relations nightmare if conservatives on the campus or in the community got wind of their ideas. Fortuitously, certain developments within the economics profession made it much easier to rationalize the exclusion of institutionalists from the faculty, particularly in doctoral programs. By the 1950s, economics had become positivist in its methodology, mathematical in its theoretical formulations, econometric in its empirical analysis, and predominantely neoclassical in its conception of the legitimate scope of the discipline. Institutional economics had come to be viewed by mainstream economists as falling outside the permissible limits of scientific discourse. This provided an apparently antiseptically clean rationale for excluding institutionalists from the faculties of "first rate" economics departments.

According to the prevailing view, the exclusion of institutionalists did not involve ideological intolerance; it was simply a straightforward matter of ensuring the professional competency of the economics faculty. Consequently, as institutionalists retired from the doctoral faculties, they were not replaced by other institutionalists. Graduate students who professed an interest in institutional economics were discouraged from pursuing the subject on the grounds that to do so would deflect them from learning "real" economics upon which their careers would ultimately depend. This view, of course, continues to prevail in the profession. The economic journalist David Warsh recently captured this mind-set with deadly accuracy in the following words:

> E. Roy Weintraub writes on neoclassical economics, which he says is a category that includes almost all the schools of mainstream economics. A few fundamental tenets hold together the neoclassical view, says Weintraub, professor of economics at Duke: that people are rational, that they maximize utility (as corporations maximize profits) and that they act independently on the basis of full and relevant information. Those who reject this core of assumptions about the effects of incentives are regarded by neoclassicals as "defenders of lost causes or kooks, misguided critics and antiscientific oddballs" (Warsh 1993).

By the end of the 1950s, the number of doctoral programs permitting the study of institutional economics had declined precipitously.[17] With the decline in the study of institutional economics at the doctoral level and the increasing isolation of those institutionalists who remained on graduate faculties, the capacity for research in the field diminished significantly. The resulting decline in scholarly output, and the profession's lack of interest in what was being produced, combined to create the void alluded to above in the publication of institutionalist books and articles from the early 1950s to the early 1970s.

This state of affairs discouraged Tool from trying to get his doctoral dissertation published. Furthermore, once he arrived at Sacramento, the challenges of academic leadership combined with his heavy teaching load crowded out time that might have been devoted to research and writing. It was not until the early 1970s, almost twenty years after the completion of his dissertation, that he was able to engage in systematic scholarly inquiry. Had his dissertation been published in the 1950s, the influence of his thinking on the development of institutional economics would have been greatly accelerated.

The dissertation, entitled "The Philosophy of Neo-Institutionalism: Veblen, Dewey, and Ayres," presents a creative synthesis and extension of the Veblen, Dewey, Ayres (and Foster) line of institutional economics.[18] As soon as it was completed, word of its existence spread rapidly among Foster's current and former students, and it immediately became an underground classic to those who had an opportunity to read it. Louis J. Junker, who was then a graduate student at the University of Wisconsin, was so impressed with Tool's dissertation that he arranged to have the wives of several fellow students retype it on ditto masters. Fifty copies were run off and distributed to friends around the country.[19]

It is not generally known that it was Marc Tool who coined the term "neoinstitutional" economics. The terminology appears for the first time in the institutionalist literature in Chapter 1 of his dissertation, where Tool offers the following self-conscious apology for adding yet another piece of terminology to the overburdened lexicon of economics.

> The writer owes the profession an apology, perhaps, for the coinage of yet another term to describe a pattern of economic and philosophical ideas. However, there seems to be no alternative term which accurately connoted the intended meaning here. "The New Economics" is typically used to refer to Keynesian economics. "The American Contribution to Economic Thought" is too inclusive a term. "Institutionalism-instrumentalism" is barbarous. Hence, indulgence is requested for the use of "neoinstitutionalism" (Tool 1955, p. 4, footnote 1).

As brash as it may have been for a doctoral candidate to offer a new piece of terminology to the profession, Tool proceeded systematically throughout the remainder of the dissertation to demonstrate the need to identify this new configuration of ideas with appropriately distinctive nomenclature.

Tool used the term again in another unpublished manuscript in 1965. It was titled "Freedom and Justice: A Neo-institutionalist View."[20] This was an article John Gambs requested he write for a book of invited essays that Gambs and Allan Gruchy were putting together on the contemporary state of institutional economics. The working title of the project was "Symposium of the Association for Evolutionary Economics." They had gathered between eight and ten articles for the book, including one written by David Hamilton. Gambs and Gruchy tried for two years to get any one of a number of publishers to accept the book. But they were unsuccessful, and the project was finally abandoned in 1967. Such were the publishing fortunes of institutionalists from the early 1950s to the early 1970s.

But if the term "neo-institutionalism" was coined in Tool's unpublished manuscripts, how did it find its way into the published literature? It was Louis J. Junker who first used the term in print in his 1968 article in the *American Journal of Economics and Sociology*, entitled "Theoretical Foundations of Neo-Institutionalism" (Junker 1968). In the first footnote of this article he cites Tool's dissertation as the source of the terminology (Ibid., p. 198). The first time the term appears in the *Journal of Economic Issues* is in Allan Gruchy's 1969 presidential address to AFEE (Gruchy 1969, p. 5). Gruchy leaves the impression that he was unaware that the term had been used before since he offered no citation in attribution to others, let alone Tool, either in this article or in his 1972 book, *Contemporary Economic Thought: The Contributions of Neo-Institutional Economics*.[21] Yet as the previous paragraph shows, Gruchy had earlier attempted to publish Tool's article for which Tool used the term "neo-institutionalism" in the title. Thus, Gruchy's failure to credit Tool with originating this terminology is puzzling, for Gruchy was always absolutely scrupulous in giving credit where credit was due. It appears that this was simply an instance in which he was uncharacteristically forgetful.

The question of who first coined the term "neoinstitutionalism" is a minor matter at best. What is significant are the philosophical insights Tool and

Gruchy bring to their treatments of neoinstitutionalism. Tool uses the term to designate the integration of the earlier institutional analysis of writers such as Veblen with John Dewey's philosophy of instrumentalism. Both Gruchy and Tool credit Clarence E. Ayres with this "creative fusion" (Tool's usage). But they give contradictory interpretations of what this integration accomplished. According to Tool, "[t]he distinguishing attribute of this neo-institutional analysis is its concern with the theory of social value" (Tool 1953, p. 4). As his dissertation clearly demonstrates, Tool's conception of the "theory of social value" is premised upon the instrumentalist rejection of the normative-positive dualism. Gruchy, on the other hand, states quite flatly that "Ayres's instrumental economics is not a normative science."[22] Throughout his entire discussion of neoinstitutionalism, Gruchy relies on a diligent observance of the normative-positive dualism without any apparent awareness that the dualism is fundamentally incompatible with the Dewey-Ayres view of the role of values in inquiry and in policy formation.[23] For institutionalists of the instrumentalist persuasion, particularly the students of J. Fagg Foster, Gruchy's 1972 treatment of neoinstitutionalism has always been viewed with a certain uneasiness.[24] In his last major treatise on institutional economics, written in 1987, Gruchy renders a commentary on the work of Ayres and Tool that is based on a much better understanding of their conception of the role of values in inquiry (Gruchy 1987, pp. 69-85). He clearly recognizes the import of Tool's use of the term "neoinstitutionalism" where he refers to Tool's "neoinstitutionalist or social value theory" (Ibid., p. 84). But even in this work, he seems not to have fully comprehended the methodological and substantive implications of Tool's "social value principle."[25]

But we cannot leave the question of the attribution of the term "neoinstitutionalism" without noting a peculiar development in the contemporary use of the term. There appears to be a European penchant to use the term "neoinstitutionalism" to refer to the "new (neoclassical) institutional" economics, even though Americans have used the term to identify a specific phase of the "old institutional" economics since 1953. See, for example Eggertsson (1990). The emergence of the term "new institutional" economics produces enough terminological mischief without the addition of "neoinstitutionalism." Since "neoinstitutionalism" has had a forty year history of usage in the American literature, it is utterly destructive to terminological clarity for the "new institutionalists" to use the term to refer to a point of view fundamentally different from that to which the term originally applied.

Most of the major themes of Marc Tool's mature scholarly output are fully anticipated in his dissertation. Accordingly, a brief revue of the organization of the dissertation is instructive. After a masterful review of the origins of neoinstitutionalism, Tool devotes one chapter each to the neoinstitutionalist theories of knowledge and human nature. Then he devotes a chapter to the theory of social change, which leads directly to the chapter on the theory of social value. He concludes the dissertation with a discussion of the implications of neoinstitutionalism for a reconsideration of a variety of theoretical and applied problems of contemporary interest in the mainstream literature.

A number of specific elements of his thesis are worth mentioning in passing. In contrast to the neoclassical view that rationality consists in constrained maximization, he identifies the neoinstitutionalist conception of rationality as the capacity of the individual to comprehend means-ends relationships. This rational capacity makes it possible for the individual to assess the consequences of his/her actions for him/herself, and, most importantly, for the community at large. This is a key concept in explaining how the individual, who has habituated traditional patterns of behavior, can become an agent in changing those traditions.

Tool also sets forth a pragmatic-instrumentalist theory of knowledge based on Dewey's *Logic: The Theory of Inquiry* (Dewey 1938). Anyone reading this discussion today can see very clearly that the rejection of logical positivism was inherent in the neoinstitutionalist literature from its inception. In contrast to mainstream writers such as Donald N. McCloskey who have finally rejected positivism fairly late in their careers,[26] neoinstitutionalists were never seduced by the positivist conception of science and its strict reliance on the normative-positive dualism. Having rejected the normative-positive dualism, Tool shows how neoinstitutionalists arrive at the belief that scientific inquiry in economics necessarily involves normative judgments. This is a methodological proposition that continues to cause controversy not only in the philosophy of science and mainstream economics, but also and among some institutionalists. Nevertheless, it is this normative thrust of neoinstitutionalist methodology that makes possible the straightforward development of social value theory. This can be most clearly seen in Tool's discussion of the progression of social value theory from Veblen through Ayres to Foster.

In his treatment of Veblen, Tool presents a *normative* Veblen whose value theory drives his powerful analysis of institutions and institutional change. Equipped with this normative reading of Veblen, Tool analyzes the "Veblenian distinction" in its many manifestations with unusual clarity and insight.[27] He recognizes that his treatment of Veblen runs contrary to the interpretations of other scholars who take Veblen's pretense of "Olympian detachment" at face value.[28] Tool is very careful to point out that although Veblen's analysis of institutional structures rests upon a normative superstructure, Veblen never made that superstructure explicit, and, indeed, he appeared for whatever reason to be "blocked by the problem" of doing so (Tool 1953, p. 186). It is the solution to this problem that constitutes Ayres's major contribution to Veblenian scholarship. Using Dewey's theory of instrumental valuation, Ayres's makes explicit Veblen's theory of value. And it is the instrumental theory of valuation that Tool employs in his examination of the "Veblenian dichotomy."

Tool's reading of both Veblen and Ayres, as well as Dewey, was greatly influenced by Foster's teaching. It is in Tool's presentation of Foster's contributions to the theory of institutional adjustment that we get the first comprehensive view of the power of Foster's ideas and a clear statement of the differences between Ayres's and Foster's treatments of the institutional dichotomy. Whereas Ayres's contribution infused the Veblenian dichotomy with a clear distinction between "ceremonial" and "instrumental" value systems, he nevertheless continued to present the Veblenian dichotomy as one of "institutions" versus "technology." Foster differed with Ayres on this construction and argued that both ceremonial and instrumental practices were found in all institutional structures. Tool puts the matter this way:

> Institutions, since they are made up of habits, are essentially static and resistant to change. But as correlated patterns of prescribed behavior, they organize behavior around the performance of particular activities. Some of these activities or functions are designated as instrumental; other activities are called ceremonial or invidious. The former kind of activity in institutions incorporates the utilization of scientific knowledge in carrying on a necessary economic or social task. The latter kind of activity in institutions obstructs the former by the insistence upon the retention of judgments based upon power, prestige, tradition, rank, and the like, as these are obtained through the institution.[29]

It is this way of viewing the institutional dichotomy that informs all of Tool's later works.

Tool concludes the paragraph in which the above quotation appears with the observation that "[t]he inclusive economic problem is the adjustment of these institutions in such a fashion as to assure an expansion of the performance of instrumental functions" (Ibid., p. 253). This is an illuminating statement. It is, in a nutshell, what Ayres meant by the term "progress." It is also the foundation upon which Tool constructs his interpretation of the "social value principle." Moreover, it offers a definition of the "economic problem" that is fundamentally different than the notion of the "allocation of scarce resources among alternative uses." It defines the economic problem in a way that places institutional change at the center of economic inquiry. And the normative import of "instrumental functions" in this definition makes the normative character of economic inquiry unambiguous.

In his dissertation, Tool's discussion of what he calls the "social value criterion" relies on Foster's definition of the concept, which is: "the continuity and instrumental efficiency of the social process." Tool (Ibid., pp. 241-42) elaborates on the meaning and significance of this notion as follows:

> Not only is this conception of value process-oriented, it is conceptually consistent with the logic of the derivation of scientific truth. As we have seen, it is part and parcel of Dewey's formulation of "instrumental logic." It is a criterion that is logically fertile; it is capable of entering into the inquiry process as an integral and interacting part of that process. Indeed, it is the criterion of judgment employed when judgments are made in scientific procedures. The

> criterion of "the continuity and instrumental efficiency of the social process" is not simply a culturally accredited elevation of the mores. There is no subsumption of a given pattern of institutional structure in the criterion. It is, therefore, a criterion which may be used to judge *among alternative* institutional structures in the effort to resolve any problematic circumstances of a social character. It is, in fact, the criterion that has been utilized to advance the arts and sciences as a part of the social process. The technological process is a fact; its character is evidentially verifiable. Its significance is common knowledge. It is the locus of value.

This paragraph captures a number of profound themes that Tool would continue to elaborate and refine in his writings two decades later. In it he identifies the nonideological character of the social value criterion in the fact that it prescribes no particular institutional structure as the right and best way of organizing social activity. Most importantly the criterion is not derivable from some set of a priori rules; it is, instead, embedded in the problem-solving processes of the community. Methodologically, Tool claims that the process of scientific inquiry that permits us to determine empirically that this is the way communities do in fact "advance the arts and sciences" is the same process of inquiry that validates the use of this criterion in judging among policy alternatives. Herein lies the rejection of the normative-positive dualism, the fundamental philosophical tenet of what Tool (but not Gruchy) identifies as the diagnostic characteristic of "neoinstitutionalism." Tracing out the implications of this normative view of economic inquiry was to become the focus of all of Tool's future efforts as a scholar.

**Tool's Career as a Productive Scholar and Editor**

In 1959 Tool attended the Ford Foundation Summer Seminar for Faculty at the University of Oregon. He found himself among kindred spirits as approximately one third of the participants were instituitonalists.[30] The seminar was run by Raymond F. Mikesell and was focused on international trade and development theories. Of that experience Tool has written that "[i]n the course of assessing the explanatory capabilities of trade and development theories of neoclassical economics, I saw, even more clearly than before, the disjunction between neoclassical theory and reality" (Tool 1992, p. 588). He returned to Sacramento with the resolve to write an institutionalist critique of orthodox development theory. The working title of the project was "The Role of Ideology in Economic Development."

Tool's involvement in the governance of the California State University system over the next fifteen years prevented him from making substantial progress on the manuscript.[31] Eventually he refocused his research on broader issues having to do with the ideologies of the major schools of economic thought in the twentieth century. The working title was changed to "Yesterday's Isms—and Beyond." In this manuscript Tool offered a detailed analysis of the failure of the theories of fascism, socialism, and (neoclassically formulated) capitalism to produce credible social value principles that would answer the question: "Which way is forward?". In contrast to the "isms," Tool set forth the non-ideological neoinstitutionalist formulation of the social value principle.

By the mid-1970s he had produced a 1,700 page manuscript, which he sent to several publishers, one of whom distributed it to seventeen different reviewers. The general response was that the book was too long, and even though it was written in clear language, accessible to undergraduates, it fell between the cracks of textbook and treatise. Finally, Goodyear Publishing Company persuaded Tool to reduce the size of the manuscript by more than half. He did so by extracting and revising the institutionalist chapters. The new, reduced manuscript, which he entitled *The Discretionary Economy: A Normative Theory of Political Economy*, was published in 1979 by Goodyear. Two years later (on September 1, 1981), Tool became the editor of the *Journal of Economic Issues*.

Tool's rapid ascendancy to the editorship of the *Journal of Economic Issues* only two years after the publication of his first book is remarkable. It was due in part to the power of the ideas he set forth in *The Discretionary Economy* and in a cluster of his articles that appeared in print within a relatively short time frame before and after the publication of the book (Tool 1977, 1978, 1980a, and 1980b). It was also due to a series of circumstances that led to mounting disaffection within AFEE and the founding of AFIT.

In 1973 Allan Gruchy and John Gambs, both of whom had been driving forces in the formation of AFEE and had served as presidents of the organization, resigned their memberships in protest of Warren Samuels's editorial handling of the *Journal of Economic Issues*. They were also displeased with the failure of the Board of Directors to support a constitutional amendment that would state the organization's purpose in terms that they felt strongly should be articulated (Gambs 1980). In the late 1970s, Samuels's editorship once again came under fire from a number of "Western" institutionalists who believed that he was not as receptive to their submissions as he should have been; they also expressed concerns similar to those of Gambs and Gruchy concerning the general editorial drift of the *Journal of Economic Issues*.[32] Samuels responded sympathetically to these complaints and made a genuine effort to publish the work of the Western institutionalists as the quality of their manuscripts permitted. But the sense of alienation among some of the Western group motivated them to propose the creation of a new organization devoted to institutional thought. At the 1978 meetings of the Western Social Science Association (WSSA) in Denver, Colorado, they were joined by a larger group of institutionalists who were not necessarily displeased with AFEE, but who believed that the time was right for the founding of a second institutionalist association that would meet in conjunction with the WSSA. Institutionalists had long dominated the economics sessions presented at the WSSA meetings, and it seemed quite natural to recognize this fact by forming an official organization to sponsor these sessions. At the 1979 meetings of the WSSA at Incline Village (Lake Tahoe), Nevada, the Association for Institutional Thought was founded.

Louis Junker organized the economics sessions for the 1979 WSSA meetings, all of which were well-attended. But the one session that drew an overflow crowd was a panel discussion of Tool's *The Discretionary Economy*. The panel participants were John C. Livingston, Rick Tilman, F. Gregory Hayden, Baldwin Ranson, and William M. Dugger.[33] The present writer was the moderator, and Tool delivered a response to the reviewer's commentaries. The Goodyear Publishing Company made complimentary copies of *The Discretionary Economy* available to all in attendance. The reviewers' commentaries were highly favorable, and the ensuing dialogue between Tool, the reviewers, and the audience had a decidedly optimistic cast to it. As the meeting came to a conclusion, one was left with the distinct impression that Tool may well have produced a programmatic statement for a renaissance in neoinstitutionalist scholarship.

The next day during the organizational meeting at which the constitution of AFIT was drafted, Tool was enthusiastically elected as AFIT's first president. The following year, at the WSSA meetings in Albuquerque, he delivered his presidential address, "The Compulsive Shift to Institutional Analysis." This paper reinforced the general view that Tool had a remarkably clear vision of the potential for the future development of institutional economics. During his year as president of AFIT, the strains between the Western instituitonalists and the AFEE Board of Directors were virtually eliminated, and AFIT and AFEE formed close associational ties which have been maintained ever since.[34] In 1980 Tool was elected to the AFEE Board of Directors.[35] When Warren Samuels retired from the editorship of the *Journal of Economic Issues*, Tool was nominated for the position by President Walter C. Neale, and the AFEE Board of Directors overwhelmingly ratified his appointment.

During his tenure as editor, Tool encouraged institutionalists contributing to the *Journal of Economic Issues* to make explicit the foundations of institutional analysis that guided their work. He did not, however, insist that they adopt a "neoinstitutionalist" methodology as he valued too highly the creative diversity found within the institutionalist literature. In summing up Tool's work as editor, John Adams made the following observation:

> His selection of papers, nurturing of younger scholars, and solicitation of important contributions to the foundations of institutional thought are all laudatory and memorable features of his stewardship. The issues appeared in timely fashion and were produced to the best standards. As the primary voice of modern American evolutionary economics, the *Journal of Economic Issues* represented under Marc's guidance, the unity and diversity that are the strengths of the association.[36]

The "unity" of which Adams speaks is to be found in the tighter focus Tool gave to the *Journal of Economic Issues*. He achieved this by maintaining a continuing dialogue with his contributors, conducting, as it were, a seminar from his editorial chair.

Tool was disinclined to mandate general themes for given issues of the *Journal of Economic Issues*, preferring instead to allow the research interests of contributors to determine the menu. However, he did on two occasions put together sets of invited papers devoted to specific themes. The first set appeared in the March 1984 issue; it was later published in hardback as *An Institutionalist Guide to Economics and Public Policy* by M. E. Sharpe (Tool 1984). Beginning with Jerry L. Petr's lucid essay, "Fundamentals of an Institutionalist Perspective on Economic Policy" (Petr 1984, pp. 1-17), the articles in this volume offered a rich sampling of institutionalist thought on a broad range of important economic policy problems. The book was addressed to lay persons and professionals alike, and it makes a splendid textbook on institutional economics.

The second set of papers appeared in two issues of the *Journal of Economic Issues* in September and December 1987. This was an enormous undertaking both in size and purpose. It was Tool's intention to produce a two volume work that would serve as a comprehensive guide to contemporary American institutionalist thought. After they appeared in the *Journal of Economic Issues*, M. E. Sharpe published the essays in a two volume hardback set under the title *Evolutionary Economics* (Tool 1988b). For this project, Tool solicited fourteen papers on the "foundations of institutional thought" (which became Volume I) and sixteen papers on "institutional theory and policy" (Volume II). It took three years (1984-87) to bring the work to completion.[37] It was clear that each author carried a heavy responsibility for trying to "get it right." An opportunity to produce a work of this importance would not present itself again within the foreseeable future. Tool's solid editorial guidance, good humor, encouragement, and infinite patience prevented more than one author from throwing in the towel. The final product is, as Tool had hoped it would be, *the* definitive work on the contemporary state of institutional economics. It is probably his crowning achievement as editor of the *Journal of Economic Issues*.

Another facet of Tool's leadership while serving as editor of the *Journal of Economic Issues* was his personal effort to establish strong professional ties with European economists interested in the evolutionary/institutionalist research program. Beginning in 1981, Tool began making regular lecture tours throughout Europe. He gave lectures and held seminars on institutional economics in Austria, Denmark, France, Finland, the Netherlands, Sweden, Switzerland, and the United Kingdom. For several years Tool held discussions with American and European institutionalists about the desirability of the formation of a European association of institutional economists. Finally, William Melody, Director of the Programme on Information and Communication Technologies at the Economic and Social Research Council in London, and F.

Gregory Hayden of the University of Nebraska organized a conference for the purpose of bringing American and European institutionalists together to present papers and to consider the possibility of forming a European association of institutional economists. The conference was held at Grim's Dyke (London), June 26-29, 1988. Thirty-three scholars attended, including Tool.[38] It was at this conference that plans were laid for the formation of the European Association for Evolutionary Political Economy (EAEPE). Geoffrey M. Hodgson (United Kingdom), who later became the General Secretary of EAEPE, agreed to organize the founding meeting of the association. That meeting, which Tool attended, was held in Keswick, England in September 1989. From that meeting forward, Tool has been active in the affairs of EAEPE and has presented papers at all of its subsequent annual meetings.[39] Among his many accomplishments, Tool takes great satisfaction in the role he played in helping to develop an international community of institutionalist scholarship. At its 1994 meetings in Copenhagen, Denmark, the European Association for Evolutionary Political Economy awarded Tool a lifetime membership in recognition of his contributions to the founding and on-going support of the association.

In addition to his responsibilities as editor of the *Journal of Economic Issues*, Tool edited a number of other books which have significantly expanded the library of institutional economics. He coedited three books with Warren Samuels that were published by Transaction Publishers in 1989: *The Methodology of Economic Thought* (Tool and Samuels 1989a); *The Economy as a System of Power* (Tool and Samuels 1989b); and *State, Society, and Corporate Power* (Tool and Samuels 1989c). All three of these books provide easy access to important works in the institutionalist literature that otherwise would be difficult for many scholars with limited library resources to locate. Working with Geoffrey Hodgson and Warren Samuels, Tool collaborated in the editing of the *Elgar Companion to Institutional and Evolutionary Economics* (Hodgson, Samuels, and Tool 1994). This is a very ambitious undertaking. Unlike the three volumes mentioned above, this work contains 176 entries (in two volumes) written especially for this publication. Among the contributors to the *Elgar Companion* are North American, British, and European scholars ranging across a spectrum of schools of thought: American ("Old") Institutionalist, Austrian, European Evolutionary, and "New Institutionalist." The purpose of this publication is to provide succinct articles on ideas and issues raised by scholars who purport to take an "evolutionary" approach to economic analysis. Given the variety and complexity of the conflicting methodologies involved, this project posed formidable challenges to the editors who also wrote several of the entries.[40] Tool originally harbored serious reservations about the undertaking, but,upon finishing the page proofs, he was guardedly optimistic that an encyclopedic publication of this type may be helpful to scholars who are trying to sort out all of the conflicting theories and methodologies that appear under the "evolutionary" rubric.

**The Meaning and Significance of Tool's Social Value Principle**

What often seems missing in discussions of Tool's social value principle is a sufficient awareness of the philosophical foundations upon which the principle is grounded. The language in which the social value principle is expressed will mean very little to those who have not followed the intellectual route Tool has taken to arrive at its formulation. What, then, is the best way to read Tool? Perhaps the most helpful answer to this question is to raise another, namely: What would political economy look like if it were based on John Dewey's theories of value, logic, human nature, society, and democracy? The answer is that it would look very much like Tool 's treatment of political economy. Obviously this view is open to challenge. Given the vagaries of hermeneutics, there are, no doubt, alternative ways to interpret Dewey's philosophy for writing political economy. Indeed, there are those who claim that Milton Friedman's methodology of "positive" economics is based on Deweyan philosophy![41] But aside from such intellectual flights of fancy, the fact is that no other economist (institutionalist or otherwise) has made the consistent effort that Tool has to base political economic analysis over a broad range of issues on Deweyan foundations. Thus to read Tool correctly, one must take Dewey seriously. Standing on the shoulders of Ayres and Foster, Tool has seen better than most the potential for a political economy founded on John Dewey's philosophy.

From his dissertation forward, all of Tool's contributions to the literature of institutional economics are of a piece. One of the most important features of his work is that it is written consistently as *political economy*. When using this term to describe Tool's work, it should be noted that neither "political" nor "economy" should be read as the dominant term. In contrast to the prevailing tendency among mainstream economists, Tool draws no invidious distinction as to which is the Queen of the social sciences and which is merely a lady-in-waiting. It makes no sense to stress one word or the other in trying to determine what he really means by "political economy."

Accordingly, Tool does not write political economy as if it were a subtopic of economics in which all political considerations are interpreted as manifestations of the rationality principle, neoclassically conceived. When applied to political behavior, the neoclassical conception of rationality blinkers political thought in such a way as to make it impossible for the "rational" political agent to act in any way other than to further his or her own vested interests or the self-serving vested interests of those the agent represents. Working with an instrumentalist conception of rationality conceived in terms of the human agent's capacity to comprehend means-ends relationships and how his or her behavior relates to that of the community as a whole, Tool is able to discuss the instrumental efficiency of the political economic system in serving the life processes of the community at large. To put it in Veblenian terms, Tool's political economy makes it possible to conceive of individuals evaluating their behavior by the standard of "whether it furthers the life process taken impersonally" (Veblen 1975, p. 99).

To be able to think effectively about the individual's relationship to the community as a whole, John Dewey believed that we must employ the "method of intelligence." "Intelligence," he said, "is associated with *judgments*; that is with selection and arrangement of means to effect consequences and with choice of what we take as our ends" (Dewey 1929, p. 213; italics in the original). Dewey's theory of democracy is an elaboration of how such judgments, woven through the fabric of democratic processes, produce social outcomes that enhance the life processes of the community. Here, then, is one of the many conceptual bridges between Veblen and Dewey that Tool incorporates in his own approach to political economy.

These considerations illuminate Tool's use of the term "discretionary" in the title of his book as well as the meaning he attaches generally to the notion of the "discretionary economy." If human discretion is rational only in the sense attributed to it in the neoclassical paradigm, then economic actors cannot live in Tool's "discretionary economy" where institutional structures are matters of social choice, not merely the unintended consequences of a multitude of individual preferences expressed in pecuniary terms in the marketplace. Neither is Tool's concept of the discretionary economy compatible with the Austrian conception of "spontaneous order."[42] For Tool there is nothing "spontaneous" about the "recreation of community." While the so-called "new institutionalists" purport to set forth a theory of the evolution of institutional structures, which presumably involves the exercise of "discretion" in the selection of alternative institutional structures, their conception of the "rational choice" involved is based exactly on the same logic they were taught by their neoclassical teachers.[43] Tool's conception of the "discretionary economy" is based on the fundamental proposition that human nature is so constituted that democratic political economic processes make it possible for the individual to engage in rational choices that are free of the normative strictures imposed by the neoclassical logic of constrained maximization. Private choices based on the maximization of utility (uniquely conceived in the mind of the individual) cannot lead to a meaningful social value principle (formulated either cardinally or ordinally). Nor do private vices lead to public virtues. The "discretionary economy" is populated by human beings who can think rationally in terms of the community and can evaluate what will advance or retard the life processes of the community.

The word "normative" in the subtitle "A Normative Theory of Political Economy" is as natural as it is necessary to Tool's conception of political economy. Philosophically it flows directly from the pragmatic instrumentalist rejection of the normative-positive dualism; methodologically, it requires that any meaningful study in political economy must confront the necessity of formulating some sort of social value principle. This is, of course, a point-of-view rejected out of hand by mainstream economists who cling to what they construe as methodological positivism. It is also clear from the criticisms leveled at Tool's work by some prominent institutionalists that the rejection of the normative-positive dualism in institutionalist methodology is not a settled issue even among institutionalists.[44]

These observations bring the discussion directly to a consideration of the content of Tool's "social value principle." It will be recalled that in his dissertation he stuck very close to Foster's conceptualization of the "social value criterion"; which was stated as "the continuity and instrumental efficiency of the social process." In later years, Foster used the shorter term "developmental continuity" (Ranson 1980). By the time he wrote *The Discretionary Economy*, Tool had considerably expanded the meaning and significance of the social value principle in searching for an answer to the question: "Which way is forward? " In answering this question, he says: "We now affirm that that direction is forward which provides for the continuity of human life and the noninvidious recreation of community through the instrumental use of knowledge" (Tool 1979, p. 293). While this statement is roughly equivalent in meaning to Foster's notion of "developmental continuity," its language is more suggestive of the normative process entailed. In elucidating the meaning and significance of the social value principle, Tool has taken pains to discuss each term in the statement in order to show the analytical frame of reference from which it is derived.[45] No attempt will be made here to reiterate that discussion. But some thematic comments concerning his terminology are in order.

In general, it must be pointed out that Tool's social value principle arises within the context of the neoinstitutionalist theory of institutional change. Two propositions of that theory are critical to understanding Tool's language "the continuity of human life." The first is Tool's treatment of the institutional dichotomy. In recognizing that institutions are composed of both instrumentally warranted and ceremonially warranted patterns of behavior, Tool places emphasis on the crucial difference between the two with respect to their relation to the continuity of life processes of the community. Following Foster, Tool argues that the continuity of life is a function of instrumentally warranted behavior. "Continuity" is here associated with the notion of "development"; thus Foster's term "developmental continuity." Instrumental patterns of behavior embody the scientific knowledge and technological processes of the community, and, as such, they are inherently developmental, requiring changes in habitual patterns of behavior. Ceremonial patterns of behavior, on the other hand, are discontinuous in the sense that they take their warrant from invidious distinctions based on status and power relationships which enforce the status quo. Unlike instrumental patterns of behavior, which can be evaluated by the criterion of "instrumental efficiency," ceremonial patterns of behavior are amenable only to a standard of "ceremonial adequacy," which is itself mystified by the prevailing ideology. While ceremonial patterns of behavior often encapsulate instrumental activities, and attempt to imitate their causal efficacy, they cannot generate them. Furthermore, they will permit only those technological innovations that can be introduced into the institutional structure without dislocating the existing patterns of power and status.

The second important proposition underpinning Tool's social value principle is the concept of minimal dislocation. Among the important implications of this concept is the idea that the "continuity of human life" cannot be sustained if institutional change significantly dislocates existing patterns of instrumentally warranted behavior. Institutional changes that produce genuine progress in human affairs involve the displacement of ceremonially warranted patterns of behavior by instrumentally warranted patterns of behavior. But because of the ceremonial encapsulation of instrumental behavior within the institutional structure, the displacement of ceremonial patterns of behavior will entail the loss of some instrumental activities. Thus it is critically important that institutional changes be so designed as to minimize the dislocation of instrumentally warranted behavior.[46]

The language "noninvidious recreation of community" embodies Tool's view that democratic processes, which are of necessity noninvidious, are vital to the policy formation that leads to institutional changes which truly "recreate community." There is no simple way to summarize all of the arguments upon which this proposition rests except to say that it is the outcome of Tool's distillation of Dewey's philosophy of democracy. It should be noted with some emphasis that neither Dewey nor Tool contend that democratic processes guarantee progress. The case for democracy cannot be made on the basis of such a claim. The value of democracy lies it is capacity to identify past mistakes and to correct them. Similarly, the language "through the instrumental use of knowledge" should not be misinterpreted as a claim of infallibility. The "warranted assertions" that Tool, following Dewey, uses as the referent for the term "knowledge" are always open to critical reappraisal, modification, or rejection. It is always assumed that even the best scientific warrant for our beliefs never entails certainty. Consequently, Tool's social value principle should not be read as a road map to Nirvana.

With all of these disclaimers duly noted, what then can be said about the meaning and significance of Tool's social value principle? The best answer to this question, it would seem, is this: the meaning of the social value principle is to be found in the neoinstitutionalist theory of institutional change which identifies progressive institutional change as the displacement of ceremonial with instrumental patterns of behavior under conditions of minimal dislocation. Its significance lies in the fact that it provides a normative frame of reference for the conduct of policy formation in the community's problem-solving processes. In sum, Tool's social value principle is a processual construct for the discovery of relevant standards of judgment by which the community can correlate behavior. It is a normative proposition which states the relevant frame of reference for the formation of value judgments without mandating their specific content.

## A Concluding Observation on Marc Tool's Contribution

In recent years Tool has returned to a line of research he identified in his dissertation as a deficiency in the contemporary literature of neoinstitutional economics. As he noted in the dissertation, neoinstitutional economics has not developed an adequate "theory of price which explains the way in which prices are actually determined under modern industrial conditions" (Tool 1953, p. 286). His latest collection of essays attempts to lay a foundation for a sustained development of institutionalist research on this topic (Tool 1995). Thus, the research agenda laid out in his dissertation forty years ago continues to guide his lifelong inquiries into evolutionary/institutionalist economics.

In conclusion, it is fair to ask: What best summarizes Marc Tool's ongoing contributions to the literature of evolutionary/instituitonal economics? Tool himself may have provided the best answer to this question during a session at the 1991 EAEPE meetings in Vienna. At the conculsion of a long exchange with Geoffrey Hodgson on the role of values in economic inquiry, Tool made the following observation: "My main concern has been to keep values on the agenda of economic inquiry."[47]

## Notes

1. The author wishes to thank Gladys P. Foster, William M. Dugger, Edythe S. Miller, and Rick Tilman for their helpful comments on an earlier version of this chapter. They are absolved of all errors of fact and interpretation that remain. The author is also grateful to Marc R. Tool for making his personal papers available for use in the endeavor and also for the years of probing conversations and written exchanges on which much of this chapter is based.

2. Aside from John Kenneth Galbraith's steady output of publications, only a few important books were produced by American institutionalists over this period. Among them were: Averitt (1968), Ayres's two books (1952) and (1961), Dorfman, et al. (1963), Dowd (1958), Gruchy, (1972), Morse (1958), Seligman, (1967), and Thompson (1967). It is not merely a matter of coincidence that the publication dates of the original and revised versions of David Hamilton's important book bracket this twenty year interval, i.e., 1953 and 1973. See Hamilton (1953 and 1973). Among the few journals that continued to publish institutionalist articles on a regular basis during this period the *American Journal of Economics and Sociology*, under the editorship of Will Lissner, must be given special mention because of Lissner's unflagging support of institutionalist scholarship through thick and thin.

3. For a more detailed discussion of the recent history of institutional economics (from 1965 to 1990), see Bush (1991, especially pp. 321-29) and Sturgeon (1981).

4. Tool (1981b, p. 17). A modified version of this paper appeared in Tool (1981a); the same idea expressed in words slightly different from those quoted appears on page 570.

5. Tool (1989). The Veblen-Commons award is the highest honor that AFEE bestows upon scholars who have made extraordinary lifetime contributions to institutional economics.

6. In addition to Tool, those of Foster's students who have made contributions to the literature of institutional economics and who have served as officers in the Association for Evolutionary Economics and the Association for Institutional Thought, and/or who have served on the editorial board of the *Journal of Economic Issues* include: Gladys Parker Foster, the late Louis J. Junker, Edythe S. Miller, Baldwin Ranson, and the present writer.

7. Baldwin Ranson compiled and edited Foster's papers and arranged to have them published as "The Papers of J. Fagg Foster" in Foster (1981). This publication has become the standard source on Foster's work. Marc Tool's exposition of Foster's ideas can be found in Tool (1953, 1977, 1979, 1986, and 1989).

8. He received his B.S. in Commerce in 1943. On December 13, 1943, he married Lilian Mae Redington, who became an elementary school teacher. They have two children: a son, Laurence Alan, born in 1949; and a daughter, Marilyn Louise, born in 1953.

9. Francis M. Myers was a student of Max C. Otto at the University of Wisconsin. Myers's *The Warfare of Democratic Ideals* (1956) offers a compelling discussion of the instrumentalist theory of democracy. In the "Preface" to his book, Myers acknowledges John C. Livingston's helpful comments on the whole manuscript. In 1972 Francis Myers, age 55, died unexpectedly from an undiagnosed intestinal blockage.

10. Several short papers that appear in the *Journal of Economic Issues* collection of Foster's works were originally written as syllabi for this course.

11. Ayres's commitment to the cause of academic freedom, however, fell somewhat short of both ACLU and AAUP standards by virtue of his opposition to allowing communists to serve on university faculties. See Breit and Culbertson, Jr. (1976, p. 17).

12. Ranson (1981, pp. 854-55). As a result of the vigorous efforts of Ayres and other members of the economics faculty, Foster, Gordon, and Peach were offered the opportunity to return to the UT faculty after the war (Breit and Culbertson, Jr. 1976, pp. 15-16). Upon hearing of Foster's firing, Kenyon College offered him a teaching position, which he accepted. In 1943, he took a job with the Federal Public Housing Authority in Cleveland, Ohio. Then, in 1944, he volunteered for military duty. After completing service in the South Pacific as a U.S. Infantry rifleman, he returned to the University of Texas where he obtained his Ph.D. in 1946. See also, Sturgeon (1986).

13. Livingston's career flourished at Sacramento. He became one of the most popular teachers on the campus and earned statewide recognition for academic leadership. He was a founding member of the Statewide Academic Senate, which represents the faculties of the (now) twenty campuses of the California State University System, and he served as its third president in 1965-66. Livingston coauthored with Robert G. Thompson *The Consent of the Governed* (1963), which became a widely used textbook. The theories of freedom and democracy embodied in this book reflect the philosophical views that Livingston and Tool came to share over the long years of their personal and professional lives together. Livingston's passionate dedication to the civil rights movement finally took the form of what is arguably one of the finest books ever written on the subject of affirmative action. His *Fair Game? Inequality and Affirmative Action* (Livingston 1979) offers a profound and innovative examination of the concepts of freedom, equality, and democracy. Livingston, an institutionalist in his broad political economic philosophy, was a founding member of the Association for Institutional Thought; and at the founding meeting of that organization, he gave the keynote address, which he called "Private Vice, Public Virtues." The speech was published posthumously (he died in July 1981 after a long struggle with lung cancer) in *The Review of Institutional Thought I* (Livingston 1981). Tool dedicated his *Essays in Social Value Theory: A*

*Neoinstitutionalist Contribution* (1986) to Livingston with the words: "Dedicated to the Memory of John C. Livingston, Scholar, Teacher, Friend, Democrat, Instrumentalist."

In relatively short order after Livingston left Denver for Sacramento, Fritz Freitag and Charles Merrifield accepted positions on the faculty of Hayward State College (now California State University, Hayward) where they taught until retirement. By the end of the 1950s, of the original group of faculty who had championed the infusion of instrumentalist philosophy in the general education curriculum at the University of Denver, only Fagg Foster and Francis Myers remained.

14. He served as the chairperson of the Department of Economics from 1971 to 1974.

15. With respect to the overwhelming moral, political, and economic issue of this era, the Vietnam War, unlike Foster and Ayres who supported U. S. intervention in Southeast Asia, Tool opposed the war. During the Sacramento State College "Teach-in on Vietnam," held on October 31, 1965, he gave a measured evaluation of American foreign policy in which he compared the U.S. failure to meet its peaceful commitments to fund economic development in the Third World with its "massive military intrusion" in Vietnam. "Of what do our *vital* interests consist? What *is* the nature and extent of our commitments? Is there an over-emphasis on military commitments, on crisis oriented activity? How long do we maintain a somewhat spurious military commitment? Do we still think that people's minds can be changed at the point of a bayonet? If our commitment in Vietnam has become primarily a matter of national honor and patriotism, then of course, reason is likely to go out the window. If the issue degenerates into a debate of whether you are for July 4th or May [1st], I say that constructive appraisal of foreign policy is impossible." The source of this quotation is from a typescript of radio station KERS's tape recording of Tool's speech, "Commitment and Credibility."

16. In 1983 he entered the "Faculty Early Retirement Program" (FERP), which permits a member of the faculty to teach one semester per academic year until full retirement. This arrangement provided Tool with badly needed time for his editorial work on the *Journal of Economic Issues*.

17. Those institutions were the Universities of Colorado, Maryland, New Mexico, Texas, and Wisconsin; Cornell University, Notre Dame, and Michigan State University.

18. In his dissertation, Tool used a hyphen in the spelling of "neo-institutionalism." In his later published work he dropped the hyphen. Except where the hyphenated spelling appears in titles, or occurs in quotations, the term will be spelled without the hyphen in this chapter.

19. For whatever reason, the dissertation was not filed with University Microfilms at the time of its completion. The inaccessibility of the dissertation is regrettable since it is a work that still can be read with great benefit even by those who are well-versed in the institutionalist literature.

20. Tool worked on this article for a better part of a year. Jack Livingston, and Robert Robinson (another colleague at Sacramento) read and commented on the manuscript. The manuscript ran 43 pages, including references.

21. Gruchy (1972, p. 16). Gruchy had not used the term in his earlier work, *Modern Economic Thought: The American Contribution* (1947). In that book, Gruchy used the terminology "holistic" economics to describe institutional thought. With respect to the question of attribution, it is interesting to note that Gruchy was scrupulous in acknowledging (on page 4) Jan Christian Smuts as having originally coined the term "holistic" in another context. The presumption that Gruchy was the first to use the term "neo-institutionalism" is readily evident in the four reviews of his *Contemporary Economic Thought: The Contribution of Neo-Institutional Economics* by Coats, Gonce, Shaffer, and Francis (1974); and in Adams (1980).

22. Gruchy (1972, p. 129). This statement is a reiteration of the position he took twenty-five years earlier in his *Modern Economic Thought* (1947). There he states (on page 598) that "[t]he holistic economists have no intention of making economics a 'normative' science, or of attempting to mix scientific and ethical analyses."

23. Aside from this complaint, Gruchy's book is, of course, a valuable contribution to an understanding of institutional economics.

24. This is not to say that Gruchy was unaware of the importance of Dewey's influence on institutional economics. He can be properly credited with offering one of the most comprehensive discussions of the "pragmatic" character of institutional thought in his earlier *Modern Economic Thought* (1947). There he gives a detailed account of Dewey's compatibility with Veblen and his influence on the work of Commons, Mitchell, and Tugwell, among others. Except for one vague footnote (p. 28), he does not discuss Ayres's work. It is clear that he did not yet fully appreciate the importance of Ayres's contribution at that time. In his 1972 work, he treats Ayres's work generously, though he fails to appreciate fully the normative implications of Ayres's methodology.

25. See his rather murky "criticisms" of Tool's social value principle (Gruchy 1987, pp. 83-85).

26. McCloskey (1989). Tool's review of the non-positivist neoinstitutionalist methodology predates Bruce Caldwell's thoughtful inquiry into the deficiencies of positivism by twenty-nine years. See Caldwell (1982).

27. Tool reprises this analysis of the Veblenian distinction in his "A Social Value Theory in Neoinstitutional Economics" (1977, pp. 824-28).

28. He specifically calls the reader's attention to Gruchy's 1947 treatise for an "alternative analysis of the Veblenian distinction" (Tool 1953, p. 186n). The "normative" Veblen is a less controversial notion today than it was when Tool wrote his dissertation. Rick Tilman, a neoinstitutionalist who is recognized as one of the nation's leading Veblenian scholars, has endorsed the legitimacy of this way of reading Veblen. See Tilman (1987), Rasmussen and Tilman (1991); Loader, Mattson, and Waddoups (1991), and Edgell and Townshend (1991).

29. Tool (1953, pp. 252-53). For a useful account of how the treatment of the "Veblenian dichotomy" changed over time from Ayres's interpretation to Foster's, and from Foster's to those of some of his students, see Waller (1982). See also Bush (1986).

30. Among the other institutionalists in attendance was Hans E. Jensen (Ph.D., University of Texas, 1961) who, in 1963, became a member of the economics faculty at the University of Tennessee at Knoxville where he was joined later by Anne Mayhew and Walter C. (Terry) Neale in 1968.

31. Beginning with the 1966 AFEE meetings, Tool was able to establish and maintain contact with other institutionalists by attending AFEE meetings on an intermittent basis. The 1966 AFEE conference was a benchmark in the professional lives of many institutionalists. In Tool's case, it brought him together with Ayres, Foster, Junker and others (including the present writer) who either had been his friends and colleagues in the past or who would become so in the years that lay ahead.

32. Among this "Western" group were Baldwin Ranson, James I. Sturgeon, and Louis Junker. On behalf of the disaffected group of Western institutionalists, James Sturgeon made a presentation to the AFEE Board of Directors in 1978 in which he outlined their concerns. It should be noted that Marc Tool never expressed displeasure with Samuels's editorship. He has always had held in high regard Samuels's scholarship and editorial endeavors. Many years after Tool had succeeded Samuels in the editorship, they began (in the late 1980s) a collaboration which continues today editing books on institutional economics.

33. Warren Samuels published five reviews of *The Discretionary Economy* by Bush, Dugger, Hayden, Ranson, and Tilman in the *Journal of Economic Issues* (Bush 1980).

34. Today almost all members of AFIT are also members of AFEE. Individuals serving as officers in AFIT often serve as officers in AFEE at some later date. In the first few years of its existence, AFIT published *The Review of Institutional Thought* (RIT), funding publication costs through institutional grants. The *RIT* published abstracts of papers presented at the annual meetings of AFIT as well as presidential addresses and a few other selected manuscripts. Only three annual volumes of the *RIT* were published: their publication dates are December 1981, 1982, and 1986. Aside from funding difficulties and production delays, it became increasingly clear to the officers of AFIT that the *Journal of Economic Issues* (JEI), under Tool's editorship, was publishing on a regular basis the better papers presented at the AFIT meetings. There was no longer any need for AFIT to struggle with the problems of producing its own journal since the *JEI* was more than

adequately meeting the publishing needs of the members of AFIT. Consequently, the publication of the *RIT* was discontinued with its third volume.

35. He had been appointed to the Editorial Board of the *Journal of Economic Issues* in 1976, and he served as a member of that board until his appointment as editor.

36. These remarks were made by John Adams (1993) in his introduction of Marc Tool on the occasion of Tool's Presidential Address to AFEE, January 6, 1993, in Anaheim, California. The author is grateful to Professor Adams for granting permission to quote from his typescript.

37. The project was launched at a dinner meeting that Tool arranged during the 1984 conference of the Association for Institutional Thought held in San Diego, California. In attendance were several of those who Tool would later appoint to an advisory committee on the project. Those who served on that committee were: Paul D. Bush (California State University, Fresno), F. Gregory Hayden (University of Nebraska), Philip A. Klein (Pennsylvania State University), Anne Mayhew and Walter C. Neale (University of Tennessee, Knoxville), and Harry M. Trebing (Michigan State University). See Tool (1988, Vol. I, pp. 2-3).

38. See Tool (1988a). The Americans in attendance were: Vernon M. Briggs (Cornell University), F. Gregory Hayden (University of Nebraska), Philip A. Klein (Pennsylvania State University), Anne Mayhew (University of Tennessee, Knoxville), Edythe S. Miller (Littleton, Colorado), Philip Mirowski (Tufts University), John Munkirs (Sangamon State University), Walter C. Neale (University of Tennessee, Knoxville), Yngve Ramstad (University of Rhode Island), Warren J. Samuels (Michigan State University), James A. Swaney (Wright State University), and Tool.

39. The following is the list of Tool's EAEPE conference papers to date: "Contributions to an Institutional Theory of Price Determination," presented in Florence, Italy, November 1990, and published in Screpanti and Hodgson (1991); "A Synthetic Analysis of Economic Systems: Continuing Questions and Institutionalist Responses," presented in Vienna, Austria, November 1991; "Administered Pricing in the Public Sector: An Institutional Approach," presented in Paris, France, November 1992; and "Institutional Adjustment and Instrumental Value: With Observation on 'Reform' in Eastern Europe," presented in Barcelona, Spain, October 1993; and "Social Cost and Social Value," presented in Copenhagen, Denmark, October 1994. The Vienna, Paris, Barcelona, and Copenhagen papers are published in Tool (1995)

40. Tool wrote articles on "John Dewey," "Clarence E. Ayres," and "Instrumental Value Theory."

41. See Wible (1984) and Abraham Hirsch and Neil Di Marchi (1990). The present writer has challenged the idea set forth by these authors that Friedman is either intentionally or unintentionally a Deweyan in his methodology. See Bush (1993, especially pp. 75-79).

42. For a valuable discussion of the difference between the Austrian and institutionalist views on the evolution of institutional structures, see Clark (1993).

43. For a recent specimen of "new institutionalist" scholarship, see Elinor Ostrom, Larry Schroeder, and Susan Wynne (1993).

44. See Gordon (1984 and 1990) and Mayhew (1987a and 1987b). For Tool's response to the criticisms of Gordon and Mayhew, see Tool (1993). A slightly different version of his replies to Gordon and Mayhew appears in Tool (1990a and 1990b).

45. He offers such elucidations in Tool (1979, pp. 293-314; and 1993, pp. 119-159).

46. Tool's EAEPE Barcelona paper addresses this problem in the context of the institutional changes taking place in Eastern Europe and the Commonwealth of Independent States. He is particularly critical of the policies advocated by Jeffrey Sachs because of their failure to account adequately for the instrumentally warranted behavioral patterns dislocated by Sach's "free market" solutions to the problems of restructuring the Polish and Russian economies. See Tool, "Institutional Adjustment and Instrumental Value: With Observations on 'Reform' in Eastern Europe, a paper presented at the EAEPE meetings, Barcelona, Spain, October 1993, published in Tool (1995).

47. The discussion referred to occurred on Saturday, November 9, 1991. Tool's extemporaneous remarks abstracted and extended the themes he developed in his paper, "A Synthetic Analysis of Economic Systems: Continuing Questions and Institutionalist Responses." The standing-room-only session, which the present writer attended, was chaired by Kurt Dopfer (Switzerland). So many people wanted to participate in the discussion, Dopfer had to beg several to withdraw their requests in order to conclude on time.

## 2. FROM NATURAL VALUE TO SOCIAL VALUE

Charles M. A. Clark[1]

Although once central to all economic theorizing, the topic of value theory seems to have become the sole province of historians of economic thought and theoretical malcontents. It would seem that John Stuart Mill's famous pronouncement on value theory ["Happily, there is nothing in the laws of Value which remains for the present or any future writer to clear up; the theory of the subject is complete" (Mill 1848, p. 299) has finally come true, with economic theorists' turning their attention to other problems and issues. This certainly is the conclusion to be drawn from the leading economics principles textbooks, where the marginal utility theory of value is taught with the theoretical elegance and confidence of established Truth. This is all very deceiving, for it is common knowledge that the marginal utility theory of value is, to say the least, an unsatisfactory "scientific" explanation of economic phenomena, especially if one applies the professed criterion of scientific legitimation (as developed by logical positivism) preached by economic theorists.

This unhappy situation was the topic of an essay by Adolph Lowe (1981) in which he answers the question "Is economic value still a problem?" by arguing that even though pure theory cannot explain empirical prices, economists still are able to merrily go about their business of explaining economic activity and offering policy advice. This lack of a theoretically satisfactory theory of value seems to have not hinder economists' attempts to understand economic problems and issues.

Lowe's willingness to abandon value theory was challenged by his most prominent student, Robert L. Heilbroner (1983), who argued that the significance of value theory is more than the mere explanation of relative prices. The theory of value, Heilbroner asserted, is concerned with the underlying order of the market, an order which is reflected, however imperfectly, in empirical prices, but which can never be fully observed in market behavior.

In this essay I argue that the truthfulness of both Lowe's critique of value theory and Heilbroner's defense are illuminated once the distinction is drawn between theories of natural value and theories of social value. Lowe's objections to past theories of value pertain to attempts at a theory of natural value, whereas, Heilbroner's defense of value theory is strengthen when it is applied to theories of social value; it is only a social theory of value that can avoid the theoretical traps elucidated by Lowe while at the same time provide the heuristic role emphasized by Heilbroner. It is the contention of this essay that the theoretical and empirical failure of the two major value traditions stems from their erroneous conception of the fundamental essence of value theory. Over the past two hundred years economic theorists have been attempting to construct an economic theory modeled after the natural sciences. It is within this research program that value theory has been developed, with the primary objective being the discovery of "natural value"—some principle in nature which can ultimately explain relative prices. The failure of this research program arises from the impossibility of the task. Value is a social phenomena and not one of nature. This statement should not be seen as reducing the significance of value theory, for it will be argued that Heilbroner is correct in placing the theory of value at the heart of economic analysis. It is merely to agree with Lowe's implicit argument, that it is impossible to adequately understand empirical prices and the underlying order of the economy independent of history and society. A theory of social value does not attempt what is impossible, the development of an invariant measure of value or natural analogue to which all economic activity is reducible. Furthermore, a theory of social value reinserts history and society into the constitution of economic thought, and thus will help to guide the future development of economic theory towards a deeper understanding of the economy.

## The Role of Value Theory

The word value in economics is most often associated with the concept of worth; a goods value is what it is worth. Normative connotations and issues have always played an important role in discussions of economic value, as they have in just about all economic questions (Lowe 1967). Although there have been numerous theories as to what determines a goods worth, and what is the relationship between worth and actual prices, almost all who have analyzed the question of value have held the opinion that the price of a good should be and is, in the long-run, determined by its worth. It is this connection between what goods are worth and what their prices are that forms the bond between the theory of value and price theory. With the rise of autonomous markets and the adoption of the natural science model for economic theorizing, economists became convinced that both values and prices were determined by the same forces, with the former being the result of the dominant and persistent (long-run) factors, while the latter was the result of these and temporary (short-run) factors. Hence, price theory's object of analysis became empirical prices, while the theory of value sought to explain the underlying ordering process operating in the economy. The connection between price theory and the theory of value thus stems from the contention that prices play an essential role in the establishment of the underlying order of the market and that there are mechanisms in the economy which cause prices to reflect this underlying order. Value theory's role is therefore to expose the logic of the economy, its underlying orderliness.

From the beginning of systematic economic theory, economists have made the distinction between the observable market phenomena of everyday prices and the deeper fundamental values[2] which act as a center of gravity for market prices. These values reflect the fundamental forces of the economy, exclusive of the temporary and transient disturbances of chance and circumstance. The connection between values and prices comes from the argument that in a market society prices perform the task of coordinating the multitude of individual behaviors into a coherent order. As Heilbroner (1988, p. 107) writes: "Prices are the means by which market societies in general, and capitalist societies in particular, establish social coherence from the otherwise uncoordinated activities of their actors. Prices link the world of action and that of order."

The second function of value theory is typically only of interest to the historian of economic thought, yet it is here that we find the lasting significance of value theory. As Heilbroner (Ibid., p. 105) has stated, value theory "powerfully influences the constitution of economic thought itself by identifying different elements within the social process as strategic for our understanding of it." Value theory not only selects which factors will become central to theoretical explanation (which is at the same time the selection of what to exclude), it also determines how these factors will be understood. The role of value theory is one of the clearest examples of Gunnar Myrdal's often stated contention of the theory driven nature of our understanding of social phenomena. If our theory states that a certain factor is fundamental, then our observation and subsequent theoretical developments will reflect this central role. Value theory gives theorists the vantage point from which they observe economic phenomena. Therefore, only phenomena which can be observed from this perspective is included in the analysis. Myrdal does not make this point as a critique of any particular theory; he merely notes that all observation is theory dependent. The prominence of value theory in economic analysis rests in its dominance of how the economy is perceived.[3]

The inability of the two major value traditions (objective and subjective) to provide an adequate theoretical explanation of empirical prices is generally accepted, yet value theory is not something which economist can live without, for it guides all theoretical research. The efforts of neoclassical economists to continue to construct a system of economic doctrines based on the marginal utility theory of value, which they cannot adequately defend, is clear evidence of the legitimation role of its theory and its "ineluctable march to obsolescence" (Galbraith 1987, p. 129).

Value theory's heuristic role exposes its necessarily normative character. Heilbroner, in his response to Lowe, outlines the various types of value theory labelling one approach as normative. The distinction between "normative" and "non-normative" theories of value is, I think, misleading, for all theories of value are normative. This is true to the extent that all theories of value incorporate criteria of judgement (Myrdal's above mentioned claim). It is also true in the sense that all theories of value are concerned, or should be concerned with, valuation, which Heilbroner notes "is a haunting but unacknowledged presence in all conceptions of value" (1988, p. 109). All economic activity is value-laden, is based on choices and actions which are expressions of values. In fact the coherence observed in economic activity stems, to a large extent, from the expression of social values as individual choices. The relationship between "values" and "valuation" is fundamental to understanding economic activity yet it is rarely included in economic analysis. Furthermore, when valuation is mentioned, it is almost exclusively at the level of the autonomous individual, as if society played no role at all. The "valuation process," that is the process by which "values" are generated is the quintessential social activity, resulting from the interaction of individuals and institutions, both in the socialization process of the individual and the process of the continued recreation of institutions.

The theory of value is necessarily normative, as all social theories are, for social theory always is concerned with both the real and the ideal. Social theory is an exposition of how things are from the perspective of how things should be. Both are essential aspects of the process by which societies continuously recreate themselves.

## The Concept of Natural Value

The history of economic theory clearly tells us that when economic theorists referred to the theory of value, their conception of value is what Adam Smith labelled "natural value," and what, following Alfred Marshall, we call long-run equilibrium prices. Essentially, they are referring to a set of prices which it is believed will bring coherence to the diverse economic activities of the individuals who make up the economy in question. The preconceptions of the originators of the theory of natural value are those of the natural law philosophy that dominated inquiry, social and natural, in the seventeenth and eighteenth centuries. At the heart of these preconceptions is the idea that society in general, and the economy in particular, had a natural order. As to the specifications of this natural order there was much disagreement. However, the belief that such an order existed was universal. The dominance of natural law philosophy on the subsequent development of economic theory, is seen in many aspects of the history of economic thought; the most obvious being in the terminology—natural value. This use of the phrase "natural value" is significant in its displacement of concepts of the natural sciences onto the understanding of the economy. In the search for a theory of value, economists have sought to develop a physical analogue for the analysis of prices and market behavior. The political and rhetorical value of the phrase "natural value" is of course very important in the understanding of the development of economic theory, for it allowed economic theory to develop under the myth of the market as a natural phenomenon (see Dugger 1989 and Appleby 1979). But for our present interest, it is the search for a non-social explanation of value, which is at the same time a search for a non-social cause of economic order, that is most significant. The approach, from Misselden to Debreu, is to treat value, that is the underlying order of the economy and the prices which reflect that order, as a function of nature and as a phenomenon of nature.

The concept of a natural order was juxtaposed with that of a social order. The natural order, with its natural values, comprises the dominant and persistent forces of the economy, whereas the social order represented the human interferences and the temporary aberrations from the natural order. As to what composed the natural order, which institutions were part of the natural order and which were the result of human interference, is, in the end, an arbitrary distinction. Most often the institutions of the natural order were those that reflected the theorist "ideal" order. The common characteristic of value theory has been the search for "value" constructs based on the preconception that "value" must flow from nature. This is seen in Misselden's "intrinsic" value; Cantillon's land theory of value; Smith-Ricardo-Sraffa's labor theory of value (that is the so called objective theory of value tradition); as well as in the Walras-Jevons-Marshall-Debreu's marginal utility theory of value (the subjective tradition). At the early stages of these value theory traditions it seems as if the theorist is looking for a common denominator which is inherent in goods, and which could be used to bring them into equality in exchange. In many ways they are like the pre-socratic philosophers, searching for the universal substance. As the traditions developed, the importance of the actual substance declined, being replaced by the metaphors of value, with the tradition being driven by the concepts displaced into the theory. Thus, as Mirowski (1989) has noted, the classical tradition had a substance conception of value whereas the neoclassical tradition had a field theory of value. Although both traditions have dropped the universal essence upon which their theories were developed (labor and utility), the path of their theoretical development has been greatly influenced by these metaphors. For our purposes, of importance is that the two traditions differed in the natural sciences upon which they relied for their metaphors and their models of what a science should be, but not in their reliance on natural metaphors.

The concept of natural value has a long history in economics. One of the earliest uses of it can be found in the Mercantilist Edward Misselden's tract *The Circle of Commerce* (1623; 1971). Misselden differentiated between natural and political exchange. Natural exchange was concerned with the intrinsic value of goods while political exchange related to "outward valuation" and is "in merchants terms called the price" (Misselden 1971, p. 97). Political exchange was determined in the short run by "circumstances of time, and place, and persons" (Ibid.). Yet these uncertainties do not lead to chaos for natural exchange regulates political exchange, that is, the intrinsic value of a good acts as the "center, where unto all exchange have their natural propension" (Ibid.).

In this early economic treatise we find many themes which play prominent roles in the discussion of value. Misselden's natural/political exchange distinction is similar to Smith's natural value/market value distinction, a distinction that is given much of the credit for providing the possibility of a scientific economics. More important for our purpose is the idea of intrinsic value, that some substance in exchangeable goods gives the good its value. The intrinsic value of a good, although not defined, is inherent in the good and is derived from nature. Although the phrase "intrinsic value" eventually is lost, the underlying concept remains. The classical conception of value asserts the idea that some substance (land [Cantillon], labor [Ricardo] or land, labor and capital [Smith]) either gives goods their value, or can be used to measure their value, and frequently both.

Adam Smith (1976, p. 65) starts his analysis of value with a typical Enlightenment parable—a "state of nature" story.

> In that early and rude state of society which precedes both the accumulation of stock and the appropriation of land, the proportion between the quantities of labour necessary for acquiring different objects seems to be the only circumstance which can afford any rule for exchanging them for one another. If among a nation of hunters, for example, it usually costs twice the labour to kill a beaver which it does to kill a deer, one beaver should naturally exchange for or be worth two deer. It is natural that what is usually the produce of two days or two hours labour, should be worth double of what is usually the produce of one day's or one hour's labour.

Elsewhere, Smith states that "Labour . . . is the real measure of the exchangeable value of all commodities" (Ibid., p. 47) and "Labour alone, . . . never varying in its own value, is alone the ultimate and real standard by which the value of all commodities can at all times and places be estimated and compared. It is their real price" (Ibid., p. 51).

Although Smith practical concern is a measure of value to use in his analysis of economic growth (a central concern of *The Wealth of Nations*), his choice of labor as the ultimate, the real source of value comes partly from the influence of John Locke's labor theory of property (Stark 1976, p. 11), particularly as to the "natural" origins of value. We will see in the next section that Smith's eventual replacement of the pure labor theory of value with a cost-of-production theory is in many ways a move from natural value to social value.

The tradition that followed Smith, from Ricardo to Sraffa, became fixated on the concept of an invariant measure of value, on a conception of value independent from society—natural value. This preconception that value is something which exists independent of society can be seen in the exclusion of history and the social environment in the determination of value, and in the desire for a non-historical explanation of prices. It is felt that one value theory should be able to explain economies independent of time or space. Thus when theorists in this tradition give the development of value theory from Smith to Ricardo to Marx to Sraffa, it is treated as a purely logical problem, as if the forces that order society and the economy are universal. The implicit assumption in any search for an invariant measure of value is that value is independent of society.[4] This is the natural value doctrine in a nutshell.

In their search for a natural, non-social, theory of value, the marginal utility theorists are following a path first set out by the classicals. Their different theory of value, as Mirowski (1989) has convincingly demonstrated, comes from the use of a different physical science theory as their guiding heuristic. They have replace substance as the basis of value with utility, with their understanding of utility coming largely from their displacement of the concept of energy.

The marginal utility theory is much more consistent in their following of the natural science model than are the classicals, which is to say they go much farther in excluding historical and social context from the analysis of economic phenomena (Clark 1992a). Walras is in many ways the leader in this movement. Walras argued at length of the similarity between economics and various branches of physics (Walras 1954, p. 71; 1909) and that pure economics was a natural science, based on natural forces (1860). He writes: "any value in exchange, once established, partakes of the character of a natural phenomena, natural in its origins, natural in its manifestations, and natural in its essence . . . (for things to) have any value at all, it is because they are scarce, that is useful and limited in quantity—both conditions being natural (Walras 1954, p. 69).[5] Walras, Jevons and Menger, as well as the other marginalists, went to great lengths to separate pure economics from historical and social factors. The marginal utility theory of value was for them a universal truth, independent of historical and social context. It was universal for them because it was based on what they considered to be forces of nature: scarcity and diminishing marginal utility.

The culmination of Walras's goal of an economics that is fully mathematical and fully emulates the natural science model is the axiomatic theory of Debreu. Debreu's depiction is thoroughly in the natural value tradition in that historical and social factors are, for the first time, entirely excluded from the argument. Whereas Walras's model was based on his conception of the Parisian Bourse, and was developed to provide the foundation of this applied and social economics, where historical and social factors did play a role in the analysis, axiomatic general equilibrium theory, as John Davis (1989) has argued, has no reference to any real concepts. That is, in the axiomatic method, the use of the terms price and commodity is not meant to imply any actual price or commodity. The validity of the theory is entirely based on the theory's logical structure. Thus we have finally completed the break between the actual economy and economic theory.

The emulation of the natural sciences by economists can only be justified if there is some force or factors, independent of society, which determines value, in both meanings being considered here, prices and order. The lack of any satisfactory theory of value from both of the two main traditions (objective/subjective) comes from the illegitimacy of treating social phenomena as if it were natural. The objective tradition requires some fixed yardstick with which it can measure commodities (labor or Sraffa's standard commodity) while the subjective utility theory necessitates a fixed hedonistic human nature impervious to exogenous influences. The failure of value theory, which Lowe so perceptively documents, in both its objective and subjective guises, stems from the necessary exclusion of history and society in the research project of "natural value." Ultimately, both traditions failed because of their adherence to a natural analogue view of value.

## From Natural Value to Social Value

The conclusion of the preceding section should not be that the theory of value has not made any important contributions towards our understanding of the economy and economic activity. There is much to be learn from both traditions in value theory, and both reflect essential truths for the understanding of market economies. The failure to find a natural regulator of prices (values) is not the failure to add insights into the operations of a market economy. From the objective tradition we get an understanding of the importance of the structure of society and production in the determination of economic activity. This can be best seen in the usefulness of input/output analysis or the insights into the problematic nature of balanced growth which are derived from Marx's analysis, especially as developed by Adolph Lowe.[6] The subjective tradition has focus attention on the problem of demand, which is neglected for the most part in classical analysis, and the importance of individual decision making in a market economy. Veblen, we should remember, praised the Austrians of his day for asking the right questions, even though he did not exactly agree with their answers.

Economic theorist's have overcome the inherent limitations of theories of "natural value" for understanding actual economies by abandoning the idealised world of "natural value" and adopting social and historical analysis in order to explain value in both sense we have been considering. In so doing they developed social theories of value. Although this is most often within their natural law preconceptions, and the addition of social and historical factors was usually seen as a sign of theoretical weakness, economists seemed compelled to explain economic and social order in social terms (further evidence of Tool's compulsive shift thesis). Equally as important is the influence of the material conditions on the creation of economic theory. The sociology of knowledge[7] teaches us that the environment, both material and intellectual, is a dominating force in the creation of theories. The influence of metaphors from the natural sciences is an example of the intellectual environment influencing theoretical developments, yet if theory is to useful, that is provide analysis which helps in the solution to particular economic problems, it is the material influences which must provide the greatest progressive force in theory development. Hence, adapting theory to explain a constantly changing reality weakens the economist, who is attempting to solve actual problems, commitment to "universals" and forces the economist to deal with "particulars," that is with historical and social factors.

Adam Smith's movement from a theory of natural value to his final cost-of-production theory of value is one example of the movement from a "natural value" theory to a practical theory of social value. Smith's adaptation of his pure labor theory of value for the material realities of his time, the fact that land, labor and capital had claims on the social product, is the victory of relevance over ideology. Smith's final theory of value argues that the actual value of a commodity is socially determined, much like St. Thomas Aquinas's just price, through a social mediation of the various claims on output. The claim is often made, most notably by Ricardo, that Smith's theory is week because natural values are determined by natural wages, rents and profits which are themselves prices in need of explanation. Yet, as Heilbroner notes (1988, p. 117) "This is not a fatal objection to cost of production as a source of order beneath the price phenomena of society, but it certainly eliminates any suggestion that this order reflects the presence of some kind of universal, objectively determined value substance." This is Lowe's implicit point, that any given price regime is determined by historical and social context and has no final term in nature.

Marx's labor theory of value might not provide an adequate theoretical explanation of prices of production, that is of natural values, but it does yield great insight into the nature and logic of capitalism. The central theme of *Das Kapital* is not that the labor content of commodities determines relative prices, but that the labor process orders the economy, that the logic of the economy is the process by which capitalist's earn profits through their employment of workers. The nature of capitalism according to Marx is the institutional arrangements of the production process: a class of owners and a class of workers, all in the setting of machine production. The logic of capitalism in Marx's theory stems from the social relations between workers and capitalist, and the relationship between man and machine. By concentrating on the capitalists extraction of surplus value from the efforts of the worker Marx has highlighted a fundamental aspect of capitalist economies. Marx is able to show how the machine production of an industrial economy generates order in the economy and provides an underlying logic for the system.

Marx never ceases to emphasize that all the relations of capitalism are social relations and he criticizes economists for treating the economy as a natural phenomena and not as social phenomena.

> Here, however, the [natural] analogy ceases. In the expression of the weight of the sugar-loaf, the iron represents a natural property common to both bodies, their weight; but in the expression of value of the linen the coat represents a supra-natural property: their value, which is something purely social. . . . The relative value-form of a commodity, . . . expresses its value-existence as something wholly different from its substance and properties, . . . this expression itself therefore indicates that it conceals a social relation. . . . One thing, however, is clear: nature does not produce on the one hand owners of money or commodities, and on the other hand men possessing nothing but their own labour-power. This relation has no basis in natural history. It is clearly the result of a past historical development (Marx 1977, p. 147; 273).

By emphasizing the social aspects of Marx's theory of value we see that his labor theory of value is very different from the classical conception for it is not the substance of labor (socially necessary labor time) which provides order to market relations, it is the historical conditions in which the worker is employed. These conditions, capitalist production, are not universal categories, nor are they given by nature. As a theory of natural value Marx's theory fails, as the abundant literature on the transformation problem attests, but as a theory of social value, both in its exposure of many of the fundamental properties of capitalism, and as the guiding heuristic for a theoretical investigation of nineteenth century capitalism, we must agree with Heilbroner's (1988, p. 121-23) assesment:

> The linkage of the concept of value—once again, an ordering presence "behind" the world of prices—to the appearance of the particular conditions under which labor becomes a commodity introduces into Marx's work an intrinsic historical aspect. Furthermore, it gives to Marxian theory a special significance in that value now becomes a category that reveals relations of hierarchy or domination that are masked by the usual vocabulary of economic discourse. For

> this reason, Marxian theory is not merely a search for the principle of "horizontal" order—an explanation of the ratios of exchange in the marketplace—but also a key to "vertical" order—the mutual relations of social classes.

Interpreted as a theory of social value, Marx's labor theory of value not only highlights the social aspects of the economy, he also provides a theory of valuation. The underlying "value" of capitalism according to Marx is that of capital expanding itself, that is money making more money. This "value" is what drives the system, legitimating all activities which support it and rejecting all which impede it. Marx thus exposes the underlying "value" of capitalism which provide the underpinning of what was then the accepted economic theory. Marx's critique of capitalism is based on a different set of value judgements and is very much a normative critique.[8]

Even the marginal utility theory of value cannot escape the sociology of knowledge, for although they more successfully excluded historical and social context from their analysis, reality still asserts itself in the creation of the marginal utility theory of value. The marginalist's great contribution to our understanding of the economy does not come from the tools they developed; it comes from their assertion that demand is an important factor in any understanding of the economy, particularly in the valuation process. The classical economists merely assume demand existed. However, by the time Jevons, Menger and Walras were writing one could not assume away demand; for the essential problems of the economy were no longer solely production related, by were instead demand related. The economy was moving away from a supply-constrained economy, where all the economic problems centered on producing more goods, to a demand-constrained economy where the economy is limited not by its ability to produce, but its ability to consume. The move to a demand constrained economy is an often neglected factor in the marginal utility revolution, althought they only understood it in relation to the firm and the individual and not in the macro-context. The marginalists were correct to insert the realm of exchange in the value problematic, that is in the social ordering process. Their system becomes irrelevant not because they asked the wrong questions, but because they were so limited by their natural law preconceptions that they were compelled to give only ahistorical and asocial answers. They could not see the true social nature of exchange. Instead they limited their analysis of exchange to Robinson Crusoe stories and other "state of nature" explanations (Clark 1991).

Arjun Appadurai (1986, p. 57), in noting the social nature of value in exchange, has stated:

> *Politics* (in the broad sense of relations, assumptions, and contests pertaining to power) is what links value and exchange in the social life of commodities. In the mundane, day-to-day, small-scale exchange of things in ordinary life, this fact is not visible, for exchange has the routine and conventionalized look of all consumer behavior. But these many ordinary dealings would

> not be possible were it not for a broad set of agreements concerning what is desirable, what a reasonable "exchange of sacrifices" comprises, and who is permitted to exercise what kind of effective demand in what circumstances. What is political about this process is not just the fact that it signifies and constitutes relations of privilege and social control. What is political about it is the constant tension between the existing framework (of price, bargaining, and so forth) and the tendency of commodities to breach these frameworks. This tension itself has its source in the fact that not all parties share the same *interests* in any specific regime of value, not are the interests of any two parties in a given exchange identical.

Both the classical and the neoclassical traditions in value theory also have strong normative elements, their pronouncements to the contrary notwithstanding. The classicals emphasis on production as the source of value is normative. It is the value judgement that whatever increases the output of society is good, that is has value. Writing in the eighteenth and nineteenth centuries, this is an understandable value judgement. The neoclassical tradition is based on the value judgement that maximizing consumer satisfaction is the basis for evaluating the economy. Again, given their environment, this is also an understandable criteria.

Theories of value are by necessity normative since they deal with criteria for selection and choice—of judgement, both by the theorist and within the economy by economic actors. If the purpose of value theory is to expose the underlying ordering forces in the economy, and society, then the theory must be a theory of social value and not of natural value, for the economy and society are not natural phenomena, organized by natural principles, but are social in their origins and in their manifestations. Furthermore, it is social institutions which generates the order in the economy and society, institutions which socializes individuals into members of a particular society, institutions which create and regulate social behavior, institutions which give coherence to the valuation process of the members of a society, and institutions which provide for collective outcomes. If our goal is to understand the dominant and persistent forces of the economy, social institutions must be our starting point and the only way to understand institutions is to examine the historical process from which they arose and through which they have evolved.

Moreover, if the final goal of economic inquiry is the assistance in economic decision making, particularly as to the ability of current economic institutions to meet the needs of society and promote the economic and social development of the community, then such inquiry must center on "values" and criteria of judgements and the consequences of these. To a certain extent this is merely being intellectually and morally honest as to the normative criteria we are using to direct our inquiry. But more fundamentally, it forces us to get to the root causes of the problems we are investigating. Economists study human actions and human actions are guided by values.

Adolph Lowe, in the essay mentioned at the beginning of this chapter, connects the well known weakness of both of the major value traditions (labor theory of value and marginal utility theory of value) to the high level of abstraction of their analysis and to the stated criteria of their analysis to explain prices independent of history. He concluded his essay by noting that the results of value theory are disappointing "because there is no ultimate determinant of empirical prices without abandoning the realm of pure analysis for that of history" (1987, p. 151) and that "the historical nature . . . [of any meaningful solution to the value problem] does not come as a surprise to those who have always conceived the economic process as embedded in a wider sociohistorical context" (Ibid., p. 148). Yet this should not be interpreted as a call for the illimination of value theory, merely an end to conceptions of "natural value" and the limiting of value theory to the explanation of relative prices. The noted decline in the importance of value theory is often explained by the common agreement as to the correct theory of value, but I think we can follow the lead of the sociology of knowledge and state that it owes more to the lack of importance competitively determined prices have in our current economy and an implicit recognition that prices are set by social agents with power. Prices may not still serve the role as the sole regulator of the economy, but the economy still has a coherence in need of explanation, and it is still the purpose of value theory to explain this institutional order.

A theory of social value is needed to direct future economic inquiry and prevent economic theory's march to irrelevance because: it will center our efforts on history and society, not nature and natural laws; it will direct our attention to social institutions and not atomistic hedonistic economic actors in a "state of nature"; and lastly, it will require an open and honest statement of the value judgements underlying both the theory and society, not the delusion of "value-free" analysis, thus promoting a more democratic and humane solution to the economic problem.

## Notes

1. The author would like to thank Marc Tool, Robert Heilbroner and William Waller for their helpful comments and suggestions.

2. Just what are the deeper fundamental values is a point of great contention. The fact that the word value has been applied in so many conflicting ways has increased the confusion surrounding investigations into value theory. I have not defined value rigidly here since, for my purposes, it is the idea of "value" and not the meaning which matters.

3. The heuristic role of value theory is nicely demonstrated in Ed Nell's paper "Value and Capital in Marxian Economics" in which he uses the Marxian notion of surplus value to illuminate various economic issues. He does not claim that the theory provides an empirical explanation, only a perspective from which we can understand the problems.

4. The Sraffian notion of an invariant measure of value relates to changes in the distribution of income. Yet I can think of nothing which would lead to a more radical change in valuation and social value than a pronounce change in the distribution of income, and the subsequent change in social power relations which would follow. For a short institutionalist analysis of Sraffian economics, particularly with respect to social value, see Clark 1992b.

# 3. INSTITUTIONALISM AND VALUE THEORY: AN IDENTITY CRISIS?

Gladys Parker Foster

> Provided the practical exigencies of modern industrial life continue of the same character as they now are, and so continue to enforce the impersonal method of knowledge, it is only a question of time when that (substantially animistic) habit of mind which proceeds on the notion of a definitive normality shall be displaced in the field of economic inquiry by that (substantially materialistic) habit of mind which seeks a comprehension of facts in terms of a cumulative sequence.
>
> Thorstein Veblen

The literature in institutional economics in recent years reveals considerable, and apparently increasing, theoretical turmoil or contentiousness, along with perhaps a greater than usual lack of cohesion. Some of this could well be ascribed to confusion resulting from the exponential growth of knowledge and information and the rapidity and momentousness of social change as the twentieth century draws to a close. Whatever its cause, it seems warranted to continue to explore the philosophy of institutional thinking and how various currents of thought relate to it.

This essay attempts to do that. The central focus is value theory, partly because the writer thinks that is the heart of institutional economics, in the Veblen-Dewey-Ayres-Foster-Tool line of development, and partly because the writer has a greater familiarity with it, from studies going back a great many years. As for the idea that value theory is and should be the central focus of institutional economics, it seems to be the richest branch of inquiry of institutional economics, in terms of the possibility of future theoretical development and also its applicability to the interpretation of events and solution of social problems. How do humans make choices? And should there not be guidance from the academy in the everyday choices humans face?

The questions chosen for discussion, necessarily brief, are absolutism, relativism, and universality; Clarence Ayres's notion of progress versus Thorstein Veblen's "blind drift;" hermeneutics; and postmodernism. Most of these questions occur as a result of, or at least center around, the effort to apply the scientific method to philosophy, to the social sciences, to aesthetics, and to morals. The effort to do this is a monumental task, considering that the great preponderance of scholarly thought throughout history has taken an approach diametrically opposed to this. Almost all philosophical inquiry, notably, has rested on the world view that there is something outside of human experience and beyond human inquiry that provides a foundation for human thought and gives us what Richard Rorty, borrowing a felicitous phrase from Nietzsche, refers to as "metaphysical comfort" (Rorty 1982, p. 166). It is inevitable that the effort described above would find the going difficult and that it would meet with some backlash. Adding to its complexity is the recurrent theme that science has been made to or allowed to assume a position unduly predominant, that it should be pushed back to a position of lower priority, or some such (see Brown 1994), about which more below.

Ayres talked in his lectures about the enormity of the idea of applying scientific theory to human behavior, saying that we are passing through a period of intellectual revolution greater in magnitude than any previous, a total crisis. The issue is, can man live by science alone? The value problem, he went on, is the heart of the crisis; economics deals with values and always has (Ayres 1950).

J. Fagg Foster also predicted in his lectures a feverish expansion of the defense of the normative/positive dichotomy as the scientific methodology threatened to gain credibility as the method of inquiry appropriate to the social sciences and to philosophy. The difficulty, he said, is that social science has always defended the prevailing ismatic structure, be it feudalism, mercantilism, socialism, capitalism, or whatever; and adoption of the scientific method means the abandonment of ismatic thinking and of any hope of validating a particular "ism" (Foster 1948).

John Dewey in a particularly fortunate passage observed that the seventeenth century witnessed the application of the new science to astronomy and general cosmology, the eighteenth century to physics and chemistry, the nineteenth to geology and the biological sciences. Is not, he went on, the establishment of the scientific view in moral and political matters the task of the twentieth century? It would make the reconstruction of philosophy an accomplished fact (Dewey

1950, p. 76).

Veblen (1991, p. 81) in 1898 had said something similar:

> Under the stress of modern technological exigencies, men's everyday habits of thought are falling into the lines that in the sciences constitute the evolutionary method; and knowledge which proceeds on a higher, more archaic plane is becoming alien and meaningless to them. The social and political sciences must follow the drift, for they are already caught in it.

The premise of this essay is that economics is about value, as Ayres said, and that particular issues connected with value are in need of reassessment. If institutional economics is to get beyond its identity crisis, it must look to value theory. A brief review of how we got here seems appropriate.

## The Development of Value Theory in Institutional Economics

Almost a hundred years ago Thorstein Veblen put forward the proposition that human beings exhibit two ways of behaving, the technological and the institutional (Veblen 1975). Although he many times denied that he was suggesting that the technological way of behaving was to be preferred, it is very difficult to escape the conclusion that he indeed was doing exactly that. It appears likely that he found no way to say so and remain "scientific." Ayres suggests that Veblen did not think the value question through to articulacy (Ayres 1950).

John Dewey, throughout a long life of writing but particularly in 1938 in *Logic: The Theory of Inquiry*, offered an instrumental criterion of judgment for evaluating choices in philosophy, human behavior, aesthetics—indeed in all kinds of choices faced in life—a criterion based on the scientific method. Dewey was at pains to divorce himself from the ancient and continuing debates about the old philosophical dualisms about mind/matter, subjective/objective, idealism/realism, theory/practice, knowing/doing, and so on. Furthermore, he wanted to put philosophy in the service of making sense out of human beings' everyday experiences and thus helping to solve social problems. The term "instrumentalism" in institutionalist thinking refers to the use of theory as an instrument in problem-solving. Unlike the Milton Friedman concept of instrumentalism as a way of achieving results without the necessity for understanding, the institutionalist view of instrumentalism *requires* understanding.

Clarence Ayres combined Veblen's insight about the two ways of behaving with Dewey's instrumentalism, locating value explicitly in the technological process identified by Veblen and identifying a tendency toward progress in the human condition (Ayres 1944).

At one point Dewey expressed regret that he had not used Ayres's word, "technology," instead of "instrumentalism," noting that Ayres was the first one to call science a mode of technology (Dewey 1946, p. 291n). Ayres, in contrast, two years earlier had said that "instrumental" was preferable to "technological" in two respects: the latter suffers from popular association with the most crudely mechanical techniques, and there is no abstract noun corresponding to "instrumentalism" by which the technological theory of economic progress might be designated, because "technology" means something else (Ayres 1944, p. 155n). Veblen in 1906 had used the following terminology: "[This] employment of scientific knowledge for useful ends is technology, in the broad sense in which the term includes, besides the machine industry proper, such branches of practice as engineering, agriculture, medicine, sanitation, and economic reforms" (Veblen 1991, p. 16).

Institutionalists continue to go back and forth about which is the preferable caption. At this point the terms are not sufficiently clearly defined (see Swaney 1989; also Atkinson 1990, p. 273; and Atkinson and Reed 1990, p. 1097). I propose to use "instrumental" and "instrumentalism" when talking about value theory, in so far as possible.

Foster extended and modified these ideas to suggest that institutions perform two kinds of functions, the instrumental and the ceremonial. The locus of value, as Ayres had argued, lies in the instrumental function. Foster set forth three principles of institutional adjustment, which he saw as applicable to societies at all times and places: technological determination, recognized interdependence, and minimal dislocation (for the best statement of these principles, see Foster 1981, pp. 932-34). Thus he asserted universal applicability, that is, applicability to the entire universe of inquiry.

Marc R. Tool drew upon these ideas to enunciate the most definitive statement on social value theory to date (Tool 1979 and 1986). He offers a value principle: act or judge in a manner to "provide for the continuity of human life and noninvidious re-creation of community through the instrumental use of knowledge" (Tool 1986, p. 10).

The instrumental theory of value, or criterion of judgment—that which tells us "which way is forward," to use Tool's apt phrase—is not an easy concept either to conceptualize or to state. As any of the above would agree, and have argued, it is tentative and provisional, like any other proposition, and subject to correction and modification and refinement as understanding develops. This frees institutionalist thought from the charge that its criterion of judgment is of the nature of an "eternal verity." It seems extraordinarily difficult to imagine any principle useful as a continuous guide in making choices that is not grounded in something outside of human experience, and as such, would be something that institutionalists could not accredit. This difficulty, it would seem, is at the heart of the recurring desire to embrace relativism or existentialism or anything that denies the possibility of the existence of "eternal verities."

**Absolutism, Relativism, and Universality**

David Hamilton describes cogently our unfortunate tendency toward "spectrum thinking," in which all people and ideas are ranged from one polar terminal to the other, with no voids or vacancies. Or, in a slightly different twist, the laissez-faire position on the right joins in full circle with the anarchist position of the left. But, he suggests, knowledge is another matter. Is there a right and left way of adding? Is a steel mill right or left? Institutional economics has been one long effort to get away from such thinking, that is, away from ideology toward knowledge (Hamilton 1991a).

Rejection of a similar way of organizing knowledge, Cartesian dualistic thinking, has been a continuing effort, clearly articulated, of William Waller. When we succumb to the Cartesian vice, he says, we are being static and nonprocessual. When we reconstruct our concepts to capture and reintegrate the complexity of human experience, we are being processual (Waller 1990, p. 900).

A dualistic concept is not appropriate for institutionalist thinking about absolutism and relativism. Absolutism is thought of by institutionalists as the belief that a standard for making judgments is to be found outside of human experience and is therefore beyond human inquiry, that is, beyond question. Relativism is likely to be thought of, at least in the extreme, as the view that there exists no way of making choices rationally about social issues because it is impossible to escape from one's cultural conditioning (see, however, Rorty 1982, pp. 166-67).

In rejecting both of these positions, institutionalists do not place them on a spectrum in which one might possibly reach a "middle ground," nor do they see them as exhausting all of the possibilities in the decision-making process.

What institutionalists seek to do is to ground a criterion in the process of inquiry, that is, to arrive at a standard of judgment by developing theory, using observation, and looking at consequences, in other words, by using the scientific method. They recognize the major contribution of relativism, that is, the insight that all judgments are made in a cultural context and that one's judgments are necessarily affected by that culture. This raises the question of how inquiry that has to be evaluated by reference to a standard can be itself the source of the standard, in the words of Baldwin Ranson (1991a, p. 843), or, as Warren Samuels puts it, whether the role of preconceptions is self-consciously self-referential. Samuels's answer is yes, that is, that indeed one cannot escape from one's culture and that therefore judgments are self-referential, system-specific, and subject to infinite regress (Samuels 1990a, p. 696; Samuels 1991b).

The answer Ranson gives, consistent with the Dewey-Ayres-Foster-Tool line of reasoning, is that the way to arrive at a standard of judgment within the process of inquiry and still avoid the logical fallacy of circularity is to treat all propositions as hypothetical and to subject them to revision as needed by observation of the consequences (Ranson 1991a, p. 844). The instrumental principle, says Tool, is not an eternal verity but a product of inquiry, a construct for inquiry and a tool for analysis and judgment (Tool 1990a and 1990b). Not an infallible method, nor an easy one, but one that is both useful and logically defensible.

Paul Dale Bush, in agreeing with this way of thinking, wisely remarks that pragmatic instrumentalists do not regard the possibility of an infinite regress to be a deficiency of the theory, all empirical and normative propositions are embedded in infinite regresses (Bush 1993). The fact that this process is not totally inhibitory of novelty, that is, of arriving at new knowledge, is evidenced by the fact that new knowledge is produced every day, by human beings, all of whom find themselves in a particular cultural situation.

Anne Mayhew raises essentially the same issue when she says that "there is no 'ought to be' that both has usefully specific meaning and transcends a particular time and place" (Mayhew 1990, p. 895). Walter C. Neale also raises the issue in seeming to deny the reality of general propositions as criteria of judgment (Neale 1990, pp. 333-44). Ranson replies by making the point that the attribute of continuity in technology is a general proposition that is logically defensible, as well as essential to making judgments, while culture-specific, that is, discontinuous, criteria will not serve (Ranson 1991b).

Confusion also surrounds the use of the word "universal." If it is used to refer to the idea of including the whole of the universe of inquiry, that is, of applicability to every member of the population in question, what Alison Dendes Renteln describes as the "least common denominator" (Renteln 1988, p. 66), as used in statistics, then indeed propositions may exist that can properly be described as "universal." For example, Foster would so describe his principles of institutional adjustment; they are applicable to societies at all times and places. Waller uses "transcultural" in the same way when he says that instrumental valuation can be applied to evaluation of the family in any culture (Waller 1990, p. 899). This usage of the word "universal" clearly does not mean that these principles are imposed from outside of human experience or outside of the process of inquiry. If, however, "universal" is thought of in some such metaphysical sense, then the word is not applicable to instrumental thinking. The Foster usage seems appropriate etymologically. The confusion, then, would seem to be one of miscommunication.

## Ayres's Progress versus Veblen's "Blind Drift"

Veblen's passage to the effect that history records more instances of "the triumph of imbecile institutions" than of peoples saving themselves (Veblen 1941, p. 25) is cited increasingly as a refutation of the idea that there is progress in human affairs. The denial, or at least the questioning, of the tendency toward progress seems to be consistent with the thrust of the postmodernist movement and with the thought of many institutionalists (see, for example, Miller 1992; Dugger and Waller 1992, pp. 6-8; Jennings and Waller 1994; Brown 1991, p. 1094; Klein 1992).

Veblen's passage by itself seems indeed supportive of such an interpretation of his thinking. However, viewed against the whole of his work, including his identification of human proclivities toward an instinct of workmanship (to which he devoted an entire book), idle curiosity, and the parental bent, the passage is not of sufficient strength to settle the question about Veblen's view of progress. Actually, one can say more than this. The whole of Veblen's work, (note the quote that introduces this essay and another in the introductory section) leads one not only to the impression that Veblen saw merit in the instrumental way of behaving but also to the impression that he saw progress in human affairs. His protestations to the contrary have a strong "tongue-in-cheek" flavor.

It seems important at this point to look a bit more closely at what is meant by instrumental behavior. Much of the difficulty associated with determining the existence of progress is attributable to the failure of institutionalists to define clearly what is meant by the instrumental process; on this point I believe that Michael Sheehan and Rick Tilman are right (Sheehan and Tilman 1992, p. 205). Ayres at times said that he was talking about a way of behaving, while at other times he said he was talking about tools and concepts, including such items as "mathematical journals and symphonic scores" (Ayres 1961, p. 278), as noted by Edythe Miller (1992, p. 120). A reading of all of his work, however, points quite clearly to a definition that sees technology (his word) as a way of behaving, as a process, and that includes not only behavior in the industrial world but also behavior in morals and in aesthetics. It is continuous and coterminous with human life. It is also developmental because each item in the process leads to something more. Basically it consists of behaving in such a way as to increase knowledge; and knowledge grows. Ayres argues that progress is indissociable from value (Ayres 1944, p. 231).

It is the idea of progress in human behavior, not progress in tools, that gives rise to some doubt. Progress in human behavior is no doubt more difficult to defend, not to mention to prove, but the fact remains that both Ayres and Foster, and others, do contend that human behavior has exhibited progress.

It is easy to fall into the common sense habit of speaking of technology as tools and concepts rather than behavior. This is done when we say that the definition of technology should include the development of the arts and sciences, or the growth of civilization, when what we should say is that human beings are behaving in a more advanced way, a more civilized way, a more knowledgeable way.

This is what Veblen seems to be saying. In speaking of capital, meaning a mass of material objects serviceable for human use, he says "these productive goods are facts of human knowledge, skill, and predilection. . . . [I]t is the human agent that changes,—his insight and his appreciation of what these things can be used for is what develops" (Veblen 1991, p. 71). He (Ibid., pp. 71-72) continues:

> The changes that take place in the mechanical contrivances are an expression of changes in the human factor. Changes in the material facts breed further change only through the human factor. It is in the human material that the continuity of development is to be looked for; and it is here, therefore, that the motor forces of the process of economic development must be studied if they are to be studied in action at all.

To make another point about instrumental value theory, there seems to be a gap, or at best an ambiguity, in institutionalist literature regarding the applicability of the scientific method to the arts. Dewey (and Ayres too) was presenting a scientific methodology that he apparently saw as applicable to the arts as well as the sciences, including the social sciences and philosophy. Looking at the arts for the moment, it seems clear that the scientific method can be applied at least in part, for example, in the use of outcomes as a guide to an assessment of the value of a work of art. But if it is possible to apply the scientific method totally to the creation of an object of art, to the exclusion of any other method, is the distinction between the arts and the sciences lost? If, on the other hand, an existential distinction remains, as I would be inclined to argue, then the objection to the unquestioned primacy of "science" has merit. It seems more satisfactory simply to see the arts and the sciences as two different ways, two media, through which to add to knowledge and understanding. Rorty suggests something similar when he remarks that "[Pragmatism] views science as one genre of literature—or . . . literature and the arts as inquiries, on the same footing as scientific inquiries" (Rorty 1982, p. xliii; see also p. 34). Would not institutionalists agree with at least the latter part of this statement? This problem seems to be involved in the concerns about treatment of the arts expressed by Waller in looking at technology and gender in institutional economics (Waller 1991), as well as by Brown (1994) and by James Sturgeon (1992, pp. 358-60).

The growth of instrumentalism is not to be confused with a teleological process, what Jennings and Waller refer to as "Big-T Teleology," meaning some ultimate purpose in the world exogenous to human behavior, which they rightly reject and which they contrast with "small-t teleology," meaning the purposeful acts of individuals. They argue, rightly, that Veblen rejected Big-T Teleology but embraced small-t teleology (Jennings and Waller 1994).

But let us be clear on this point. Big-T Teleology, which we reject, is not the same as the dynamic of instrumental change, or the growth of knowledge described by Ayres. The dynamic that Ayres talked about is not imposed by some outside metaphysical purpose but occurs because of the tendency of humans to add to knowledge, new knowledge being built upon previous knowledge and, if wrong, being subject to correction.

As Ayres explains, achievements are to be judged "in terms of their fructifying effect upon further achievement in the same, and related, fields. A great painting is one that furthers the art of painting. A great symphony is one that ushers in a new era in music. A great scientific discovery is one that opens up new fields of discovery" (Ayres 1949, pp. 19-20). In the area of economics, the result is an improvement in the standard of living.

Ayres and others who believe in the dynamic inherent in the instrumental process look for evidence in the entire history of human beings from the time Adam and Eve first tasted of the fruit of the tree of knowledge and had to start making judgments about right and wrong. What is the evidence?

On the negative side of the question, anyone can provide a list of some of the horrors of the last decade of the twentieth century, such as ethnic hatreds and atrocities against neighbors, guns in schools, riots in Los Angeles, organized terrorism, widespread starvation. Not to mention the presumed effects of the law of entropy and limited resources (for a constructive opposite way to look at entropy, see Weinel and Crossland 1989, pp. 804-06).

But there is all of human history to consider.

Look at disease, life expectancy, health, development of the arts and sciences, mobility, libraries, universities, communication, education, problem-solving capacity, democracy, civil rights, Mozart, space exploration, photography, the differential calculus, nutrition, sanitation, housing, plumbing, electricity, the theater, freedom (that is, enlargement of the area of discretion), control over the environment, diminished risk. These suggest a trend line slanting upward, rather than downward, to the right, albeit with ups and downs along the way. All of these considerations involve human behavior; they do not exist without human activity. Human beings behave better today because they have the experience of the entire human race to draw on for guidance.

As further evidence of progress one can ponder, along with Ayres, the day when "lords enjoyed first night rights with every bride" (Ayres 1944, p. 244), or, along with Robert Heilbroner, the condition of workers of both sexes, stripped to the waist, in the mines of Durham or Northumberland (Heilbroner 1970, p. 41).

Another difficulty with assessing progress is that the words we use to describe progress, words such as "civilization," "development," "flourishing," and the like, are sufficiently ambiguous and lacking in precision that one could, and some will, argue that one person's "development" is another person's "retrogression."

This should not be allowed to stand as a debate-stopper. The words do have meaning and are sufficiently clear to be useful for purposes of communication.

When a historian says that the Tang dynasty in China saw a development of the arts, we have a pretty good idea of what is meant, and furthermore we approve of it.

Ironically, the idea of value and progress is likely to be better understood by the "man/woman in the street" than by academics. The great mass of the population know when their lives are improving: there is no great mystery about this theory of value that seems so difficult for intellectuals to grasp. It is not reserved for the great defining moments in life, but is the criterion used in everyday experience in solving problems in the community, such as where to put solid waste, how to prepare children to enter school, how to lessen auto pollution, and so on. It is also applicable to individual decision-making, as, for example, choosing the appropriate fabric for a child's sleepwear, or choosing what tool to use in carpentry. It has to do with serviceability for human life, with a rising standard of living, with the application of the scientific method rather than reliance on the gods, or on fate. This does not mean that its application is always clear and simple, nor that is always productive, far from it. It does not make of life a rose garden. It does not lead to utopia. As one problem is solved, new problems await or develop, forever as far as we can tell. But it is something that the great mass of people understand well enough to accredit it and, more often than not, to act on it.

Kenneth Boulding had both vision and a way of speaking understandably. In talking about evolutionary economics, he remarks that evolution and development are almost the same word (Boulding 1981, p. 85). The evolutionary system opens up the possibility for very large improvements in public policy. This is the result of the more realistic appraisals of actual futures corresponding to various decisions, and also of an evolutionary learning process by which "bad" values are slowly reduced, even as error is reduced in our images of the world. In all ecosystems there is likely to be an empty niche at a higher level of complexity but not at a lower one. These asymmetries give direction to evolution, both in biology and in social systems, and give us hope for improvement.

> [Progress is] painfully slow and intermittent, interspersed with catastrophes and reversals, but there is a strong case for believing that in the long run *it is built into the system*, providing there is not an ultimate and irretrievable catastrophe. We should never forget, however, that from the human point of view progress is improvement in the state of persons. . . . We can go to the moon . . . but if in the interval we have not, by well-judged and well-criticized human values, increased the quality of life of persons, it is not progress (Ibid., pp. 194-95; italics mine).

Finally, to conclude this section about progress, Ayres is frequently misrepresented as holding the view that progress is inevitable. To the contrary, he states again and again that it is by no means certain (see, for example, Ayres 1944, pp. 120-21, 250, 294; 1961, p. 227; 1950). What he is saying is that the nature of the instrumental process and the entire history of the human race give evidence that there has been progress and that it is more likely than not to continue. The evidence to him is substantial, if not overwhelming.

It is true that both Ayres and Foster were strongly optimistic on this score, even to the point of indulging in frequent rhetorical excess, but both frequently expressed pessimism as well. The point here is that the entirety of the work of both reveals clearly their view that the expectation of progress was "warrantably assertible," but, like any other proposition, tentative and open to continued inquiry.

## Hermeneutics and Institutional Economics

A discussion of hermeneutics is included in this essay because it seems to contain in it the idea that it is not possible to compare paradigms, or at least that it is better to get beyond this and talk about something else.

Usually defined as the theory of interpretation, hermeneutics is a response to a recognition of the difficulty of communication involved when the participants do not have a shared tradition or world view. Like institutional thought, hermeneutics rejects self-evident certainties and inapplicable dualisms and suggests tendencies toward open-endedness, process, pluralism, and pragmatism.

Philip Mirowski explains that hermeneutics concentrates on the role of shared tradition as the locus of continuity and quality control in the interpretative process. It is a response to the gridlock of communication that often results when strongly disparate perspectives confront one another; it arose from the experience of trying to "get into the other person's head" (Mirowski 1987, p. 1010 [1988a]).

Brice R. Wachterhauser sees history and language functioning as both conditions and limits of all understanding. He hints at a philosophical problem similar to that faced by institutionalists when he observes that since history and language are transitory, they serve as a special type of transcendental conditioning, which, because they are transitory, "necessarily evade a final theoretical account of how they function in this transcendental capacity" (Wachterhauser 1986, p. 6). What we are, he goes on, cannot be reduced to a human nature that is the same in all historical circumstances, but rather,

> [W]ho we are is a function of the historical circumstances and community we find ourselves in, the historical language we speak, the historically evolving habits and practices we appropriate, the temporally conditioned problems we take seriously, and the historically conditioned choices we make. . . . In short, hermeneutics defends the ontological claim that human beings are their history (Ibid.).

Much of hermeneutical thinking has been embedded in institutional thinking all along. Ann Jennings and William Waller suggest a strong affinity in their interpretation of Veblen's concept of cultural evolution as an unfolding hermeneutic process. They proceed to go beyond this in suggesting a combination of culture and hermeneutics as perhaps providing a way to find what they call a middle ground between Veblen's "blind drift" and Ayres's faith in progress (Jennings and Waller 1994). Mirowski sees an affinity between hermeneutics and John R. Commons's "transaction," a complex social phenomenon in which conflicts of interest and interpretation are endemic (Mirowski 1987, pp. 1026-27 [1988a]).

To go back to Wachterhauser's concern about transcendental principles, in most discussions of hermeneutics the notion of metaphysical foundations or the possibility of a court of final appeal is either scoffed at or explicitly denied. Rorty gives great credit to Dewey for trying to get beyond the unanswerable questions of philosophy, beyond ontology and toward participation in community. The current movement to make the social sciences "hermeneutical" is applauded by Rorty if it refers to vocabulary or conversation rather than to a special method. As is frequent in such discussions, there is a wariness about science as well as about fundamental principles.

This highlights the importance of the singular contribution of Dewey. He was trying to do something that arguably had not been done before in philosophy and has not been done since except by those who get their inspiration from him: to identify a way to find validity in orderly inquiry into inquiry, that is, logic, without basing it on some outside force that is beyond human scrutiny. It is extraordinarily difficult for human beings to free themselves from the need for certainty, for "metaphysical comfort," as Dewey explained so clearly (Dewey 1929). But, alas, it seems equally difficult for us, especially for academics, to accept the possibility of finding guiding principles on which we can base inquiry without the fear that we have surrendered to metaphysics or eternal verities. If it is not called scientific, then it is metaphysical, and therefore suspect. But if it is called scientific, then it is suspect too.

Hermeneutics has a view of human nature that institutionalists can accept in part but not wholly. The idea that human beings "make themselves" will find a sympathetic ear among institutionalists. But most institutionalists will find continuing factors in human nature as well. Does it not go without saying that granting that human beings exist means also granting that there is such a thing as human nature, that is, that there are continuing attributes in human beings that permit identification of them as human beings? Institutionalists would probably largely agree, for example, that human beings in all societies use tools and language.

Institutionalists could well accept a hermeneutic philosophy if it were to be understood as incorporating Dewey's logic. Such seems not to be the case, however, at this point. Along with a rejection of metaphysics, the hermeneutical philosophy seems to find it necessary to reject any logic that provides guidance in evaluating cultures of different times and places. But there is much in hermeneutical thinking that can be, and indeed already has been, incorporated into institutional thought.

**Postmodernism and Institutional Economics**

Postmodernism is said to have started in architecture; it now seems to have extended to virtually all fields. A look at postmodernism is included in this essay largely for the same reason that hermeneutics is included, namely to explore what it has to with value theory.

In philosophy and the social sciences, postmodernism is described by Doug Brown as a perspective on the world rather than an epistemological paradigm or an analytical framework like institutionalism. It is a response to the fragmentation, heterogeneity, speed, diversity, discontinuity, and chaos of today's life. It is a rejection of modernism—of the science, knowledge, belief in essences and in a common human nature, in absolute truths and universal values that characterized it. Postmodernism disputes this confidence in progress and knowledge (Brown 1994).

The postmodern capitalistic system appears to create more and more differences rather than commonalities. It has created a proliferation of heterogeneous life experiences among people once thought to have a lot in common. Life is becoming more differentiated, particularized, individualized, and customized, and this forces us to accept limitations on our ability to fully comprehend the world, in contrast to the "enlightenment" of modernism. There are no teleological forces operating behind the scenes, there are no universal essences or unifying tendencies in today's capitalism. The postmodern world is one of insecurity, apprehension, instability, and bewilderment. The number of diverse experiences we are exposed to expands tremendously. Postmodern living creates a profound identity crisis. Our traditions are destroyed, our lifestyles are diversified. We find less basis for shared experiences and common meanings with others. Communication becomes more important. Postmodernism is the manifestation of the freedom/insecurity compulsion in fast-forward. For postmodern philosophers such as Michel Foucault, Jean-Francois Lyotard, and Richard Rorty, life experiences and the meanings associated with them are destabilized, and knowledge and truth are called into question (Ibid.).

The epistemology of postmodernism says that society is going nowhere in particular, that the knower is part of the known, that knowledge is provisional, and that we have to be our own foundation. From all of this Brown feels, and I agree, that at least much of institutional thinking is postmodern.

Brown explores very thoughtfully to what extent this is true. He thinks the epistemology of postmodernism points toward reliance on instrumental value theory and Dewey's pragmatism (Brown 1994, pp. 43, 44). He also writes approvingly of Ayres's effort "to go beyond postmodernism by attempting to ground his view of universal values in the technological dimension of the life process" (Brown 1991, p. 1099). In general, however, while Brown is clearly sympathetic with Ayres's genuine effort to get beyond moral relativism, he cannot grant that technology is in fact uniting us in a valuation process based on shared meanings (Ibid., pp. 1100-01).

David Ruccio is helpful in pointing out postmodernist effects on economics, most of which will be immediately recognizable by institutionalists, having to do with criticizing the mainstream epistemological position on such issues as equilibrium, uncertainty, and rationality and with analyzing the multiple languages, metaphors, and strategies of persuasion used by contemporary economists. He goes on to suggest that value is a concept constituted within discourse rather than something that is said to exist "out there" (Ruccio 1991, pp. 502, 507).

Warren Samuels, in a very thoughtful and "hermeneutic" analysis, outlines a proposal or synthesis that affirms the importance both of epistemology and its limits and of the analysis of discourse. The epistemological status of statements and theories does not exhaust their meaning; they must also be comprehended as linguistic and rhetorical, that is, discursive, phenomena. Epistemology has to do with truth, which he defines as what we accept as confident knowledge, while discourse analysis has to with meaning. This does not mean that "anything goes;" it does mean that the burden is on human beings to choose (Samuels 1991a).

## Concluding Thoughts

In reading much of the often abstruse literature on philosophy, one sometimes finds it tempting to join Rorty in the hope that a "post-philosophy" period might be realized. But it is better to continue with Dewey in the effort not to discard philosophy but to get beyond the old unanswerable dualisms and to work toward fashioning a philosophy that can help to make sense out of the everyday lives of the great mass of human beings. Both Dewey and John Maynard Keynes tried to do this, that is, to explain human experience in terms meaningful to the community in order that the community could proceed rationally to solve its problems (see Keynes 1921; G. P. Foster 1991a).

A large part of the necessary content of philosophy is the development of a unified and consistent theory of value. The instrumentalist theory of value developed by institutionalism is admittedly imperfect, provisional, and tentative. But it is warrantably assertible and clearly useful. Some criterion is essential, and if not instrumentalism, then what? If a better one is available, by all means let it be put forward.

One thought that emerges from the look at postmodernism is that the laments of postmodernists sound much like the laments of philosophers at least since the time of the ancient Greeks. It seems very easy to think that one's own time is the most confusing and turbulent ever.

Another thought is that the explosion of knowledge and social change has become so overwhelming that it becomes increasingly difficult to organize it, either for analysis or for policy-making, much less to understand it. This encourages a tendency to go too far in the direction of nihilism, in the feeling that the individual is adrift in a boundless sea without a compass. It is perhaps more important than ever to see that life is not just "a dance of the atoms," to perceive that there is in fact some order and pattern in the universe, and to continue to try to identify the continuing factors. It is not warranted to discard all of the philosophy of the eighteenth-century apostles of reason, morality, and progress based on the growth of knowledge (see Randall 1926, pp. 365-86).

Better to recognize that one is not adrift without a compass but rather that one has all of the experience of the past to provide guidance, as Veblen and Dewey and Ayres tried to tell us, and to combine this with an effort to use discourse to try to enhance meaning, along with Foucault, Rorty, and other postmodernists.

# 4. THE URGENCY OF SOCIAL VALUE THEORY IN POSTMODERN CAPITALISM

Doug Brown

> We are in the epoch of simultaneity: we are in the epoch of juxtaposition, the epoch of the near and far, of the side-by-side, of the dispersed. We are at a moment, I believe, when our experience of the world is less that of a long life developing through time than that of a network that connects points and intersects with its own skein.
>
> Michel Foucault 1967

> We survey conditions, make the wisest choice we can; we act, and we must trust the rest to fate, fortune or providence.
>
> John Dewey 1929

## Introduction

The above statement by Michel Foucault, whose work is generally associated with the development of postmodernism in contemporary philosophy, speaks to the unsettling and disorienting experience of everyday life encountered by much of the world at the close of the twentieth century. His words reveal a profound loss of confidence in "truth," a skepticism about knowledge, and an insecurity about progress. Foucault speaks with an emotional depth and conveys that sense of decenteredness commonly associated with postmodernism.

Postmodernism is in many respects a philosophical extrapolation from the human condition Foucault describes above. The confusion and discontinuity of contemporary life that these words describe also anticipate the fundamental question posed by Marc Tool and the institutional tradition of social value theory: Which direction is forward? If Foucault's assessment is at all accurate, and if it does in some way attest to the postmodern condition today, then there is some urgency for social value theory. Postmodernism questions whether or not we can ever know which way is "forward." Institutionalists have spent the better part of the last century trying to answer that.

Yet the fears of life, the lack of foundation, and loss of cognitive mooring that Foucault suggests here are no more than what John Dewey battled in the "quest for certainty." In the postmodern world of today, with the fragmentation, decenteredness, insecurities, and uncertainties that Foucault announces, Dewey's statement above provides the instrumental response. We do not give up the struggle in the "epoch of simultaneity" but rather "survey the conditions" and "make the wisest choice we can." The way forward as Tool suggests is "that which provides for the continuity of human life and the noninvidious re-creation of community through the instrumental use of knowledge," and as Dewey said "knowing goes forward by means of doing" (Tool 1979, p. 293; Dewey 1929, p. 290).

The questions posed by postmodernism tend to undermine the entire notion of social theory, its legitimacy, its credibility, and its efficacy. Postmodernism is in many respects re-asking the questions under somewhat more difficult conditions that institutionalists since Veblen have been trying to answer. Postmodernism may be the current version of what Clarence Ayres called the "pestilence of moral agnosticism" (Ayres 1961, p. 42). Ayres also said that it is the "dissociation of truth and value that defines the moral crisis of the twentieth century" (Ibid., p. 49). Postmodernism is not a rehashing of the truth-value dichotomy but suggests that there is no way out of this moral crisis, and yet again, this is where Dewey's pragmatism, institutionalist instrumentalism, and Tool's social value theory make a contribution in a time of urgency.

**Is There Anything New About Postmodernism?**

The fact that postmodernism is asking questions today that institutionalists have been trying to answer for the last half-century should not cause us to dismiss postmodernism with a simple wave of the hand. Although much of the postmodern issue in epistemology is concerned with the "uncertainty" of truth and knowledge that Dewey tackled, postmodernism represents some additional and deeper issues resulting from the very dramatic cultural and social transformation now taking place in the global economy.

Postmodernism is a neologism, and as such Michael Rosenthal recently suggested that it may have "vagued itself out" (Rosenthal 1992, p. 102). He may be right, as it has been a term used in intellectual circles with a certain *nouveau chic* popularity. People like to use it and talk about it, but nobody knows exactly what it is. He adds, that "when we cut through the fanfare, what this often boils down to is an affirmation of plurality and complexity, something we can all gladly endorse, but which does not seem to require the firepower of postmodernism to give it expression" (Ibid., p. 101). However, he correctly concludes that "the transformations in social and economic life that underlie theories of the postmodern, such as the new economies of information, new global organizations of commodity production, the impact of new technologies on work life and the impact of just-in-time production on job security as well as commodity consumption—all of this continues to take shape around us, continues to cry out for understanding" (Ibid., p. 104). It is this "cry for understanding," a consequence of the current cultural crisis of postmodern capitalism, to which social value theory can respond.

There have been some novel applications of postmodernism also dotting the economics landscape. As Philip Mirowski recently asked: "If it is a hallmark of postmodernism to deny the text has a single fixed and stable referent, then what if the 'economy' were treated in a similar manner?" (Mirowski 1991, p. 565). In this same issue of the *Journal of Post Keynesian Economics*, David Ruccio states that "postmodernism has begun to reshape economics: first, by criticizing modernist epistemological positions, and in general the way economists write and talk about the work they do; then by challenging the content of economics and the particular way modernist economists treat such issues as equilibrium, uncertainty, or rationality" (Ruccio 1991, p. 502; see also Samuels 1990 and Klamer, et al 1988). One is, however, tempted to respond that institutional economics has been doing precisely what Mirowski and Ruccio are currently suggesting.

Institutional economics, beginning with Veblen, clearly does have a postmodern flavor to it (Brown 1991 and 1992). This is because both institutional economics and postmodern epistemology take a similar approach to the uncertainty of truth and knowledge. Both reject the modern science and Cartesian notion that a "God's eye view" of the world is obtainable for service as an ultimate foundation of legitimacy. Jean-Francois Lyotard in his *Postmodern Condition* states that such a privileged perspective is not possible, and therefore knowledge is limited and tentative.

In agreement with institutionalists he says that "the fact remains that knowledge has no final legitimacy outside of serving the goals envisioned by the practical subject, the autonomous collectivity" (Lyotard 1984, p. 36). The question is whether or not he would agree with Dewey that therefore "knowing is advanced by doing." Social value theory plays an important role here, because it does not leave us in the postmodern dilemma of doing nothing for lack of a universal foundation for legitimacy.

Cornel West maintains that the fragmentation and decentering effects of the cultural crisis of postmodern capitalism cause a "walking nihilism," because much of what postmodernism characterizes is a breakdown in "structures of meaning" (West 1988, p. 286). Social value theory is aimed at preventing just this sort of "walking nihilism" and "moral agnosticism." As Wittgenstein stated, under postmodern conditions, "philosophy leaves everything as it is" (Wittgenstein 1965, p. 124).

Kate Soper paints a caricature of this postmodern dilemma of the value issue. There are the absolutists and the relativists. It is this dilemma that she caricatures that social value theory and the work of Marc Tool and those that preceded him seeks to overcome:

> On the one side there are the dogged metaphysicians, a fierce and burly crew stalwartly defending various bedrocks and foundations by means of an assortment of trusty but clankingly mechanical concepts such as 'class,' 'materialism,' 'humanism,' 'literary merit,' 'transcendence' and so forth. Then on the other side we have the feline ironists and revellers in relativism, dancing lightheartedly upon the waters of *difference*, deflecting all foundationalist blows with an adroitly directed ludic laser beam. Masters of situationalist strategy, they sidestep the heavy military engagement by refusing to do anything but play (Soper 1991, p. 122).

Yet there is a "reconstructive wing" of postmodernism as Steven Best and Douglas Kellner suggest "that uses postmodern insights to reconstruct critical social theory and radical politics" (Best and Kellner 1991, p. 257). Many who have been influenced by postmodern ideas and who have felt the decentering effects of the current cultural crisis of postmodern capitalism, but who also do not want to submit to "walking nihilism" are part of this reconstructive wing.

Social value theory is a direction in which to turn. Marc Tool has perceived this in economics as well. He says that there is a "paradigm shift" occurring, and some of the new directions "are similar to or compatible with the positions institutional theorists (Thorstein Veblen, Clarence Ayres, Gardiner Means, and so forth) have been evolving over this century" (Tool 1986, p. 182). Richard Rorty argues that there is "still an air of provincialism about pragmatism. Peirce, James, and Dewey are studied mainly in their native land, the United States" (Rorty 1990, p. 1). Many analytic and continental philosophers "are content to shrug off pragmatism" (Ibid.). Yet Rorty is hopeful that with the postmodern drift, philosophers and social theorists who are still committed to social change and a criterion for "which direction is forward," will move toward pragmatism and Dewey, Peirce, and James will get the credit they deserve. Social value theory stands at the contemporary frontline—not as an answer to all the postmodern queries but as a tool to be used.

**The Cultural Transformation Of Postmodern Capitalism**

So what is *new* about postmodernism are the particular global, political-economic conditions that give rise to it. Postmodernism is the label describing the cultural reaction to the globalization of capitalism, which itself is being driven by the high-technology revolution. This is a change in capitalism that is structural but is not equivalent to, at least at this point in time, a shift to a post-capitalist society. It is not a system change but a "global shift" that is deep enough to create a major social and cultural crisis (see Dicken 1992).

There are two separable dimensions to this transformation that are interrelated and both byproducts of the high-tech revolution in communications, computerization, and electronics: 1) a factor mobility-based drift to global laissez-faire capitalism, and 2) a shift in mass production and mass consumption from homogeneous to heterogeneous needs, products, and lifestyles. Together these two phenomena are causing a whole host of globally metastasizing symptoms including increased anxiety, insecurity, community fragmentation, cultural dislocation, and multicultural congestion. It is as Foucault suggests in the epigraph to this chapter: the epoch of the "near and far," of the "side by side," and of the "dispersed."

What has previously been spatially distant and separated is now together. What has previously been together is now divorced. There is both novel integration in the international economy coupled with social disintegration. Both are occurring simultaneously. What was a half-century ago common to cultures, communities, peoples and places is now fragmented, particular, differentiated, and diversified. What was also culturally specific, historically unique, and well-defined is now blurred, uncommonly recombined, pastiche, and an unrecognizable blend of "fuzzy sets."

With respect to the first dimension of the transformation, Karl Polanyi's thesis in *The Great Transformation* is insightful (Polanyi 1944, 1965 ed; see also Brown 1992). Polanyi argued that the drift toward a self-regulating market economy in the 19th century created so much insecurity and disruption people intuitively reacted by seeking protection from the vagaries of these market forces. They organized unions, both business and labor lobbied the state for protective legislation, they built trusts, and sought out all kinds of novel means to get some control over blind market forces. The result in the 20th century was the welfare state and social democratic capitalism. As Polanyi suggested laissez-faire was a negative utopia that existed only in the theories of neoclassical economists. Thus, in Polanyi's terms, the "disembedding" of the economy that tended to create laissez-faire was met with "re-embedding" forces of the "protective response" of society. Negotiated contracts, social democracy and the welfare state, and global U.S. hegemony all tended to "re-embed" economic activity during the post-WW II period. This measure of stability was achieved primarily through efforts at the domestic level, while at the international level the nation-state system led by the unrivaled dominance of the U.S. maintained a stable system based upon international *trade* rather than *global production.*

The high-tech revolution has now helped to produce a truly global, integrated, accelerated, and intensely competitive capitalism in which the old "re-embedding" institutions are being undermined. As Adolph Lowe (1988, p. 36) states:

> Perhaps the 'malaise' about which social and clinical psychologists complain today has its roots in a rate of change that greatly overtaxes mental and even nervous capacity. A similar discrepancy between the speed of change and the capacity for adaptation affects the *institutions* that the liberal era has bequeathed to us.

As the previous "re-embedding" and protective institutions are eaten away by the globalization of production, we enter a new and far more frightening condition of global "disembedding" of economic activity (see Dicken 1992; Lash and Urry 1987; Block 1990; Ross and Trachte 1990). Ross and Trachte refer to the globalization of capitalism, that is postmodern capitalism, as the "New Leviathan." The globalized system of capitalism has become such because the high-tech revolution has dramatically accelerated the mobility of all factors of production, while at the same time shortening the planning horizon of TNCs and speeding up the decision-making process. More supply and demand decisions can be made more quickly in this globalized market system.

"Yet the irony of the New Leviathan is that its individual agents, global firms, and financial institutions, are not sovereigns but severely constrained competitors committed to the *economic* war of each against all" (Ross and Trachte 1990, p. 2). Peter Dicken says "a key feature of the postwar period has been the development and intensification of *global competition* in virtually every industry, both old and new" (Dicken 1992, p. 430). Likewise, Lash and Urry refer to this as the "end of organized capitalism" (Lash and Urry 1987). To the extent today that impersonal, self-regulating markets work more quickly over a broader geographic scope, they tend to organize behavior. But this is not what Lash and Urry want to depict by their analysis. What they mean by the "end of organized capitalism" is the end of the stability fostered by the quasi re-embedded character of the post-WW II institutional system.

Dicken (1992, p. 1) adds that it is now a "multipolar system" of "turbulence and volatility":

> We live in a period of major economic change; an era of *turbulence and volatility* in which economic life in general is being restructured and reorganized both rapidly and fundamentally. We live in a world of increasing complexity, interconnectedness and volatility; a world in which the lives and livelihoods of every one of us are bound up with processes operating at a global scale.

Polanyi described these same disruptive and socially destructive byproducts of the original disembedding of economy from society that occurred between the 16th and 19th centuries. The 20th century witnessed a period of domestic attempts at tempering self-regulation with weak and often fleeting re-embedding and protective institutional mechanisms.

Now the century closes with turbulence and volatility driven by new production and distribution systems that are not only global in nature but produce "social heterogeneity" rather than "massified homogeneity" typical of earlier mass industrial-production technologies. The literature describing the new production systems that are part of postmodern capitalism verges on overwhelming. New descriptive labels are proliferating. There is "post-Fordism," "flexible accumulation," "flexible specialization," "just-in-time production," "lean production," "space-shrinking technologies," "time-space compression," and "economies of scope" rather than of scale (see Harvey 1989 and 1991; Dicken 1992; Rosenthal 1991; MacEwan 1991; Gordon 1988; Freeman 1987).

The second dimension of the current economic transformation, although it like the drift toward global laissez-faire is also driven by technological changes, is still separable from the first. The technological changes underway are not only bringing the world within the orbit of global self-regulating markets that both integrate in some areas (Los Angeles—the "capitol of the third world") and fragment in others (the breakdown of the nuclear family), but they are also creating a new round of diversity in virtually all aspects of life. As Feher and Heller (1988, p. 142) note:

> The specter of 'mass society' in which everyone likes the same, needs the same, practices the same, was a short intermezzo in Europe and North America. What has indeed emerged is not the standardization and unification of consumption, but rather the enormous pluralization of tastes, practices, enjoyments and needs.

For the last century and a half the technologies available were ones that could only produce cost-effectively for standardized and uniform needs. To profitably produce for "mass markets" the products had to be standardized. There was a sense clearly evident in Marx and followed up by the hippie movement in the 1960s that populations living under this type of capitalism were or would eventually become more and more alike: homogeneous working (or middle class) class people, doing the same jobs, going to work at the same time, wearing the same clothes, living in identical "ticky-tacky" suburban houses (Levitown), driving the same cars, and living the same, boring middle class lifestyle! John Kenneth Galbraith raised this point in *The Affluent Society* and *The New Industrial State*, and Herbert Marcuse discussed this in his appropriately-titled *One-Dimensional Man*. Homogeneity and one-dimensionality were seen by the 1960s to be the "essence" of capitalism.

By today's vantage point that would appear to have been a wrong judgment. The new technologies allow firms to tailor production to "niche markets" using "just-in-time" production techniques and "flexible specialization" (Harvey 1991, p. 67). With the ability to differentiate products comes the ability to differentiate needs on an ever-finer basis. As needs become more diversified, consumer capitalism takes on a more diverse appearance. Lifestyles become more differentiated and diversified. Multiplicity, pluralization, cross-cultural combinations of diverse tastes and preferences have all been accommodated by the system's capacity for "mass customization." What is most important to emphasize in this process is that, although this is still a system of consumerism in which the "good life" continues to be embraced as the "goods" life, *the means by which people can define themselves and their interests differently from one another has increased.* Postmodern capitalism is a global multicultural pastiche of social heterogeneity.

This has been made possible, if not directly caused by, the high-tech revolution. As Dicken (1992, p. 5) states:

> Both old and new industries are involved in this re-sorting of the global jigsaw puzzle in ways which also reflect the development of technologies of transport and communities, of corporate organization and of the production process. The technology of production itself is undergoing substantial and far-reaching change as the emphasis on large-scale, mass production, assembly-line techniques is shifting to a more flexible production technology.

As David Harvey states "economies of scale" have been replaced by "economies of scope" (1989, p. 155; 1991, p. 76). Flexibility is the key focus and goal. Fred Block suggests that "it is now generally understood that there is a sharp contrast between what was called automation in the late 1950s and early 1960s and the current phase of automation, which is characterized by increasing flexibility" (Block 1990, p. 94).

But the heterogeneity of life today is not merely one of cosmetic differences in consumption. In production, the drift is away from standardized occupations and the stylized image of masses of bluecollar, white, male wage-workers droning away in a machine-orchestrated factory. Not only is the working class diversifying in consumption but is doing so in production as well. The sociological composition of working people is becoming more diverse and complex as the nature of production shifts to "post-Fordism:"

> of all the new 'post'-words, post-Fordism is the one most directly concerned with technology. Theorists of post-Fordism interpret the contemporary world in light of a movement away from large-scale mass production and toward production under conditions that are often called 'flexible specialization.' The Fordist model of production was Henry Ford's assembly line, where a mass work force produced large batches of goods using large-scale machinery designed for only that purpose. The post-Fordist model, by contrast, implies an insecure, retrainable work force, producing smaller batches of goods in computerized, reprogrammable machinery, in response to a variegated and unpredictable consumer market (Rosenthal 1991, p. 80-81; see also Dicken 1992, p. 116).

Work and occupations have diversified. The people in the workplace have become more diverse in race, class, ethnicity, age, gender and cultural contour. About all they have in common is that they offer their labor for wages. This is surely not the makings of class consciousness and solidarity as Marx hoped.

The cultural transformation of postmodern capitalism in both its global laissez-faire and social heterogeneity dimensions does not create commonality of interests, meanings, or values. Possibly, in the sense that we are all wage-workers, there is one other common condition besides the identity crisis, stress, and anxiety that are increasingly universal: "Those fortunate enough, however, to be citizens of temporarily rich countries should not be lulled into a false sense of security. What First World people increasingly have in common with those of the Third World is vulnerability" (Knippers Black 1992, pp. 12-13).

According to Fredric Jameson what we have as a common experience of postmodern living is "discontinuity," decenteredness,and "psychic fragmentation" (Jameson 1988, p. 14). From the perspective of social value theory, the values that these experiences imply is not at all clear. To have fear and insecurity in common when at the same time people cannot identify the sources of these feelings due to "psychic fragmentation" does not suggest optimism. For Jameson, what is happening in this "postmodern space" we inhabit is "the loss of our ability to position ourselves within this space and cognitively map it" (Ibid., p. 7). We then experience a rather profound type of permanent identity crisis, and as Harvey puts it, "to what space do I as an individual belong?" (Harvey 1991, p. 77).

This is the cultural context in which postmodern philosophy comes into existence, and this is what also forces the urgency of social value theory. If "psychic fragmentation" is what people of the "earth island" have in common, then "which way is forward?" is not very clear.

## Postmodern Philosophical Challenges

Although the neologism, postmodernism, is one that has come into popular usage only within the last two or three decades, as a reaction to Enlightenment modernism, postmodern thought is at least a century old. Friedrich Nietzsche is usually considered one of the earliest postmodern thinkers. As Best and Kellner (1991, pp. 27-28) suggest:

> Postmodern theory however, is not merely a French phenomenon but has attained international scope. This is fitting because, as noted, German thinkers like Nietzsche and Heidegger already began the attack on traditional concepts and modes of philosophy. The American philosopher William James championed a radical pluralism and John Dewey attacked most of the presuppositions of traditional philosophy and social theory, while calling for their reconstruction.

Because postmodern thought is a reaction to the modernist faith that somehow within the anarchy of the unbridled profit-seeking market system there is order, rationality, and eternal and universal verities, it is only logical that skeptical souls such as Nietzsche would challenge this faith.

For as far back as the emergence of capitalism and what Polanyi called the "disembedding of the economy from society," there has been a schizophrenic dichotomy between the experienced reality of capitalist blind market forces and the cognitive rationality of equilibrium and order assigned to the invisible hand. At the level of experience for many people capitalism is insecurity, impersonal and uncertain market forces, dislocation, vicious competition, dehumanization and alienation. Yet at the level of reason and Descartes' *cogito*, it is presumed to be just the opposite. For modernists capitalism is self-equilibrating harmony, balance, rationality, and teleology. Modernists have suggested that skeptics like Nietzsche should distinguish between the irrationality of appearance and the "rationality of the essence" of capitalism, that is modern life.

Of course to grasp the "essence" of modern life, science was to be of great service. With the scientific perspective, one was supposed to be able to take a "God's eye view of the world," that is, a perspective that is outside the object of investigation, objective, and totalizing. From this vantage point, the scientist could rightfully comprehend the essence of the system. Thus, "things aren't as bad as they might appear." As Ruccio states, "modern thought can be understood as a long tradition—stretching from Descartes, through the Enlightenment, to the most recent focus of modernist literature and economics—of gradually transferring to a creative human subject the attributes traditionally associated with the divine subject" (Ruccio 1991, p. 500).

So for modernism, the point of science and inquiry is to pierce the veil of mystification that binds us to experiences of absurdity, irrationality, and anarchy and reveal the essential nature of modern living. The essential nature of modern living is order, universal truths, progress, emancipation, and once people come to recognize the essence of *what is* then truth will reign, history is transcended, and reason will prevail.

Much of modernist thinking is not only based upon the scientific method and Cartesian dualism but is also situated within "grand narratives" or "meta-narratives." The grand narrative "purports to be a privileged discourse capable of situating, characterizing, and evaluating all other discourses, but not itself infected by the historicity and contingency that render first-order discourses potentially distorted and in need of legitimation" (Fraser and Nicholson 1988, p. 87).

Of course this sounds very Hegelian, and naturally, both Marx and the classical economists were modernists in this sense. As Enlightenment modernists they "took it as axiomatic that there was only one possible answer to any question. From this it followed that the world could be controlled and rationally ordered if we could only picture and represent it rightly" (Harvey 1989, p. 27).

Therefore, the modernist vision of salvation by science, of eternal essences and universal truths has had its detractors before the current cultural crisis brought it all to the surface by way of global laissez-faire and post-Fordist heterogeneity. As Lyotard declared, grand narratives are out, that is, that there is "incredulity" toward them today (Lyotard 1984, p. xxiv). The danger here is that consequently, "anything goes" is in. As Feher and Heller (1988, p. 2) state:

> The grand narrative recounts the story (of who we are, from where, and going where) with an overtly causal, covertly teleological self-confidence. But those dwelling in the postmodern political condition feel themselves to be after the entire story, strict causality, secret teleology, omniscient and transcendent narrator and its promise of a happy ending in a cosmic or historic sense.

Postmodernism, as it has come into vogue today is a very diverse, and probably for that specific reason, a very vague but emotional reaction to the epistemological confidence of modernism. Much of what has been said by Foucault, Derrida, and Lyotard concerns the lack of foundation for all kinds of theorizing in both the natural and social sciences. Cornel West states that "what we call postmodern philosophy today is precisely about questioning the foundational authority of science" (West 1988, p. 272). Best and Kellner suggest that there is a "broad array of postmodern perspectives and positions," yet they all

> tend to explode the boundaries between the various established academic disciplines—such as philosophy, social theory, economics, literature—and produce a new kind of supradisciplinary discourse. Postmodern theorists criticize the ideals of representation, truth, rationality, system, foundation, certainty, and coherence typical of much of modern theory. As Hassan puts it, postmodern theories are part of a culture of 'unmaking' whose key principles include: 'decreation, disintegration, deconstruction, decentrement, displacement, difference, discontinuity, disjunction, disappearance, decomposition, de-definition, demystification, detotalization, delegitimation' (Best and Kellner 1991, p. 256; see Hassan 1987, 92).

The deconstruction of modernist epistemology also leads to the idea that the irrational is present alongside the rational, and that the Cartesian subject is never fully outside the object of its investigation (Ruccio 1991, pp. 500-1). The contradictions and paradoxes that result from the recognition that we are always *within* whatever we are looking at were announced by existentialists a half-century ago, particularly through their search for the origin of absurdity.

Dewey's rejection of representationalism in epistemology is likewise based upon his rejection of Cartesian dualism and the spectator theory of knowledge. Richard Rorty (1990, p. 2) adds that

> only what Dewey called a spectator theory of knowledge can lead one to think that metaphysics, empirical science, or some other discipline might someday penetrate through the veil of appearances and allow us to glimpse things as they are in themselves. For that theory assumes

> that there is something like what Hilary Putnam called a 'God's-eye view' of things. A God's-eye view is one that is irrelevant to our needs and our practices.

What has happened with the deconstructivist attack on modernism is that truth becomes limited, uncertain, tentative. There are no universals, no irreducible core essences, no identifiable commonalities that are eternal, and no ultimate foundations for our political practices and our values (see Fraser and Nicholson 1988, p. 85). So the "relativist logic" of postmodernism is "inherently self-stultifying" (Soper 1991, p. 120).

This is the point at which social value theory makes its contribution, because the postmodernists "are delivered into a condition of theoretical paralysis: they can neither argue for the 'truth' or knowledge status of the forms of argument they have employed to expose the mistakes and self-delusions of foundationalist metaphysics, nor lay claim to any emancipatory values in liberating a left politics from the disquieting assimilations of identity concealed within its collectivist and humanist 'grand narrative'" (Ibid., p. 120).

## The Urgency of Social Value Theory

Not only have there been critics of modernism before the contemporary postmodernists, but there have been those who also have tried to rescue social theory from the authoritarian and objectivist effects of modernism and the "moral agnosticism" of the postmodern critique. There are precedents for the kind of theorizing done by Veblen, Dewey, Peirce, James, and other early institutionalists. Clearly the work of Heidegger, Sartre, and Merleau-Ponty are in this genre, and the development of hermeneutics is as well. Best and Kellner suggest that this kind of "third way" approach "calls for theory to be reflexive and self-critical, aware of its presuppositions, interests, and limitations. This tradition is thus non-dogmatic and open to disconfirmation and revision, eschewing the quest for certainty, foundations, and universal laws" (Best and Kellner 1991, p. 257).

What this is suggesting is what institutionalists have called instrumentalism, social value theory, pragmatism, and "evolutionary economics." What Best and Kellner describe here is what Marc Tool states as the basis for his approach in *The Discretionary Economy*, and the collection of articles in *Essays in Social Value Theory*.

It has been suggested that many postmodern theorists, such as Lyotard, go "too quickly from the premise that philosophy cannot ground social criticism to the conclusion that criticism itself must be local, ad hoc, and untheoretical" (Fraser and Nicholson 1988, p. 90). In other words, they see no "third way" between objectivism and relativism. This nihilistic dimension to postmodernism implies that it "throws out the baby of large historical narrative with the bathwater of philosophical metanarrative and the baby of social-theoretical analysis of large-scale inequalities with the bathwater of Marxian class theory" (Ibid.).

Yet Harvey says that there are other postmodernists who have been able to find a progressive dimension to postmodernism in which there is an "intermediate niche for political and intellectual life which spurns grand narrative but which does cultivate the possibility of limited action" (Harvey 1989, p. 351). This was earlier referred to as the "reconstructive wing" of postmodernism. Social value theory for institutionalism is the "intermediate niche," and it represents a major contribution toward finding our way out of "walking nihilism" and "moral agnosticism."

As Chantel Mouffe states, "affirming that one cannot provide an ultimate rational foundation for any given system of values does not imply that one considers all views to be equal" (Mouffe 1988, p. 37). Social value theory and instrumentalism are based upon the belief that judgments can be made without recourse to ultimate rational foundations. Ayres asked "what hope is there for a community whose intellectual leaders not only cannot demonstrate the superiority of their own way of life over that of any other people but have convinced themselves that no such demonstration is intellectually possible?" (Ayres 1961, p. 49). If the baby is thrown out with the bathwater as mentioned above then Ayres' fear is valid. If no effort is made to carve an intermediate niche or third way in the current turmoil of the postmodern cultural crisis then the problems of the twenty-first century will only be worse.

The postmodern critique of modernism makes sense, and this is what Dewey argued in *The Quest for Certainty*. Based upon what has been described here as modernism and the postmodern critique of it, it should be clear to the institutionalist reader that the approach of institutionalists from Veblen and Dewey to Marc Tool is an approach that is well-suited to the challenge of postmodern capitalism and its cultural crisis.

Postmodernism raises the same questions today that Dewey (1929, pp. 6-7) raised in 1929:

> All activity deals with individualized and unique situations which are never exactly duplicable and about which, accordingly, no complete assurance is possible. All activity, moreover, involves change. The intellect, however, according to the traditional doctrine, may grasp universal Being, and Being which is universal is fixed and immutable. Wherever there is practical activity we human beings are involved as partakers in the issue. All the fear, disesteem and lack of confidence which gather about the thought of ourselves, cluster also about the thought of the actions in which we are partners. Man's distrust of himself has caused him to desire to get beyond and above himself; in pure knowledge he has thought he could attain this self-transcendence.

Thus, as Veblen, Dewey, Ayres, Foster, and Tool have pointed out the quest for certainty is admirable but certainty is unobtainable. Today's postmodernism is an open philosophical admission of this. And this in-itself is progressive so long as it does not submit to moral agnosticism and walking nihilism. Pragmatism, instrumentalism, and social value theory are not aimed at overcoming uncertainty but at judging "which direction is forward" given the actuality of uncertainty.

Many postmodern theorists are coming to the conclusion that American pragmatism (and by inference social value theory) is the way out (see West 1988; Rorty 1990). It is the third way and intermediate niche suggested by David Harvey. Instrumentalism and social value theory are a way of doing theory and working for progressive social change without certainty—in an age of uncertainty. As Bill Dugger (1989, pp. 14-15) comments:

> the truth, itself, is a process. The pragmatic or instrumental truth is not something that is found. It is not discovered once and for always. It is a democratic and participatory process. The truth is to be found in action. Existing through action, the truth is instrumental—and existential.

Liebhafsky also states that "rather than seeking final truths, institutional economists seek knowledge to shape institutional change through operational concepts permitting problem solving in reality. Accomplishment of their purpose . . . is not possible within the framework of an analysis in which natural forces are deduced to lead to the values inherent in an ideal" (Liebhafsky 1993, p. 750). Given the global changes leading us into the twenty-first century, there is little hope that "natural forces" will lead us anywhere but into greater turmoil and violence—certainly not to "values inherent in an ideal." Therefore, the urgency of social value theory exists as a demand for those wanting to shape change in a humanizing and democratizing direction for a sustainable and socially-just world in the next century.

## Conclusion

The type of capitalism that corresponded to the development of modernist thought is now evolving in a much different direction. Modernist confidence in teleological social progress, in universalizing tendencies, and in eternal, intrinsic and essential truths was based on that specific tendency of capitalism to integrate and mold economic and political behavior in the direction of self-regulating markets. Yet this particular tendency to bring all behavior into conformity with the logic of the competitive pursuit of economic self-interest has also been accompanied by the counter-tendency to disrupt, disintegrate, and fragment traditional cultural patterns.

The market system, in other words, has both the integrating, harmonizing tendency of subordinating life activity to the invisible hand of blind competitive market forces, and it also has the fragmenting tendency of destroying all barriers to its logic. It harmonizes and integrates while it dislocates and disembeds.

Modernist thinking situated itself on the side of the integrating effects of the market system. It saw method in the madness. It had faith that the "market pattern," as Polanyi called it, would win out. In the twentieth century the stabilizing, social democratic and Keynesian policies coupled with the mass production, Fordist technologies of homogeneity reinforced the modernist faith.

Of course, there were others who focused more on the disintegrating, dislocating, and otherwise anarchic tendency of capitalism. Institutionalists have been one such group along with Nietzsche and some existentialists. Now that capitalism is in a new transformative period, characterized by global disembedding and social heterogeneity, postmodernism surfaces to challenge the modernist faith in truth, progress, and universal essences.

Modernist rationality corresponds to a capitalism that no longer exists. It was a capitalism that had a measure of order, of homogeneity and standardization of life, of balance, routine, and integration. Postmodern capitalism is much different, and it gives rise to a healthy skepticism about eternal and universal truths and progress. Pragmatism, instrumentalism, and social value theory, because they are rooted in the disintegrating and fragmenting tendency of capitalism, are appropriate modes of inquiry for the postmodern condition of the twenty-first century.

Best and Kellner suggest that we need a "multidimensional critical postmodern social theory" that is therefore "multiperspectival" (Best and Kellner 1991, p. 272). Social value theory is precisely this. As Liebhafsky suggests, "pragmatic truth is relative, depends on current knowledge, and changes as knowledge improves in response to changes in man's physical and social environment" (Liebhafsky 1993, p. 748). Instrumentalism also is open-ended, based upon the means-ends continuum, warranted assertability, and so on. As Tool concludes, the institutionalist "instrumental value principle offers no utopian solution; it is no panacea. It is no magic elixir which if taken in prescribed doses will clear up economic and political aches and ills without inquiry and vigorous social action" (Tool 1979, p. 299).

The postmodern condition is real. This is a period of turbulence and volatility, of multiplicity, diversity, and decenteredness. It has shaken our confidence in progress, unanchored our existence, and set us lose in a world of global confusion and cultural crisis. The temptation to resignation and moral agnosticism is strong. Social value theory's urgency is a result of this. Dewey was correct in 1929 when he stated that uncertainty is part of our existence. At best we retain the modernist set of values comprised of democracy, equality, and freedom; survey the landscape; make the best decisions we can; and forge ahead in what we take to be that direction most in sink with these values.

# 5. PRAGMATISM AS A NORMATIVE THEORY OF SOCIAL VALUE AND ECONOMIC ETHICS

Lewis E. Hill and Roger M. Troub

Pragmatism may be defined as that philosophy which holds that all reality has practical consequences and that, therefore, certainly the best way and perhaps the only way to know and to understand true reality is through the consideration of practical consequences. It is commonly supposed by those scholars who misunderstand and misinterpret pragmatism that this philosophy is based on cultural relativism and is, therefore, completely devoid of all normative and ethical content (Lutz 1985, p. 169). It is the purpose of this essay to advocate vociferously and to support vigorously the contrary view that normative and ethical considerations inhere in pragmatism and that a valid and reliable normative theory of social value and economic ethics can be induced from the pragmatic philosophy.

Pragmatism is the only major philosophical system that is uniquely American. It originated in the United States where it grew out of the historical experience of the American people on their western frontier. Life on the American frontier was a constant struggle for survival, which required many hard choices among alternatives that had to be judged according to their practical consequences. Moreover, the resulting knowledge and understanding of reality had to be used to solve practical problems. In this manner, pragmatism emerged from the historical milieu of the United States to become the folk philosophy of the American people (Kalen 1933).

This implicit and informal folk philosophy was transformed into an explicit and formal system by Charles Sanders Peirce, who captured the essence of pragmatism in his well known imperative ". . . consider what effects, which might conceivably have practical bearings, we conceive the object of our conception to have. Then, our conception of these effects is the whole of our conception of the object" (Peirce 1958, p. 124). Peirce always insisted that the meaning of a concept, proposition, or idea could be correctly specified and truly understood only in terms of the practical consequences which it implies for the conduct of life (Ibid., pp. 180-202). Pragmatism is empirical, rather than rationalistic, in its epistemology and inductive, rather than deductive, in its logic.

Peirce developed logical definitions of truth and reality. Peirce defined truth as the final conclusion that all competent investigators would reach if they studied the problem long enough; he defined reality as the object to which the true conclusion applies: "This great law is embodied in the conception of truth and reality. The opinion which is fated to be ultimately agreed to by all who investigate is what we mean by the truth, and the object represented by this opinion is the real" (Ibid., p. 133).

Peirce's normative theory of value and ethics is induced from his philosophy of religion. He defined religion as a perception and recognition of First Cause and Final Cause and of "a relation to that Absolute of the individual's self, as a relative being" (Ibid., pp. 350-351). Peirce always conceived religion to be a dynamic pattern of behavior and life style; he never conceived religion to be a set of ecclesiastical dogmas and doctrines which are not only completely static, but also extremely narrow. According to Peirce's philosophy of religion, Christianity is differentiated from other religions by the Doctrine of the two Ways: the Way of Life symbolizes love and the other creative propensities of the human personality; the Way of Death symbolizes hatred and the other destructive propensities of the human personality (Ibid., pp. 353-357). The Way of Life motivates the creative and benevolent behavior which becomes the essence of social value; the Way of Death motivates the destructive and malevolent behavior which becomes the essence of social disvalue. Economic ethics are a set of rules of conduct which require socioeconomic behavior that is compatible with social value and prohibit socioeconomic behavior that is incompatible with social value. Peirce (Ibid., p. 355) has summarized his normative theory of social value and economic ethics very succinctly in the following quotation:

> Now what is this Way of Life? Again I appeal to the universal Christian conscience to testify that it is simply love. As far as it is contracted to a rule of ethics, it is: Love God, and love your neighbor; "on these two commandants hang all the law and the prophets."

Peirce's version of pragmatism was modified and popularized by William James, who introduced the instrumental epistemology into the pragmatic philosophy. According to this epistemology, the truth of an idea should be judged according to what it does, rather than according to what it says. In order to be judged to be true, an idea must not only correspond to some external reality, but also prove to be useful to us in helping us to relate to that external reality. True ideas help us to distinguish between the good and the bad aspects of reality, to establish a harmonious relationship with reality, and to use reality to achieve our objectives and goals. Conversely, false ideas confuse and deceive us in such a manner and to such an extent that they lead us into a disharmonious relationship with reality and prevent us from achieving our objectives and goals. All true ideas are useful; all useful ideas are true. The truth of an idea is a prediction that it will be useful; the usefulness of an idea is the verification of its truth. This line of reasoning led James to assert that truth is nothing more nor less than mere expediency in our patterns of thought (James 1908, pp. 197-238).

James rejected all metaphysical or absolute criteria for judging religious ideas to be true or false. Entirely to the contrary, he consistently used his instrumental epistemology to evaluate the truth of ideas concerning religion in exactly the same manner that he used this epistemology to evaluate ideas that concern all of the other aspects of our experience. If a person finds his religious ideas to be useful to him in relating to reality, then these ideas are true. But if a person does not find his religious ideas useful to him in relating to reality, then these ideas are false. This instrumental analysis led James to distinguish between "tough-minded" and "tender-minded" people. The tough-minded people are the ones who are so strong and so secure that they do not need religious ideas to help them to relate to reality; therefore, they evaluate religious ideas to be false. The tender-minded people are the ones who are so weak and so insecure that they need religious ideas to help them to relate to reality; therefore, they evaluate religious ideas to be true (Ibid., pp. 273-301). James (Ibid.) concludes his discussion of religion with the following quotation:

> But if you are neither tough nor tender in an extreme and radical sense, but mixes as most of us are, it may seem to you that the type of pluralistic and moralistic religion that I have offered is as good a religious synthesis as you are likely to find. Between the two extremes of crude naturalism on the one hand and transcendental absolution on the other, you may find that what I take the liberty of calling the pragmatistic or melioristic type of theism is exactly what you require.

This pragmatistic or melioristic religion became the basis for James' normative theory of social value. James rejected the idea of cultural determinism; rather, he contended that a cause-and-effect relationship exists between the actions of an individual reformer and socioeconomic progress. According to the doctrine of meliorism, which James induced from his philosophy of religion, each person has an inherent personal responsibility and a social obligation to meliorate the dangerous and drastic conditions that threaten the survival of contemporary civilization. In this manner, the doctrine of meliorism transforms James' pragmatism from a theory of individual behavior into a theory social behavior. If pragmatism is a theory of social behavior, then it can easily be expanded and elaborated into a normative theory of social value and economic ethics.

John Dewey continued to lead pragmatism in the direction of instrumentalism. He agreed with James that a true idea must not only correspond to reality, but also prove to be useful in dealing with reality. But, Dewey extended the analysis to its ultimate conclusion by seeking answers to two questions: one concerning the origin of true ideas; the other concerning the purpose for which true ideas should be used. True ideas originate from logical or scientific inquiry, which is open, unbiased, systematic, and creative. True ideas are intellectual tools or instruments to be used for the purpose of solving important practical problems. The instrumental process always begins with the utilization of logical or scientific inquiry to induce true ideas from experience; it always ends with the instrumental application of true ideas to the solution of important practical problems (Dewey 1938, pp. 101-117).

Dewey also developed an instrumental or operational theory of normative value. He believed that ordinary people are entirely capable of using inductive logic to make true value judgments concerning the goodness or badness of practical consequences. These judgments of normative value are made in exactly the same way and for exactly the same purpose as judgments of positive fact. Both judgments of normative value and judgments of positive fact are made through the use of inductive logic to provide a basis for decisions concerning a future course of action. Judgments of normative value, like judgments of positive fact, are induced from previous experience and verified by reference to subsequent experience (Ibid., pp. 157-180). In other words, people learn from previous experience how to make valid normative value judgments and how to apply these value judgments through the instrumental process to the solution of practical problems. They also learn how to verify both the validity of the normative value judgments and the effectiveness of the problem solutions by reference to subsequent experience. This instrumental or operational interpretation was expanded and elaborated into Dewey's normative theory of social value (Dewey 1939b).

The instrumental theory of normative value implies a social interpretation of morality, which becomes the axiological basis of an instrumental system of ethics. According to Dewey, "Morals is connected with actualities of existence, not with ideals, ends and obligations independent of concrete actualities" (Dewey 1957, p. 329). He believed that the established churches had lost their ability creatively to integrate the individual person with an infinite whole and had become nothing more than an institutionalization of mythical superstition, irrational dogmas, and liturgical ceremonies. The true basis of morality must be found through scientific inquiry into the social aspects of human behavior.

Morality involves the harmonizing of incompatibilities in the social environment and the solving of problems involving social relationships. Moral actions are expressions of the human awareness of the ties that bind each person to all mankind. A system of instrumental ethics can be induced from this social interpretation of morality (Ibid., pp. 314-332).

Another approach to formulating a normative theory of social value has been sought by Jacob Bronowski, a distinguished scientist who became an equally distinguished pragmatic philosopher. Bronowski has taken a very strong position that the scientific method implies a set of normative values which are not only created by the scientific method, but also necessary for continued scientific progress. According to Bronowski, the whole purpose of scientific inquiry is to discover and publish the truth; therefore, *truth* is the first value of science. But the quest for the truth requires independence of thought and action; therefore, *independence* is the second value of science. Independence of thought and action produces originality; therefore, *originality* is the third value of science. Originality brings dissent; therefore, *dissent* is the fourth value of science (Bronowski 1965, pp. 40-62).

Dissent is a hallmark of freedom; therefore, *freedom* is the fifth value of science. Freedom is protected by tolerance; therefore, *tolerance* is the sixth value of science. Tolerance characterizes democracy; therefore, *democracy* is the seventh value of science. Finally, democracy presupposes a sense of human dignity, therefore, *a sense of human dignity* is the ultimate value of science. Bronowski based his normative theory of social value on the sense of human dignity, which he considered to be the most important of all human values (Ibid., pp. 60-69).

Bronowski enlarged this pragmatic theory of normative value from a theory of social value into a theory of ethics by alleging that the practical consequences of historical progress tend to reward ethically good behavior and to punish ethically bad behavior (Ibid., p. 54):

> Is it really true that the wicked prosper? In the convulsions of nations, have tyrannies outlived their meeker rivals? Rome has not survived the Christian martyrs. Machiavelli in *The Prince* was impressed by the triumphs of the Borgias, and he has impressed us; but were they in fact either successful or enviable? Was the fate of Hitler and Mussolini better? And even in the short perspective of our own street, do we really find that the cheats have the best of it? Or are we merely yielding to the comforting belief that, because one of our neighbors flourishes, he is *ipso facto* wicked.

Pragmatism provides the philosophical basis for the institutional school of economic thought; therefore, institutional economics is an extension of the pragmatic philosophy into the social sciences. Institutional economics may be defined as a pragmatic theory of socioeconomic and politicoeconomic behavior, derived empirically through the application of inductive logic to qualitative and quantitative historical facts, and applied instrumentally to the solution of practical problems. Institutional economics utilizes an empirical epistemology and an inductive logic; it emphasizes the historical methodology. The purpose of institutionalism is to solve practical socioeconomic and politicoeconomic problems. Institutional economics has always included and emphasized normative theory; institutionalists have always demonstrated a strong interest in social value and economic ethics.

Thorstein B. Veblen, the brilliantly radical Norwegian-American economic philosopher and social critic, originated the institutional school of economic thought during the early twentieth century. Although Veblen explicitly denied any intent to formulate a normative theory of social value, his scholarly works not only clearly implied the existence of such a theory, but also definitely imputed substantive content to it. He always held that the human personality is divided into opposite and offsetting sets of instincts and propensities: an affirmative set which motivates good behavior; and a negative set which motivates bad behavior (Tool 1977, pp. 824-828). He dealt with the negative aspects of the human personality in his first book, *The Theory of the Leisure Class* (1899); he developed the affirmative aspects in his third book, *The Instinct of Workmanship* (1914). Veblen contrasted the affirmative and negative personality traits in *The Theory of Business Enterprise* (1904) and in *The Engineers and the Price System* (1963). This juxtaposing of the good and bad aspects of the human personality become the basis of the Veblenian dichotomy, which distinguished between the affirmative and negative instincts and propensities which motivate human behavior. Veblen found value in the affirmative instincts and in the creative, productive, and useful patterns of technological or instrumental behavior which they motivate; he found disvalue in the negative instincts and in the destructive, exploitative, and wasteful patterns of institutional or ceremonial behavior which they motivate (Tool 1977, pp. 824-828). This Veblenian dichotomy has become the basis of the normative theory of social value and economic ethics which implicitly inheres in all institutional economic theory.

Veblen's greatest disciple was Clarence E. Ayres, who not only extended and elaborated the Veblenian tradition of institutional economics, but also synthesized and integrated this tradition with Dewey's philosophical tradition of instrumental pragmatism. Ayres accepted the Veblenian dichotomy between the affirmative and negative aspects of the human personality and utilized it as the basis of both his theory of economic causation and his theory of normative value. In his theory of economic causation, Ayres analyzed the structure and functioning of the economy as a conflict between an inherently dynamic technology, which causes all progressive change, and inherently static institutions, which inhibit and resist progressive change (Ayres 1944, pp. 105-202). In his theory of normative value, Ayres analyzed human behavior as a conflict between the creative propensities of the human personality, which motivate productive and useful technological or instrumental behavior, and the destructive propensities, which motivate exploitative and wasteful institutional or ceremonial behavior. Ayres then generalized his theory of normative value by formulating his concept of the technological or instrumental life process and by utilizing this concept, to symbolize and to summarize the creative propensities of the human personality and the affirmative patterns of human behavior that they motivate. This technological or instrumental life process has brought the human species from being a naked and hungry savage struggling for survival against great odds and into the abundance, comfort, and security of modern civilization. Moreover, the life process is the basis for all truly normative value judgments; it is the standard by reference to which all normative value judgments are evaluated to be true or false (Ibid., pp. 205-230). Clarence Ayres has written: "It is in this, the life process of mankind, that values arise . . . . When we judge a thing to be good or bad, or an action to be right or wrong, what we mean is that, in our opinion, the thing or act in question will, or will not, serve to advance the life process insofar as we can envision it" (1961, p. 113f.).

Ayres also integrated Veblen's institutional theory of normative value with Dewey's instrumental philosophy of normative value. The senior author of this essay has argued in another paper (Hill and Owen 1984) that Dewey's theory of normative value was entirely procedural. Dewey not only insisted that ordinary people are thoroughly competent to make completely valid normative value judgments, but also specified a procedure through which they could make these judgments (Dewey 1938, pp. 101-117, 159-180, and 220-244; Dewey 1939b). Dewey, however, never presumed to dictate to these ordinary people anything concerning the substantive content of their value judgments. Ayres completed Dewey's theory of normative value by providing a substantive content for it. Ayres' concept of the technological or instrumental life process provides the substance of the pragmatic theory of normative value which is necessary to transform Dewey's procedural theory into Ayres' substantive theory, which specifies a real norm or standard for ethical economic behavior (Hill and Owen). This institutionalist or instrumentalist theory of normative value has become the philosophical basis of the pragmatic theory of social value and economic ethics.

One of Ayres' ablest students and most faithful disciples was J. Fagg Foster, who had a remarkable impact on institutional economics largely through the oral tradition that he created over his long career at the University of Denver. Foster's normative theory of social value specified the manner in which institutional structures must be adjusted to the dynamically progressive technology in order to achieve instrumental efficiency in behavioral patterns. Foster articulated a set of three principles which facilitated optimally beneficial institutional adjustments. The first was the principle of technological determination, which held that a socioeconomic problem can be solved only if the institutional aspects of the problem can be brought into an instrumentally efficient correlation with the technological aspects of the problem. The second was the principle of recognized interdependence, which held "that the immediate pattern of any institutional adjustment is specified by the pattern of interdependencies recognized by the members of the institution" (Foster 1981, p. 933). The third was the principle of minimal dislocation, which held that all institutional adjustments should be incorporated into the culture in such a manner as to minimize the disruptive effects on the institutional structure of that culture. These three principles of institutional adjustment constitute the essence of Foster's normative theory of social value (Ibid., pp. 929-935).

Foster's normative theory of social value implies a code of ethics which mandates instrumentally efficient patterns of behavior in order to facilitate the required institutional adjustments to the dynamic technology and to promote the technological or instrumental life process. But there are practical constraints on the magnitude of the institutional adjustments that can be introduced into the culture; therefore, ethical people should seek to determine the maximum amount of institutional change that can be tolerated by the system. In the light of this determination, it would be unethical to do nothing or to do too little for the purpose of facilitating the necessary institutional adjustment. But it would be equally unethical to attempt to force unfeasible change which might cause intolerable dislocations and maladjustments in the system. Ethical behavior requires inquiry into the relationship between "what is" and "what ought to be" in order to facilitate the adjustments that are necessary to achieve a continuous improvement in human welfare (Ibid., pp. 893-895).

Marc R. Tool, a protege of Foster, has written extensively on the subject of social value theory (1977; 1978; 1979; 1983; 1986), and he has always acknowledged his intellectual indebtedness to his mentor. A major thrust of Tool's work has been the formulation of an explicit statement of a general criterion of judgment that can become the basis for making decisions concerning normative value. Tool's criterion of judgment holds that social value is to be found in that course of action "which provides for the continuity of human life and the noninvidious recreation of community through the instrumental use of knowledge" (Tool 1979, p. 293). This criterion of judgment is well known among institutional economists and has been widely but not universally accepted. Tool has addressed two underdeveloped areas in pragmatic value theory: the "operationality issue," and the "evolutionary compass issue."

By providing a general, overarching criterion, Tool greatly improves the operationality of pragmatic social value theory. It improves the communication of the nature of pragmatic value theory and thereby its potential for explicit acceptance and use in particular contexts. Moreover, by specifying explicit elements (continuity of human life and the noninvidious recreation of community through the instrumental use of knowledge) Tool's criterion more clearly identifies ethical and non-ethical behavior. Tool goes further to identify such things as promotion of freedom "as genuine choice for all" (emancipation), equality "as discretionary dignity" (right to be and belong), and justice "as instrumental involvement" (participation in democratic social decision-making processes) as currently warranted derivative aspects of his social value criterion (Ibid., pp. 320-336).

The "evolutionary compass issue" involves the necessity to distinguish between progressive change and regressive change. Everyone agrees that the life process is evolutionary. Theories of cultural evolution provide very good explanations of the social change and evolutionary progress that inhere in past events, but they neither predict nor preordain the course of future events or the direction of cultural change. However, human inquiry, discretion, and effort can identify new "ends in view," choose among them, and seek to achieve the one which is most likely to create progressive change. It is our belief that Tool's criterion of judgment provides a valuable intellectual instrument which can prove to be extremely useful in identifying progressive change and distinguishing it from regressive change (Ibid., pp. 292-314).

Tools's normative theory of social value can be implemented only through the application of instrumental ethics. Tool warns against both ethical relativism and ethical absolutism. Ethical relativists pursue a situational ethic which is devoid of general social applicability. Ethical absolutists utilize immutable ultimates which transcend human experience (Ibid., p. 289):

> Ethical absolutists are not on the way; they have already arrived. Evolutionary theorists are always enroute; their destination is always provisional and intermediary; their destinations or arrivals are departure points for further reflective travels.
>
> A criterion of judgment must be sought elsewhere than in the either-or boxes of the relativists and the absolutists. The ambivalence of the former and the certitude of the latter are in differing ways crippling.

From his application of instrumental value theory, Tool draws broad conclusions concerning ethical behavior. Citizens of a democratic nation, such as the United States, have an ethical obligation to themselves continuously to seek self-growth and self-development to the fullest possible extent. The purpose of this self-growth and self-development is to acquire the skills of critical thinking, logical inquiry, and articulate communication which are necessary for effective participation in the process of democratic self-government (Ibid., pp. 253-263). Then each citizen has an ethical obligation to participate fully, effectively, and creatively in the democratic political process in such a manner and to such an extent as to facilitate and to promote "the community of human life and the noninvidious recreation of community through the instrumental use of knowledge" (Ibid., p. 293).

It is our conclusion that pragmatism and institutionalism imply a normative theory of social value and economic ethics. The emergence of this normative theory of value and ethics has been traced from Charles Sanders Peirce, through

William James and John Dewey, to Jacob Bronowski. The further development of this theory and its application to institutional economics has been traced from Thorstein B. Veblen, through Clarence E. Ayres and J. Fagg Foster, to Marc R. Tool. It is our conviction that pragmatism provides the strongest philosophical basis for normative theory and that this normative theory of social value and economic ethics is a powerful intellectual instrument which should be utilized in the formulation and evaluation of socioeconomic and politicoeconomic policy.

# 6. EFFICIENCY VERSUS EQUITY: A FALSE DICHOTOMY?

Glen Atkinson



Marc Tool has made a convincing argument that, over the last sixty years, economists have been compelled to do institutional analysis. The compelling forces have been the problems and situations facing people trying to improve their material circumstances. The world-wide depression of the 1930s was the event that broke "the pervasive grip of the Marshallian/Hicksian orthodoxy on the minds and hearts of an increasing number of economists and policy makers" (Tool 1981a, p. 569). Other events such as World War II, de-colonization, and rapid advances in technology have caused the shift to institutional analysis to continue. A major point made by Tool is that these structural shifts in the economy have compelled policy makers to be concerned with normative issues as they consider questions of efficiency. If economists failed to respond to the concerns of policy makers, the discipline would be left out of the most important public debates. The orthodoxy Tool referred to posed a trade off between equity and efficiency; equity enhancements necessarily impose an opportunity cost in terms of efficiency. The shift to institutional analysis is a recognition of the fact that the relationship between equity and efficiency is much more complicated than a simple trade-off. The characteristics of that relationship will be explored in this chapter.

## The Compulsive Shift and the Forces Working Against It

All schools of economics are concerned with creating conditions to improve the material well-being of the population, though their definitions of the necessary conditions and the characteristics of material do differ. Nevertheless efficiency is a vital concern of economic inquiry. Even though the orthodoxy has included institutional questions in their analysis, equity concerns still play second fiddle to efficiency. The logic of the market rests on the notion that because exchange between two individuals is voluntary, then each party must have gained or they would not have consented to the swap. Therefore, allocative efficiency is improved because the market responded to the preferences of the individuals who, alone, can rank their own preferences. This is all there is to rational behavior; an individual can rank his preferences. Allocative efficiency is maximized when preferences that are able to be registered in the market are prioritized by market processes and satisfied in order. Any other outcome would necessarily be based on non-voluntary choices, or coercion, which would do harm to someone. Since we cannot make interpersonal comparisons, it is concluded that efficiency would be reduced by such choices.

The story does not end with allocative efficiency, however. These goods and services in the optimal allocative mix are produced with scarce resources which are also exchanged in their relevant markets. Productive efficiency is achieved when goods in the allocative mix are produced with the lowest cost combination of resources purchased in the relevant markets. If a resource which is not owned can be used in production, then it is free and should be exploited. Economic efficiency requires both allocative and productive efficiency. Owners of more productive resources will have relatively high earnings, and will be able to register their preferences in the goods market more heavily than those with less productive resources. Accordingly, efficiency and equity problems are solved simultaneously with no societal constraints. The solutions of rational individual markets have been aggregated into a social welfare function which demonstrates that social policy cannot improve on the performance of smoothly working markets. An aggregation of individual "welfare functions'" becomes a social welfare function without the aid of any institutions other than markets.

All economists know this story, and institutionalists have spent a great deal of time exposing the circularity of the logic. That is not my present intention, because I believe institutional theory has advanced well beyond the stage of criticizing alternative paradigms to the point of using and evaluating our own theory. My point in retelling this story is to remind us of how appealing the message is. No amount of facts and logic will unseat such an appealing foundation for belief. Marc Tool was correct; the change had to be compelled by circumstances. As a theoretical instrument, it has proven inadequate to the tasks it has been assigned. Because such powerful interests and deeply held beliefs have been challenged, the change has been more of a drift than a shift. As Douglass North put it "to abandon neoclassical theory is to abandon economics as a science" (North 1978, p. 974). We need to learn from other scientific disciplines that science is not a particular paradigm. Richard Feynman, a Nobel award winning physicist, concluded that science is "a kind of scientific integrity, a principle of scientific thought that corresponds to a kind of utter honesty—a kind of leaning over backwards" (Feynman 1985, p. 311). It makes it very difficult to shift to a new method of analysis if the method itself is confused with truth as North and other neoclassicals tend to do.

Traditional neoclassical price theory, and its extension to welfare theory, has been concerned with choices made within a given rules structure, but as we have had to alter institutions to deal with new circumstances, we have found that efficiency and equity cannot be so neatly separated. A change in rules is about changes in rights, which directly involves questions of equity in addition to concerns about allocative and productive efficiency. The discussion of health care reform, which is high on the political policy agenda in the 1990s, will require a delicate balance of equity and efficiency considerations, but this does imply a simple trade-off between the two. As Allan Schmid reminds us the question of whose interests counts will be asked throughout the debate (Schmid 1987, pp. 251-252). In any ongoing system, such as health care, there are vested interests and those attempting to become vested. It distorts the legitimacy of the debating process to characterize any of these as special interests since all interests are special to one group or another, but it does help to make a distinction between vested and non-vested groups. (Academics with tenure or seeking tenure cannot be too smug in castigating special or vested interests.) The question becomes why are some groups vested and some left out? What happens to the performance of the system if some of the vested groups have their rights diluted by the inclusion of others or alternatively, how do we judge the performance of the system if the excluded remain excluded? It is obvious that in such debates we cannot hope to find a position of global efficiency as is searched for in modern welfare theory because some interests will be exposed to the rights of others (Ibid.).

It is these kinds of issues which have compelled economists to deal directly with institutional analysis, and institutional change must correlate equity and efficiency concerns. It then follows that a theory of value resting on individual preference will not be sufficient to study institutional development. Instead an explicit social theory of value is required for intelligent policy analysis (Tool 1977). Orthodox economists have attempted to ward off or minimize these concerns by developing theories of occasional market failure. Public choice economists have taken this a step further by the deployment of standard rational models to show that choice theory is the same for rules as for goods and resources. From this perspective we can now simply add a market for institutions to the general orthodox system (see Field 1979; Schmid 1987; and Atkinson 1983 for critiques of these attempts to save orthodoxy). Even a group which has labelled themselves "New Institutionalists" have appeared on the scene to study institutional development. This group led by Oliver Williamson would turn over control of institutional design to existing organizations under the rubric of "private economic ordering" (See Williamson 1985 for a statement of private ordering and Simon 1991 and Dugger 1983 and 1990 for a critique). Although orthodoxy has been compelled to include the study of institutional change in their inquiry, they have a strong vested interest in doing it on their own terms. Thus it will likely continue to be a compulsive drift, rather than a shift.

There are powerful voices in the mainstream who do clearly see the compelling forces. The editors of *The Economic Journal* asked a group of distinguished (orthodox) economists to speculate about the direction economic theory will take in the next century. These pieces were published in the January 1991 issue of that journal, which marked the beginning of the second century of its publication. Several of the authors echoed Tool's claim of a compulsive shift. One of the better written articles was written by Frank Hahn who believes that we will see the end of theory which relies on deducing implications from a small number of axioms because we have learned that the economy is much too complex to be captured by such theorizing. As Hahn said the present state of economic inquiry is "theoretically as well as empirically unsatisfactory" (Hahn 1991, p. 47). The axiomatic logic will probably be replaced by historical and evolutionary theorizing according to Hahn. He does recognize the difficulty of embarking on this shift noting "it is unlikely that those with the temperament and facilities of the mid-twentieth century theorists will find this a congenial road" (Ibid.). I interpret this to mean there will be a great deal of reluctance to do what is necessary because of the heavy hand of custom and tradition. Perhaps we need an institutional analysis of the compulsive shift. Hahn, unlike Tool, believes that the shift will be brought on by "an increasing realization by theorists that radical changes in questions and methods are required if we are to deliver, not practical, but theoretically useful results" (Ibid.). Tool is more interested in the instrumental use of theory to assist in the solution of actual problems.

Ray Marshall made much of this distinction between theoretical consistency and policy relevance in remarks upon receipt of the 1993 Veblen-Commons award, and concluded that "good economics will respect rigor but will not sacrifice rigor for relevance" (Marshall 1993, p. 319). Similar to Tool, Marshall concluded that the obsession with rigor rather than relevance will diminish the appeal of neoclassical theory. Much of the basis of Marshall's conclusion is that efficient markets require "rules that are transparent, fair and enforceable" (Ibid., p. 311). Hence, efficiency and equity are inseparable as I understand Marshall's remarks.

It would seem that institutional economists would have been recognized as the scholars with the method to undertake the inquiry needed to solve the emerging problems. To some extent our position was usurped by the pretenders of institutional analysis described above. Also there are not enough Institutionalists on doctoral granting faculties; we are not vested. But that was perhaps only part of the problem. The debate Institutionalists have engaged in over the last ten or fifteen years regarding social value theory might be considered an indication that as a group we were not ready to lead the public study of institutional change. The content and function of a social value theory has been hotly debated among Institutionalists for the past decade, and a resolution to this debate appears to be in sight. This debate, sparked by Marc Tool's attempt to spell out valuation criteria, has probably prepared us to be more effective participants in public policy analysis, but we will still have to deal with the heavy hand of custom and power of vested interests which define what is appropriate economics.

As related above, it will be difficult to get orthodox economists to make the shift they will need to make in order to become effective participants in public policy discussions, because of the powerful cultural heritage of orthodoxy and orthodoxy still considers questions of social value to be out of bounds. As Charles Schultze characterized the situation, "When you dig deep down economists are afraid of being sociologists. The one thing we have going for us is the premise that individuals act rationally in trying to satisfy their preferences. That is an incredibly powerful tool, because you can model it" (Quoted in Kuttner 1985, p. 76). True science is not about maintaining inappropriate deterministic models, but we recognize the power of custom on any going concern including the science of economics. This powerful force cannot simply be dismissed because vested interests are in a better position than those trying to become vested, especially when they have such a seductive message of efficiency determined by voluntary choices in a decentralized system.

However I believe institutional economists are probably in a better position to become influential in policy than ever, regardless of the powerful forces working against a true paradigm shift. I believe there are two reasons for the improved lot of institutional economists. First, there are the compelling forces described by Marc Tool. Second, the debates over the concept of an institutional social value theory which have been printed in the *Journal of Economic Issues* have sharpened our own understanding of the theory and method of institutional economics. A synthesis of ideas by contributors too numerous to name have advanced the theory of institutional economics well beyond where it stood before the debates began. In the next section I will outline my understanding of this synthesis without going through a blow-by-blow account of the debates. This will be followed by a section of discussion on the improved social value theory which allows institutionalists to treat efficiency and equity issues without the use of the trade-off dichotomy of orthodoxy.

**Pragmatic Value Theory**

Institutionalists do not find the concept of equilibrium very useful in understanding institutional development and economic change. Orthodox economic theory is ahistorical, and perhaps even anti-historical, as we notice the elimination of economic history and history of economic thought from the very standardized curriculum. The core concept of institutional economics is process or cumulative causation rather than tendency to equilibrium. As Wendell Gordon has observed if our task is to understand ongoing processes, "the starting point is realizing there is no starting point; there is no starting point in the sense of initial conditions knowable to us" (Gordon 1992, p. 891). Our starting point is someone believes there is an economic problem that requires an institutional adjustment. For instance, many believe there is a health care problem which needs to be fixed. That is a starting point, which will be followed by many statements of the problem. Medical professionals, insurance professionals, young families, senior citizens, homosexuals, and probably an increasing number of research economists, will offer statements of the problem. If we see this as a problem emerging in an ongoing process we will appreciate that the vested interests do not have an inherent claim, but they do have the advantage of custom. But these vested interests are being challenged by people's expectations of the possibilities of the going concern we know as the medical profession. The problem is partially the result the successes of medical technology and our partial collectivization of health care expenses through employment health care plans. The past and reasonable expectations of future performance are important aspects of problem solving. Reasonable expectations are in part shaped by the progress made in the past as well as better practices observed elsewhere in the world.

This process is not moved by atomistic individuals, or by a group of individuals described in an organization chart, but by individuals interacting in going concerns. These going concerns are held together by working rules which are subject to change by the participants in the going concern or a body with authority or influence over this going concern. Institutional economics is the economics of going concerns, which is collective action in control, expansion and liberation of individual action (Commons 1950, p. 21). These individuals are not secondary to the collective as in totalitarian economies, because they have the ability to shape, influence and resist changes in the working rules which define their rights and duties. But since others, inside and outside the going concern, have different purposes and goals, there is conflict as well as harmony. It is the understanding of the process of artificial selection and modification of working rules to handle emerging economic problems that is the method of institutional policy analysis. This process inevitably involves coercion as well as consent. It is this recognition that consent alone cannot bring about a harmony of interests in every case that distinguishes institutional economics from Pareto orthodoxy.

Collective action, public and private, will limit some interests as it expands and liberates others. It is the honest recognition of collective coercion which requires a social value theory to assist public policy analysis, and this value theory begins with the question: whose interests counts? Anything other than an open inquiry into coercive actions would be dangerous indeed. It is certainly more appealing to rely on an economic system governed by consent and voluntary exchange, but such a myth protects the status quo. On the other hand, we have to respect the orderly processes of the going concern, and not disrupt it without due regard to its place in the modified order and the relationship it has to other going concerns. I think this is, in part, what Fagg Foster meant by the principles of recognized mutual interdependence and minimal dislocation (Foster 1981, pp. 940-41).

This brings us to the concept of pragmatic problem solving. A problem is a recognition that there is a difference between what is and what ought to be in a particular situation. Fagg Foster defined an institution as prescribed patterns of correlated behavior. Economic problems are recognized when there are conflicts between two or more interacting institutions or between a technological innovation and the institution which harnesses the technology (Ibid.). According to Foster all economic policy is about institutional adjustment. Scientists and engineers solve problems, within an institutional system, by improving or adapting technology. As social scientists we advise on institutional development. What ought to be is not checked against some eternal verity or some criteria external to human knowledge and experience. It is also not checked against some ideal structure as is laissez-faire orthodoxy. What ought to be for economists is how to get the most out of productive capacity by improving on the institutional structure through which technology works. The institutions are the delivery system of technology. Technology which cannot be delivered is no more effective than technology which does not exist. Institutions do matter. The system is efficient if we are able to get the maximum delivery of technical capacity. If it were this simple though, we would not need a value theory either. The value theory is needed to determine to whom do we deliver the fruits of our technical capacity and on what terms and conditions.

## Valuation as Process

Although, Wendell Gordon reminds us, there is no beginning point in an ongoing process, we must begin problem solving analysis somewhere. The most appropriate point to begin institutional analysis is with a particular problematic situation. However we must remember that this particular problem probably results from the solution to an earlier problem. Institutional analysis frames a problem as the need to align an institution with a new technology or with other relevant institutions. If the problem could be solved by voluntary action or customary behavior there would be no need for deliberative collective action to alter an institution. Therefore, it is almost certain that the action to solve the problem will have negative consequences for some, or it would have been solved by voluntary agreement. This clearly indicates that the logic of voluntary exchange is inadequate to the task of understanding the collective action of institutional change and development. Considerations of equity issues, then, are as central to institutional analysis as are considerations of efficiency. The shift to institutional analysis cannot be made, therefore, without a theory of the process of social valuation rather than a simple aggregation of preferences of individuals.

It follows that the effectiveness of institutional reform cannot be judged on the same criteria as are used to judge individual exchange within a given institutional structure. The call for a public policy to change or develop an institution is a recognition that there is a performance problem, and the correction can only be evaluated within the context of the problem and the purpose of the proposed policy. Institutionalists have also concluded that there can be more than one statement of the problem by various participants affected by the institution and its reform. The valuation problem includes how to reach some working agreement on the nature of the problem and how to solve the problem given the working agreement. In a pluralistic society it is important to determine who will be included in the discourse on defining the problem and shaping a solution to the defined problem. Access and effective participation in the problem solving system is critical to whose interest will count as well as what constitutes an efficient outcome. For example, attorneys can conclude that the poor have few legal problems because very few poor people show up in their offices. Furthermore, from an exchange efficiency standpoint it is better for the court to spend months of court time and legal resources settling the Howard Hughes estate case because it has a higher value as determined by the market than hundreds of smaller civil and criminal cases which were crowded out. Efficiency, as well as equity, is determined by whose interest we consider.

A second part of the problem is to determine the best means to solve the problem once we have reached a working agreement. This is a much easier and straight-forward set of considerations than the former. Unfortunately, this part of the deliberation is all that some seem to refer to when they consider rational public policy. The best and the brightest in the Kennedy administration, for example, thought their problem of efficiency was limited to getting the most bang for the buck, rather than seeking to know if the bang was agreed to by those required to participate in delivering the bang. Too often institutionalists who state that the valuation problem is limited to concluding that a sharp knife is better than a dull knife reduce the valuing process to this step.

William Waller and Linda Robertson have helped us to see the problem of limiting problem solving analysis to only one aspect as some institutionalists have done (Waller and Robertson 1991). A problem cannot be solved until there is some working definition of the problem that is widely shared and that working definition is developed through public discourse. It is the only after development of a working definition that purposeful action can occur. They do not suggest that these two aspects are actually separable in a real world situation, but the separation aids analysis.

Marc Tool has said "that direction is forward which provides for the continuity of human life and the noninvidious recreation of community through the instrumental use of knowledge" (Tool 1979, p. 293). Without the continuation of human life there would be no human problems to solve and without community, discourse would be impossible. If, as Waller and Robertson have argued, a problem cannot be solved, instrumentally or otherwise, until it has been defined through discourse, then community is critical. Who is included in the community and how effectively they can exercise voice will determine what we mean by the instrumental use of knowledge. If women, racial or religious minorities or homosexuals are excluded from participation in discourse, then the problem will be framed without considering their interest. Using the orthodox definition of efficiency, various states of efficiency can be reached depending on whose interests are included or excluded. Thus, invidious distinctions can determine which efficiency solution is chosen.

What has bothered many institutional economists about the statement of Tool's criteria is that they cannot be made instrumentally effective in particular problematic situations. It seems to be suggested that harmonious solutions can be generally found in the face of conflict. As institutional economists we need to make it clear that we are not considering only Pareto efficient adjustments. Also, in the face of conflict where the solution cannot be arrived at voluntarily, the problem cannot be resolved by objective analysis alone. For example, orthodox analysts argue that the creation of the North American Free Trade Area will improve market efficiency, but the act of creating NAFTA is not consistent with Pareto criteria because some will be harmed in the process of integration. On the other hand, Tool's general criteria only establish the conditions by which we could establish channels of discourse to negotiate the complex particulars of a NAFTA. In other words effective discourse which can lead to negotiation requires a community. In the case of NAFTA the problem begins with the need to create a community in order to carry on the discourse of the creation and continued evolution of the created institution, NAFTA. However, whatever the outcome, some people will clearly lose. It is important if economists are to advise in institutional adjustment processes, that they make the community aware of the consequences on the losers. And it is important to disclose that the proposed changes are experimental and will, no doubt, have to be modified to deal with the conditions the original changes bring about.

This process of valuation by discourse is consistent with the reasonable value process developed by John R. Commons. The concept of reasonable value is collective and historical, whereas the rationalistic idea was individualistic, intellectual and static (Commons 1961, p. 682). In rejecting the individualistic notion of value, subjective criteria are also rejected. But because reasonable value is grounded in collective and historical processes, the objective-subjective distinction is not helpful. Objective analysis can help describe the evaluation of whether or not we are moving toward the solution a problem after we have arrived at a working definition of a problem. The usual definition of objective does not, however, sufficiently describe the process of settling on the agreement of what the problem is, but neither does the definition of subjective. The problem of institutional adjustment is not similar to an individual choosing cheddar or swiss cheese. Commons argued that if we based our reasons for institutional adjustment on the evidence offered by the investigation of transactions of many going concerns, then we do not have to rely on individualistic, subjective emotions (Ibid., pp 739-740). The notion of the distinction between subjective and objective is based on individualistic thinking, and does not sufficiently describe the valuation process of evolutionary going concerns. The valuation process of collective action is so different from the valuation process of individual choosing that we need different tools. Such dichotomies as subjective-objective and efficiency-equity must be applied with great caution.

If we do not take care, the compulsive shift will simply be another neoclassical synthesis with emphasis on neoclassical. I do not mean to argue that the shift to institutional analysis is doomed. There is much evidence that there is a recognition by many orthodox economists that the prevailing paradigm is inadequate. Since the pain of the shift to institutional analysis will be great for those in the mainstream, it will be a considerably long evolutionary period for institutional analysis to become orthodox.

## Conclusions

Many in the economics profession believe that the only way to remain engaged in public policy analysis is to embrace institutional analysis. Unfortunately, for many that means nothing more than including transactions cost in their paradigm. Others have simply expanded the individualistic exchange paradigm to expose rent seeking which could have been done with Ricardian economics. Most seem to agree with Douglass North that to abandon neoclassical economics is to abandon economics as a science. That position seems to be based on the notion that efficiency can be objectively discovered, but equity is simply a matter of subjective tastes. It is my contention that scientific institutional analysis cannot begin until we find a research framework which is not supported by such dichotomies as subjective-objective and efficiency-equity. Scientific institutional analysis will not begin with the subjective preferences of individuals, but with the processes of going concerns. It must be recognized that the economics of collective action, or the economics of going concerns, can be a very dangerous prospect for individuals because these going concerns define the quality of life for affected individuals. It should, then, be obvious that the process of social valuation is a central part of institutional analysis. That does not mean that economists establish the criteria of valuation in specific situations, but that they listen to the social discourse to discover the purposes of different interests. It is also appropriate to point out which interests were and were not served by the collective action of institutional adjustment.

The general criteria of social valuation listed by Marc Tool are not operational criteria which can be applied in specific instances, but they do establish necessary conditions to guide collective action toward efficient and equitable (reasonable) outcomes. There will not be complete agreement on the working definition of the problem because there often are many overlapping and conflicting interests. Also, there will not always be agreement on the means to solve an agreed on problem because the patterns of evidence are not that simple (Foster 1981, p. 963). Tool's criteria, though, are stated in a way to remind us that institutional adjustment is a process. That means the study of institutional adjustment begins with the investigation of the customs and purposes of going concerns. Tool's criteria seem to recognize that the going concern shapes individual choices and actions. However, we would overstate the case for instrumental use of knowledge if we failed to point out that most decisions and actions are routine and customary. What we are concerned with in institutional analysis is the deliberate action to reshape a going concern to the extent that it will have desirable and harmful consequences on various individual participants as well as non-participants affected by the going concern.

If we agree with Waller and Robertson that problem solving involves discourse over time, then we can escape the dichotomy of subjectivism and objectivism and realize that an efficient solution to a problem must also be considered a fair solution. That is the difference between rational and reasonable.

# 7. THE INSTRUMENTAL VALUE PRINCIPLE AND ITS ROLE

Warren J. Samuels

This chapter considers the instrumental value principle, the concept with which Marc Tool is so closely associated. It advances a particular argument concerning its role, strengths and limits.

## The Instrumental Value Principle

We begin with the principle of Fagg Foster and Marc Tool, that we should do or choose that which provides for the continuity of human life and the noninvidious recreation of community through the instrumental use of knowledge. With respect to this principle, based on the foregoing analysis, I want to argue that (1) it comports with the view that science inevitably involves both positive and normative premises; (2) economics is willy nilly a participant in and a contributor to the social valuation process, in part through its selective positive definition of reality and in part through its selective normative premises; (3) the principle embodies pluralistic values long associated with institutionalism (as well as certain valuational movements of thought in post-Enlightenment Western society); (4) the principle is not an absolute comprised of eternal verities but a framework of discourse and policy analysis; (5) human choice must inexorably be exercised in the use of the principle; (6) amplification and application of the principle is always provisional; (7) in association with it the Veblenian dichotomy (not discussed here), comprehended in terms of ceremonialism versus instrumentalism, is not self-subsistent and independently and conclusively generative of policy implications but can be used as a dichotomous framework of discourse and policy analysis; (8) the terms and implications of the dichotomy can be used as serious pointers to policy, but policy which is relative to circumstances as well as to specification of the terms of the principle; and (9) Commons's "reasonable value" and Veblenian "instrumental value" are not mutually exclusive but correlative, each dealing with different aspects of the valuational process both furthering and helped along by the instrumental value principle (also not discussed here).

This is not to say that all institutionalists either do or must adhere to the instrumental value principle, or for that matter to instrumental valuation itself (Ramstad 1989, p. 765).[1] Nor does it imply that all who use it will derive identical and nonconflicting policy implications. The principle is a tool of policy analysis in a discretionary economy. Policy is inexorably made willy nilly leading to the social reconstruction of economic reality. Policy is normative, and the instrumental value principle is a tool to facilitate discourse and policy analysis. It is nothing but, as Alfred Marshall and John Maynard Keynes argued, an organon of inquiry, a technique of analysis which leads its user to conclusions which are logically correct in and on the terms of the principle and not necessarily to conclusions immediately and unequivocally applicable to policy. The implications for policy are derived from both the principle itself and the use(s) made of it. The policy implications thereby reflect the mode of discourse and general values ensconced within the principle—notably when coupled with the Veblenian dichotomy, which, apropos of the phrase "instrumental use of knowledge" is already incorporated in the principle—but especially reflect the supplemental understandings and values brought to the principle by the analyst.

This specifically means, first, that the particular substantive content of such terms of the principle as "we," "continuity of human life," "noninvidious," "recreation of community," and "instrumental use of knowledge" must be provided through the valuational process. Precisely who "we" are and who constitutes "community" must be worked out, in a world of nation states (and other political divisions of power) and in which the complexities of hierarchy versus equality, not to mention freedom versus control, are enormous and subtle. What constitutes the "continuity of human life" has aspects which are both simple and complex, aspects which are also subjective and subject to selective perception; aspects which also must be worked out. So too with "noninvidious" and the "recreation of community." All these terms involve comparisons and judgments which can lead to quite different implications for policy.

This also means that both the substantive content attributed to each of these terms and the policy implications reached with the use of the principle are tentative and provisional, always subject to change. What constitutes "progressive" institutional change, what constitutes dislocation of the life processes of the community, what constitutes preservation of the continuity of the life process of the community, what constitutes minimization of the dislocation of instrumentally warranted patterns of behavior, what constitutes instrumental institutional adjustment (Bush 1989)—all of this must be worked out and is subject to both selective perception and change. In this process of "working out" two operative elements must be noted: First, the channeling of analysis by adoption and use of the principle, in juxtaposition to other principles and to philosophies other than instrumental valuation; and second, the impact of culture and received institutions on the specific content attributed to terms identified at the beginning of this paragraph. These terms are not self-subsistent and self-revealing; they are given meaning by people (the problem, again is which people). In short, the life process must be worked out. That Veblen may have had something particular in mind as to what constituted the life process, in a manner relevant to discourse and policy analysis, is much less important than his identification of the need for people to work out the meaning of the life process.

The lesson here is that insofar as analysts make assumptions about what constitutes the life process (and the other terms of the principle), and they must do so, they contribute to the process of working out its meaning. To the extent that the work of policy analysts tends to foreclose that process and to substitute their own premises and preferences for those of actual economic and social actors, they are engaged in activities which may well tend to conflict with the principle itself—though determination of when such foreclosure, substitution and conflict exists (or exists dysfunctionally) is itself something that has to be worked out. Perhaps no more subtle aspect of the provisional and working-out character of instrumental valuation and of the instrumental valuation can be found.

The precise content of the Foster-Tool instrumental value principle is less important than the role which the theory of instrumental valuation, as I understand it, adduces to it, discussed in the next subsection. For now, let me say only that its importance resides in the putative help it provides in promoting certain values, help which, as indicated just above, requires supplementary human valuation of alternatives in order to give pragmatic operational meaning to its terms.

Actually, I personally have mixed feelings about the principle. On the one hand, I am not overly impressed with its specific language, essentially because of its ambiguity. Moreover, other more or less equally functional and impressive formulations can be found in the relevant literature. On the other hand, it does make values explicit, and I certainly applaud the specific sentiments and values expressed in it: the principle is useful for focusing discussion and promoting a free, open, pluralist, liberal, democratic society. In this respect, the principle does go pretty far in expressing the "constellation of shared beliefs" in the "invisible college" formed by institutional economists (Ramstad 1989, p. 764). This is true so long as one does not read either eternal verities or specific policy implications into it. It is not always clear what specific policies will, under varying conditions, either unequivocally or problematically advance the cause of a free, open, pluralist, liberal, democratic society, in part because the relationship(s) of means to ends will not be clear and in part because "the patterns of evidence are not always that simple" (Atkinson and Reed 1991, p. 1140, a quote from Foster).[2] Such details need to be worked out in a processual manner. One can only take the principle so far—as Gordon (1990, p. 881; see also Sheehan and Tilman 1992, p. 203) argues, "A single brief principle that can orient the process is not part of the scheme of things," —but the values which it promotes are laudatory.

Several aspects of the foregoing need to be elaborated, particularly the more recent views of Tool himself, especially his responses to critics. We will find that he sometimes seems to be writing as if the instrumental value principle is self-subsistent but at other times recognizes both that it must be worked out and its provisional and processual character, the latter position apparently more fundamentally. There are passages in which Tool (and others) seem to feel that the instrumental value principle is itself capable of being used to "differentiat[e] . . . institutions and practices that are progressive and non-invidious, and that promote serviceability from those that are ceremonial and invidious and that promote mere vendibility" (Hickerson 1987, p. 1128). But there are other passages in which it is recognized that it is not the principle but people who engaged in valuation, perhaps with the aid of the principle who make (not find) the distinction in particular cases. And, again, it seems to be that latter which are more fundamental—though clearly some instrumentalists, perhaps Tool himself, would prefer otherwise. For these latter folks, instrumental valuation is transcendental and the instrumental value principle, itself embodying the values of instrumental valuation, has something of a self-subsistent and self-applying character. And they may not be entirely wrong, particularly when one compares and contrasts the principle to some other principles, notably those ensconced in the conventional ideological "isms." In this view, choices are just choices (the phrase is Louis Junker's, quoted by Hickerson 1987, p. 1131), but some advance instrumentalism and others do not. This is a position with which it is difficult to disagree in principle (especially once one recalls that institutionalists acknowledge both deliberative and non-deliberative decision making), but which must also encompass the point that the determination of when a choice does and does not advance instrumentalism must itself be worked out, for it too is a matter of choice.

One aspect has to do with specificity of application. Sheehan and Tilman (1992, p. 205 and passim) aver that "a greater degree of value specificity is essential if instrumental valuation is to have more lucidity and applicability than it presently possesses as well as avoid charges of value diffusity and opportunism." Yes and no. Specificity is nice for determinacy and closure. But both can be presumptuous and foreclosing. With a variety of ends-in-view, intermediate criteria or principles, means-ends relations, evidence, and interpretation of each, it is illusory to believe that complete and objective consistency and homogeneity is possible. Different principles will rise above the others at different times.[3] Call it value diffusity and opportunism, even adhocism, but pragmatism must yield such diversity, especially in a free, open, liberal, pluralist, democratic society. Indeed, Sheehan and Tilman (Ibid., p. 203) go on to recognize, in the very next sentence, that:

> It is important that neoinstitutionalists recognize that the development of their own social value principle is part of an evolutionary process whose incompleteness at this state itself constitutes in Dewey's words, a "problematic situation" whose adequate resolution will always lies in the future. The social value principle is thus a matter of an ongoing, revising synthesis.

Inasmuch as all valuation, perhaps even all thought, commences with problematic situations, and problematicity itself is a continuing stimulus to reform and changing values, one can expect neither consistency=uniformity=homogeneity nor continuity, at best a provisionally worked-out solution (Koch 1992).

This brings me to the necessity of choice in a world of complexity, heterogeneity, and change. The instrumental value principle is neither self-subsistent nor self-applying. The instrumental value process to which it has been offered as a principle is very much a process in which things have to be worked, and reworked, out. The process is explorative and emergent. The values operative within it are at one both hypothetical and experimental, and provisional and tentative (Sheehan and Tilman 1992, p. 200, attributing the first pair to Foster and the second to unnamed others).

As Bush (1991, p. 340, emphasis added) has perceptively concluded,

> Tool's social value principle, far from being an eternal verity that is beyond inquiry, is an overriding normative implication entailed in the logic of the institutionalist analysis of the process of institutional change. As such, it is subject to critique and revision as any other instrumentally warranted assertion set forth in scientific inquiry.

This is essentially correct, once it is recognized that the social, or instrumental, value principle does not exhaust the institutionalist analysis of the process of institutional change. The instrumental value principle has both positive and normative facets. On the one hand, it relates to "an explanation of the process of institutional change" (Bush 1987, p. 1107). On the other, it affirms certain valuational criteria relating to the working out of that process (criteria ensconced within both the principle itself and the roles which it performs; see below).

As Hickerson (1987, p. 1127) indicates "not all valuations are equally valid or legitimate . . . some of the valuations imprinted upon thought by cultural and systemic phenomena are patently and demonstrably false and misleading" with regard to "bettering" the life process. The present point is that it remains to be determined through the valuational process which valuations are and which are not legitimate. Not all culturally impose valuations are bad; choice must be made among them. Valuations are not per se legitimate and illicit; valuations are judgments of legitimacy or illegitimacy which emerge from the decision making, or valuational, process and are subject to change. As distasteful as it may be to some to read the words, it is "all" a matter of choice—though, as indicated above, value perceptions and choices are influenced by social conditions. Even the meaning and application of the terms of the expression used above— "a free, open, liberal, pluralist, democratic society" —must be worked out. This is particularly apposite because advocates of the social value principle envision it as instrumental to the realization of a free, open, liberal, pluralist, democratic society.

Considerations like these have been emphasized by Wendell Gordon. Gordon, as I interpret him, responded to a perception that adherents to the instrumental value principle believed not only that it was central to institutional economics but that it was by itself capable of normatively distinguishing between desirable and undesirable social arrangements. Gordon rejected the view that it is simply a matter of applying the principle to determine what provided or did not provide for the continuity of human life and the noninvidious recreation of community through the instrumental use of knowledge. Gordon argues that the principle is none of these things, and he is correct. Inasmuch as Tool now seems to concur with Gordon's position, as will be seen below, the result is an approach to instrumental valuation congruent with the interpretation given above.

Gordon commences his principal article on the subject with the claim that "a social value principle, criterion of judgment, or value referent, which states a simple basic concept or two for use in judging instruments, ends, and values, is not a a basic characteristic" of institutional economics (Gordon 1990, p. 879). He also commences his article with the claim that "the assumption of such a definitive characteristic violates the flexible, self-correcting value judgment concept of instrumentalism, the proposition that changing conditions may change criteria of choice" (Ibid., p. 879). The latter argument is repeated both in the middle of the article, "A single, brief principle that can orient the process is not part of the scheme of things (Ibid., p. 881)" and at the end of the article:

> The concept of a social value principle, which represents an effort to state the definitive, desirable characteristics of society in a nutshell, runs counter to the instrumental concept involving continuing reappraisal of the worthwhileness of both tools and goals, means and ends. And beside that, we do not know what the universe is all about anyway. let us continue to be inquiring and skeptical and interested in trying to improve things. (Ibid., p. 885)

The implication that all this needs to be worked out, through social processes which are inexorably cultural in character, is obvious. Not so obvious is the clause within the instrumental value principle which calls for the instrumental use of knowledge. What Tool is trying to accomplish with it is affirmation of instrumentalism. What Gordon is trying to accomplish is affirmation of the problematic nature of instrumentalism—the instrumental use of knowledge—itself, and that just as instrumentalism does not exhaust institutionalist inquiry, so too Tool's particular instrumental value principle does not exhaust instrumentalist valuation.

Of course, Tool also affirms several specific values, notably the noninvidious recreation of community. And it is with regard to those values that Gordon insists that advocates would be seen as "prone to the making of cavalier value judgments" (Ibid., p. 880), that Deweyian "ends-in-view do not involve an effort to identify principles of permanent validity that should guide all decision-making" (Ibid.), and so on.

Gordon (Ibid., p. 881) recognized the principal problem, which may have been due to different beliefs or misinterpretation:

> Sometimes, it seems to this writer that Tool is offering the social value principle as a definitive eternal verity or truth. At other times it seems that, in deference to the instrumental logic, he is offering the desirability of the continuity of human life and the noninvidious recreation of community as provisional value judgments that are subject to reappraisal.

And he quotes Tool to this effect, that the principle is "provisional and tentative."

In his subsequent article on the processual character of instrumentalism, Gordon (1992, pp. 897, 899) states the fundamental points.

> The valuation theory being presented here means that at each state in ongoing process, we are viewing matters and attitudes from the perspective of our then prevailing conception of their worthwhileness.

> And we can be continually reconsidering the meaning of improvement as we learn more about what we and the universe are all about. . . . an ongoing struggle to effect change that is worthwhile in terms of our continually revised ideas as to what is worthwhile. . . . the organization through which we are working to implement changes we believe to be desirable is itself subject to change as an aspect of the ongoing process.

What needs to be emphasized are the phrases "from the perspective of our then prevailing conception of their worthwhileness" and "we believe to be desirable," for it is they which incorporate the problematicity of the content of the valuational process. It is this problematicity which is agreed upon, as we have seen, by all participants in the controversy, for example, by Sheehan and Tilman (1992, p. 205) when they write that the development of the social value principle "is part of an evolutionary process whose incompleteness at this stage itself constitutes, in Dewey's words, a 'problematic situation' whose adequate resolution will always lie in the future. Indeed, "futurity" was one of Commons's greatest insights, namely, that although we think and decide largely in terms derived past experience, the meaning of our decisions lies in the future, the future made in part through those decisions.

Before turning to Marc Tool's recent work, let us note some examples of alternative formulations of basic value propositions by institutionalists. Bush (1987; 1989; 1991) emphasizes such criteria as recognition of interdependence and minimal dislocation. Gordon (1992, p. 243) suggests such values as "(1) a decent minimum income for all, (2) getting along pleasantly with others, (3) constructive self-expression that will make the individual proud of his or her behavior, and (4) various kinds of security against violence, illness, and war." As Gordon says, Tool's is "a similar but different pattern of value judgments." Once again, the precise meaning and details of applicability of all such criteria and values would need to be worked out—and working out would inexorably involve cultural inputs. As Gordon puts it elsewhere but with regard to the same values, "the identity, nature, and role of the matters in this list are subject to continuing change" (Gordon 1990, p. 881).

Turning finally to Tool, we find that in his reply to Gordon he states:

> Is the instrumental principle an 'eternal verity?' If by eternal verity is meant a given truth that is beyond inquiry and has no evidential grounding, or an ethical absolute that is rooted in some religious dictum, received doctrine, or otherwise unchallengeable source, the instrumental principle is not an eternal verity. The instrumental principle is rather a product of inquiry and remains subject to revision or abandonment by further inquiry. It has no standing except as a construct for inquiry and as a tool for analysis and judgment. Its relevance is repeatedly tested by its incorporation in, and guidance of, inquiry and its use as a judgmental standard in problem solving (Tool 1990a, p. 1110).

All this should have been obvious. But it had not been, in part because one could read or hear Tool seemingly affirming that the principle was singularly dispositive of questions of policy. I say this with some "authority," because I heard and read Tool in precisely such a manner. But that hearing and that reading were wrong; whether the error was due to the producer or the consumer of the words should now be irrelevant—although I am quite prepared to plead mea culpa. Indeed, now that we have been done the road so conflictually travelled, one might wonder what the controversy has been all about. Whatever one's answer to that question, one conclusion seems evident: Instrumental analysis, even about instrumental analysis itself, is not so simple—which is what Gordon and Tool, et al, seem now to be agreeing upon after all.

Tool (1990a, pp. 1110, 1112, 1118, 1120) elaborates his view of the instrumental value principle in part as follows:

> The instrumental value principle is rather a product of inquiry and remains subject to revision or abandonment by further inquiry. It has no standing except as a construct for inquiry and as a tool for analysis and judgment. Its relevance is repeatedly tested by its incorporation in, and guidance of, inquiry and its use as a judgmental standard in problem solving. . . . it is derived exclusively from the experience continuum of people and . . . it articulates what often has historically been

> meant by progress, reform, or betterment. . . . it is a product of inquiry; it may be modified or replaced by subsequent inquiry. . . . The formulation here is thus provisional and exploratory. . . . The scholar's role is not, of course, to decide for the community what is best for the community; rather, it is to help the community understand why instrumental judgments are better than noninstrumental judgments. . . . Institutionalists believe they can demonstrate that the greater the level of democratic participation, the higher is the probability of instrumentally valued judgments being made in the formulation and implementation of economic policy. . . . What is novel about the instrumentalist position . . . is that . . . criteria must themselves remain as objects of inquiry. We really do have to appraise principles of appraisal.

Tool could not be clearer about all this. Whatever misapprehension existed in the past, there should be no question that the principle is neither self-subsistent, capable itself of determining policy issues, nor an eternal verity.

The same position is taken in Tool 1993a and in his Presidential Address to the Association for Evolutionary Economics (1993b). In the former, he says that the instrumental value principle is a way of coming to understand and appraise the character of causal determinants of economic problems. It is a tool, a construct of inquiry, and as such it is an evolutionary as well as processual construct. While it is a judgmental standard for inquiry and conduct, it is not a conclusive universal touchstone; it offers no shortcuts, no panaceas, no prefigured or simple solutions. There is nothing routine or automatic about it. Its conclusions—the conclusions reached with its use—are provisional. It is an attempt, in the tradition of Gunnar Myrdal, to make explicit the normative premises of institutional analysis (Tool 1993b, paraphrased).

In his Presidential Address, Tool thus acknowledges (in the context of pricing theory) that discretionary agents are engaged in a running appraisal of principles of appraisal; that constructs to facilitate instrumentalist evaluation and assessment are constructs, however useful; and so on, in an application somewhat further elaborative of the positions he recently had come to state so carefully.

In clarifying his position, perhaps in large part due to the pointed arguments of his critics, Tool exemplifies Dugger's (1993, p. 1) description of instrumentalism:

> Instrumentalism is open ended and evolutionary. No instrumentalist has ever attempted a final formulation of instrumentalism and none will ever do so, for to do so would be to move outside of the instrumentalist tradition.

As Dugger says apropos of Ayres, "He searched for a universal criterion of judgment and made a significant contribution. And yet, he was too bound by his own time and place" (Ibid., p. 9). Recognition of this, rather than the ceremonial elevation of any formulation of principle, is one key to instrumentalism.

### The Role of the Principle

The crux of the matter, therefore, becomes this: What is the operative significance of the instrumental value principle? The answer, I believe, resides in the two roles of the principle.

The first role is to advance the realization of a free, open, pluralist, liberal, democratic society (hereinafter called pluralist). These values are shared by most if not all other schools of economic thought and indeed are endemic to modern Western civilization, albeit frequently violated in practice (given all sorts of judgments as to what these values mean both in the abstract and in practice). The values are shared with neoclassicism, although, in the minds of many institutionalist (and other) critics, neoclassicism has a tendency to reify and reinforce established institutions and power structure—although "continuity" is part of Tool's instrumental value principle. At any rate, the values have been part of the mindset of institutionalists since Veblen and Commons, notwithstanding differences of conceptualization and application.

Commons's view is neatly summarized by Selig Perlman's (1952, p. 411) statement in which he affirms Commons as

> the father of a labor struggle theory which is not a class struggle theory in the Marxian sense. It is not a struggle by the rising group to liquidate the old class or to raze the social structure which the latter controlled, but essaying instead to add to the old edifice new and spacious wings to serve as the dwelling places of the customs of the ruling class.

The second role of the principle is to advance deliberative over nondeliberative decision making. Institutionalists, as we have seen, identify both modes of decision making as characteristic of economic and social life. But institutionalists concur, oddly enough, with the Menger-Hayek view that institutions which are essentially nondeliberative, which have in some sense developed organically, and are matters of custom and habit, should be and in fact are subjected to deliberative critique as to their suitability, that is, be considered and revised instrumentally/pragmatically. Pragmatism and instrumentalism mean conscious confrontation with problematic situations, principles as instruments to be tested in action, and social reconstruction through experimentation (Koch 1992). This means that the cutting edge of change transpires both nondeliberatively and deliberatively, and that the application of human reason not only distinctively constitutes the latter but is lauded as preeminent. This also means that instrumental valuation is a matter of inquiry and the inquiry which it contemplates is conscious and deliberative. As Waller and Robertson (1993) argue, the purpose of inquiry and discourse is to provide reasoned decisions as a contribution to the process of addressing problems; otherwise there is no reason for inquiry. This process of inquiry will be ultimately culture bound but sufficiently self-aware of its cultural context and content to be self-examining and self-critical, that is, self-corrective.

In both respects, the instrumental value principle is a manifestation of or emanation from post-Enlightenment ways of thought and society. (It is interesting to speculate how much post-modernism is an outgrowth of modernism in these regards, but that is another story.)

The questions then arise with regard to nondeliberative decision making, Whose customs and habits are to count?, and with regard to deliberative decision making, "Whose cognitive choices and interests are to count? The instrumentalist answer derives from the two roles of the principle: In each case, the answers turn on what is deemed to promote pluralism and instrumentalism (deliberative decision making) itself.

The problem of balancing continuity and change is manifest in the instrumental value principle itself. So also, though more implicitly, are the problems of balancing freedom and control, and hierarchy and equality. The instrumentalist position is that deliberative decision making is necessary, if only because reliance on nondeliberative decision making tends to reinforce hierarchy, and thereby give effect to the decisions made by upper-level hegemonic powers. This is so even though decisions as to means and ends with regard to pluralism still have to be worked out. In a certain sense, the central problem is, Who is to modify the working rules? Instrumentalism affirms the value of not leaving it to the already entrenched power holders. Thus pluralism informs deliberative decision making and deliberative decision making informs pluralism. A key role, therefore, of the instrumental value principle is to both permit and facilitate, as well as to channel along pluralist directions, critique of established arrangements (what else extant is there to critique?; we must start from where we are). It is also a critique that affirms that the determination of the existence of "problems" is not to be made by upper-level hegemonic powers alone, but in a democratic, hence deliberative manner ("blind," or noncognitive decision making, signifies allowing choice to remain in the hands of the already powerful). Again, the two roles inform each other.[4]

The same conclusion is reached when one recognizes that although purpose is not given to man and society, purpose still must inform policy and the social reconstruction of society. To affirm, therefore, the necessity of purpose[5] is to query, Whose purpose?, therefore to emphasize the necessity of choice, and therefore to query, Whose choices? The instrumentalist approach to the decision making process emphasizes pluralism and deliberativeness as two sides of the same coin.

The emphasis on pluralism means that no single solution can be adequate for all; that individuals must be free to associate freely to form alliances and coalitions and that each of these must respect (though not necessarily give effect to) each other's self-definition and interests and be democratically constructed; that something reasonably constituting an equality of rights be sought; and, inter alia, that serious and effective efforts be made to identify and remove injustice (paraphrasing Brown 1993).

The emphasis on deliberative over nondeliberative, as not just a matter of description but of fundamental orientation and policy, is pervasive in the relevant literature and arises in numerous contexts, indicating its fundamental as well as robust significance. It is found for, example, in David Hamilton's (1986, p. 531) statement that "The technological process is an irreverent one and a liberating one, in that it focuses on problem solving rather than on adherence to ideology and ancient prescriptive." Clearly the emphasis is on the conscious evaluation and potential reform of institutions rather than their unquestioning continuance.

The point is explicit in three of Atkinson's (1987, pp. 192, 193) statements. The first is a quote from Dewey, that "intelligence is the instrument of social well-being and advancement." The second is that "Change is not back to some stationary state, but is brought about with intelligent human action guided by expected, desired future consequences of that action."[6] Thirdly, Atkinson writes that because "society is not made up of groups who share the same interests, . . institutionalists encourage widespread participation in decision-making processes" (Ibid., p. 193), an articulation of (1) pluralist decision making, (2) deliberative decision making, and (3) how the former may require the latter.[7]

The point is made emphatically by Hickerson (1987, p. 1131; see also 1132) when he writes about that "ordered and purposeful conduct" which "arises when responses to problematic situations are measured and assessed in consideration of the future consequences of present action, rather than simply carried out impulsively or instinctually." Hickerson also identifies "reflective inquiry" as the basis of plans of action (Ibid., p. 1133). So that when he writes that "The instrumental value principle . . . facilitates the process of valuing" (Ibid., p. 1138), he clearly has conscious, deliberative policy analysis in mind.

Emphasis on deliberative decision making is evident in Tool's statements, the first apropos of a quotation from Albert Guerard, that "'thought' refers to a running dialogue between reason and experience" and that Foster recognized "that genuine freedom must include choice among institutional options" (Tool 1982, pp. 351; 352).

It is implicit, too, in all those who maintain that "When a problem arises—if people do not like the way things are going or find life frustrating—they set about changing the old system and the values implicit in it. They do this by experimenting with new ways and by discovering from their experiences with the new ways whether the new ways are better than the old ones in solving the problems and alleviating the frustrations. Learning-by-testing is the way people solve their problems . . ." (Neale 1982, p. 364).

Waller (1988, p. 667; also quoted by Tool 1990b, p. 279) thus describes what he considers to be "radical institutionalism" as "critical analysis aimed at accurately describing the working of an economic system with the intent of purposefully altering that system toward more democratic and participatory social structures and practice." The combination of deliberative decision-making and pluralism is obvious. That there is a radical institutionalism different in any meaningful way from institutionalism in general as to its emphasis on both conscious purpose and democratization is doubtful, but the emphasis on purposeful social change is central to Waller's position (see also Ibid., p. 673).

It is part of the mind-set of institutionalists to rebuke mainstream neoclassical economists for believing or pretending that their theory is value free and for constructing deterministic analyses which seem, first, to obviate all human choice but nondeliberative decision making and, second, to facilitate the reaching of noninterventionist, status quo-reinforcing policy implications.

Bush (1991, p. 337; see also 1987, p. 1080 and passim) makes the point a bit differently. He argues that "Since it is the instrumentalist view that inquiry cannot proceed without valuation, 'objectivity' depends on making those value judgments that keep the path of inquiry open and subject to identifying and correcting errors." Obviously implicit in this statement (and others cited here) is the deliberativist practice of making values explicit.

The emphasis on deliberativeness is implicit in, if not central to, Gordon's (1990, p. 885) already quoted statement, "Let us continue to be inquiring and skeptical and interested in trying to improve things." For "inquiring" means nothing if not deliberative inquiry as both a supplement and a substitute for nondeliberative decision-making/traditional culture. This is the same implication reached when one considers Tool's (1990a, p. 273) statement that "intelligent action needs to be applied on a continuous basis to effect institutional adjustment to new technological situations."

The emphasis on deliberativeness is one reason, perhaps the most fundamental reason, why some institutionalists favor "economic planning." Two points here: first, not all those in favor of planning have the same idea as to what it would entail; and second, not all institutionalists agree that elaborate planning is desirable. However, all institutionalists would agree, I think, that effective planning, largely hierarchical in structure, is already being undertaken through governmental and nongovernmental means, and that democratization requires opening up that process and rendering it accountable—again, the joint emphasis on pluralism and deliberativeness, with the sense that emphasis on nondeliberative decision making is a mask for oligarchic decision making.[8]

From a different angle but to the same deliberativist effect, Ramstad (1989, p. 763, emphasis in original; see also p. 774n.18) writes that from the Mitchellian institutionalist viewpoint "it is apparent that the function of economic knowledge—the sum of provisionally accepted facts, concepts, theories, models, and so on—is to show how 'interacting forces' and the existing patterns of 'burdens and benefits' are related, with an eye toward being able thereby to determine *how, in a specific context*, the governing 'working rules,' that is, the governing institutions, can be modified or 'adjusted' so that the actual pattern of 'burdens and benefits' *can in fact* be made 'better.'"

In his Presidential Address, Tool emphasizes that choice involves criteria (or standards) that "are, at least initially, products of deliberative reflection; they are in some measure discretionary" (Tool 1993b, p. 3).[9] Moreover, Tool calls attention to the role of power, namely, those "individuals and institutions that possess the power to determine whether . . . knowledge is introduced into the economy and if so in what ways and on what terms" (Ibid., p. 11). The crux of deliberative social critique, therefore, is rejection of the tendency to believe that "the fact of possession of power is . . . a sufficient justification for its existence" (Ibid., p. 13). In another recent paper Tool emphasizes seeking "accountability for those exercising control" (Tool 1993a, p. 8); change in the structure of society as "a consequence of human deliberation and control" (Ibid., p. 11); that "An unreflective decision to perpetuate the status quo" involves the reaffirmation of "what is" as "what ought to be" (Ibid., p. 12); and the deliberative use of policy to solve problems and thereby reconstitute the social and economic institutional fabric (Ibid., p. 15).

Finally, the significance of the instrumental principle in terms of both pluralism and deliberativeness has been stressed by Dugger as constituting the core of Tool's contribution to and version of institutionalism. Dugger argues that Tool has made "democratic participation the central element of social value theory" (Dugger 1993, p. 1). Interestingly, Dugger interprets Tool as having moved beyond Ayres's focus on technology to democratic participation on the basis of the issues—civil rights, women's' rights, and environmentalism—of the 1960s and beyond. "While Ayres located instrumental value in the technological process; Tool locates instrumental value in the democratic process (Ibid., pp. 13-14)—an intellectual revolution of considerable significance for institutionalism, obscured by the use of technology as a proxy for instrumentalism. Dugger concludes that the "central elements" of Tool's instrumentalism are "(1) the human capacity to think critically about experience and (2) "the democratic quest" to apply that capacity to the solution of social problems" (Ibid., p. 5). Therein resides the social roles of the instrumental value principle, according to Tool.

## Notes

1. Sheehan and Tilman (1992, p. 198) argue that "instrumental valuation is the linchpin that today holds the neoinstitutional movement in economics together." One can make the case that, ideological and teleological formulations notwithstanding, all human decision is, at least in some respects, instrumental, so that *pro tanto* instrumental valuation can be "equated with the human life process itself" (Ramstad 1989, p. 766; see 772n7). Gordon (1992, p. 898) quotes Ayres, that "This naturalistic, instrumental, technological theory of value is not 'mere' theory. As I have already said and will continue to repeat, it is not a theory of how value judgments ought to be made. It is an account of how we do, now and always, actually evaluate the things we value."

Such should not negate the fact of the co-existence of deliberative and nondeliberative decision making, that is, of culture and "rational" or conscious choice. On the relation of instrumental and reasonable value, see below.

2. One example: A diffusion of power by one criterion may represent a concentration of power by an other criterion, in part because "power" is so complex a phenomenon. And the determination of which criterion is/should be paramount is likewise a matter of means-ends and evidential controversy.

3. Bush (1991, p. 338) provides a wonderful example illustrating problematicity using the problem of allocating educational resources: "An important valuation to be made is to determine who should have access to higher education. While there may be some neoclassicists who would disagree, institutionalists would say that the individual's 'ability to pay' would not be an appropriate standard to apply in determining access to educational services. In other words, the value judgment—in the sense of selecting a standard of judgment -- would be to reject the 'ability to pay' as an instrumentally warranted criterion in making this valuation. A standard such as the 'ability to learn' might seem more appropriate. But the rejection of 'ability to pay' as a standard of judgment in this problematic context does not constitute a judgment of its appropriateness as a standard of judgment in other problematic contexts. For example, with respect to the question of how the tax burden to finance higher education might be fairly distributed, the 'ability to pay' criterion may be found to be instrumentally warranted." Notice two things: first, the meta-criterion as to using ability-to-pay is what promotes pluralistic democracy; and second, the determination of "instrumentally warranted" is not based on any intrinsic quality of a criterion but is a matter of designation through valuation.

4. Thus Munkirs (1988, p. 1041) writes that instrumental reasoning democratizes hierarchy by "fostering greater and greater participation in organizational decision-making processes. That is, instrumental ways of knowing and doing slowly but surely tend to undermine the hierarchical political, economic, and religious types of behavior patterns that emanate from our a priori/ceremonial cultural heritages."

5. Hickerson (1987, p. 1128), among others, emphasizes Dewey's recognition of "the purposeful and problem-directed nature of social inquiry."

6. Atkinson then makes the Shackellian point that "The future continues to unfold as we continue to act" (p. 193).

7. Atkinson also notes that "Veblen was skeptical about the use of law as a tool of social reform, while Commons assigned it a major role in directing progressive social change" (1987, p. 201), a distinction that may well reflect more Veblen's mood (leading him to doubt how much deliberative change can be achieved through collective action) and lack of experience in worldly affairs akin to that of Commons, than to any fundamental opposition by him. More apropos of the present discussion, with its emphasis on deliberative critique of the status quo, Hickerson (1987, p. 1126) affirmatively quotes Tool that "much if not most" of Veblen's "scholarly work was directed to a fundamental critique of prevailing social customs and business practices and the theory that gave each its credibility."

8. Bush (1989, p. 460) writes that "This does not mean that 'progressive' institutional change cannot involve significant challenges to the power and status of entrenched vested interests. But it does mean that due regard must be taken of the fact . . . that the hegemonic influence of such vested interests is manifested in habits of thought and behavior of ordinary persons going about the routine business of the life of the community. Minimal dislocation is quite consistent with a good deal of social strife as the institutional changes associated with evolution of collective bargaining and the civil rights movement demonstrate." Clearly (1) what constitutes "due regard" and acceptably "minimal dislocation" must be worked out; (2) the conflicts of continuity with change and of freedom and control are deeply intertwined; and (3) no contemplation is given to the utter destruction of nondeliberative institutions and social control by the elevation, at the margin (deeply and lengthily) of deliberative over nondeliberative social control. Hickerson (1987, p. 1137) writes that adoption of instrumentalism "would entail a democratization of the twisted system that presently exists, wherein knowledge and information are controlled by vested interests and distorted by corporate media."

# 8. THE INSTRUMENTAL EFFICIENCY OF SOCIAL VALUE THEORY

Edythe S. Miller

Institutional economics is well recognized as a heterodox body of thought. From this, it often is concluded that the system consists largely or completely of dissent from mainstream theory.[1] Irrespective of the stance taken on this matter, it correctly is surmised that a group of economists thus engaged in critical inquiry will from time to time experience internal differences. Although institutional economics contains a central core of ideas, differences in interpretation and analysis exist.

A current controversy within institutional economics involves the question of the "social value principle" proposed by Marc Tool. Tool posits as the criterion of social value "the continuity of human life and the noninvidious re-creation of community through the instrumental use of knowledge" (for example, Tool 1979, p. 293; 1986, pp. 50, 55-6). Tool clearly apprehends the social value principle as fully consistent with and grounded in the pragmatic philosophy of Charles S. Peirce and John Dewey as further expounded in the economic works of Thorstein Veblen, Clarence E. Ayres, J. Fagg Foster, and others. More specifically, in a sense Tool's social value principle may be viewed as progeny of the union wrought by Ayres between the Veblenian dichotomy and Dewey's instrumentalism, as augmented by Foster's principle of instrumental efficiency.

The debate concerning Tool's social value principle has a number of components, including the fundamental question of the appropriate function and purpose of theory. It encompasses the issue of whether science generally, and economics specifically, is positive or normative; that is, whether valuing and problem solving are appropriate functions of economics. If economics is a positive science, it follows that economics should not be involved in problem solving. In that case, one cannot reach the question of whether the standard proposed by Tool is reasonable, or of whether the validity of theory is related to the validity of its consequences in application. If economics is a positive science, a social value principle clearly is irrelevant.

The cohering factors in institutionalism are partially matters of context and perspective, a view of the economic world that at the same time sets institutionalism apart from orthodoxy and gives to it its distinctive quality. An inquiry into the beliefs that bind institutionalism as a school will serve both as useful staging ground for examination of internal differences and as a means of clarification of these issues. The caveats should be added that not all institutional economists will find the portrayal of institutional general core concepts agreeable, and that there may be even less agreement upon specific detail.

## The Central Concepts of Institutional Thought

A fundamental aspect of the institutional perspective is its view of the economic world as processual and evolutionary—a system in a state of dynamic flux rather than one of episodic and equilibrating stasis. Unlike mainstream theory, institutionalism looks to ongoing process, and not solely to initiation and consummation as its field of study.

Accordingly, human personality is viewed as influenced by culture. Individuals are not envisaged as materializing as fully formed bundles of innate preferences. That is, human consciousness is perceived as shaped by life experience including the mix of beliefs accepted as social norms of conduct. Moreover, in contrast to the orthodox perception of individuals as "rational economic" entities, a view mocked by Veblen as depicting persons as "homogeneous globules of desire of happiness," humans are viewed as variously motivated; complex creatures moved to action by various incentives including, but not limited to, that of self-interested hedonism.

Individual personality thus is perceived as a complex combination of habit, custom, avarice, envy, fear of and curiosity about the unknown, and other equally intricate and tangled inborn and acquired traits. Institutionalism views individuals as at the same time creations and creators of, participants in and observers of the social milieu. Accordingly, it roundly rejects the individualism, rationality and maximization that anchor mainstream economics. In doing so, it denies that individuals are solely passive receptors, reacting mechanically to economic signals. Humans are conceived as active, purposive players in social and economic affairs.

Thus, institutionalism is both processual, in its evolutionary perspective, and holistic, in that it apprehends the interdependence, interrelatedness and interactivity of the parts (individual participants in the process) and the whole (the culture, broadly conceived). As opposed to the atomism depicted by orthodox schools of thought, this perspective sees interconnectivity, a view of individuals as essentially bound, both to each other through various types of relationships, and to the culture.

Institutionalism thus substitutes a multi-directional flow among and between individuals and the culture for the one way upward flow of economic orthodoxy. It perceives humans as culturally shaped, and at the same time actively engaged in changing the culture through individual and collective action. The teleology inherent in the orthodox concept of a "natural order" moved by a body of "natural law" propelling the economy toward a specified end is rejected. The animism that sees purpose in that natural order also is repudiated. That is, institutionalism denies the existence of an antecedent reality, "a consistent propensity tending to some spiritually legitimate end" (Veblen 1961, p. 61), with that end point established by the conventional ideal; that is, the prevailing common-sense of the community. Institutionalists contend that the social process is open-ended, that worldly conditions are the result of human choices, both informed and uninformed; that is, of the application of organized intelligence, as culturally conditioned.

Dewey draws a distinction between reason and intelligence that is paralleled by Veblen's differentiation of "sufficient reason" and "efficient cause." In both pairings, the former term refers to an *a priori* method of knowing based upon logical deduction from underlying general principle, the latter to a method based upon the factual recognition of causal connection. Belief in the existence of an ulterior general law involves the assumption of order in the universe that specifies indisputable guiding principles susceptible to human perception through the application of reason. Examples from mainstream economics include such general categories as the profit maximizing firm and the utility maximizing consumer from which are derived principles of efficient markets and consumer sovereignty.

The orthodox perspective, which encompasses positivism, accommodates a vision of the mind as, in Richard Rorty's telling phrase, "a mirror of nature." Rorty describes traditional philosophy as captive to an interpretation of the mind "as a great mirror, containing various representations . . . capable of being studied by pure, nonempirical methods" (Rorty 1979, p. 12). Orthodox logical positivism discerns "natural" laws and regularities that underlie truth and reality, that are "given" from outside the system and susceptible to human cognition (that is, accurate representation) through *a priori* reasoning. Thus, the emphasis is upon description and prediction as opposed to prescription. The "given" truth and reality of orthodoxy is indistinguishable from the conventional wisdom, that is, from a *status quo* to which truth and merit is ascribed. It follows that social action to effect change is unacceptable.

Against such methods is posited the pragmatic and institutional method of the use of intelligence as opposed to "reason." The method is one of causal reasoning, of analysis in terms of cause and effect. These opposing methods—the use of reason and of intelligence, of sufficient reason and efficient cause—are the basis of the so-called Veblenian dichotomy. The former term is based in some form of authority—custom, convention, fashion, power, coercion, law. The latter is a matter of the application of organized human intelligence to get from an unsatisfactory here to a demonstrably more satisfactory there; that is, to solve human problems.

Veblen apprehends all human thought and behavior as infused with opposing characteristics of authority and intelligence; that is, as accommodating simultaneously the ceremonial and instrumental or (as they are haplessly characterized) the institutional and technological. Human choice is governed simultaneously by both. Both are evident in all human activity and human organization. They jointly control mundane choices about housing, education, and vocation. Their influence is felt in all such human organizations as the family, the school, the church, the laboratory, and the learned professions.

At the risk of belaboring the point, in the above example the laboratory or the classroom would seem least amenable to the influence of the ceremonial. Nevertheless even here, where inquiry is held to be valued above all else, custom also is honored, considerations of rank, status and professional reputation abound, there is deference to a received wisdom, even while scholarship is valued. These conflicting tendencies are not distinct or separately distinguishable; they infuse and shape each other. Formal social organization—for example, the family, the university, the market—are not ceremonial or instrumental, but interactively both.

David Hamilton describes canoe-building in the Trobriand Islands where "[m]atter-of-fact adzing took place in conjunction with bull-roaring which gave to the matter-of-fact activity, ceremonial adequacy" (Hamilton 1986, p. 528). It is important to note that the intention in citing such examples is not to denigrate primitive cultures. It is rather to distinguish the instrumental and ceremonial and to establish parallels between practices in primitive and contemporary cultures. As will be further developed below, all cultures have their cherished prejudices holding similar time honored standing and serving similar time honored functions as that of bull-roaring in the Trobriand Islands. The referencing of other cultures occurs not to impugn them but because, as Veblen often observes, myth and magic are more easily recognizable when viewed from outside a familiar cultural context. It is evident to a contemporary audience that, in the case of Hamilton's Trobriand Islanders, the matter-of-fact adzing contributes to canoe building, the more honored activity of bull-roaring gives to the instrumental activity conventional approval and acceptability, conferring on the process ceremonial adequacy. Moreover, as Ayres frequently points out, the ceremonial practices simulate the technological; that is, they lay claim to causal efficacy (Ayres 1944, pp. 159-69).

Matter-of-fact methods change as a function of the development of technology and other understanding. Technological advance occurs by building upon the knowledge of the past, by—as Ayres indicated—combination and permutation. Instrumental learning is developmental. It expands upon an existing body of knowledge by reasoning from cause to effect about methods of accomplishing worldly tasks. Technical matter-of-fact knowledge continuously is reformulated and reconfigured. New techniques and processes are developed as recombinations and additions to the intelligence contained in a current base of knowledge. It goes without saying that the larger that base, the greater the potential for combination and permutation. It is a matter of building upon, of reaching beyond, of determining "what works" to achieve particular results. That process may be thwarted by ceremonial behavior; for example, by obstacles put forth by those with a vested interest in maintaining the *status quo*.

The ceremonial, in contrast, is replacemental. In our own day, the "captains" of industry and "lords" of finance, replace former keepers of the faith and provide the requisite ceremonial adequacy for industrial organization. In contemporary society, economic well-being is attributed to speculators and financiers, as in other cultures it is ascribed to bull-roarers, rather than to the advance of worldly knowledge that makes it possible. In any period, the prevailing economic hierarchy is credited for economic progress (see Hamilton 1991, pp. 555-57).

All cultures practice such culture-specific forms of magic. Industrial growth and productivity is attributed to specific institutional structures and their ranking functionaries. Each culture has its keepers of the faith and the myth, apprehended as responsible for an achieved level of life. The ceremonial is culture-specific precisely because it is replacemental. The group accredited for economic progress changes, but the fact of such attribution continues. Thus, in one society clerics are the recipients, in another it is the entrepreneurs.

Every culture also accepts matter-of-fact knowledge. The ability reasonably to make judgments of value and prescribe is dependent upon the ability to develop and adopt matter-of-fact explanations, and techniques to achieve particular ends-in-view. The aim is understanding, with understanding linked indissolubly to prescription for problem solving. It is the question of prescription upon which the current dissent is centered.

## Institutionalism and Moral Agnosticism

Within institutionalism, objections are raised to prescription by economists basically on two grounds: that economists are not qualified for this role, and/or that their attempts to do so amount to overreaching. It is maintained, first of all, that economists are not competent to prescribe policy because of knowledge limitations, including an inability sufficiently to distance themselves from their culture to evaluate and prescribe objectively and critically. It also is contended that prescription by economists is inappropriate—an act of arrogance. It is a task that should be left to others.

The contention that economists are too much creatures of their culture to be capable of objective observation contains the inference that because "knowledge is socially constructed" and "[i]nquiry . . . a social process" (Waller and Robertson 1991, p. 1047), understanding is inescapably contaminated by cultural factors. This translates into a perceived insuperable barrier to scientific evaluation and prescription. Evaluation and prescription is viewed as an expression of individual cultural bias (Samuels 1990). The ability to engage in description and analysis, activities that are just as surely informed by the values of the economist-observer, is not similarly questioned.

It is further professed that economists who view policy prescription as a valid role display a certain arrogance, that the assumption of a prescriptive role is an act of hubris. The charge is essentially that of elitism; that is, that economists who would prescribe policy hold themselves above others and are attempting to substitute their values for those of "legitimate" policy-makers. Economists, it is asserted, "should be diffident and exercise restraint in making policy recommendations, lest they foreclose the operation of actual decision-making processes and substitute their own preferences for those of economic actors" (Samuels 1993, p. 237; on this point, see also Ramstad 1989, p. 766). It follows that economists should confine their role to that of descriptive analysis.

The "arrogance of prescriptivism" (Samuels 1991, p. 515) is attributed in some measure to traits of personality. There exist, it is claimed, two types of people: "those who require determinacy and closure, and those who can tolerate ambiguity and open-endedness" (Ibid., p. 511). It is evident that in this view, the closure-craving economists are those who define their discipline as normative, whereas ethical relativists are identified as capable of accepting uncertainty and indeterminacy.

It should be noted, however, that all institutional economics, normative as well as positive, involves description. It is evident that prescription cannot be undertaken in its absence. In addition, prescription will seem to many to be implicit in description. It also is arguable that description loses its edge, if not its reason for being, if not employed for critical and thereby prescriptive purposes. It should be recognized, however, that economists who maintain that policy prescription is a legitimate professional obligation do not do so out of conviction that they, and they alone, possess certain knowledge. To the contrary, they do so in full recognition that uncertainty is endemic to the human condition, and that the possession of absolute knowledge is not within their grasp, nor that of anyone else.

Policy prescription by economists is criticized on a number of additional grounds. Normative economics is described as suffused with an explicit anti-cultural bias, and as verging on a "dangerous ethnocentrism" (Mayhew 1987, p. 602). It is contended that "the emphasis, particularly by Veblen, on the imbecile nature of institutions has resulted in a tendency for his followers to dismiss the need to describe and analyze culture patterns" (Ibid., p. 599).

It is not entirely clear if the criticism is that institutionalism has not focussed sufficiently upon cultures other than that of contemporary business enterprise, that the focus on other cultures has been insufficiently sympathetic, or that the cultural bias of the analyst precludes even objective description, much less dispassionate evaluation of the cultures of others. It is important to recognize that the focus upon imbecile institutions is misperceived if it is viewed as directed negatively toward cultures that do not resemble, because they do not resemble, that of the analyst. Assessment is not directed toward cultures at all, but toward specific patterns of activity; toward the differentiated magic and myth that exist in all cultures, including those of contemporary societies, and the causal reasoning that combats them. Inter-cultural parallels are drawn for the sake of better distinguishing the ceremonial and instrumental aspects of all cultures. It is not apparent how attention to imbecile institutions results in a slighting of description and analysis. Nor is it evident why it should produce an "anti-cultural bias," much less the suggested ethnocentrism.

The contention appears to be a misapprehension of how the mode of institutionalists who accept a normative role comports with a Veblenian investigatory prototype. Not only have followers of Veblen not dismissed analysis of culture patterns, they have focussed on it, in the view of some, excessively. What, after all, is the case study, so important to institutional economics, if not a description and analysis of patterns of culture?

Some additional criticism of policy prescription by institutional economists include the following: It is maintained that cultural relativism is misunderstood. Cultural relativism, it is said, is the "inter-cultural equivalent of openness to trial and error." It also constitutes an acknowledgement that "we do not know we are right . . . that those other people might be right; that we might try some of their values in formulating . . . policies" (Neale 1990, p. 342).

In response, it should be pointed out that virtually all institutionalists do not simply admit of, but insist upon, the use of methods of trial-and-error. Indeed, it is fundamental to the perspective. Most also would be sympathetic to an openness to the practices and values of others. It is, of course, quite another matter if it is an insistence upon the acceptance of or neutrality toward values based upon authority and myth that is involved.

And finally, it is concluded that its predilection for making value judgments is one reason that institutional economics does not command the respect it deserves within the profession (Gordon 1984, p. 380). It should go without saying (even putting aside the question of whether such "do as we say, not as we do" prescriptions, generally accepted only as parental prerogative, also should be tolerated when advanced under the banner of orthodox practice) that when it comes to questions of theoretical validity, theory formulation should not (even if it too often does) hinge on professional respectability.

## Alternative Foundations of Knowledge in Economic Science

Some years ago, Charles Wilber and Robert Harrison examined the theoretical foundations of institutional economics, as distinguished from that of standard theory. They contrasted the formalism and mechanical adjustment processes of economic orthodoxy with the techniques of story telling and pattern modelling of institutional thought, concluding that where the purpose of orthodox logical positivism is prediction, that of the pattern model is understanding (Wilber and Harrison 1978, p. 77).

The distinction is enriched if viewed within the context of alternative conceptions of the foundation of knowledge found in institutional and neoclassical theory. When Veblen calls for the replacement of the principle of sufficient reason with that of efficient cause, he notes that this shifts the basis of knowledge from a subjective to an objective footing (Veblen 1941, p. 323). This is a statement of a realistic foundation of knowledge. Peirce rejects as a means of "fixing belief" accepted methods of his day (and ours) founded in tenacity (faith), authority and *a priorism*, and calls instead for the use of a method founded in an "external permanency;" that is, in "something upon which our thinking has no effect." He adds:

> There are real things, whose characters are entirely independent of our opinions about them . . . and, though our sensations [of these things] are as different as our relations to the objects, yet, by taking advantage of the laws of perception, we can ascertain . . . how things really are.

Peirce calls this method of "fixing belief" the method "of reality" and adds: "This is the only one of the four methods which presents any distinction of a right and a wrong way" (Peirce 1958, pp. 107-8).

Integral to its acceptance of the method of reality is the exception taken by institutionalism to the chain of cartesian dualisms (after Rene Descartes, the 17th century philosopher who proposed the taxonomy) that constitutes one of the pillars of orthodox philosophy and economics. Cartesian dualisms posit specific paired terms in various categories of human experience as separate and independent of each other. In this formulation, associated categorical concepts such as thought and action, reason and experience, knowing and doing, theory and practice, means and ends, fact and value, the objective and subjective, and the positive and normative, are perceived as discrete and independent facets of the human experience. This interpretation is rejected by institutionalism. Institutionalists maintain, to the contrary, that the terms in each of these pairings are interactive and interdependent. Thus, means influence and even determine ends, we know through doing, experience and action inform and are informed by reason and thought, objective facts are suffused with subjective values, the normative permeates the positive, and so forth. It follows, if only by implication, that you *can* get an ought from an is. It appears, indeed, that this is the only condition from which "an ought" is derivable.

Institutionalists reject the drawing of similar distinctions when it comes to such categories of knowledge as the ideal and the empirical, and such bases of valuing as the absolute and the relative. These distinctions also involve misspecifications because the terms again are presented as exclusive alternatives; that is, as either-or categories. That abstract thought is essential to understanding is indisputable. However, the proposition that "inquiry is a social construct," while beyond dispute, does not nullify the existence of a real world, independent of our perception of it. The choice presented between idealism and empiricism unduly constricts the field.

Nor is it valid to posit absolute and relative value as self-contained alternatives. That facts are colored by values and that inquiry is value-laden cannot be gainsaid. Inescapably, each of us views the world through a personal prism. Nor can our knowledge be complete, both because of human limitations, and because the constant interaction of humans with their environment means that each is subject to continuous change. That there are no absolutes underlying social reality, however, is not an indication that relativism is a valid foundation of knowledge or value. The choice presented between absolutism and relativism, like that between idealism and empiricism, is false.

An alternative to reliance upon an absolute or relative standard of value is adoption of what Dewey describes as "warranted assertability," or, to use Rorty's apt phrase, "what we are justified in believing" (Rorty 1979, p. 9) as a criterion. There are understandings and methods that have passed the test of time and experience. These are not to be viewed as eternally valid truths. They rather are to be adopted as tentative working hypotheses. That truth is not absolute is not an intimation that truth is relative. The present state of knowledge supplies superior and inferior means of dealing with problems.

Needless to say, we cannot state with certainty that the apparently reasonable will be, or will remain, the genuinely workable. That is why unremitting inquiry and experimentation play so important a role in the institutionalist paradigm. Knowing is a function of doing, that is itself a function of knowing. Policy implementation is an inherent part of the learning process. Policies must continuously be reevaluated in light of their consequences as a result of application to a problem at hand, and adjusted accordingly.

The organization of industry that Veblen describes in *The Theory of Business Enterprise*, his distinction between pecuniary and industrial employment, the tendencies toward "conscientious withholding of efficiency," are factual conditions of life that have factual consequences for human well-being. A recognition of the realistic basis of knowledge is implicit in John R. Commons' identification of collective action as in restraint, liberation and expansion of individual action (Commons 1961, p. 73; see also Ramstad 1986, pp. 1089-92), a recognition that there exists a social category (including a public interest) that is different from, and more than, individual aggregation. Commons' plea for changes in working rules to help make capitalism "good" (cited in Ramstad 1989, p. 768) is an acknowledgement of the existence of the unequal distribution of power and the potential for its abuse in our society.

Commons' reliance upon judicial determination for dispute resolution is an intimation of his recognition of the lack of a revealed absolute truth. The courts present a means of testing competing claims in an accessible and public arena, of permitting all contenders to have a voice in a process that is open to public view. It is not a perfect mechanism, by any means. But, in the absence of revealed wisdom, what is a preferred alternative?

When Gunnar Myrdal analyzes the "American Dilemma," and when he sets forth the principle of circular causation, he is describing tangible problems with genuine consequences for human life and experience. The discussion by John Kenneth Galbraith of public squalor amidst private affluence is a harbinger of the future deterioration of our urban centers. John Maynard Keynes' refusal to bend to mainstream insistence that "in the long run" widespread unemployment is a self-healing condition and, in any event, is one that is amenable to cure by the simple expedient of individual employer-employee negotiation, takes account of tangible realities. Each of these works contains a clear recognition of the real, factual world, and a clear statement of right and wrong. In each, analysis includes an explicit or implicit prescriptive stance.

The existence of real world objects and phenomena is independent of our perception of them (Miller 1991, p. 1000). Included among these are social and economic afflictions, and more and less appropriate means to their relief. It is undeniable that culture-specific problems exist. That they are culture-specific, however, is not an indication that they may be ignored as idiosyncratic. There are substantiated solutions to many problems that should not be dismissed, cultural mores to the contrary notwithstanding. Slavery is wrong, irrespective of the cultural context. It is wrong to permit inadequate health and sanitary measures and facilities to cause disease and death when they are preventable. Extant cultural conditions do not make conditions such as these acceptable.

Under such circumstances, it is reasonable to give expression to statements of right and wrong. Statements of right and wrong are verifiable.

It also is possible to identify problems that transcend culture: barriers to full participation and self-realization, abuses of economic and political power that take shape as exploitation and coercion. For example, the existence of poverty, in a society in which productive capacity is repressed in order to maintain price, is improper. Conditions such as these are impediments to social and economic functioning irrespective of the culture in which they occur. Incomplete knowledge may limit our ability to solve problems, and cultural specifics may limit the approaches that will be successful in combatting them. This does not alter the fact that, irrespective of social context, appraisal in terms of consequences for the human condition is both possible and appropriate. Nor are these conditions necessarily susceptible to melioration through specific individual action or inaction. If conditions are to be changed, collective action often must be undertaken. To take no position on these questions is, in effect, to take a position in favor of their perpetuation.

Indeed, the stipulation that the economist *qua* economist take no position on these matters strains credulity. Individuals, including economists *qua* economists, are active and purposive creatures. They are not capable of separating their various selves—to speak with one voice as economist and another as citizen. The record would seem to reveal, moreover, that most do not, in fact, even attempt to achieve such separation. The assignment to economists of a neutral role assigns to them a role akin to that ascribed consumers in neoclassical economics; that of inert and passive receptors of signals, a role that is no more supportable in the former than in the latter instance.

This is not to suggest that economists do not have biases. The very questions they choose to explore is a reflection of those biases. Nor is it suggested that economists should not attempt, as possible, to subdue their biases and engage their subject matters as objectively as possible. It often is remarked that part of Veblen's genius is his ability to distance himself from his subject matter and to view it from the point of view of an outsider and as if it were a distant (in time and place) domain. At the least, and as Myrdal is well known to have stated, values should be specified. This is so whether the analyst is engaged in prescription or description. However, to deny economists a role in policy prescription because their knowledge is limited and their objectivity blemished is analogous to an admonition to physicians not to attempt cures because their understanding of the causes of illness is incomplete, and because they are biased against disease.

The Veblenian dichotomy, as noted, distinguishes two sets of underlying bases for thought and action, the ceremonial and the instrumental. The ceremonial is founded in authority, faith, custom, and power. Much of Veblen's work is devoted to a demonstration of the existence and character of the honorific in such areas as "higher learning," business enterprise, and the leisure class. The instrumental, in contrast, has as its basis causal reasoning.

Within the means-end-means continuum that admits of no final ends, Veblen identifies a number of self-reinforcing human propensities that underlie instrumental efficiency. These are designated idle curiosity, the instinct of workmanship, and the parental bent. The case could be made that each of these is an analogue; idle curiosity for free inquiry, the instinct of workmanship for causal reasoning and experimentation, and the parental bent for caring, compassion, connectedness. At bottom, the parental bent may also be viewed as an analogue for problem solving, for it is through problem solving that we recognize and reinforce our human connectedness and common humanity, and improve the social realm that humans share.

It is important to recognize, further, that instrumental reasoning is essentially a method, and that method is the method of science. The method of science includes openness to the beliefs and opinions of others, a respect for diversity and dissent, and the use of experimentation (Bronowski 1965, pp. 60-68). Thought control is antithetical to scientific advance. Opinions do not assume the "worth" of their bearers, their validity must be established. Validity is established by "doing" that in itself changes the "knowing" that will in turn change future "doing." It is in large measure because such interactivity may have unanticipated consequences—for example, the effects of inventions, innovations and associated changes in organizational structure on customs and folkways—that institutionalism maintains that the future is unknowable and rejects a predictive role for economics. This is the reason too that experimentation and adjustment in light of consequences assume such continuing importance.

Instrumental value theory is not a means of imposing the values of the analyst upon society. The statement that there are "better" and "worse" methods of addressing problems, even if they are not self-evident or even as yet fully identified, simply amounts to acknowledgement that all opinions are not equal, and that taste *is*, after all, worth disputing. This is, perhaps, most fully apprehended by institutional economists whose work is in the applied fields. In the case of applied institutional economics, there is no alternative to the study of "brute irreducible facts," a reliance which roughly translates into a case study approach and equates, broadly speaking, to Wilber and Harrison's pattern modelling and storytelling.

The case study approach amounts simply to bringing to bear upon analysis of the situation at hand the facts of experience. Institutional economists historically have relied, in the broadest sense of the term, upon a case study approach. For example, some contemporary institutional analyses in this vein look to such questions as the consequences of the application of a "supply side" model to the macro-economy (Klein 1983; Petr 1983); the results of a sole, some say obsessive, focus by successive Republican and Democratic administrations upon deficit reduction (Foster 1994); the effects for lesser developed countries of bending to the insistence of lending authorities that they "tighten their belts" before receiving loans (Junker 1967). In each of these cases the consequences of particular policies, an indication of their validity or invalidity, will only be revealed by investigation of actual experience. The implications of current deregulation and privatization policies for economic concentration, stability, and consumer welfare is appreciated only by examination of actual cases (Trebing 1986; Miller 1993). The connotation for the wider economy of recent employment innovations; that is, of widespread cost-cutting by firms, and the adoption of a prototype of a contingent labor force, will not be apparent in the absence of detailed investigation. In each of these fields, and the many others in which orthodox prescriptions predominate, fact-based inquiries are required to evaluate consequences. Characteristically, fact-based inquiries contain implicit or explicit statements of value.

Toilers in these applied institutional vineyards make economic value judgments every day of their lives. The judgments are different—and more difficult to reach—than the judgments made by orthodoxy. Mainstream economists, despite their protestations to the contrary, also are actively and continuously valuing in each of these and other fields.

Judgments of value are more difficult for institutional than for orthodox economists precisely because the mainstream is not required to employ a case study approach or, indeed, to so much as glance at the facts, prior to prescribing policy. Criteria of judgment are based upon principle, not upon facts, nor upon the experienced consequences of policy. Orthodoxy does not get an ought from an is, but from some higher realm. Value judgments are based upon whether the policies are perceived to move us closer to a market solution, and/or reduce the role of government or other collectivities. If they are viewed as doing so, the policy is adjudged "good;" if not, it is pronounced "bad."

The social value principle does not supply simple answers to all questions. Nor are the policy prescriptions of institutional economics made of cloth cut to fit a predetermined pattern, irrespective of problem shape, context or texture. Institutional thought bases policy prescription upon the facts of the case, and the result sought; a matter, not of individual preference, but of perceived reasonableness and workability. If the objective is not achieved or is not proven beneficial, the policy is open to change. In the case of mainstream economics, in the name of value neutrality, an active policy stance is taken, that is invariant to the problem at hand. Irrespective of circumstance, a laissez-faire, hands-off approach is advocated. The approach is justified by denial of the existence of the problem—in effect, economic practice as reality denial.

The denial is evident in almost every field. For example, unemployment is not a problem, because in this perspective involuntary unemployment does not exist. All unemployment is viewed as voluntary, and individually curable by acceptance of a lower wage. Employers and employees are viewed as relative equals. Moreover, the specification of the "natural" rate of unemployment always may be revised. Economic concentration is not a problem because the model assumes a competitive economy. Even in concentrated markets, it is claimed, firms will act "as if" markets were competitive, disciplined by potential competition. The existence of power consistently is denied.

**Conclusion**

Individual efficiency is at the heart of orthodox economics. It is measured pecuniarily, facilitating summation for aggregative purposes. The sum of individual efficiencies is presumed to aggregate to an economy-wide total. The concept of instrumental efficiency employed by institutional economics, in contrast, is social. Tool's "noninvidious re-creation of community through the instrumental use of knowledge" can be read in no other way. It focusses upon the functioning of the social whole; a functioning that, in turn, facilitates or impedes individual activity.

Social efficiency is measured in real, rather than in pecuniary, terms. Efficiency is identified with the consequences, in terms of serviceability and reasonableness, of the application of particular policies to specific problems. It is a matter of how well the community can be made to work for its inhabitants; the extent to which productive participation, the realization of potential, the nurture and protection of the vulnerable and powerless is facilitated; and the extent to which polarization and isolation is thwarted. That instrumental efficiency is difficult to quantify does not indicate that it should be rejected as a criterion. Despite neoclassical affirmations to the contrary, Pareto efficiency is hardly a model of precision and clarity, and yet is widely accepted as a standard.

To an extent, institutional value theory has been misapprehended. It is a very different thing to say that we should acknowledge and apprize ourselves of the values of other cultures, and to say that all opinions are equally valid, or that their validity cannot be determined. It is not elitism, and does not constitute the imposition of the values of the analyst upon society, to call for the use of the unique perspective that institutionalism brings to economics to help solve human problems. The institutional perspective acknowledges that assessments of reasonableness may be incorrect. It recognizes that instrumental efficiency does not provide simple copybook solutions to every problem. For that reason, and because it also is recognized that the future is not predictable, assessment of policies is in terms of result, and experimentation is relied upon for improvement of methods. That is, institutionalism looks forward to consequences, rather than backward to absolute principles, to evaluate policy.

Institutional economics also recognizes that there are problems beyond individual control that require collective solution. For example, when it comes to social control of business, while recognizing that efficiencies sometimes inhere in scale, it also is acknowledged that concentration and integration involve an augmentation of market power. Yet, individuals are relatively powerless to act independently in the face of concentrated power. The existence of concentrated power requires the exercise of social control. In respect to the labor market, and even absent considerations of the macro-implications of large scale wage decreases, it is understood that the association between wage decreases and employment levels may be ambiguous.

We have recognized since at least the publication of Keynes' *General Theory* that it is not always possible for the laborer to cure individual unemployment by accepting a lower wage. Only the money wage is even partially within the control of the individual wage-earner. But a decrease in the money wage does not ensure a decrease in the real wage. Thus, individual attempts to maintain conditions of reasonably full employment often are fruitless—social action may be required. Similar caveats apply in the case of individual attempts to ensure a safe and humane workplace, or to achieve a decontaminated food supply, or to maintain a healthy environment.

Institutional economics does not attempt to discover or create a perfect system. It leaves the search for perfection to the more utopian practitioners of the art of economics, such as the neoclassicists. It recognizes that the real world often is untidy. It also apprehends that despite the best of intentions and efforts, the economy never will be problem free, and that, in fact, new problems inhere even in successful correctives. In place of perfection, institutional economics pursues reasonableness and serviceability. And that, it seems to me, is both the essence and the promise of social value theory.

## Notes

1. Orthodox economists tend to view institutionalism as little more than dissent from the mainstream, a view that institutional economists roundly reject. Institutionalists perceive institutionalism instead as a body of thought that presents an alternative perspective to that of orthodoxy, a perspective that includes dissent from mainstream beliefs and prescriptions as but one component of its general theoretical framework.

# 9. INSTRUMENTAL VALUATION IN A DEMOCRATIC SOCIETY

Philip A. Klein

There is no area in institutional economics more critical than the approach to value and the valuation process. At the same time, despite the many efforts which have been made to delineate the instrumental theory of value, and despite a common core of views toward instrumental valuation which are not really in dispute, the subject in many ways remains unclear and even controversial. This is particularly true if one attempts to push the implications of instrumental valuation as commonly expressed to their logical conclusion or to apply the theory in new areas. This paper is an effort to make a modest contribution toward clarifying some of these implications of instrumental value.

## Instrumental Value—Dewey and Ayres

It is generally agreed that instrumental valuation is an outgrowth of the work of John Dewey. He noted that the word "value" itself involves ambiguity, both as a noun and as a verb. "To value" something involves subjective feelings in the commonly used sense of the word. Says Dewey, "If, however, the question is raised whether the subject-matter is *worthy* of being directly enjoyed . . . then there is a problematic situation involving inquiry and judgment. On such occasions to *value* means to weigh, appraise, estimate: *to evaluate*—a distinctly intellectual operation" (Dewey 1938, p. 172).

Dewey goes on to suggest that evaluation is a process with consequences which need to be surveyed. "We have to investigate connections—usually that of cause-effect. Connections are then formulated in abstract generalized conceptual propositions, in rules, principles, laws. . . . Consequently, in order to obtain a grounded final judgment there has also to be evaluation or appraisal of principles" (Ibid., p. 173).

Dewey contributed several other critical strains to institutional value theory. He commented that "rationality is an affair of the relation of means and consequences, not of fixed first principles "and he was careful to note that he was referring to "ends-in-view," thereby contributing the means-end continuum to the discussion (Ibid., p. 9). The essential nature of this continuum permeated all scientific advance for Dewey. "The Newtonian formula of gravitation comprehended the Copernican conceptions, and the laws of Kepler in a new comprehensive theory" (Ibid., p. 455). Thus the means-end continuum is clearly related both to scientific progress and to the evaluative process which underlay it in Dewey's perspective.

Finally, and perhaps most important of all, from Dewey came the notion that human inquiry cannot be *wertfrei*. The learning process is indivisible. The process of expanding the true is coterminous with expanding the good. Thus from its very beginning institutionalism eschewed the normative-positive dichotomy.

Irving Louis Horowitz expressed the institutionalist position with respect to this dichotomy very well some years ago as part of a broader consideration of positivism. He (Horowitz 1976, pp. 51-52) wrote:

> Positivist method realized at least one central aim: that method should be so constructed as to allow for internal validation. The price, willingly paid, for realizing this aim was abandoning social prescription. Political science became isolated from politics as such; sociology became segregated from social welfare; and economic theory became isolated from the economic system.
>
> For mainstream economists, value neutrality went up as a cry in the night, itself to become an ultimate value. The purer methodology became in positivist thought, the less applications it seemed to have to those questions of value the philosopher was dedicated to resolve. This factor, coupled as it was with the inability to recognize its own valuation base, made positivism a tool lacking in human purpose.

This view toward the normative-positive dichotomy certainly colored Ayres' thinking, as indeed it does that of succeeding (including the current) generations of institutionalists. But it is important to recall that the overall perspective and the insight about the nature of progress which it embodies, is explicitly a part of the Dewey legacy.

The great fear of Ayres was that *values* would get mixed up with *mores*, which led to "mores nihilism"—"good" is whatever a given society chooses to call good. Good, like truth, is not relative; good is a dimension of value and valuation, and being instrumental, is universal. In this connection John Dewey asserts, ". . . there is nothing whatever that methodologically (*qua* judgment) marks off 'value-judgments' from conclusions reached in astronomical, chemical, or biological inquiries" (Lepley 1949, p. 77). Thus value judgments are reached by a process not different from the rest of developments in these fields (to which Dewey could certainly have added economics). Dewey added, "Only by taking facts ascertained in these subjects into account can we determine the conditions and consequences of given valuations, and without such determination 'judgment' occurs only as pure myth" (Ibid.). Here explicitly Dewey makes clear that instrumental value involves a universal process of expanding human knowledge and this process is sharply antithetical to the institutional, the magical, the ceremonial and the mythic.

Dewey makes the universality and the inescapable simultaneity of the process by which the "isness" of our world and the "oughtness" of our view of that world expand strikingly clear by quoting approvingly a statement that "moral evaluations 'must draw from the whole of man's knowledge . . .'" (Ibid.). These bedrock Deweyian views on value form an indispensable part of the essential institutionalist core.

For example, Tool, speaking for most institutionalists, writes critically of Pareto optimality on grounds that "what is becomes a criterion of what ought to be" (Tool and Samuels 1989a, p. 103). But clearly if the two cannot be dissociated, the institutionalist question is, what are appropriate grounds for ascertaining "oughtness?" The implication of our consideration of Dewey is that "oughtness" and "isness" are part of the same process. We come full circle to the realization anew that the positive and the normative are part and parcel of the analytical process, and that involves "instrumental valuation." Then the question becomes, "Can we state clearly what that means?" Ayres surely felt he could and did.

Ayres' greatest contribution, many would argue, was to combine Dewey's instrumentalism (including the means-end continuum) with the Veblenian dichotomy. Seminal as the dichotomy is in the development of the institutionalist perspective and methodology, it can be argued that Ayres also acquired from Veblen a rather unremittingly pejorative view of the role of institutions. Whether this was entirely appropriate we shall consider below.

Ayres was relentlessly tool-oriented. In discussing the meaning of value, Ayres (1944, pp. 222-223) wrote:

> Mankind is a tool-using species. All that man has done and thought and felt has been achieved by the use of tools. The continuity of civilization is the continuity of tools . . . . Economic value is no exception to this rule . . . . The criterion of every economic judgment is 'keeping the machines running.'

What Ayres thus makes clear is that "keeping the machines running" is coterminous with continuing the life process. This central Ayres thesis deserves some consideration. "For every individual and for the community the criterion of value is the continuation of the life process—keeping the machines running" (Ibid., p. 230). This is the critical dimension of instrumental value—its universality.

"True values are trans-cultural—they are the same for all men—because they are interrelated. All are manifestations of the same process, the life process of mankind" (Ibid., p. 167). In the value principal that Ayres placed at the heart of institutionalism this universality means that the true, the beautiful, the good, and the efficient are not only coterminous but are derived from the same dynamic and universal technological continuum. Said Ayres (1961, p. 206): "Truth is not merely that which works. Only what works is true, and it works only because it is true. Technology persists and advances because technical processes are the same for everybody. Only insofar as all men are free and equal can their works persist and advance. Equality before the law is a direct reflection of equality before the tool." The "tool," of course, is a broad and sweeping metaphor for the knowing-and-doing-and-imagining process which is the core of "the life process" which human endeavor, including economic, attempts to "enhance." It is the inherent conflict between this source of value and the institutionally filtered perspective toward it taken by individual societal groups which is at the heart of the discussion in this paper.

## The Role Of Institutions

This brings us to the next problem, "What is the role of institutions?" Ayres in discussing cause and effect as between tool-using and "the spirit world" refers to Knight's statement that fundamental to understanding economic process is the notion of "some . . . absolute and inscrutable type of a 'causality' by which technology drags behind it and 'determines' other phases of social change" (Ibid., p. 169). Ayres makes clear that the dynamic technology "drags ceremonial behavior along in its wake . . . . Sociologists quite commonly employ the word 'lag' to refer to this phenomenon. Far from being inscrutable, this also is an objectively verifiable feature of ceremonial behavior, quite as objective as a tool" (Ibid., p. 170). The term "cultural lag," is well known in sociology.[1]

Ayres' view of this process comes through in almost everything he writes. The economy is a cultural manifestation of a dynamic society. As Gruchy notes, "Ayres' theory of culture is associated with a technological interpretation of cultural development. Changes in the technological basis of human culture shape the institutional superstructure in the long run . . . the institutional structure is resistant to change . . . . The cultural process is continuously affected by the lag between institutional and cultural change" (Gruchy 1972, p. 96).[2] The lag between technological and institutional change, as Gruchy clarifies, exists because "outmoded institutional arrangements become obstacles which must be removed before a satisfactory adjustment between the institutional and technological aspects of our culture can be achieved" (Ibid.).

Ayres summarized his view: "The history of the human race is that of a perpetual opposition of these forces, the dynamic force of technology continually making for change, and the static force of ceremony—status, mores, and legendary belief—opposing change" (Ayres 1944, p. 176).

It is clear that in Ayres it is quite literally true that the ultimate and absolute source of value emerges from the machine process. The notions of "efficiency" which enable one to pronounce one process or tool "better" than another constitute the origin of the perspective utilized to pronounce on all human value questions.

The essence of instrumental valuation is, therefore, the broadening of the logic of technological progress as epitomized in the development of industrial technology to encompass not only science but ultimately all knowledge and the way in which the process of human valuation has developed in the past and will continue to do so in the future.

Do institutions play a "technological" role? Recent institutionalists speak in terms of the instrumental qualities of institutions, a view that would have been met with derision by Ayres. The question is nonetheless worth asking.

Ayres' discussion of institutions was, as noted, almost invariably pejorative. Almost all the terms he utilized in discussing institutions—myth, magic, superstition, ceremony, and the human traits they gave rise to—rank, status, pecuniary emphasis,—stress their inhibitory or technology-thwarting nature.

One rarely finds qualifying statements such as Gruchy's (1972, p. 296) "Although social and political factors cannot be ignored, the major active factor that gives momentum to the economic process is its changing, proliferating industrial technology and the science on which this technology is based." One can fairly say that while Ayres would not "ignore" political and social factors, progress was almost invariably a matter of waiting for such factors to be pushed into adapting to the fruits of technological progress. For Ayres progress was made in spite of social and political factors.

Can institutions be "technologically useful?" I think the answer is yes, if we qualify the statement carefully. Ayres' great fear was that instrumental valuation—a universal process—would be tripped up in folkways, mores, superstition, ceremony, magic, and other aspects of human behavior which are not universal but very particularistic. They in fact are grounded in individual societies from which they gain their sanction and their authority. For Ayres, the distinction is fundamental. The process of technological acceptance is a process by which institutions must adapt so as to encompass technological change. Ayres made much of this. Nonetheless, there is a sense in which some societal structures are necessary for "housing" even "universal" technological progress in particular social settings.

Despite the "past binding" nature of institutions, of belief systems and attitudes, of political and social relations, it is also true that without *some* set of beliefs or attitudes, *some* societal relations, *some* "habitual modes of conduct" it would be quite impossible for society to function at all. The problem is not with belief systems *per se*, but with their failure smoothly and continuously to adjust in light of technological progress.[3]

That being the case, Ayres, it may be argued, recognized an implicitly supportive role which institutional arrangements play. Institutional adjustment is an essential part of progress. Technological innovation can never lead to "progress" if it occurs in a social vacuum. Ayres recognized that institutional acceptance is, therefore, an integral part of turning technological progress into a functioning part of society.

Institutional support is a requirement customarily for the incorporation of technological change into any society. As such there is an important role for institutions to play in the way in which the dynamic process of technological progress, from which instrumental value emanates, is incorporated into particular societies around the world.

**Are there Remaining Ambiguities?**

For Ayres, we have seen, value means continuity and continuity is essentially the elaborate ramifications of the tool process, preeminently universal. We avoid "mores nihilism." The universality of instrumental valuation is an essential link which all institutionalists share. At the same time, there is an ambiguity in instrumental valuation which all institutionalists' formulation of it reflects. There is one word in all statements of instrumental valuation which needs clarification because it lacks precision. For Ayres and Commons the word was "reasonable." Ayres spoke of moving "toward a reasonable society" (Ayres 1961). For Commons, too, the objective was "*reasonable* value." Yngve Ramstad characterizes Commons' major work on institutional economics as one in which Commons calls Veblen's major error to be "a failure to arrive at a concept of Reasonable Value."[4]

But what is "reasonable" and how is it defined? Hayek would no doubt argue that avoiding "the road to serfdom" would constitute a "reasonable" societal objective. For Marx achieving the classless society would similarly have seemed "reasonable." For many modern mainstream economists "freeing the market" constitutes "reasonable" public policy. All agree, in short, that policy should be reasonable. The problem is in giving teeth to the notion of reasonableness, and Ayres tried to do this through his analysis and discussion of instrumental value theory grounded as it is in terms of that which "keeps the machines running."

At that, this basic Ayresian criterion as a standard of value is a good deal clearer than the associated Ayresian view that all matters of esthetics, taste, and judgement are at bottom reducible to a variant of instrumental efficiency. Thus he frequently writes of works of art, of music, poetry, etc., as though they are appropriately dissected analytically in the same value terms as economic questions. There is but one standard of value—the instrumental standard. Indeed, he goes further: the standard of value is inherent in the tools themselves. Therefore, truth, beauty, and efficiency are all part of the same value continuum.

Fagg Foster, following Ayres, tries to remove the possibility of ambiguities in a universal instrumental valuation standard by emphasizing efficiency as its bedrock basis. He suggests that economics is concerned with "the process of providing the means of human life and experience," and that most particularly for economics this involves "the institutional aspects of the productive process," and that "a problem arises when that process ceases to be carried forward at the level of efficiency indicated by the current state of the industrial arts" (Foster in Tool and Samuels 1989a, pp. 353; 354). Clearly by "the institutional aspects" Foster refers to the inhibitory. Accordingly, if it were true that "what is" is right, there could be no economic problem. Value theory is concerned with the criterion for determining "what ought to be." Foster concludes "The evidence . . . drives us rationally to the inescapable conclusion that our only choice is to accept economic efficiency in the instrumental sense as our criterion of judgement, our theory of value" (Ibid., p. 359).

Foster argues (with Ayres) then that the valuation criterion applied to the tool process is identical with the valuational criterion applied generally. Both argue that valuation as in choosing the better wrench is coterminous with valuation as in judging art, music, literature, or political strategies. It is all well and good to claim, as did Ayres, that there is a simple standard of choice involved and indeed that all valuation is instrumental valuation, the adjective being useful in reminding us of the origins of the value principle we apply generally. Detailing instrumental value in aesthetics lacks a comprehensible equivalent of "efficiency," although the assertion that the question, "What is good?" in aesthetics, as in the choice of the better wrench, has comprehensible dimensions based on the progress of the instrumental basis of each art, is at least a promising beginning. Art and music critics will surely argue that their criticism has a sounder (an instrumental value) basis than simply what they "like."

For Tool the objective of progress is a "*non-invidious*" society (see Tool 1979, pp. 292-300). But who and what defines invidious? How is it defined? Although Tool tends to discuss invidiousness in social terms, he declares that noninvidiousness itself is a corollary ethical concept for progress in racial and sexual matters. It seems clear that a non-invidious society is for Tool at bottom a society without impediments to the societal incorporation of the fruits of technological progress for all participants to the full extent to which each participant is capable of benefitting from them. Thus Tool's view is essentially consistent with Ayres'.

In Tool's view, the basic worth of all individuals does not mean the equal worth of all individuals. "All individuals cannot equally take advantage of the ongoing fruits of technological progress. Invidious valuation bases human worth on "the invidious use of race, sex, ethnicity, color, wealth, ownership, rank, age, power, etc." (Ibid., p. 295). Denigration, at bottom, involves denial of equal access to the potential for human betterment deriving from the technological continuum.

This may make the matter as clear as it can be, but it does not in my judgment, provide an easy answer to all questions which may arise. Ayres might dispute this; Tool probably would not. I suspect, for example, that most institutionalists are pro-choice in the abortion debate, and would be unhappy if told that the pro-choice position treats fetuses as a class in an "invidious" way. But surely it does. Surely it implies that fetuses (a term which one supposes technologically applies to human organisms from the moment of conception to the moment before birth) do not "enhance human life" to the same extent that their parents do. Or if one decides that they do, that too represents a standard of enhancement which is controversial. If one concludes that by enhancing human life Veblen meant extant or born life, this is, even if true, conjecture. (On the other hand, it seems instrumentally clear that by no stretch of logic can being *both* pro-choice and indifferent to the societal treatment of the new born be regarded as anything but both illogical and a violation of the instrumental value principal. Hence some invidious judgements must be being made).

In short, even after one factors in a standard of instrumental valuation, *a la* Ayres, derived from the combination of Dewey's means-ends continuum (instrumentalism), and the Veblenian dichotomy, it is not entirely clear that one has a standard of valuation deriving from the "enhancement of human life" criterion which is so unambiguous that no gray areas remain. At the very least, the task of clarifying through application the instrumental value criterion is a never-ending one.

Thus, for example, when Tool defines "invidious" in instrumental terms and argues that "Invidious judgments, by fostering interpersonal and inter-group conflict, directly threaten continuity of instrumental economic, political, and social functions" (Ibid., 309) he must hope to have found a way of separating instrumental (non-invidious) from invidious valuation for most human concerns. He does indeed go on to suggest that race riots, religious conflict, "overt discrimination," and a whole host of other ugly social and political activities "make the task of 'recreating community' virtually impossible."

Ayres claimed as noted earlier that choosing the "best wrench" is choice on the same continuum as choosing the best music, resolving a racial or religious dispute, or, for that matter, the problem of choosing the "correct" economic policy. The solution to all these problems, we have seen, is found for both Ayres and Foster by asking which of the alternatives is "instrumentally most efficient?" Tool would ask which contributes most to creating a "non-invidious community?"

Veblen would have asked more generally which "enhances the life process" most? All these formulations, while helpful, still require precise definition, as well as application to specific circumstances. Presumably we may all agree on the "ideal" outcome of macroeconomic policy—we should like non-inflationary growth which kept all factors of production employed fully save for the irreducible frictional or seasonal unemployment. This would provide the optimal growth rate and, if we factor in technological progress, keep our economy as fully competitive in the world as current resources and the state of the industrial arts permit. Have we resolved all our value problems here?

The difficulty with the Foster position is that while he eschews "invidious" and "reasonable" he still falls back on "economic efficiency" as the diagnostic implement with which to discern value and to distinguish what ought to be from what ought not to be. Mainstream economists revere efficiency and still manage to distinguish normative from positive in a way which institutionalists find unacceptable.

Economic policy in terms of ends-in-view is not in dispute. What is in dispute is the efficacy of means to achieve ends-in-view. A central theme of this paper is that factoring "democracy" in as a bedrock principle, merely complicates an already complicated issue.

This is very tricky terrain. "Enhancing the life process," we have argued, may have been unambiguous to Veblen, just as a "reasonable society" was for Ayres. The universality of instrumental valuation is unambiguous enough. Discerning it in individual instances, however, may nonetheless be complicated by institutional incrustations, which need to be confronted by all analysts.

Consider the race riots in Detroit in the 1940s. They were surely destructive in the short-run of the process of "recreating community." They may also have been unavoidable, or ultimately an essential part of the civil rights struggle. I judge the march on Selma in the 1950s (mostly non-violent) was not inconsistent with recreating community. What of the violent Los Angeles riots of the early 1990s? One can argue that out of that caldron came the anguished voice of Rodney King asking a pure "non-invidious recreation of community" question, "Can't we all get along?" But to the extent that the riots were a violent response to a court verdict by no means easily viewed as compatible with current societal values and was, moreover a verdict which gave rise to death, looting, wanton destruction, etc., the answer, even from a believer in violence as a method of making social progress, is not so clear. One could multiply examples of ambiguity from many social sciences in defining "invidious." World War II was "clearly" an effort to reduce "invidious" (i.e., Nazi) judgments. What of the Viet Nam War?

One could raise questions of this nature in connection with current debates about euthanasia, school busing, the use of nuclear energy, etc., all of which may still be difficult to resolve even with the aid of the instrumental value theory.

One can debate the wisdom perhaps of all violent social protest. There has always been debate about the efficiency of both violent and non-violent social protest. Putting this in a Tool-Foster context, it becomes a debate about the most efficient ways to free the community to accept non-invidiously the fruits of technological progress.

All these questions are broadly "economic" (i.e., they have resource allocation implications) and appropriate for economists to debate. Many (e.g., family planning) are concerned—directly or indirectly—with the ideal rate at which the supply of human inputs should be introduced into the production process. More broadly they concern the ratio of "hands" to "mouths"—surely among other things, an economic question. Is the task of efficient allocation ("economizing") to produce as best we can for the rate at which the population happens to be growing, or should the rate of population growth be coordinated with the rate of technological progress and the rate at which this allows for the maintenance of any given standard of living? (This is, in effect, applying the usual "Third World" approach to all economies).

What is very clear, as the discussion above underscores, is how many areas customarily regarded as *non-economic*, are an integral part of an instrumental value-based approach to economic analysis. Institutionalists would agree that these are legitimate areas for concern, and that institutionalist economic theorists have—and accept willingly—a responsibility to consider such matters. Institutionalists do not assume pressing societal matters away, no matter how complex they may be. We are as far from the normative-eschewing "positive" economics of the mainstream as we can get! The discussion, therefore, is a validation of the critical Ayresian insistence that the instrumental value principal is universal and is thus useful in all areas where human beings discuss the worth of things, that is their ability to enhance human life.

In sum, we conclude that we may still ask, "Does the instrumental value principle invariably point the way *clearly* and *unambiguously* in all controversies involving allocation?" Clarence Ayres would have had no problems with this question. Emphatically, he thought that it did. Modern institutionalists are totally united in concluding that "leaving it to the market" most particularly does *not* dispose of all allocational matters and that, indeed, all allocation emerging from market prices requires monitoring by an exogenous authority. "The public interest" must always be raised as independent standard against which market allocation is judged. (This is the preeminent job of government in a democratic economy, presumably assisted by expert economists utilizing their expertise in the service of society). In particular, mainstream stratagems to avoid facing up to this necessity for societal monitoring applying instrumental valuation through such devices as reliance on Pareto optimality or cost-benefit analysis are explicitly avoided. As such we might be left with very inadequate and slender reeds on which to rely. But having said all this, we may still conclude that even instrumental valuation, while it avoids the huge pitfalls of the easy out, is not always immediately and transparently clear and that applying it to emergent areas of concern is a never ending requirement for progress—both economic and non-economic.

## "Emergent Valuation"—Two Aspects

### *The Technological Continuum and Valuation*

In the more or less continuous unrolling of the technological process new aspects of "value" and valuation are, as has just been considered, always making their appearance. From Veblen and the Veblenian dichotomy we know that there are resistances to "progress." But in addition to "resistances" as we have just seen, there is the matter of recognizing "better" or what "enhances" life when it is confronted.

For Ayres we have seen there was never any problem about determining "better." When it was not acted on he attributed it to the "mores," superstition, myth, etc. All those things included in "ceremonialism" were pejorative. There was a clear "Bad." In short, recognizing "progress" for Ayres was not something to dwell on—the internal logic of instrumental valuation clarified what one meant by emergent valuation. Rather in the manner of our modern penchant for labelling Keynes' multiplier an "instantaneous" multiplier, in contrast to the "period multiplier" which corresponds to "reality," we may label Ayresian technological advance as recognizable instantaneously by those who applied the instrumental value principal, no matter how long it may take for this potential progress to be introduced into the actual economy. Presumably this also describes the current state of analytical affairs when a Commons follower confronts what is reasonable, a Fosterian what is efficient, or a Tool follower confronts what is invidious. The instrumental value principle provides all with a standard for making these judgments.

If, thus, technological progress were and is abundantly clearly defined for Ayres and other institutionalists, it is arguably less clear today in social and political intercourse. It is this difficulty which explains both the continued insistence of mainstream economists on separating the normative from the positive, and the complexity of public debate about many policy issues. What is at issue, of course, is nothing less than explaining why the technological and the institutional can and do fail to correspond (at best) and conflict (at worst).

I have over the years often employed the term "emergent valuation" to connote the manner in which dynamic societal valuation grows out of the technological process. I now realize that instrumental valuation is in fact a two stage process and the two stages need carefully to be distinguished. When Ayres referred to instrumental or technological valuing we have noted that he assumed that a trained institutionalist could easily perceive the steady accretion of knowledge produced by instrumental valuation. In this institutionalists would implicitly accept the implications of Galbraith's "conventional wisdom"—it is what institutionalists, understanding instrumental valuation—can throw off. More generally, the conventional wisdom is shorthand for the limitations of static institutions, which are, in turn, what prevent technological progress from being instantaneously incorporated into all economic activity.

More recently, institutionalists have concentrated on elaborating the distinction between the technological and the ceremonial. Implicit in these discussions, as we have noted above for Ayres, was the notion that institutionalists can tell the difference. When Tool talks about "the non-invidious recreation of community" he considers many clarifying examples of what is invidious and what is non-invidious. When Petr characterized institutionalism as "values driven" it is implicitly assumed that institutionalists can recognize "values" when they see them. Petr similarly described institutionalists among other things, as "instrumental" and "technologically focussed." The same comment must be applied. Apparently institutionalists all agree that they can themselves easily distinguish the technological from the ceremonial or the instrumental from the non-instrumental.

In the same vein when institutionalists assert that the criterion of value is not whether it conforms to a pre-established pattern but rather is "Does it enhance human life" the same comment is applicable. We considered this earlier, and concluded that presumably institutionalists can tell. We have all many times referred to the value problem in these terms, following Veblen's famous comment about "enhancing the life process." What is the problem here? Earlier we saw that neo-classical economists no doubt would argue that "leaving it to the market" enhances human life. We tread on the danger of "mores nihilism" about which Ayres warned us. Do we need to find or do we already have some way of discerning what **really** enhances human life? Galbraith avoids this institutionally produced myopia. In his differentiation of conventional wisdom from "true" wisdom, it is crystal clear (if always by implication) that he at least has avoided these traps. Galbraith is never ensnared in the conventional wisdom so that if he pronounces on what is instrumental there is no danger that he, too, is engaged in specious (ceremonial) reasoning. He avoids what Ayres would have derided as the "Cretan dilemma." ("All Cretans are liars").

Miller reminds us that institutionalists reject the neo-classical perspective based on dualities (Miller 1989). We do not distinguish rigidly between essence and existence, between reason and experience, theory and practice, thought and action, knowing and doing, means and ends, deduction and induction, normative and positive. But we *do* distinguish sharply between technological and institutional, between instrumental and ceremonial. Often these distinctions are perfectly clear. On occasion, as we saw earlier, some of this can get us in trouble—e.g., the family is an institution but surely caring for the young is a technological necessity. Many institutions serve technological purposes. Whether Ayres (or even later institutionalists) paid enough attention to this aspect of institutions is debatable. We do today view structural institutions as encompasing both instrumental and ceremonial behavior.[5]

In any case, the point to be made is that institutionalists profess to discern clearly when instrumental or technological progress is being made because they apply assiduously the tests that we have been at pains to develop by which one can distinguish the instrumental from the institutional.

We can conclude, therefore, that for institutionalists instrumental value was derived by Ayres via Dewey and that despite ambiguities, can be infused with a reasonably precise meaning derived from the process of judging efficiency in the tool process. As one student has pointed out for Dewey, ". . . value and valuing are regarded as observable phenomena carried on within the social process through the application of intelligence and action to problematic situations. They are not transcendent, isolated, or subjective. Emergent values, rather, are objectively tested to determine their success or failure in resolving problematic situations" (Hickerson 1988, p. 178). Ayres recognized that the dichotomy's ultimate use was in the valuing process and so became particularly critical when it was combined in the means-ends continuum. As Hickerson notes, "Ayres made a clear distinction between genuine values, which are the technological stuff of experience, and ceremonial values, which are the product of cultural mores, and institutionalized rank, status, and authority" (Ibid., p. 179).

This first aspect to emergent valuation seems reasonably clear. It refers to the change in value resultant from the technological process itself.

*Emergent Value in a Democratic Society*

The second aspect to "emergent valuation" refers to the actual incorporation of that change into the important value system of the community. This requires us to consider the Veblenian dichotomy—technological change and institutional resistance—in the framework of political democracy. Earlier institutionalists clearly have argued that a criterion for determining what is "good" and what is "bad" can be derived from the technological process and that this criterion is the only criterion which ultimately can be supported by logic, by reason, and by historical analysis. Moreover, this criterion is universal. But having said all this, we must nonetheless add that any *democratic* society cannot force either new technology or the implications of new technology upon its participants until such time as they themselves influenced either by the power of their own senses to observe and appreciate directly and thus to be persuaded of the "correctness" of the new instrumental valuation emanating from the technological continuum or else to be persuaded (i.e., seduced) by clever and charismatic leaders. One way or the other participants and demonstrators would probably be willing to accept it. Earlier I offered the term, the "value floor," to the values embodied in ongoing society at any given time. The value floor reflects current societal values—"for the collective ought" (Klein 1984). Valuation changes derived from technological progress customarily precede changes in the value floor because of institutional resistances to changes in societal values. There is, in more conventional terminology, a role for the teacher and/or the leader to play in facilitating the acceptance of new technology in a democratic society.

Until such time as one of these routes to acceptance has been traversed, there is—presumably observable—in this society 1) new implications or insights which are part of instrumental valuation derived from the ongoing technological process, 2) a failure of societal institutions as yet to have altered and adjusted so as to incorporate into ongoing life the new implications of technological progress, and 3) the clear implication that citizens in this society have, therefore, not yet sanctioned technologically derived change which would represent "progress" or the furtherance of "good" economic policy. The requirements of democracy, we have asserted, however, require that this society live by whatever is institutionally sanctioned until such time as either charismatic expertise or dawning public insight permit politically sanctioned change. While Ayres often referred to institutional resistance, and equally often referred to the technological continuum as the locus of value, he treated scarcely at all the process by which a *democratic* society overcomes institutional resistance to incorporate the fruits of technology into the active values of ongoing society.

## Technological Change, Democratic Acceptance, and Cultural Lag

Institutionalists in the Ayres tradition attribute the failure of technological progress to be incorporated into society's conventional mode of doing things more or less promptly to two factors: (1) to the Veblenian notion of "imbecile institutions," which can thwart or stop the implementation of technologically sanctioned new ways of doings things for long periods of time, and (2) the failure to accept may similarly be the result of Veblenian "vested interests." In this sense the two pragmatic stages to the instrumental valuation process are first new valuation (a new step in the means-end-continuum) must be extant—i.e., the technological process must have proceeded to a new point where this change in the valuation process can be discerned. But second, the now explicitly existing insight, relationship, possibility, change in conclusion, etc., which constitutes the new stage in technological progress (is *technologically* emergent valuation) must still be accepted by society. The only alternative is an authoritarian society in which the Authority makes all decisions itself or else appoints a Designated

Monitor of Instrumental Valuation to announce periodically those changes in society which technological progress has produced. Time, therefore, must elapse between these two aspects of "emergence." Pasteur "discovered" bacteria—a part of the technological process—but that occurred sometime before the French were willing to accept it to the extent of actually boiling milk (acceptance of the progress). The cathode ray tube was "discovered" by De Forest some time before television sets were actually introduced into the economy, etc. I, in common with many other institutionalists, have in the past used "emergence" to mean the physical appearance of knowledge about bacteria in milk, the existence of the first cathode ray tube, etc. Institutionalists have always, been at pains, however, to note then that society did not accept technologically "emerging value" immediately.

One could of course speak of emergent value as the acceptance of the results of the latest technological progress by a given society. In this sense the phrase refers to the rate at which new technological insights are incorporated into given societies. The two emergences are different however.

In any case, the critical point is that no democratic society can appoint a Values Czar charged to "see" emerging technological truths and to pronounce upon them for everyone else. John Kenneth Galbraith we saw earlier handled this problem in his introduction of the term "the conventional wisdom" by in effect appointing himself Value Czar and implicitly concluding that most everyone but himself was warped by the "conventional wisdom" (see Galbraith 1958). Similarly Ayres did not make this point complicated—he almost always wrote as though what constituted "progress" in instrumental value terms was invariably fairly simple to discern. Experimentation usually led to self-evident results. Other institutionalists do not get concerned about this. Commons could tell the "reasonable" from the "unreasonable"; Tool easily differentiates the "invidious" from the "non-invidious." "Mores nihilism" is not a fate that many institutionalists fear for instrumental valuation. Still, the price of democracy is clearly that we bumble and stumble along making "progress" as fast as **both** the technological continuum makes it physically or logically possible **and** society incorporates the fruits of the process into its ways of doing. The latter is, I take it, what Ayres thought Veblen added to Dewey's instrumental valuation. The dichotomy refers to the genesis of resistance to technology and to the strategy for progress required to effect the changes technological progress pointed to.

The canard that democracy is never "efficient" and frequently messy surely applies.

### Democracy as a Value

Ayres, we have implied, did not talk very much about democracy. (An exception would be in the last few pages of *Towards A Reasonable Society*). Significantly, in that work, the "values of an industrial society," which he spells out in chapter length discussions include, freedom, equality, security, abundance, and excellence—but not democracy. He did talk about technological imperatives and about the way in which the rightness or wrongness of things was a manifestation of the efficient or the inefficient. The tools themselves and the tool process, we have seen, are for Ayres the locus of value.

I have always contemplated the technological process in the context of a democratic society. In such a society, recognizing that information is not perfect, communication channels are not necessarily unclogged, etc., we can advocate moving toward open channels and "perfect knowledge" in an effort to make the two aspects of "emergence" closer together temporally. But in the meantime we can do no better than put some questions of "value" before the citizens and ask in open elections or referenda what they accept and what they don't. In this sense the institutionalist's devotion to technological progress is held hostage to the same "lack of perfect information" which bedevils the enshrinement of perfect competition for the mainstream micro-theorist! Democracy requires that we live under an imperfect system, with rules derived from past technological times which still have institutional sanction (there must be a place to consider technological progress and institutional resistance-call it "cultural lag" if you want). One of the freedoms which is a constituent part of democracy is the "freedom to be wrong"—that is to proceed in ways which can no longer be technologically sanctioned—that is, optimal.

In the discussion previously alluded to Ayres does not consider what is optimal short run "progress" if the technological and the freedom components of the industrial way of life are in conflict. While in such circumstances it is clear that "imbecile institutions" would prevail for some time, it is not clear that violating the freedom principle would improve the industrial way of life. Along with the triumph of imbecile institutions in this circumstance, Dale Bush would probably clarify the situation significantly by suggesting that "technological progress" was "ceremonially encapsulated" here (Bush in Tool 1988, p. 444).

Ayres may talk all he likes about how clearly "value" emerges from the technological process itself—that all value questions should be decided on precisely the same basis that "a worker chooses the 'right' wrench." But it is still true (as indeed elsewhere he recognizes when he quotes Veblen's "triumph of imbecile institutions" for very long periods of time), that no one has yet devised a system in which to make the introduction of new technology smooth, if not painless. That would require that citizens, as suggested earlier, anoint someone with the power or the right or the duty to pronounce on value questions as they emerge from the technological process. The alternative would be a "law" that all manifestations of technological progress must immediately be accepted by all. We have already seen that democracies appoint no Value Czar to tell them what is currently the instrumentally "correct" path in a given situation. It may be "clear" (and the application of the instrumental value principle—see below—ought to help enormously), but democracy requires that technological choices—no matter how clear or how instrumentally tuned in they may be—must nonetheless await societal sanctioning before they can be implemented.

This may be what some call "cultural lag." By "emergent valuation" I certainly do not mean that we vote on questions of instrumental value. The valuation process (the valuation process) has its own integrity. I do mean that society can progress no faster than the rate at which the instrumental values emerging from the technological continuum can be or are accepted by the citizens of a democracy. (This is the political science version of "technological progress overcoming institutional resistance.")

"Emergent" is perhaps not the best word. We have argued that ultimately instrumental value "emerges" twice. First it emerges from the technological continuum. But such valuation and/or its implications may or may not be understood by the society in which it emerges and if understood it may or may not be accepted. Ayres, of course, talked about "the strategy of progress." But always this strategy was discussed in terms of ways to "reveal" the insights of technological change, with often the implicit suggestion that revealed truth—because it has been revealed—will be accepted because it obviously *is* truth.

The inevitability of technological progress and of societal incorporation of technological progress are, therefore, not the same thing. But they are clearly linked. Moreover one can certainly argue that democracy itself is a part of instrumental valuation. Democracy and the institutionalists' penchant for it are not institutional, but a part of the strategy for progress viewed instrumentally.

To elevate democratic decision making to a central place in the development of economic policy is more than Ayres ever attempted. But his view can be inferred. It is not by chance that he included "freedom" in his list of requirements for a reasonable society. While he would, as has been noted, have regarded it as totally confusing to speak of the technological role of institutions, he clearly felt that genuinely free choice (as opposed to Friedmanesque free choice in a power-and-wealth-distorted market) was a critical part of a "reasonable society." The only conclusion is that, in spite of the fact that progress is slowed by institutional resistance and the necessity to overcome it before technological change is an active part of society, nonetheless *how* the fruits of technological progress are made viable is critical. I have often written about the rate at which the public comes to see what is instrumental. (It is "emergent valuation" in the second sense). The object of sound public policy devoted to instrumental valuation is to reduce the time it takes for the fruits of technological progress in all areas to be accepted by the participants in a given society. In doing this Ayres thought the use of demonstration represented the fastest way. Nothing will convince the public, say, that round wheels are more efficient than square wheels faster than a demonstration with both kinds of wheels. More complicated cases are less rapidly assimilated.

**Instrumental Valuation, Democracy and Public Policy**

Ayres always wrote as though instrumental valuation was always or almost always potentially convincing through demonstration. As we have seen, it seems fairly clear however, that thinking—even "instrumentally"—about issues such as, say, abortion, euthanasia, affirmative action, the appropriate degree of environmental protection, etc., is anything but simple. Even if we go a step further and argue that the instrumental way to attack such issues is to ask in each case, "What is the path which most enhances human life?" the decisions are far from easy. (The American Civil Liberties Union not too long ago had a very contentious national meeting in which their long-held view that "free speech" is the preeminent value came into conflict with their more recently announced view that safety and advancement for women in society must be supported. In that discussion the devotees of the latter position prevailed).

Does this kind of discussion lead inexorably to being charged—as Ayres might say—with "mores nihilism?, and that worrying about these things mean's that one's view of instrumental valuation will slide into a sea of relativism?

Not necessarily. It does mean that we must realize that "thinking instrumentally" is not invariably as intuitively obvious as some would assert. By sticking to easy cases the complexities are buried. Thus by distinguishing what "really" causes the rain from the American Indian's rain dance (a favorite Ayres analogy) Ayres made it childishly simple to distinguish what is "fact-based" from what is not fact-based. Edythe Miller (1989) approves of Jerry Petr's (1984, p. 4) emphasis on "fact based" institutionalism at the same time that she rejects the duality involved in efforts to distinguish theory and practice. This makes sense if one means that theory unrelated to facts is irrelevant. A major contention among institutionalists has always been that the critical link for theory must be to policy and problems in the "real world." Elegant theorizing made possible by extensive assumptions about the world and which, therefore, were not explained by the theory means often that the usefulness of the theory in explaining the world is severely curtailed (a point made *ad nauseam* by institutionalists concerning mainstream theory, especially price theory). This is strong ground on which to distinguish fact based theory from "unreal theory." In terms of the duality it must mean that the useful theory must be sufficiently fact based so that it explains a significant part of "practice." The only comment we add is to reiterate a point made earlier—that Ayres customarily employed examples that were obvious and in the real world such may not always be the case. It is fine, as we have underscored, to ask, "What enhances human life?" The answer may sometimes require much consideration.

Marc Tool relates instrumental valuation to democracy this way: "Democracy is a necessary, but not sufficient, criterion in choosing among alternatives . . . . The fact that an institutional choice (e.g., to establish a national medical-insurance program, to reimpose the death penalty, to expand nuclear fission energy installations) is made by majority vote, directly or indirectly, does not necessarily mean that the 'continuity of human life and the non-invidious re-creation of community through the instrumental use of knowledge' is therewith being served. Majorities may be wrong, as we are often reminded by elitists" (Tool 1979, p. 307). Tool is, in effect, noting as we did earlier that "emergent valuation" is a two stage process in a democracy.

Right and wrong are not decided by majority vote—or even by elitists. They are decided by application of the social value principle. (That is to say, if one begins with the Veblenian dichotomy and combines it with Dewey's theory of value, including Dewey's means-end continuum, one arrives at Ayres' notion of "progress," which is quite unambiguous). Certainly in Ayres' hands there could never be debate about what direction was "ahead," what one meant by "progress," or which of two alternatives was technologically superior.

Says Tool: "The instrumental value theory . . . does indeed identify the public interest, and democracy is the most efficient process thus far conceived through which to achieve some approximation thereof" (Ibid.). We would agree, but this statement must be carefully interpreted. It means that democracy is more efficient than any elitist authoritarian system. (Either it takes less time to achieve a given result and/or it is less likely to be manipulated in devious directions that are neither technologically justified nor in the public interest). (One can imagine a Gosplan headed by a Values Czar, which might be charged with implementing the fruits of technological progress into projects and procedures charged with furthering the public interest in light of advancing technology). It offers a way to monitor what majorities approve in light of what technological progress would permit. But it does not eliminate the difference pointed to earlier—namely Veblen's "imbecile institution" possibility and the modern version—that for long periods of time "better" ways to do things can be known about but not implemented because majorities for their own reasons—good, bad, and indifferent—refuse to sanction them. This is a lag of some sort brought about by the resistance of institutional structures to adapt to possibilities which nonetheless are newly available technologically.

### Emergent Value in A Democracy—Residual Problems

The problems with which we wrestle, accordingly, in considering instrumental valuation in a democratic society necessarily include:

1. Developing better ways in which to state the limits to assumption permissible in theorizing.

2. Considering whether or not we can make more convincing than we have our conviction that theory must at all times be the handservant to real world problems.

3. Closely related, stressing convincingly that placing theory in the service of problems is the path down which the distinction between theory and practice can be reduced or even eliminated.

4. Considering whether there are ways to refine the notion of "life enhancement" so that the instrumental can be more readily distinguished from the ceremonial for the many cases where the distinction is not as obvious as the myth vs. reality, magic vs. scientific examples which historically institutionalists—perhaps simplistically—have employed to make the distinction.

5. Where we can clearly identify instrumental and so give explicit meaning to emergent instrumental value, facing squarely the question, "How shall we relate this kind of "emergence" to the kind that is involved in democratic acceptance of the implications of instrumental valuation?"

6. Rethinking carefully the conventional distinction between the technological and the institutional with a view to asking ourselves whether or not the necessary positive role of *both* in introducing technological progress into the ongoing system ought not to be acknowledged squarely at the same time that the technological basis for defining both value and progress is underscored, along with the inhibitory role which extant institutions at any given time frequently play in the process of actual societal incorporation or activation of technological developments.

## Conclusions

It can be argued that the key to the value question for institutionalists revolves around the Veblenian notion of "enhancing human life." This realization, however, by no means disposes of all critical issues, but it offers a guide for the path down which questions can be resolved.

It may be that one problem with Ayresian instrumental valuation is that he made it sound as if there were no problems, no grey areas, no questions which one needed to ponder. Ayres seemed to suggest, that putting the emphasis on "freedom," "equality," "security," "abundance," and "excellence" pointed presumably to an unambiguous path for the resolution of every allocative question which could confront an economy as it sought to pursue "the industrial way of life"[6] (Ayres 1961). We have suggested that Ayres may have promised more than can be delivered (a suggestion which would probably have infuriated Ayres). Ayres made it appear that out of the tool process itself all value questions could easily be resolved. Thus he deliberately used terminology which reinforced this position. The "instrumental" way involved "reason"—not "superstition." "Myths," "mores," "magic," and "status" were clearly part of the institutional drag on "the knowing and doing process." He recognized that it is easier to make these distinctions in cultures far removed from one's own. But painting the problem as he did made it easier for one's own culture than may always be the case. It is not entirely clear that other later institutionalists have avoided this pitfall. We have argued that both Commons' "reasonable" value and Tool's "non-invidious" recreation of community come without a clear standard with which necessarily to differentiate always and in all situations that which is "instrumental" from that which is not.

But if one holds as the instrumental criterion the conscious effort to use as the standard the question whether in fact a proposed course of action or policy or attitude will enhance human life or not, one has at least a way to begin. This is the essential perspective which has historically held together institutionalists of all sorts, regardless of the positions on which they may differ. The question now is how best to advance beyond this point?

The answer is difficult because one can argue that "enhancing human life" begs the question. (This may simply be a confession that as a standard it is appropriate but lacks sufficient specificity). Even so, institutionalists can well ask, what are the current alternatives?

In sum, the standards of valuation (or alternatives to choosing one) available to us include:

1. Try definitionally not to choose at all a valuation base, despite being "free to choose." This is Friedman's position. Economic analysis is *wertfrei*.

2. Accept neoclassical standards of choice.
   a. The old view would be Pareto Optimality.
   b. The new view would perhaps be Cost Benefit analysis.
   (Institutionalists reject both, but for different reasons).

3. God's will—a non-economic standard, except perhaps in connection with the social economics reflected in various Papal Encyclicals. One asserts that

a given course of action, policy, or attitude is "God's Will." A slippery standard in the non-economic world (God's Will, like beauty, is too often seen to be in the eye of the beholder). Without considering this alternative in detail, suffice it to say that it resolves few if any of the problems institutionalists regard as fundamental. Even algebra problems must be "solved for X."

4. "Leave it to the market." This is a positive version of Number l. Many economists eschewing formal welfare theory operate in their application of economic theory as though market allocation *per se* is good because it emerges from the market. Thus "market incentives" are imbued with "good" because they are part of market allocation, which in turn is definitionally good, and the distribution of income, power, goods, and "satisfaction" is good because it is derived from market allocation and not from "command" decisions.

5. Let command decisions make these judgements. With the disintegration of the Soviet Union, equating "good" with the decisions of central planners has been largely discredited. China, Cuba, and a few other places may still argue that societal "good" can be centrally decreed.

6. Instrumental value-institutionalists embrace this option, "warts and all." Instrumental value must be regarded as "emergent" in two senses:
   a. It is dynamic—hence constantly emerging—because technological choices are based on dynamic technology.
   b. It is emergent because a significant part of instrumental valuation is that it must be democratically incorporated into the social process. "Lags" are a part of the process, therefore, of democratic incorporation of the fruits of technological progress into ongoing society.

In this connection, it may well be that ultimately institutionalists will amend the Veblenian dichotomy, useful as it is, to ascribe a positive role to at least some institutions, providing a necessary social structure within which unfolding technology can be housed.

## Notes

1. In *An American Dilemma* (1944, p. 1388) Gunnar Myrdal refers to Hortense Powdermaker's use of the term "lag" in speaking of the process of acculturation.

2. In the quote, I believe Gruchy mis-spoke. He meant to say "the lag between institutional and technological change."

3. See Paul D. Bush, "Theory of Institutional Change," in Tool 1988b. Bush calls this institutional adjustment process "ceremonial encapsulation," (p. 144). They can also be "future binding" when vested interests control technological innovations so as to increase their control.

4. Yngve Ramstad (1989, p. 768). He was, of course, referring to John R. Commons' *Institutional Economics, Its Place in Political Economy* (1934).

5. For a discussion of this distinction cf. Hamilton (1986), Miller (1989), and Klein and Miller (forthcoming).

6. The references are all to the basic structure employed in Ayres (1961).

# 10. COMPULSIVE SHIFT or CULTURAL BLIND DRIFT? LITERARY THEORY, CRITICAL RHETORIC, FEMINIST THEORY AND INSTITUTIONAL ECONOMICS

William Waller

Clearly one of the central organizing foci of Marc Tool's contributions to institutional thought is the thesis put forward in his 1980 Presidential address to the Association for Institutional Thought where he argued that a compulsive shift towards institutional analysis was underway. He argued that the reactionary counter revolution going on at that time would not overtake this tendency (Tool 1986, p. 181-202). I think it is relatively safe to say that Tool's observation was correct, but that some qualification and elaboration is required. The qualification is as follows—the move towards institutional analysis has occurred, but it has not been a move to *institutional economics*. Since Tool's address the movement away from mainstream orthodoxy has increased. However the dominant tendency remains away from (or beyond) orthodoxy, not towards institutionalism. This tendency can be demonstrated by: 1) The increased interest in heterodox traditions, the proliferation (or fragmentation) of heterodox positions, and the creation of new proto-schools of thought—all building on themes recognizable within institutionalism. This increased interest in heterodoxy manifests itself in the formation of new scholarly organizations, the founding of new journals, and expanded discussions of institutionalist themes in existing journals within heterodoxy. 2) The serious reconsideration of the methodology of positive economics within the mainstream and the widespread consternation about and interest in reopening the question of methodology by mainstream and heterodox methodologists, historians of thought, economic historians and those interested in the philosophical foundations of economics. 3) The increased interest by orthodox economists in the creation of social institutions, the processes of institutional adjustment, and the evolution of economic systems. This interest can be seen by the growth of such sub-fields as public choice, transactions cost analysis, law and economics, and property rights theorizing increasingly identified as the "new institutionalism." 4) The increased interest in conservative alternatives to orthodox economics such as Austrian economics.

I do not intend to defend Tool's thesis. In many ways I wish to assert it and move beyond it. The reason for this approach is straightforward. Most economist's seem to be moving in the direction of institutional analysis, but the name or label "institutional" is carefully avoided. Institutional economics is simply not reputable within the mainstream, thus the name is avoided by newcomers who naively think that mainstream practitioners will accept their "new" or "novel" approach. As institutionalists well know this strategy has been tried by many and has no appreciable effect—however, this is not a sufficient reason not to try it again. I assume our neoclassical colleagues are intelligent, well-intended scholars who simply cannot hear or read us intelligibly because of incommensurability between our paradigms. Possibly someone will overcome the incommensurability, but it is more likely that the drift toward institutional analysis will cause the various frameworks to slowly evolve to the point of minimal commensurability—at such a point conversation might begin afresh.

There are scholars with whom this incommensurability poses less of a problem. It is to these others I wish to draw institutionalist's attention. Further I wish to argue that some of these other scholars, because of shared preanalytic intellectual assumptions, are also making a compulsive shift to institutional analysis. Moreover they lack an historical animosity toward either the subject matter or the name of "institutional economics." These other scholars fall within the "fields" of literary theory, critical rhetoric and feminist theory. I will take each of these in turn. But first a few preliminaries.

## Non-foundationalism in Institutionalism and Postmodernism

A number of writers have drawn attention to common interests between institutionalism and what is often referred to as postmodernism (Brown 1991; Jennings and Waller 1993; Mirowski 1989; Olson 1991; Samuels 1990, 1993; Sebberson 1990; Waller and Robertson 1991, 1992). In particular what most of these writers have noted was the common rejection of foundationalism in institutionalism and postmodernism. In order for this to be intelligible a brief discussion of what I mean by postmodernism is necessary. To begin, foundationalism has been and largely remains the dominant perspective underlying Western epistemology since the Enlightenment. Scholars who are foundationalists in their inquiry believe that immutable foundational principles exist or can be discovered upon which deductive and inductive logic are applied to find true knowledge, meaning knowledge that is isomorphically correspondent to existential reality and thus is true and incorrigible. The techniques and methodological precepts emerging from this position are what McCloskey identifies as modernism, precepts that we commonly associate with cookbook versions of "the scientific method" and "the methodology of positive economics." This understanding of inquiry has been effectively buried among methodologically preoccupied neoclassical economists and many heterodox economists (McCloskey 1985). However, I suspect that most neoclassical practitioners and many economists in heterodox traditions still subscribe to some formulation of foundationalism or modernism and are unaware of either the critique or emerging consensus (at least among cultural inquirers) on the unsustainability of foundationalism. This is unsurprising since foundationalists approaches dominate popular perceptions of science and scholarly inquiry, largely due to the exclusively foundationalist character of primary, secondary and most (science and social science) higher education.

The rejection of modernism or foundationalism hardly constitutes a definition of a scholarly program and as such most of what comes under the diverse rubric "postmodernism" approaches inquiry from other traditions. It can be argued that shared "Cartesian anxiety" or recognition of the "Cartesian vice" is all that these diverse approaches to inquiry really have in common.[1]

It is almost impossible to define postmodernism without entering into the specific debates within and among the many strands of thought.[2] Since I am writing to an audience that is largely unconcerned with the details and minutia of these debates I will focus on those aspect of postmodern thought that in my view share common ground epistemologically, methodologically, and in terms of praxis with pragmatism and hermeneutics.[3] The rationale for doing so is quite straightforward—these approaches to inquiry are complementary (in some formulations, see Diesing 1991) and as Mirowski has argued constitute the philosophical basis of institutional economics (Mirowski 1988). We will be exploring scholarly programs that share at the very basic epistemological level some commonalities that allows for productive discourse and the possibility of commensurability between institutionalist inquiry and particular strands of postmodern inquiry.

## Literary Theory

### *Introduction (translation or obfuscation?)*

Literary theory comes in all different kinds and varieties. It is often striking to scholars trained in the social or natural sciences that scholars in the disciplines traditionally referred to as the Humanities are both so preoccupied and sophisticated regarding epistemology and that interest in epistemological questions is omnipresent among these scholars. I have come to understand through collaborative work with humanists that they are equally baffled by the treatment of epistemology and methodology as specialties (and relatively unfavored specialties at that) in the social and natural sciences. They are similarly amazed by the indifference and ignorance of such issues by practitioners in the social and natural sciences. In many ways the Humanities are about epistemology and methodology and the content of particular texts is the terrain on which this inquiry takes place. Understood in this way it seem less odd to suggest that literary theory could provide insight into epistemological and methodological issues in the social and natural sciences, though as we shall see the substantive content of the terrain upon which the inquiry is conducted is important.

All literary theory concerns the reading and interpreting of texts. Close reading and "explication of texts," usually spoken in French for invidious reasons, constitute essential components of literary analysis and scholarship. So far this is pretty obvious. The central issues are which approach to close reading a text is employed in interpreting (or alternately—in "reading") specific texts and what is the epistemological status of that interpretation (or reading); this is the contested terrain.[4]

A book (or other physical manifestation of a text) is a cultural artifact, as is its content. But the text is also a form of communication between the author and the reader. When a text leaves the author's hands the author's control over the text is diminished if not ended. The control of the text shifts partially, if not totally, to the reader.[5]

As I write this text I have a particular audience within institutional economics in mind. The purpose of writing the text is, for me, quite clear. What I want to say is evolving as I construct the text. I will alter and reconstruct this text several times before you, the reader ever see it. You will then read it. If you are a member of the intended audience I expect that my intended meaning will be clearly and effectively communicated to you. The members of my intended audience are members of the same school of thought in economics in the mid-1990's, all of whom are trained in both neoclassical and institutional economics and are familiar with the broad contours of the American economy, American culture and the Western intellectual tradition. We all share at least that context for this text. But others will read this text as well. They come from other contexts and may construct other interpretations building on their different understanding. Moreover, I might not be as clear as I had hoped. The ambiguities of language and my own skill as a writer may mean that my intended audience interprets this text differently than I intended. This leads to two simple but fundamental questions that any reader can ask about any text: What did the author mean? and What does the text mean? Depending on the reader there is no necessary correspondence between the answers to these two questions. Though both of these questions are important, they are important for different purposes. Thus the purpose of a particular form of inquiry is a crucial aspect in determining the correct question, and consequently, the appropriate technique for answering that question.

To return to literary theory, both of these questions are asked of texts. The first question implies an approach that requires the exploration of a text from within a reconstruction of author's context and purpose to the degree such a reconstruction is possible. It is the imperfect character of the reconstruction that leads to the multiplicity of possible and plausible answers to the question concerning the author's meaning. This is fertile ground for intellectual controversy. The second question requires another approach, that is the construction of a meaning for a text from the context and purpose of the reader—which of course can lead to a nearly infinite multiplicity of meanings and contexts. The potential for controversy and disagreement inherent in this approach makes controversy within the first approach seem relatively trivial in comparison.

I have avoided jargon for a long time now. This latter approach to the reading and interpretation of texts; where the reader's context and purpose are the foundation of the interpretation and where the only constraint on that interpretation is whether or not the text will support the interpretation (and not whether it corresponds in any way with the author's intent or context, or the traditional or community consensus on the meaning of the text) is called a "reading." The method of deconstruction, which may include many alternative "readings" of a text, is the process of breaking a text down to reveal its implicit assumptions and embedded contradictions. Debates over the legitimacy of this approach to texts have gone on in literary theory for some time. I will argue however, that this controversy is overblown and relatively unimportant.

*The Purpose of "Readings"/Interpretation*

To begin with it requires neither Santayana's over-quoted authority or much thought to establish that the study of the past is important, including both the author's intent and the culture's consensus or range of thought on the meaning of texts from the past. It is equally obvious that when we read texts we will understand them and interpret them in the context of our own experience. Thus, if a text supports an interpretation by an individual within a particular culture, at a particular time—fine. This same approach can also be used for contemporaneous texts. But more is at stake. Foucault and others have constructed an argument that interpretation is the basis of knowledge and thus all knowledge is relative and is power (Foucault 1980). Presumably power is the ability to determine, reinforce, construct and legitimize meaning. This is nontrivial, but in and of itself does not affect the legitimacy of "deconstruction" as a methodology for literary interpretation. The issue it raises is the purpose of the scholarship or interpretation.

If the purpose of an interpretation is to establish or reinforce a particular class of or a singular interpretation as dominant, and as a result influence the members of a culture's understanding of that culture or reinforces a cultural hierarchy—enforcing invidious distinctions, precluding other interpretations or reinforcing cultural mythology,—then it is both a mode of acquiring and enforcing power through the establishment of cultural hegemony. This understanding of interpretation as knowledge/power constructs a nihilistic and paralyzed view of cultural interpretation and action. Every "reading" reflects (or projects) the reader's idiosyncratic, unassailable, non-comparable, non-evaluative knowledge/power, and has the same status as any other "reading." This relativism is only sustainable in two circumstances. The first is if all interpreters conclude that all interpretations that are supported by the text are equally valid for all purposes. This is silly. It assumes that cultures have no valuational mechanisms and that people within those cultures are unable to critically reflect upon the implications and meanings of their cultural values systems. Put simply, cultural relativism implies neither ethical paralysis or moral agnosticism. It does imply that cultural value systems are self-referential and self-reflexive, but for institutionalists this is hardly novel (Mayhew 1987; Neale 1987; Samuels 1990).

The second possibility for sustaining extreme evaluative relativism is if the interpreters really believe that the inability to judge objectively between interpretations means that the only purpose of interpretation is to entertain or converse with others doing interpretation. This position has been put forward by Stanley Fish (and is implicit in the work of Donald McCloskey) as a similarity between literary theory and economics (Fish in Klamer, McCloskey and Solow 1988). However the act of writing down these interpretations belies this position. Frankly, why bother? If there is no greater meaning than entertainment and to receive the applause of your audience, why preserve it beyond the contextual moment? The act of publishing as a book of essays on literary criticism suggest and implies a permanence that is utterly unwarranted by the purpose of entertainment. Could it be that even the most vapid deconstructionist unconsciously senses that there might be something in their work that transcends personal interpretation and speaks in a meaningful, if not objective, way about the human condition?

If I understand George Steiner correctly in his book *Real Presences*, this is his argument. It is not our ability to say anything with certainty about reality or of transcendent value regarding the human condition that drives us to write, communicate, and interpret, but the possibility that we might—through our efforts—make a contribution to a larger human understanding of what motivates and has motivated people throughout time to record their thoughts. When we read a text with the same intent—to see if it informs us about our lives, the nature of human existence, or the commonality of the human experience—it is not the certainty that it will, but the possibility that it might, that make the experience and sharing it with others valuable beyond its entertainment value. Thus we can and do judge among "readings" /interpretations as better and worse; the real question is better and worse for what purpose. This criteria is referred to as performativity and is very controversial among postmodernists—it means judgment made on the basis of pragmatic performance or outcome. It is seen by them as limiting (Rosenau 1992, p. xiii).

Thus literary theory offers several ways for reading texts that support both a historical approach and a multiplicity of interpretations that encourages novelty, diversity and experimentation. Its historicism can either be a beginning of cultural understanding, interpretation and reinterpretation; or a sterile exercise in textual exegesis resulting in reification of texts and sterile sepulchral studies. This sterile extreme is not dissimilar to the trap the German Historical School in economics fell into or with economist's penchant for argument about what Keynes, Marx, Smith, Veblen etc., *ad nauseam* "really" meant. Alternately at the other extreme in literary theory is a trivial deconstructionist focus on endless critique (deconstruction) and/or (re)interpretation for the purpose of entertaining other critics and interpreters. This corresponds to the purpose of economics actually practiced by too many economists of all types—causing the endless production of stylized arguments to receive the applause of similar minded economists.

The consequences of a generalized acceptance by society of the extreme deconstructionist tendency (meaning a refusal to evaluate because of the impossibility of either an objective or disinterested interpretation) in literary theory would be to eliminate the possibility of texts to influence community identity in a conscious way—a form of cultural blind drift.[6] The consequence of this extreme evaluative relativism in economics is the same, as Veblen noted, blind drift. But there is a difference (I will argue a difference in level and immediacy of impact, but not of kind). People and cultures can read and interpret a text or not, but human life and society (economy) are not only coterminous, but indistinct (we can separate them analytically, but not existentially) and immediate. If you don't like a book you can refuse to read it, both individually and as a culture, but if you don't like your culture (and as a result your own enculturation) you can't leave it; it is part of your own identity even if you physically remove yourself to another geographic location or consciously revolt against it.

*Are Texts and Economies Different?*

This raises the issue of the importance of the difference between the subject matter of literary theory and social science. Many literary theorists and cultural critics would argue that their methods are applicable to social analysis. I would agree with this position. But there is a difference between the deconstructionist approach to literature and applying this approach to social phenomena. Unlike many others within the sciences and social sciences my argument is that the difference is one of level of analysis or immediacy of impact, but not of substance. I need to elaborate on this difference in some detail.

Literary theory and postmodernism are often dismissed by social theorists, particularly those wedded to "materialist" social theories. This is an argument often, but by no means exclusively, put forward by Marxist theorists. The argument against postmodernism (and deconstruction) in the social realm notes that the economy, as a system and as social processes, exists regardless of the particular way in which we interpret or understand it. This position is often presented as a reassertion of realism in the face of instrumentalism, an argument for the possibility of objectivity against the irrationality of subjective interpretation, or an argument for a strict demarcation between science and nonscience. In fact there are many variants, but they all have one thing in common—an appeal to a dualistic conception of inquiry that is unsustainable in the non-foundationalist framework that literary critics (and as we shall see institutionalists, critical rhetoricians and many feminists theorists) ground their inquiry. These objections are not illogical or inchoate within the traditions that generate them. But foundationalist's miss the point that such arguments are irrelevant (in fact, they are non-arguments) to non-foundationalists; they attack premises that are not present in the construction of the non-foundationalist approach to inquiry.

This in no way implies that adoption of non-foundationalist methods of inquiry will lead to massive irrationality in economic or social inquiry. The existential economy puts limits on the range of acceptable interpretations of it. Put simply, the real economy serves as an external constraint on the discourse. The economy is not universal—it is socially constructed, but that construction includes constraints that are binding within the temporal context of the present. And at the level of individual interpretations and actions this is particularly true. Contrast the external constraints in economic analysis with the external constraints and limits on literary theory. The only constraint is what the text will support.[7]

Foundationalist and materialist critics then draw obvious conclusions of the following type. If Alan Greenspan misinterprets the economy a crisis may follow as a result of his ability to affect the real economy through policy. However, if J. Hillis Miller (a literary critic) misinterprets Hawthorne, so what?

The only consequence is more articles and dissertations within the closed confines of a discourse community of other literary critics (see especially Robertson 1993).[8]

There are two problems with this argument. The first is that both the economy and literature are cultural artifacts. Thus the same limits on interpretations that affect our ability to interpret one aspect of the culture, affect our ability to interpret other aspects of that culture—though admittedly at a different level of social importance. Put simply Greenspan's ability to make effective his interpretation of the economy through policy is immediate and profound. But remember Keynes's warning in *The General Theory* concerning madmen in authority being the intellectual slaves of some long dead academic scribbler (Keynes 1964). Greenspan may be today's madman in authority, but it is just as likely that J. Hillis Miller or Stanley Fish are the academic scribblers to whom the future's madmen pay homage.

Put directly, literary interpretation is part of our culture and the interpretation of texts surely affects the construction of future texts and their interpretation. Cumulative causation insures that this process will have consequences for the evolution and reconstruction of our culture. The future reconstruction of culture will determine the parameters that define and place limits upon both literary interpretation and the interpretation of the economy.

The second problem with the foundationalist/materialist argument is of a different sort. Analytic philosophy often poses a fairly linear relationship among ontology, epistemology and methodology. Nonfoundationlists sometimes uncouple them altogether. I would argue, if space allowed, that the relationship is more complex. Preliminary assumptions about the ontology of phenomena are made that condition the methodology of inquiry. However the fruit of that inquiry can only be interpreted within the context of an epistemological framework that suggests what it is possible to know. Thus while ontology does not determine epistemology at least the working hypotheses about the nature of being, what it is possible to know and how inquiry can be conducted are hermeneutically related in all inquiry. This issue has been addressed in the work of the philosopher Roy Bhaskar in ways consistent with realism (Bhaskar 1989). I find the work of Usakli Maki in this regard very helpful in incorporating a realist perspective on cultural constructed phenomena (Maki 1993). This allows us to avoid the extreme interpretive relativism of deconstructionist approaches.

This raises problems in the area of value theory in economics. Deconstructionist approaches, by virtue of arguing that all perspectives or social locations or social lenses are only partial, or inherently distorted, or a reflection of social power, are advocating a form of interpretive methodological individualism. There is nothing intrinsically radical about this, in fact deconstructionist method can be called into the service of any interpretation because it lacks a social value theory.

Materialists object to this because there is an objective criterion of value in their framework. However institutionalists' view value systems as culturally constructed and thus self-referential and relative. This approach does not mean that values are irrelevant, the subject of individual whim, dispensable or incapable of being consciously re-evaluated and altered. Within literary theory cultural relativism has allowed many to slide down the slippery slope to ethical relativism and moral agnosticism. I would argue that it need not do so and that critical rhetoric provides the valuational grounding of literary theory—I shall return to this point later.

Thus the method of literary theory in its middle ground is the interpretation of culture from its artifacts, namely texts. I will argue that institutionalism is similarly the pragmatic and hermeneutic interpretation of texts—where the evolving culture and economy are the text. Interestingly we can get some assistance from another related branch of the humanities, namely critical rhetoric. Literary theory is about the interpretation of texts, and the related discipline of critical rhetoric focuses on the social construction of texts.

## Critical Rhetoric

Critical rhetoric is currently engaged in the process of defining itself as a discipline. Rhetoric has been an area of study and contemplation throughout human history. Critical rhetoric encompasses this history and augments it. As I understand critical rhetoric, it encompasses instruction in writing, research on the teaching of writing, the study of writing as a form of thinking, and the social construction and use of texts as a cultural process. Thus it retains its historical emphasis on the teaching of writing, but reemphasizes that writing takes place in a cultural context for specific purposes that affect the way it is constructed, read, interpreted and used. This modern view of critical rhetoric makes important connections between the social construction of texts, the cultural interpretation of texts, the cultural use of texts and the unity of creation and praxis in cultural communication. As such it is a convenient connector between literary theory and scholarly work in the field of communication thus bringing together the interests of both the humanities and social sciences concerning the creation, interpretation and use of texts.

Donald McCloskey's important work on the rhetoric of economics reflects the growing recognition of the connection between how we think about the world and how we both share and construct those thoughts through writing. This, of course, is a core insight in the work of Charles Peirce (Peirce 1958) and deeply influenced all of Veblen's work (Veblen 1964; Tilman 1992; Dorfman 1934).

One of the central insights of critical rhetoric is that all thinking and writing takes place in a cultural context. This cultural process begins with a writer who is a fully acculturated person and an audience who is also fully acculturated. The beginning of sharing your thoughts with others is their presence as an audience. The audience must have something in common with the writer or the attempt at communication will fail. Ordinarily a writer and their audience have a tremendous amount of shared understanding, just as my intended audience and I have. But this is not always the case, nor is it necessary. What is necessary, is that the writer and the audience must have something in common as a foundation for the beginning of conversation or discourse. This would be the case in a situation of first contact between members of previously unknown (to one another's) cultures. The only thing they have in common is a desire to try to communicate—that is a beginning, but it is also fraught with danger and potential for failure. Within a culture, however, it is usually the case that a tremendous amount of explicit and tacit understanding is present and can be taken for granted at least at the beginning of a conversation (Waller and Robertson 1991).

Among the most fundamental reasons for communication or engaging in discourse is a perception of dissatisfaction with the status quo. In the simplest and earliest case our cry as a baby can be understood this way. Sometimes this is referred to as cognitive dissonance. While this term is useful for communicating the motivation for thought, action and communication, it is a bit off-putting for social analysis since it refers to situations as mundane as the desire to know someone (or oneself) better, at one extreme, to the recognition of a profound and destructive crisis (this could include individual, community, cultural, world, or spiritual crises).

## Literary Theory, Critical Rhetoric and Institutionalism

My brief interpretive comments on literary theory and critical rhetoric are very suggestive of matters of mutual concern with institutionalism, but I would like to suggest a closer tie, one that gives greater credence to my assertion of a compulsive shift to institutional analysis.

The foundation of knowledge and knowing in postmodern literary theory, critical rhetoric and institutional economics is culture. Knowing is constructed from cultural experience. The concept of culture is central to these three forms of inquiry—they reject the possibility (though not the categories) of objective (positive) or subjective (normative) knowledge and construct a *tertium quid*, a middle ground, of a process of establishing warranted assertability.[9] The foundations of their epistemology and methodology are pragmatism.

As a consequence, cultural and individual valuations and valuational processes are both an object of inquiry and an aspect of inquiry. The similarity between the notion of cognitive dissonance and John Dewey's description of a problem as the perception of a difference between the way things are and the way they ought to be, is to my mind overwhelming and shows that understanding the motivation of inquiry and the valuational aspects of inquiry are the same for all three areas of inquiry.[10]

These shared underpinnings are responsible for additional similarities between these areas of inquiry. For example, both literary theorists and institutional economists have been engaged in a complicated discussion of cultural relativism and its implications for social analysis and inquiry in general (Hoksbergen 1994). Moreover critical rhetoric suggests a fruitful way out to resolve this controversy—through treating social valuation as discourse (Waller and Robertson 1991). These shared aspects of inquiry also point out why literary theorists have found the work of Thorstein Veblen so useful and have no difficulty understanding it, in contrast with neoclassical economists who so consistently misunderstand and ignore his work (Waller and Robertson 1990).

Showing the shared epistemological and methodological underpinnings of postmodern literary theory, critical rhetoric, and institutional economics establishes a shared foundation and provides a basis for the assertion of convergence. But I believe we are looking at more than a similarity in the praxis of inquiry. The analysis of texts by hermeneutic processes involve reading the text for the purpose of answering questions; it is engaging in a conversation with and about the text. The reading and interpretations suggests new understandings and new questions that generate rereading and reinterpreting of the text. This process involves questioning, reading, interpreting, sharing the interpretation, followed by new questions in light of the sharing rereading and resharing of the new or revised interpretations. It is a dialogical process of inquiry within a community of inquirers who share some cultural preconceptions. This process, whether undertake by an individual scholar or a community of inquirers is sometimes called a hermeneutic circle. The interpretations generated are provisional, but purposeful in that the continuation of the process and resolution of problems defines the inquiry.

Ann Jennings and I have argued elsewhere that Veblen's conception of an evolutionary economics treats inquiry as a cultural hermeneutic: a self-reflexive, self-referential process of inquiry where the culture in general and the economy in particular are the texts. We (Jennings and Waller 1994, p. 1002) write:

> . . . Veblen was interested in a theory of *endogenous* cumulative causation. All terms in the process are to be explained by, take their meaning from, and be "stated in terms of the process itself" (Veblen 1991, p. 77). Veblen's view of culture might be described as hermeneutic insofar as all meaning is self-reflexive and stems from the complex interrelatedness of the system itself. In hermeneutic systems, there are no disconnected terms, no exogenous constants, no supersystemic "selection mechanisms." This does not suggest that there are no "external terms" at all, or that novelty cannot enter hermeneutic systems "from outside." Rather, "external" influences *must enter* the system to matter, and will have their "character" determined within the relationships of the hermeneutic system.

We argue that Veblen's conception of evolutionary economics involves constructing a culturally based understanding and explanatory framework for the cultural processes of provisioning—a framework he recognized would constantly change as a result of dynamic processes generated within the culture. For Veblen and for institutionalists the culture and the appropriate mode of inquiry for understanding the culture are a cultural hermeneutic. It is a process of ongoing interpretation and reinterpretation of a text, the process concurrently reconstructs the text as a result of the reinterpretation, of which the inquiry itself is an intrinsic part.

I have already argued that the epistemological and methodological underpinnings of the modes of inquiry employed in literary theory, critical rhetoric and institutional economics are, if not the same, at least commensurable. By arguing that the method of institutional economics is that of interpreting an evolutionary cultural hermeneutic process and is itself part of that evolving hermeneutic process, I am arguing that the method or techniques of institutional economics are essentially the same as those of postmodern literary theory and critical rhetoric.

The last apparent major difference between these forms of inquiry is the subject matter of the inquiry, what I referred to earlier as the terrain on which the epistemology, methodology, and method are practiced in the process of inquiry. I will argue that this last level of difference is only a difference in the "level of analysis" and that all three modes of inquiry are moving in the direction of encompassing the others, critical rhetoric again provides the *tertium quid.*

Literary texts are cultural artifacts, so are economies. Texts are constructed within cultures—so are economies. All of the subjects of inquiry are cultural artifacts. Critical rhetoric focuses on the valuational and cultural processes leading to the construction and use of these texts in cultures. But the techniques of literary theory have spread beyond written texts to the analysis of other products of culture—art, film, theater, music, critical essays, and importantly elements of popular culture—indeed everything is a text. Critical rhetoric focuses on the construction of these artifacts and their social use. But culture is a unified whole, only analytically separable. So as the process of inquiry is expanding to include a broader definition of what is a text and critical rhetoric focuses on the social processes that generate the ever-enlarging category of text, the interconnected character of culture will require that the intersection of those matters traditionally demarcated as economics with the social production of texts must come under scrutiny. Similarly, as economics generally (most obviously in neoclassical economics in the work of McCloskey, and in institutional economics in the work of Sebberson, Lewis, Waller and Robertson, Mirowski, Neale and Samuels) becomes more involved in exploring the interrelationship between the economy, how we think about the economy, and how we share our understanding of the economy, we come closer to the kind of work being done in literary theory and critical rhetoric. Moreover the interconnected character of cultural analysis and its tendency to spread across interconnections serves not just as a suggestion, but as an imperative for institutional economics to move into the areas of cultural analysis heretofore the province of literary theory, critical rhetoric, and the humanities generally.

From these many areas of common interest and concern, I believe it is safe to conclude that postmodern literary theory and critical rhetoric are shifting in the direction of institutional analysis. Since they have no preconceived aversion to institutional economics, fruitful conversation with scholars in these disciplines is possible and of course desirable. But it would be equally correct to conclude that institutional analysis is making a compulsive shift toward cultural analysis of the type done in literary theory and critical rhetoric. Who is moving towards whom is a matter of designating a starting point and this is both arbitrary and distinctly unpostmodern. What is important is the convergence and shared concerns.

I have argued that there is a strong epistemological similarity among scholars in literary theory, critical rhetoric and economics. These shared conceptions of the nature and status of knowledge and inquiry form a common ground upon which fruitful intellectual exchange can occur. This similarity in epistemology leads to methodological similarity as well. The upshot is that the application of methods of cultural critique and analysis will cause these groups of scholars to produce qualitatively identical analyses concerning different, but converging subject matter. Currently, however, the subject matter of literary theory and institutional thought are quite distant, thus the bridge or middle ground of critical rhetoric is the more likely location for the interdisciplinary conversation.

Feminist scholarship is inherently interdisciplinary, thus feminist theory could as easily be feminist literary theory as feminist economics. It is beyond the scope of this paper to trace the individual connections across this feminist matrix of interconnected inquiry. The immense breadth of feminist theory has two important implications for this paper. 1) Some, but certainly not all, feminist theory shares the epistemological conceptions discussed earlier in this paper. This makes for easy connections to what I have already discussed. 2) The phenomena considered the legitimate subject matter of feminist theory already includes the economy, thus providing a common ground between institutional economics and feminist theory, not unlike that provided by critical rhetoric, that will facilitate intellectual sharing.

## Feminist Theory

There are many different varieties of feminist theory. There are some obvious connections that emerge from the intersection of feminism and literary theory, but they are not what I will focus on in this essay. Instead I will discuss elements of this intellectual movement of direct relevance to my argument that there is a compulsive shift to institutional analysis. Specifically I will focus on some developments in feminist philosophy, philosophy of science and feminist history that have a particular resonance with institutionalism. There are three areas of similarity of key importance: the rejection of dualisms, the understanding of knowledge as socially constructed, and the rejection of economism.

*Rejecting Dualisms*

The core of the similarity between feminist theory and institutionalism is the shared understanding of the problems arising from the use of dualistic categories. The world is; but our consciousness compels us to create ways of understanding it (and as a result we change it). We do this using the language we all acquire, and all of its ready-made components, to construct categories. When we acquire language as a child we incorporate the most common sets of categories into our consciousness in an uncritical way. Thus these categories seem natural and normal. Moreover they form the archetypes that we use in the further construction of categories for the more sophisticated inquiry we conduct as we mature. Categories similar to those "natural" ones occur to us easily. In fact, categorization schema that are similar in structure to the archetypal ones seem intuitively correct to us most of the time.

Susan Bordo, in her book *The Flight to Objectivity*, notes that the particular use of dualistic categories expounded by Descartes has become the primary mode of categorization in Western epistemology and been very important in shaping the Western intellectual tradition. Moreover Descartes' use of a system of dualistic categories was motivated in part by considerations of gender (Bordo 1987, pp. 93-4; 97-118). Descartes particular formulation is of interest because of its continuing intellectual influence. But Bordo's analysis of Descartes also shows that Descartes' dualism is not the only or the natural way of constructing categories, thus the preference for, or selection of, any particular categorization scheme reflects culturally conditioned tastes and choices. They are neither natural or objective.

To question dualisms is not to question all categorization schema involving the use of two categories. Mary Douglas recalls that Durkheim's suggestion that primitive categorization comes from direction: up/down, right/left, etc. (Douglas 1986)—could also lead one to ask if the fact that we have two hands suggests categorization by two? Sexual reproduction similarly suggests categorization by two. The difference between simple categorizations and dualisms are: A dualism is a reified categorization schema where all of the things being categorized are placed into one or the other of the two mutually exclusive categories (a Cartesian attribute according to Bordo). However, these two mutually exclusive categories taken together are universally inclusive (or collectively exhaustive—for those preferring statistical terminology) of the things being categorized. Eventually these reified categories stand in as labels for the things they categorize, ultimately becoming so identified as to confound the category and the thing. Often in scholarly discourse the category then becomes the object of inquiry, independent of the things it was constructed to include. When this occurs the inquiry may, to paraphrase Barbara Wootton, become pure mathematics or logical manipulation but is more likely pure nonsense (Wootton 1950, pp. 25-26). In many ways neoclassical economic theory is the study of reified categories divorced from the real existential economic phenomena whose study the categories were constructed to facilitate. It is not surprising that the manipulation of symbols, once loosed from the phenomena they were intended to describe, take on a life of their own devoid of any referential meaning and lose the ability to generate meaningful results.

Descartes' use of a body/mind dualism and its association by him and subsequent scholars with additional dualisms has tremendously influenced the development of the Western intellectual tradition and the development of our languages to the extent that it is hard to speak or write without invoking dualisms. Ann Jennings has extended Bordo's insight and clarified the dualistic construction of our understanding of the economy/family dualism and related it to a whole system of dualisms that mutually define and construct social relationships in our society (Jennings 1990). Bordo notes that the mind/body dualism central to Descartes is related to his dualistic categorization of rationality/emotional (irrationality) and masculine/feminine. To this Jennings adds a contemporary complex of reified dualisms that systematically structure our thoughts and actions regarding society. Jennings argues that these dualisms are central to the construction (and continual reconstruction) of both society and inquiry. This system begins with:

mind/body

to which Descartes argued the following dualisms were related ontologically and socially:

rational/emotional
masculine/feminine.

But

rational/emotional

also constructs and defines the following dualisms:

objective/subjective
positive/normative
fact/value
is/ought
means/ends

as socially and culturally meaningful and interrelated constructs. These constructs are especially important in prescribing the social organization and meaning of inquiry. This system of dualisms undergird Western epistemology and are linked in complex ways to the related system of dualisms focusing on the social nexus of

masculine/feminine

which includes:

public/private
economy/family
material/moral
historical/natural
active/passive

all of which are central to defining and constructing social hierarchy in our culture. We will see later that the foundational dualistic construction between

individual/society

is related in similar ways to this cultural matrix of dualisms and taken together creates an economistic understanding of society that is rejected by both feminist theory and institutional theory.

Jennings explains the historic development of these dualisms into a system of double dualisms that support our current cultural understanding of inquiry and social relationships as normal and natural, if not inevitable. Once understood as a social construction of meaning, we can consider alternative ways of structuring our understanding of this system and each of its component dualisms. This critique of dualism has moved many feminists in the direction of analyses that institutionalists should be very comfortable with and should find very useful. Of particular importance are Sandra Harding's views on the philosophy of science.

*Knowledge as Culturally Constructed*

Sandra Harding, in her two books *The Science Question in Feminism* and *Whose Science? Whose Knowledge?*, has argued that the dualistic view of objectivity embodied in modern science is gendered and unsustainable. In the *Science Question* she argues that science as usual is marred by gendered constructions of meaning that impede women's participation in science, alter inquiry through the choice of research programs that are pursued, the way that inquiry is conducted, and how results are interpreted. She argues in this book for a scientific pluralism; encouraging inquirers from many perspectives to engage in inquiry and to engage in the sharing, debating, interpreting, reinterpreting, and reconciling disagreements regarding results. It should be noted that this is the dialectical discourse that critical rhetoric suggests as the best model for inquiry. The notion that alternative interpretive systems lead to different results in not new. Nor is the notion that engaging in debate and conversation aimed at resolving differences or integrating results is useful and furthers inquiry. But it does fly in the face of what we culturally define as science, meaning the pursuit of objective knowledge. Harding concedes the importance of the cultural perception of objectivity in the success of science as both a pragmatic problem solving process and as a social institution. But in my view her critique of androcentric science provides a *prima facie* case for the abandonment of objectivity.

Analytic philosophers could read Harding's arguments as a rejection of realism. While I would argue that Harding's views on epistemology are certainly an assault of foundationalism, I believe she is arguing for a process view of inquiry whose purpose is to find out how the world (universe, cosmos) works. In fact, institutionalists will recognize Harding's view of science as a self-correcting cultural process, the purpose of which is finding/constructing matter-of-fact knowledge that is self-referential, self-reflexive and culturally constructed. Harding's views are very much in the tradition of Peirce, Veblen and Dewey's view of inquiry as the pursuit of warranted knowledge. Harding, like the institutionalists, recognizes that a real world exists and the purpose of inquiry is to find out about it, while acknowledging that all knowledge is inevitably mediated by culture. Rather than abandoning the pursuit of knowledge, both she and institutionalists see the diversity within and among cultures as expanding the potential perspectives brought to the process, thus enriching and furthering the pursuit of knowledge (Jennings and Waller 1993). Neither see it as a retreat into epistemological relativism or irrationality.

### *The Individual/Social Dualism and Economism*

If the critique of dualism and the recognition of inquiry as a cultural process combined with the implication that knowledge is socially constructed are the first two components of a shift towards institutional analysis, the third is the recognition and critique of economism.

Both Thorstein Veblen (Jennings and Waller 1993) and Karl Polanyi (Waller and Jennings 1991) argued that the separation of aspects of human experience into economic and non-economic was always artificial, and often extremely arbitrary. Ann Jennings has also noted the implications of the particular distinction between the economic and non-economic in our society for the construction of gender roles, specifically the designation of the roles and activities of women as not part of the economy (Jennings 1992).

The construction of women's roles and thus their identities in our culture as simultaneously familial and non-economic has profound consequences. This is because our pecuniary society determines social status, identity and value by where a person is "located" in the "economic" sphere. These consequences include not just limitations of women's economic opportunity, but also the devaluation of the activities prescribed by women's non-economic designation and limitations upon women's full participation as a public persons in economic society. There are additional consequences stemming from economism not as specifically gendered in character. For example we tend to view all social policy as economically motivated and evaluate its consequences, if not only, at least primarily in pecuniary terms. We ignore our social, intellectual, cultural and artistic development as indicators of cultural well-being and focus instead, on economic statistics of dubious importance and even silly economic symbols—such as the quarterly trade balance and the Dow-Jones Industrial average, respectively.

To understand the relationship between economism and the individual/social dualism we need to explore the origins of our particular use of individualism. It would be historically inaccurate to argue that individualism is the foundation of Western notions of democracy. However, I believe it is not too far off the mark to argue that modern democratic political forms and the expansion of political and civil rights in the West, has resulted from using the notion of the individual to establish compelling cultural claims for political and civil rights.

In a society where the political primacy and authority of a landed aristocracy is based on upon a claim of divine right, and where that claim is supported by an institutionalized religious hierarchy that is widely accepted as legitimate, all arguments for political participation and civil liberties must address the issue of divine authorization. Society in feudal Europe was the divinely authorized status quo. Thus by arguing that the same divine authority (God) endowed each individual within that social order with certain inviolable characteristics or properties, among them certain political rights, and that this same divine authority (God) specifically prohibited the political agents of the status quo (the landed aristocracy) from encroaching upon these rights (they are inalienable), democratic social theorists powerfully coopted potent cultural meanings and symbols and used them first to establish and then defend the expansion of political and civil rights to larger numbers of people. Not only did this argument establish the individual as separate in some important political ways from feudal society, it also established that separation as the result of divine creation. Thus the individual/society dualism was in some sense not only reified, but deified.

The historic success of this argument has many consequences for contemporary society. First, as noted above, it established and legitimized the separation of the individual and society, thus paving the way for the reification of this distinction into a dualism. Second, it led to speculation on the character, number and extent of those divine attributes. While we began with life, liberty and the pursuit of happiness, we quickly added the pursuit of property. Eventually this rights discourse led to extensive elaboration of political, civil, and social rights that flow from this divine authority. The attribution of these properties or rights as endowments from our creator suggest a fixed, divinely constructed and immutable human nature. Thus there are fixed aspects to the human condition, beginning with political rights, but logically extending to the human spirit, and thus the motivation and criteria of action and judgement of human beings. The transformation of divine authority into natural rights is masterfully argued by Carl Becker in his classic *The Heavenly City of the Eighteenth Century Philosophers*, and need not be rearticulated here. But this transformation from a divinely constructed human character to a not so divinely but equally fixed human nature, is the foundation for universal behavioral assumptions thought to be both applicable and appropriate for understanding human behavior in all times and places. Veblen argues in his "Preconceptions of Economics" articles that this natural rights philosophy forms the foundation of Adam Smith's natural philosophy and economics, this is where economic "man" comes from.

Unless Adam Smith and the early classical economists were startlingly different from their contemporaries, economic man was just that—male. The current use of *homo economicus* is more complicated. Ann Jennings, Julie Nelson and Elizabeth Fox-Genovese (a feminist institutional economist, a feminist neoclassical economist and a feminist historian, respectively) would all argue the this construct is deeply gendered. Quite honestly, I am a bit ambivalent in one regard with this characterization; *homo economicus* is so devoid of culture, socialization, and any characteristics we identify as human why dignify the construct with a gender, any gender?

The cultural segregation of individual rights from society continued even after significant evolution of the social order in Western Europe (and its colonial outposts) beyond feudalism. In fact the autonomous "individual" has become an important cultural symbol resulting in the reification of the individual/social dualism. Two consequences of the reification of this dualism that I will focus on are: 1) Its importance in promoting economism. 2) Its importance in defining gender roles.

In neoclassical and Austrian economics the individual is the primary economic agent. In neoclassical economics, the individual "naturally" maximizes their well-being whether it is defined in terms of satisfaction or profits. The assumption of rationality, defined as individual agents behaving as if maximizing some objective function, is an extension of natural rights and the belief in a natural order. Clearly the tautological character of the assumption brooks no empirical evidence or refutation. The behavioral imperative of rational calculation of individual well-being and action based on that calculation transcends conscious decision, it is a specie characteristic, whether grounded in nature or divine creation.

Only the Austrian school within economics pursues this position in a coherent and logical way. They recognize the complexity of the social realm because of the interaction and uncertainty real human activity entails. So they focus on that which (as a result of fixed human nature) is certain—individual motivation. They explore the logic of these individual imperatives in economic matters, often acknowledging the tautological character of their individualism. Yet they recognize that social complexity disallows simple (or even sophisticated) aggregation—thus they eschew mathematical reasoning in economics and critique neoclassical economics for using mathematical aggregation as both reductionist and logically insupportable. In this judgement they are correct. Once the individual/society dualism is accepted, the dualistic boundary cannot be ignored.[11] Neoclassical economists use this belief in an immutable human nature in a logically inconsistent way and only when it is convenient (see Boland and Caldwell in section 5 of Caldwell 1984). The most generous interpretation is also one I believe is correct, *homo economicus* and maximization generally are used because they are heuristically useful and not because they are believed to be fundamental properties of human behavior by neoclassical economists.

Nevertheless the consequence of the individual/social dualism's primacy in our cultural symbols and in the dominant mode of economic reasoning, is to define the individual in our pecuniary society increasingly in terms of their economic roles while ignoring their political, familial and other cultural roles. Moreover, in pecuniary society where social value and status are defined in terms of economic roles, a process begins where all social roles are redefined in terms of economic structures, roles, behavior and activities, hence economism.

Economism causes us to view all cultural and social activity through the lens of its impact on the economy as it is culturally conceived. Moreover the value of these cultural and social (and in fact, all other) activities are judged in terms of their relationship to the economy. Education is perceived in terms of its contribution of a trained workforce and technology that can be employed to facilitate business interests. Politics is recast as enabling the economy to function at its culturally defined optimum. All things are measured by their pecuniary value.

William Dugger argues that when economic institutions become hegemonic they subvert the values, activities, legitimization and resources of other social institutions in society (Dugger 1980; 1984; 1989). Not only has this occurred regarding our major social institutions, but it has happened in the scholarly realm as well. The intellectual imperialism of the economics discipline is well documented, moreover the increasing tendency toward emulation of economics in the other social sciences (through mathematical formalization, statistical analyses of questionable validity and even the uncritical importation of economic models into their analyses) attests to the power of both economism and scientism. This has to do with the prestige and status of the subject matter, much more that the success of the economics discipline in either actually informing common understanding of the economy or contributing to solving real problems.

### *Economism and Fox-Genovese's Cultural Critique of Individualism*

At this juncture the work of Jennings and Elizabeth Fox-Genovese complement one another. Jennings argues that economism drives economic theorizing and social understanding, thus ignoring and devaluing other aspects of human life. She also argues that part of this process is to define and devalue women's social activities, including women's participation in the social provisioning process, as not part of the economy. In Jennings analysis the dualistic understanding of culture that we currently hold includes three interrelated dualisms:

masculine/feminine
economy/society
individual/society

Where masculine roles are associated with the economy and thus are of high value and status. Of course women whose roles are defined as "not economic" are associated with society. But the individual is also associated with the economy and is thus masculine in our economistic understanding of the world.

Fox-Genovese's analysis, in her controversial book *Feminism Without Illusions*, complements Jennings. Her book is not a critique of economism *per se*. Instead she produces a cultural critique of individualism. She argues that in Western culture patriarchy has associated the activities and roles of women with community (society) and devalued them through its espousal of individualism (Fox-Genovese 1991, pp. 36-51). The "individual" is of course constructed (really selected) from the activities and roles of the culturally dominant white male, thereby constructing the archetypal Western identity. Thus personhood in an economic, political and cultural sense is denied to women and of course any people who are not white males. The construction of the individual as white male is simultaneously the construction of everyone else's cultural identity as "other."

Fox-Genoves's cultural critique shares the institutionalists' understanding of culture as a hermeneutic, where humans are simultaneously products and producers of culture, and where our understanding of the material environment cannot be separated from the culturally constructed intellectual apparatus we use to understand it. Put simply the materialist/idealist dualism is as artificial and false as the rest of the reified dualisms discussed in this paper.

The point here is that many feminist cultural critics reject dualistic understandings of society, embrace the concept of culture in a sophisticated way and thus are not limited by androcentric notions of inquiry. This pushes them in the direction of institutional analysis. However, in many ways they are moving beyond institutionalists. Since most institutionalists are trained as economists and since we choose that field of inquiry because of a preexisting economistic bias or urge, we often focus and thus limit institutional analysis to inquiry into economic processes (though admittedly much more broadly defined than our neoclassical colleagues). We need to read more broadly, and of greater significance, we need to locate our own inquiry in a larger conception of institutional analysis. I think feminist theory offers a congenial, but critical audience for us to reach as well as providing interesting and thoughtful analyses from which we can benefit.

Additionally a growing number of economist are beginning to read feminist theory. This is having some impact on neoclassical economists. It is not possible for neoclassical economics to incorporate feminism. Gender is a cultural phenomenon. Since the economic agent—the individual—is conceived prior to culture, or as if culture did not exist, neoclassical economics would have to develop separate microeconomic theories of economic agents of gender M and gender F (or possibly blue microeconomics and pink microeconomics). The behavioral assumptions would have to be different (otherwise why do it?) and then justified on some precultural grounds. This will cause some neoclassical economists to shift in the direction of institutional analysis as it has for many feminists from marxist economics backgrounds, indeed this seems to be the case already (Nelson 1990).

## Conclusion

It would take a volume of textual exegesis of truly monumental proportions to fully establish my argument. I have not taken that path, instead I have provided a sketch of the convergence of literary theory, critical rhetoric and feminist theory with institutional economics is what is called for to begin a dialogue among scholars in these different fields of inquiry.

I would add that in addition to the scholarly trends beyond the confines of the economics discipline that are shifts toward institutional analysis, similar shifts reflecting many of the same scholarly influences are at work in mainstream economics. As I have just mentioned feminist economists are likely to continue down this path. Also Donald McCloskey's rejection of modernism is a rejection of the most common forms of dualism operative within economic methodology.

Douglas North's recent work on the development of institutions is also much closer to recognizable institutional analysis than his earlier work (North 1990). This holds promise that some of the participants in the neoclassically inspired "new institutionalism" movement may also be experiencing a compulsive shift to institutional analysis. Similarly, much of what is done under the rubrics of Post Keynesian economics, neo- and post- marxist economics, Social Economics, Socio-economics, industrial relations, and many analysts focusing on structural economic change (the self-described "structuralists") also exhibit this tendency toward convergence in some aspects of their analyses.

What does this say to or about institutionalism? Oddly almost nothing. Many groups outside the economics profession have never heard of institutional economics; while economists who have heard of it, consciously avoid the label, because to be labelled a heretic is to lose the potential to influence the mainstream culture. This is a genuine problem if we seek to affect the direction of our society or at the very least assist in solving problems.

I see two types of interrelated action for institutionalists to follow that may address this issue. Communicate with scholars in different disciplines. This requires that you have something useful to say to them. They will listen. It helps that neoclassical economics is undecipherable to the uninitiated and appears deeply trivial when translated for them. The next two types of actions concern what kind of scholarship we engage in and share. I would argue that we have enough meta-theory and enough empirical work. This is not to suggest that we should stop these forms of scholarship, but when we are all collectively engaged in history of thought, methodological debating and sepulchral studies—we may have a great time, but no one else cares. Empirical work abounds, data everywhere, but very few useful ways of organizing it. We must continue doing empirical work, but if it never transcends the particular it makes only a transient impact.

We need to theorize. I mean big theory and little theory. Tool's work on the relationship between democracy and instrumental valuation processes is theory (Tool 1979). It is a statement of a cultural generalization that transcends the particular.

Because we recognize that theory is cultural, we also recognize that it bound to a particular context. On occasion the continuity of culture provides for continued relevance of generalizations and the process of continual re-evaluation and reinterpretation allows for us to disregard that which has become irrelevant. Moreover, old theory reinterpreted in new contexts is often the catalyst for constructing a new, more relevant theory in the new cultural context.

Because we have a good understanding of the tentative nature and lack of permanence or universality of theory, we should not abandon it as an activity. If we build a theoretical foundation that is useful in organizing our understanding of culture, flexible enough to accommodate change and provides compelling suggestions for solutions to our problems, institutional analysis will be reinvigorated.

Moreover, when we theorize we do not need particularly good foresight, much less perfect foresight, of its eventual impact. We only need to build the best theory we can in the context and world we live in now. There will always be both anticipated and unanticipated consequences.

We have to decide why we engage in inquiry. By expanding our range of inquiry to include other perspectives that share our epistemological and methodological approach, a larger conversation concerning our most pressing problems can begin. Cultures evolve through the cumulative impact of the small changes we all make adding up to a qualitative change. All of the scholarly work discussed in this paper began at the margin of a traditional discipline. Some of this scholarship has made inroads in the academy and is already impacting our culture. Institutional economics is unlikely to make inroads within the discipline of economics because to do so would be to successfully challenge the hegemony of neoclassical orthodoxy. So we will remain on the margins. But we have two things we can make work for us: The intractable problems of the day encourage people to look for solutions. Ultimately this is the source of the compulsive shift to institutional analysis. The second is the strategy outlined in this paper—put simply, go where "they" (neoclassical orthodoxy) aren't. Work to solve problems with those who are open-minded. This will not bring us status or recognition, but we might develop some useful theories and solve a few problems.

## Notes

1. Institutionalists will recognize "cartesian anxiety" as Dewey's "quest for certainty." The "cartesian vice" is the conceptual consequences that follow from the anxiety—usually constructed as reified dualisms.

2. Pauline Marie Rosenau has done an admirable job of sorting through the many strands of postmodernism and in explaining both the ideas and introducing the uninitiated to the almost impenetrable jargon used within and among the many strands of postmodern thought in her book *Post-Modernism and the Social Sciences* 1992.

3. Both Bordo and Rorty make explicit connections to pragmatism and Dewey in particular. Mirowski makes a strong argument for Peirce's perspective. European writers generally understate or overlook pragmatism.

4. Postmodern literary theorists prefer the term "reading" to "interpretation." However, such usage would be more confusing than helpful for my purposes and audience.

5. The status of the "author" is itself a central issue in this discourse. I am indebted to my colleague Clare Battista and Matthew Allison for the opportunity to read their working paper, "The Political Economy of Literary Production and Professional Authorship," for its insightful and concise discussion of these issues.

6. Interestingly all texts would become exclusively writerly texts and no text would be readerly texts—an oddly dualistic construction—suggesting that this extreme position is itself not postmodern.

7. The "internal" constraints are the cultural artifacts—language, concepts, norms, traditions, and myths—that tend to push our thinking down some (usually familiar) paths and not others. I also wish to be clear that culture is a interconnected whole and that the "external"/"internal" categorization is employed heuristically and does not indicate any ontological difference among cultural constraints.

8. Linda Robertson has addressed this problem specifically in a fascinating paper entitled, "Social Circles: Being a Report on J. Hillis Miller's Campus Visitation."

9. This assertion is controversial among postmodern literary critics (see also footnote 1). I would note that these scholars do choose some texts over others to deconstruct, some scholars over others to respond to, and some commentary to publish over others not published. Dewey, in *Theory of Valuation*, noted not that instrumental valuation was how people should value, but that it was one of the ways they did value. Clearly some criteria of better and worse—that are cultural, local, non-universal, non-objective and clearly contextual—are being used by literary theorists. It is the application of such contextual, local criteria that I am identifying as warranted assertability specifically and pragmatism generally.

10. Again I will assert that postmodern literary theorists offer readings of texts with some purposeful intent. Presumably they choose to present a particular reading because it is heretofore absent from the conversation—if for no other reason to continue the conversation.

11. Any effective critique of Austrian economics must reject the ontology of the individual/social dualism which is the basis of their methodological individualism or to assail the logic of each of their individual arguments (since they often import minor premises from neoclassical economics rather uncritically). Both of these approaches are very time consuming and unlikely to alter the belief structure of an Austrian economists.

# 11. STRUCTURAL CHANGE AND THE COMPULSIVE SHIFT TO INSTITUTIONAL ANALYSIS

Charles J. Whalen

In his Presidential Address to the Association for Institutional Thought, Marc R. Tool (1981) reflected on economic science since World War I and described what he saw as evidence of a "compulsive shift" to institutional analysis. "The shift is compulsive," he stated, "in the sense that the necessity of claiming pertinence to crucial problems of the day compels movement out of and beyond the mainstream conventional wisdom" (Tool 1981, p. 570). Three examples of this shift were discussed in Tool's address: John Maynard Keynes's work in response to capitalist instability; Arthur M. Okun's stagflation research; and microeconomic work on human nature and motivation by Harvey Liebenstein and Herbert A. Simon.

Tool acknowledged in his closing paragraph that it was premature to claim "a compulsive shift . . . is in fact under way." But "suggestions of drift and indicative shift are not premature" he maintained. His conclusion also asked his audience to "make their own assessments and, perhaps, extensions" of the compulsive-shift argument (Tool 1981, p. 588). This chapter is a response to that suggestion.

In this chapter I argue that U.S. structural economic change is a contemporary problem leading many who try to address it to move in the institutionalist direction. Confronting structural change in a way that produces detailed policy advice and innovative recommendations is nearly impossible for conventional economics. Thus, the recent work on deindustrialization and falling

U.S. competitiveness enables us to extend and assess Tool's notion of a compulsive shift toward institutional analysis.

The chapter is divided into six major sections. The first describes America's disappointing economic performance since the early 1970s. The second discusses why conventional economics has trouble recognizing and responding to the structural changes now affecting our economic system. The third section describes the shift to institutional analysis by researchers seeking to confront structural change. The fourth outlines a structural-change analysis of postwar U.S. economic performance. The fifth section considers whether abandoning economic orthodoxy can and should be avoided by structural-change analysts. The concluding section provides both a summary and a brief discussion of the future of economics.

## A Disappointing Performance

The performance of America's economy has troubled most domestic observers since the early 1970s. President Ronald Reagan's Commission on Industrial Competitiveness stated the following in its 1985 report: "A close look at U.S. performance during the past two decades reveals a declining ability to compete—a trend that, if not reversed, will lead to a lower standard of living and fewer opportunities for all Americans" (President's Commission 1985, p. 11). A similar body, the bipartisan Competitiveness Policy Council (CPC), reached the same conclusion in 1992: "America's economic competitiveness, defined as our ability to produce goods and services that meet the test of international markets while our citizens earn a standard of living that is both rising and sustainable over the long run, is eroding slowly but steadily" (CPC 1992a, p. 1). The present section reviews some of the evidence that has caused such concern and disappointment.

### *Surveying the Waste Land*

An excellent source of information on post-World War II trends in U.S. economic performance is *After the Waste Land* (*AWL*), by Samuel Bowles, David M. Gordon, and Thomas E. Weisskopf. That volume compares performance during 1973-1988 to the period 1948-1973. The comparison reveals: (a) that our average annual unemployment rate rose from 4.8 to 7.2 percent; (b) that our average annual real-output growth rate fell from 3.8 to 2.7 percent; and (c) that our average annual rate of growth in private investment fell from 4.0 to 3.0 percent. Other data presented in *AWL* indicate that the most recent of these periods has also been an era of stagnant worker earnings, increasing income inequality, higher real-interest rates, and lower after-tax corporate profits, productivity growth, and capacity utilization (Bowles et al. 1990).

A more recent work by Wallace C. Peterson (1991) presents similar evidence on U.S. economic activity. In fact, Peterson maintains that if average worker and family incomes are used as the determining criteria for the economy's state of health, then "the economy has been in a depressed state since 1973." Peterson's "Silent Depression" thesis rests on trends in three variables: (a) real weekly earnings (in the private nonagricultural economy) since 1947; (b) changes in median family income (measured in constant dollars) during the same period; and (c) the path of productivity changes since the end of World War II (Peterson 1991, p. 29). Each is briefly considered in turn.

Real weekly earnings of the average American grew at an annual rate of about 1.84 percent from 1947 through 1973. Since 1973, however, weekly earnings have actually *fallen* at a rate of 1.22 percent per year. "Thus, seventeen years after the watershed year of 1973 and in spite of the vaunted prosperity of the Reagan years, the real weekly income of a worker in 1990 was 19.1 percent *below* the level reached in 1973" (Ibid., p. 30).

Median family income, meanwhile, grew at an annual average rate of 2.72 percent from 1947 through 1973. This growth slowed to 0.04 percent for the years 1974 through 1988. Peterson (Ibid.) concludes:

> Continued increases in the numbers of working wives and mothers was the factor that saved real family income from an actual decline during these years. This practical stagnation in family income also explains why the generation that has come of age in the last decade doubts that their standard of living will even reach that of their parents, let alone exceed it.

Finally, labor productivity in the nonfarm business sector grew at an annual average rate of 2.51 percent from 1948 through 1973. Productivity dropped to 0.83 percent a year during the next decade and rose only to an annual average rate of 1.28 percent during the post-1982 expansion. It would take fifty-five years for output to double at this rate, nearly twice as long as at the early postwar (i.e., 1948-1973) rate (Ibid).

*The Cuomo Commission*

An even more recent discussion of America's economic difficulties since the early 1970s is offered in a 1992 report by the Cuomo Commission on Competitiveness. It identifies "ten signs of the nation's distress." They are: (1) insufficient public and private investment (relative to past levels and the levels found in other nations); (2) lagging productivity and a loss of manufacturing and technological leadership; (3) a persistent trade deficit; (4) rising levels of public and private indebtedness; (5) a weak financial sector; (6) a health care system in crisis; (7) chronic poverty; (8) slow national economic growth; (9) high unemployment and underemployment; and (10) declining middle-class incomes and growing inequality (Cuomo Commission 1992, pp. 6-23).

Like the Reagan Commission (on Industrial Competitiveness) and the CPC, the Cuomo Commission concludes that "the present deficiencies in our economic system are not small and isolated, but deep and systemic." In fact, the Cuomo report states that rebuilding economic strength will require both a comprehensive national strategy and a major reform of our public policies and economic institutions (Ibid., pp. 23-34). The aforementioned reports of Peterson, Bowles and his colleagues, the CPC, and the Reagan and Cuomo Commissions contain many differences. Nevertheless, all these works share a fundamental belief: that our present economic system is no longer a reliable foundation for U.S. prosperity.

## Orthodoxy and a "Nonexistent Trend"

America's economic experience since the early 1970s has involved such a sharp break from early postwar performance, and has been disappointing in so many areas, that many analysts have searched for a structural-change explanation to our problems. Conventional economics, however, was not designed to consider such change. As George J. Stigler noted, "Standard economic theory almost always takes the institutions of a time as given, and does not often assist in explaining their changes. The user of economic theory is therefore pressed to study structure, not change" (1984, p. 307).

### *Change? What Change?*

There are actually a number of reasons why standard economics has difficulty recognizing and responding to structural changes in the real-world economy. One reason, as Stigler suggested, is that most orthodox analyses derive a price-system equilibrium from initial conditions. Such analyses have simply no room for questions of structural change.

Another reason is that professional training leaves the economist concerned almost exclusively with the equilibrium-derivation process, not the realism of particular conditions. Moreover, Milton Friedman (1953) has been interpreted by most conventional economists as giving them a license to knowingly employ unrealistic assumptions—even when seeking to undertake work with real-world relevance. Consequently, structural changes in the actual economy are usually considered insignificant and ignored.

Perhaps the most important reason why conventional economics seldom addresses structural change, however, is that self-equilibration is implicit in mainstream analyses. This preconception suggests that both national and world economies will, in the absence of government "interference," adjust on their own when confronted with structural change. Keynesians can stretch the self-regulation viewpoint enough to justify countercyclical macro policy, but on matters of secular change these economists are usually as laissez-faire as those in the more conservative branches of neoclassicalism.

*Deindustrialization? What Deindustrialization?*

Proponents of a structural-change perspective toward America's economic problems often talk about the "deindustrialization" of America. Some use this term to describe a major loss of U.S. leadership in manufacturing. But in recent years "deindustrialization" has been used in a broader sense—to indicate that America has failed to adapt to global developments in a way that permits overall national economic prosperity. Either way, believers in "deindustrialization" are structuralists. They view deindustrialization as a symptom of deep-seated structural problems, problems that will not be cured by conventional macroeconomic measures.

Most economists have been unsympathetic to the structuralist viewpoint. In fact, mainstream economists took the lead in the attack on deindustrialization. This attack was simple: "America has not been deindustrializing." Deindustrialization, as Charles L. Schultze wrote in 1983, is "a nonexistent trend" (Schultze 1983, p. 4).

Schultze's widely-cited essay on deindustrialization and industrial policy acknowledged that the U.S. has some industries with structural problems. But he maintained "they are not typical of American industry generally." Schultze added: "There is no evidence that in periods of reasonably normal prosperity American labor and capital are incapable of making the gradual transitions that are always required in a dynamic economy" (Ibid., p. 5). In short, the mainstream has insisted on dismissing structural change and redirecting attention toward traditional macro problems and tools—especially the business cycle, countercyclical policy, budget deficits, and the value of the U.S. dollar.[1]

## The Shift to Institutional Analysis

Many economists have remained wedded to the conventional view of our economy. But an increasing number have found this perspective insufficient in the past few years. These economists represent the latest group of scholars to experience the compulsive shift to institutional analysis.

*Beyond Macroeconomics*

Perhaps the most high-profile convert to structuralism in recent years is the

Director of the Institute for International Economics, C. Fred Bergsten. Bergsten was a senior fellow at the Brookings Institution in the 1970s and served as an assistant secretary of the Treasury under President Carter. He has chaired the CPC since 1991.

Bergsten was not a proponent of structuralist views in the 1970s and 1980s. Instead, he advocated conventional macro policies, especially manipulation of exchange rates. But the 1992 CPC report explicitly rejects reducing our exchange rate as a strategy to stimulate exports. Bergsten (quoted in Rowen 1992, p. 17) explained his new view as follows:

> I've changed my thinking for two reasons. First, it is clear that macroeconomic policy alone didn't work. Second, I would now say that structural and other micro issues are more important than I thought.[2]

*The CPC Analysis*

Bergsten's CPC is a quadripartite body divided equally among business, labor, government (federal and state), and public representatives, with members appointed (in 1991) by the White House and Congress. The Council's 1992 report concluded "that the immediate problems of the American economy have resulted to a large extent from its fundamental long-term difficulties." It also indicated that rebuilding prosperity requires a program that addresses our system's "underlying problems" (CPC 1992b, p. 1).

The three major underlying problems identified by the 1992 CPC report are: short-termism; perverse incentives; and an absence of global thinking. "Short-termism" refers to this nation's proclivity to think and act short-term (in both the private and public sectors) while our global competitors "plan and execute their actions against far more extended time horizons" (Ibid., p. 11). "Perverse incentives" refers to the numerous features of our national policies, educational system and financial markets that encourage activity detrimental to the nation's long-term economic security.[3] Finally, "an absence of global thinking" refers to the CPC belief that Americans have not yet fully realized that today's competition is global and "that American competitiveness can be effectively sustained only if [all sectors] respond to that reality" (Ibid., p. 15).

The CPC also identified two barriers to the development and implementation of an effective response to America's economic difficulties. One is the fact that today's problems involve a slow erosion of economic strength rather than a sudden crisis: "Pluralistic democratic societies such as ours—perhaps especially ours—are not adept at responding to 'termites in the woodwork.'" The other barrier is "excessive confidence in our competitiveness." In particular, the 1992 CPC report stated: "[S]ome Americans seem to believe that American resources and institutions are inherently the best in the world. This view may have been accurate at one time but is now in doubt in some key areas" (Ibid., p. 7).

## The American Economy in Transition

The bipartisan and multipartite nature of the CPC lends credibility to the structuralist viewpoint. But the 1992 CPC report does not offer a comprehensive and systematic analysis of the rise and demise of our postwar U.S. economic system. Taken as a whole, however, the structural-change literature—which rests on an institutionalist methodological foundation—does offer such an analysis.[4] This entire analysis cannot be presented in the present chapter, but an outline is possible. This section provides such an outline.[5]

### *The Postwar System*

From the close of our Civil War to the end of World War II, U.S. workers, employers and public officials struggled to devise a coherent set of economic arrangements that would be not only mutually reinforcing but also compatible with the technological, demographic, political, and cultural aspects of American society. The task was a formidable one. There were always conflicting views on the appropriate setup. Moreover, the environment into which this system had to fit was constantly changing.

The need for a coherent system, however, was widely recognized. The nation seemed inherently prone to boom and bust cycles, and competitive practices and wage cutting seemed to only make matters worse. As one business leader summarized the private-sector view at the turn-of-the-century, "The old idea that we were raised under, that competition is the life of trade, is exploded" (Bruchey 1990, p. 343).

After much trial and error, our nation acquired a manageable institutional balance in the mid-1940s. This system provided the foundation for an unparalleled period of U.S. prosperity and growth, from the end of World War II through the 1960s. The system produced prosperity and stability because its pieces functioned in a complementary manner—and because the entire setup was compatible with the world environment in which it operated.

The American "postwar system" was located in a world economy dominated by U.S. firms and stabilized by the Bretton Woods agreement. Domestic product and labor markets, however, were of primary importance. Further, most major industries were dominated by a few large corporations with significant market power.

These corporations employed mass-production processes, hierarchical and bureaucratic organizational structures, and "scientific management" (an approach to determining the nature of work that involved task specialization and simplification, a comprehensive set of work rules, and detailed monitoring of job and firm performance). The result was a sharp distinction between management and labor—between "thinkers" (including supervisors) and "doers."

The labor movement was also an important actor in this early postwar era. It accepted and adapted to both the structure and work environment of mass-production enterprises. Planning and coordinating production was left entirely in the hands of corporate officials. Labor organizations sought instead to improve wages and working conditions through collective bargaining. These terms and conditions were spelled out in union-management contracts, contracts that also formalized the work rules produced by scientific management.

Union membership peaked in the mid-1950s at a level of about 35 percent of the non-agricultural work force. Still, industrial-relations research conducted by MIT's Sloan School indicates that "collective bargaining served as the most significant source of innovation in employee relations" during the 25 year period beginning in 1945 (Kochan et al. 1986, p. 5).[6] In particular, unions exerted a "threat" effect on non-union enterprises and a "spillover" effect upon unorganized portions (including many managerial levels) of unionized firms.

The federal government also played a major role in the postwar system due to its industry, labor and macroeconomic policies. Through trade associations and by other means, industries have been engaging in various forms of coordination throughout this century. But the Great Depression and two world wars brought the public sector into this process as well, a fact discussed in Robert Reich's *The Next American Frontier*.[7] As Reich notes, this "industrial policy"—involving numerous public agencies, commissions, and advisory boards—was "ad hoc, largely hidden from public view, organized by industry, and dominated by the largest firms" (Reich 1983, p. 111). It was also an important part of postwar efforts to stabilize investment and output in an economy based on high-volume production.

In the realm of labor policies, the government provided a legal foundation that formalized the collective-bargaining process, and it engaged in some direct regulation of working conditions (i.e., minimum wages, child-labor laws, etc.). The collective-bargaining law was strongly favored by industrialists seeking to avoid development of a more radical U.S. labor movement.[8] The workplace regulations, meanwhile, involved both an antipoverty dimension and an effort to stabilize consumer spending.

Finally, the federal government employed monetary and fiscal policies in an effort to counteract swings in the business cycle. Since the New Deal was unable to produce either a significantly more centralized or decentralized economy (it sought both at different times), the best U.S. policymakers could do was use public expenditures to compensate for major changes in private spending. Annual budget balancing was replaced by countercyclical budgeting in an effort to equate revenue and spending over the course of the business cycle.

*The End of Hegemony*

Since the postwar system was designed primarily to minimize economic fluctuations, America organized for stability not adaptation. We created a structure unprepared to adapt in a changing world. This was not a serious problem initially, and various domestic and international developments affecting the context and functioning of our system could be ignored.

By the 1970s, however, such developments exerted an increasing amount of pressure on our economy. The institutions and practices of our postwar system were quickly becoming obsolete. The era of American economic hegemony had come to a close.

Important domestic developments contributing to the erosion of our postwar system include the evolution of an increasingly-fragile financial structure and shifts in the composition and expectations of the labor force.[9] But the most important element identified by nearly all contributors to the structural-change literature has been the evolution of a new global-economic context. As the President's Commission on Industrial Competitiveness wrote in 1985, "the global economy has been transformed around us" (President's Commission 1985, p. 1).

The 1970s saw the unmistakable arrival of a major challenge to U.S. firms in world markets. Discussions of "Pax Americana" gave way to expressions of concern regarding "the new international competition," especially from Europe and Japan. Moreover, postwar technologies made it easier than ever for firms everywhere to undertake and coordinate world-wide operations. Product markets, production, and financial activity all quickly became internationalized.

Many U.S. enterprises tried to take advantage of this new environment by producing and selling more abroad. The amount of our Gross National Product accounted for by international trade rose from 9 percent in 1950 to 25 percent in 1980 (Marshall 1987, p. 12). But foreign enterprises were doing the same. Indeed, corporations from abroad often made a special effort to target the large, home markets of our most profitable industrial giants.

The effectiveness of many U.S. economic-system elements began to diminish significantly in the face of intense international competition. For example, collective bargaining lost its relevance and social impact; the domestic link between high wages, consumer demand and profits was severed by global capitalism; and macroeconomic policies became less powerful and more difficult to manage in the face of world-wide transactions. The postwar system was beginning to unravel—and nearly all indicators of economic performance were signaling the need for new strategies in both the private and public sectors.

*The Corporate Response*

Corporations responded with "paper entrepreneurialism," an assault on unions (and labor costs in general), and—when necessary—a call for government protection. Paper entrepreneurialism is described by Reich (1983, p. 141) as a version of scientific management so extreme that business executives lose all connection with the corporate level at which production occurs. Instead of reacting to the economic crisis with technological or institutional innovations related to the production of goods and services—responses that would often require huge investments and only yield returns in future years—firms chose instead to rely on financial and accounting gimmicks to make short-term gains.

In short, corporate leaders unfamiliar with production and unable to find "patient" sources of capital (due to short-term performance pressures) increasingly made industry into a plaything for finance. The result was a de-emphasis of production that Sony Chairman Akio Morita called the "hollowing of America." By buying firms instead of investing in research and development, and by selling advanced technology to foreign competitors instead of using it to exploit a comparative advantage, corporate America transformed us into a "casino society." In Morita's words, "The U.S. is abandoning its status as an industrial power" (quoted in Jonas 1986, p. 56).

*Government's Response*

From a historical perspective, government's response has been surprisingly consistent throughout the past two decades. Corporate taxes and the progressivity of personal taxes fell steadily since the early 1970s. Tight monetary policies were an important part of the federal reaction to our economic situation since the beginning of the Nixon Administration.

In addition, there have been a series of post-1970 policies designed to check the power of labor, deregulate key segments of the economy, and increase our reliance upon the initiative of private enterprises. Ronald Reagan may have made this strategy more explicit, but most elements were well underway even before he and George Bush entered the White House. As difficult as it may be for some to recall (given the rhetoric of more than a decade), Jimmy Carter—the "outsider" from Georgia—appointed Paul Volcker, unleashed the deregulation craze, and oversaw reductions in both social spending and corporate and capital-gains taxes.

The federal government also resorted to its own form of paper entrepreneurialism. It reconstructed (or eliminated) statistics, employed an array of budget tricks, sold assets to raise cash, and regularly (and knowingly) adopted unrealistic economic projections. Many of these practices were clearly unwise from a long-run perspective, but Washington officials—like corporate executives under quarterly pressure from Wall Street—seldom felt it possible to look even a few weeks beyond the next election.[10]

*Labor's Response*

Employees have had little recourse in the wake of the aforementioned developments. Though the burden has certainly fallen most heavily upon blue-collar workers, even professionals and managers have been displaced in significant numbers due to their firms' reduced market shares and corporate restructuring. Most unorganized workers at all ranks have submitted to job loss and benefit reductions rather quietly.

Unions, meanwhile, have adopted a primarily defensive posture. In an era of widespread concession bargaining, organized labor has often fought hard merely to retain representation rights and the jobs of members. Labor-management cooperation, gainsharing, and worker-participation initiatives have received renewed attention in some unions, but there is much distrust of management and many leaders prefer traditional industrial-relations approaches and practices.

*Chaos, Stagnation and Decline*

It has now been two decades since our economy's major actors began to respond to the obsolescence of the early postwar system. Unfortunately, they have been two decades of chaos, stagnation and decline. Today, instead of a solid foundation for future progress we have a mountain of immediate problems and—in many ways—a weaker, less competitive economy. Our responses—often motivated by an attempt to avoid addressing the structural roots of our problems—have made matters worse.[11]

Instead of accepting further decline, structuralists believe America can adapt to the present global economic environment in a way that rebuilds prosperity. But rebuilding prosperity requires "more than just marginal reforms or superficial change" (Bergsten, quoted in CPC 1992c, p. 4). Indeed, it requires a coherent national strategy and a comprehensive form of restructuring—restructuring that increases skills, productivity, product quality, and industrial innovation.[12] Perhaps President Bill Clinton will seek to move the U.S. in this direction during the second half of his term. At present (early September 1994), however, one finds little evidence of such an effort.

## Is Orthodoxy Beyond Repair?

Some economists have recently looked for ways to accommodate structuralist concerns and policy recommendations within conventional economics. These efforts usually focus on issues of market failure or economic dynamics. The present section discusses such attempts and the need for a more complete break from neoclassicalism.

*Market Failure*

A 1981 report by the U.S. Office of Technology Assessment (OTA) identified three types of market failure providing rationales for the sectoral policies advocated by structuralists. One type involves externalities. For example, the OTA noted that government funding of research and development (R&D) might be justified because social returns to R&D may exceed private returns (OTA 1981, p. 175).

Public goods engender another type of market failure. In particular, national security and defense were mentioned as fundamental public-goods categories by the OTA. If the output of a particular industry—such as steel or semiconductors—is vital to national security, then "government intervention may be needed to maintain socially desirable levels of production," wrote the OTA staff (Ibid., p. 176).

A third type of market failure is produced by market imperfections. Product-market imperfections may involve barriers to entry or other evidence of a deviation from competitive conditions. Capital-market imperfections may stem from poor information about small firms and/or innovative projects. And labor-market imperfections can include the lack of portable pensions, skill or geographical barriers to worker relocation, and rigid wage differentials across industries or occupations. "Such imperfections," the OTA noted, "can become an important rationale" for a wide range of selective policies (Ibid., pp. 176-179).[13]

*Economic Dynamics*

Like market failure, issues involving economic dynamics provide a potential justification for sectoral interventions and other structuralist policies. For example, a new approach to international economics emphasizes the fact that "the pattern of international trade and specialization reflects historical circumstances rather than underlying national strengths." This means, as Paul Krugman has acknowledged, that "government policies can in principle shape this pattern to the benefit of their domestic economies" (Krugman 1990, p. 109). In short, the move from traditional international economics to this new view can be viewed as shifting from a "static" to a "dynamic" conception of comparative advantage—and opens the door to moving from a "free-trade" to a "strategic-trade" policy stance.[14]

Economic dynamics also provide a rationale for structural policies when one recognizes that real-world adjustments take time and that it is possible, at least in theory, for government action to facilitate ("speed-up") such adjustments.

Schultze may remain convinced that nothing more than macro policies are needed to allow U.S. economic actors to adjust effectively to changing conditions in a dynamic world, but other mainstream economists are not so sure. Robert Z. Lawrence, for example, acknowledges that America needs more than laissez-faire and free trade to promote "efficient domestic adjustment" to recent changes in the global economic environment (Lawrence 1984, pp. 122-123). Indeed, one can envision a host of policies that could be employed to promote industrial, labor-market, and community adjustment.[15]

*Unanswered Questions*

The aforementioned efforts to accommodate structuralist concerns and policies within standard economics should be welcomed by institutional economists. Any evidence that economists in the mainstream are working to keep in touch with the critical issues of our day must be considered good news for both economics and public policy. Nevertheless, when conventional economics addresses such matters it often produces more questions than it can answer.

For example, what types of R&D spending are most appropriate for a given nation at a particular point in history—and how much spending is "enough?" Yes, we should use cost-benefit analysis here, but neoclassical theory alone tells us nothing about particular costs and benefits. What we need is an understanding of reality—in the form of empirical data, scientific information, international comparisons, and case-study reports. Standard theory, with its attention to market clearing and the suggestion that realistic assumptions are unimportant, pulls us in precisely the wrong direction.

Similarly, neoclassicalism can neither identify a "vital industry" nor the "socially desirable level of production" in such an industry. It tells us nothing about the nature of particular market imperfections. And it offers no details on the best way to devise a policy to overcome imperfections, capture a competitive advantage, or promote positive economic adjustment. All these unaddressed issues require analyses that reflect a deep understanding of institutional reality and the passage of historical time. In short, they demand a shift from orthodoxy to institutionalism.

*Institutional Balance, Not Market Equilibrium*

The preceding discussion suggests that the proper foundation for attention to structural-economic change is a framework emphasizing institutional balance, not price-system equilibrium. Rather than explaining our structural problems in terms of market failure and adjustment dynamics, we should instead seek to understand such difficulties as results of "the way the nation organizes itself" for economic activity (Reich 1983, p. 119). The mainstream preconception that economic order emerges spontaneously from voluntary market activity must be supplanted by an understanding of the need for institutional adjustment to regulate and coordinate social provisioning.[16]

A focus on institutional balance instead of market equilibrium is important not only because this perspective engenders historical and institutionally-oriented economic analyses but also because it replaces the mainstream's notion of a "corrective" state with institutionalism's "creative" state. This view frees economists from the powerful spell of laissez-faire ideology and allows us to fully recognize that the government is an inseparable part of our economy. In fact, institutionalists stress that the public sector plays an essential role in helping to both define economic "order" and determine the methods most appropriate for establishing it.[17]

## Conclusion: The Future of Economics

This chapter has indicated that what Tool described in 1981 as a "compulsive shift" to institutional analysis has continued to the present. In recent years, many economists have become increasingly dissatisfied with U.S. economic performance and have sought to explain our problems with a structural-change argument. Their account of our troubles involves a major departure from both standard theory and traditional neoclassical policy recommendations.

### *The Successor to Orthodoxy?*

In "The Compulsive Shift to Institutional Analysis," Tool called for extensions of his argument. But he (Tool 1981, p. 570) also wrote:

> Will we, a decade or so hence, hear all economists proclaim they are institutionalists? Perhaps not, but intellectual honesty and consistency might recommend such an assertion. If the cases herein discussed turn out to be representative of the whole, institutionalism may well become the successor to neoclassical orthodoxy, although probably under another name.

In fact, however, the shift to institutional analysis described in the present chapter is *not* representative of the trend of contemporary economics.

A few months after publication of Tool's "compulsive shift" essay, Wassily Leontief described academic economics as a discipline in "splendid isolation" due to its detachment from reality and emphasis on market equilibrium. Moreover, Leontief suggested this state is likely to be maintained for some time because methods used to impose "intellectual discipline" in economics are not unlike "those employed by the Marines . . . on Parris Island" (Leontief 1982, p. 105). Unfortunately, Leontief's prediction was more accurate than that of Tool. Academic economists have successfully marginalized all forms of heterodox economics.

Unconventional economists have often taken the lead in practical problem solving. But—as this chapter indicates—orthodoxy has learned to follow well enough to avoid being cast aside as entirely irrelevant. Besides, only standard theory offers the rigor and elegance most economists now demand (often above all else) from work in their discipline. Indeed, "institutionalism" has become a pejorative in the economics field.

*Institutional Analysis in the Next Century*

The 21st Century is likely to open with neoclassicalism in the same position of dominance it holds today. Nevertheless, institutional analysis will probably survive, under one name or another. This work will survive because practical economic problems are not likely to disappear and institutionalism is inherently a policy-oriented and problem-solving perspective.

Structuralist research represents one of the newest forms of institutional analysis. This research offers an explanation of recent U.S. economic performance and provides a point of departure for applied work that should be of great interest to policymakers. Such efforts may not help institutionalism overthrow neoclassical economics, but they just might help us obtain something much more important—a revitalized national economy.

**Notes**

1. For evidence that mainstream economics remains wedded to a macroeconomic explanation of (and a macroeconomic-policy solution to) U.S. economic problems, see Krugman (1990) and Blecker (1992).

2. Another high-profile economist to make a bit of a conversion to institutional analysis as a result of studying U.S. competitiveness is Robert M. Solow. In the late 1980s, Solow served as Vice-Chairman to the MIT Commission on Industrial Productivity. That group reported in 1989 "that macroeconomic manipulation alone cannot solve the nation's productive-performance problem" (Dertouzos et al. 1989, p. 35). Both the analysis and recommendations of the MIT Commission go far beyond macro issues and policies. Their 1989 report is unquestionably structuralist in orientation.

3. Examples of perverse incentives identified by the CPC include the following: "Our tax laws penalize saving, provide little inducement for investment, indeed tilt investment away from productive capital equipment, and favor consumption and debt. . . . There is inadequate linkage between the long-term performance of our corporations and the compensation of their managers or their boards of directors" (CPC 1992a, pp. 13-14).

4. Unlike orthodox economic analysis, structuralist research is holistic, processual, nonteleological, and pragmatic. For an explanation of why structuralism is "institutional" analysis, see Whalen (1993a).

5. This discussion of the American economy in transition is based on the following structuralist works: Blecker (1992); Bluestone and Harrison (1982); Bowles et al. (1990); Commission on the Skills of the American Workforce (1990); Committee on New American Realities (1990); Competitiveness Policy Council (1992a); Council on Competitiveness (1987); Cuomo Commission (1988; 1992); Dertouzos et al. (1989); Economic Strategy Institute (1990; 1992); Graham (1992); Harrison and Bluestone (1988); Hayes and Abernathy (1980); Kochan et al. (1986); Kochan and Piore

(1984); Marshall (1987); Marshall and Tucker (1992); President's Commission (1985); Piore (1982a); Piore and Sabel (1984); Reich (1983); and Thurow (1985; 1992).

6. Major union-membership losses did not occur until the 1970s.

7. See Reich (1983, pp. 83-105).

8. For a discussion of business's role in passing the National Labor Relations Act, see Ferguson (1984, pp. 87-88).

9. For discussions of the evolution of an increasingly-fragile financial structure, see Wolfson (1990) and Minsky (1986). For discussions of shifts in the composition and expectations of the labor force, see Marshall (1983) and Heckscher (1988).

10. For insight into public-sector "paper entrepreneurialism" during the Reagan era, see Stockman (1987). For a short list of budget gimmickry, see Mufson (1990).

11. This chapter was written in early 1993 and revised slightly in the late summer of 1994. Since then, observers have tended to de-emphasize competitiveness concerns and stress the impressive nature of America's economic recovery since 1992. Nevertheless, our U.S. Trade deficit continues to widen and wage stagnation and growing income inequality remain serious concerns.

12. Readers interested in structuralist policy recommendations should consult the works listed in note number five above. See also Whalen (1993b).

13. See Lawrence (1984, pp. 117-145) for an additional discussion of how structural economic policies can correct market failures.

14. In *The Age of Diminished Expectations*, Krugman explains that the new international economics provides "an argument for a limited government industrial policy consisting of carefully targeted subsidies" (Krugman 1990, pp. 110-111). While this certainly does not justify all forms of "managed" trade, it is clearly a major departure from the strict laissez-faire perspective of traditional trade theory. As Robert Kuttner noted in 1991, this "new view" radically alters trade debates "for it removes the presumption that nations like Japan, which practices strategic trade, cannot, by definition, be improving their welfare" (Kuttner 1991, p. 121).

15. See OTA (1981, pp. 178-179); Lawrence (1984, pp. 122-133); and Magaziner and Reich (1983) for discussions regarding specific policies designed to promote economic adjustment.

16. For two similar perspectives on the matter of institutional adjustment versus price-system equilibrium, see Ramstad (1985, p. 509) and Piore (1982b, p. 6).

17. See Whalen (1992) for a further discussion of differences between orthodoxy's "corrective" state and the institutionalist conception of a "creative" state.

# 12. BEYOND TECHNOLOGY TO DEMOCRACY: THE TOOL LEGACY IN INSTRUMENTALISM

William M. Dugger[1]

## Introduction

This chapter compares the instrumentalism of Clarence E. Ayres and Marc R. Tool. Both work in the tradition of John Dewey and Thorstein Veblen. However, Tool has picked up where Ayres left off and has moved instrumentalism beyond the Ayresian foundation. In particular, the Ayresian formulation of instrumentalism was made without the insights gained from the 1960s; while Tool's contributions were made in full recognition of what the turbulent 1960s taught us. Technological progress was the central concept in Ayres's instrumentalism. Tool's more recent instrumentalism includes technological progress, but in dealing with the revolutionary upsurges of the 1960s, Tool makes democratic participation the central element of social value theory. Therein lies the Tool legacy.

Instrumentalism is open ended and evolutionary. No instrumentalist has ever attempted a final formulation of instrumentalism and none will ever do so, for to do so would be to move outside of the instrumentalist tradition. Being an accomplished instrumentalist, Ayres could not have considered his instrumentalism to be definitive and final. Economies, cultures, and politics have all changed dramatically since Ayres. Instrumentalism has changed too. Marc Tool has reformulated instrumentalism in light of continued experience. To highlight that reformulation, Tool's instrumentalism will be compared and contrasted with Ayres's instrumentalism.

Ayres and Tool differ in six important ways. First, the structures of Ayresian and Toolian instrumentalism are composed of different elements. Second, Tool omits the frontier hypothesis from his analysis. Third, Ayres and Tool explain the nature and origin of institutional resistance differently. Fourth, Tool's locus of value is not the same as Ayres's. Fifth, the central problem of their age is different for Tool and Ayres. Sixth, Tool emphasizes democracy far more than Ayres.

The differences are due to the continued evolution of instrumentalism in light of human experience. They are not due to any invidious differences between Ayres and Tool. Tool has an advantage over Ayres simply because Tool has had the benefit of experiencing the tumultuous 1960s and their aftermath. Neither is "better" than the other, but Tool's work does represent an advance because it reflects additional evolutionary experience. The structure of Ayres's instrumentalism is influenced by the age in which he constructed it. The same is true of Tool. The "Age of Ayres" and the "Age of Tool" are strikingly different.

## The Structure of Ayres's and Tool's Instrumentalism

### *The Age of Ayres: America's Rise to Affluence*

Ayres wrote several books early in his career, but he first pulled together the elements of his instrumentalism in 1944 with his book *The Theory of Economic Progress*. His next book was *The Industrial Economy*, published in 1952. His last major contribution to instrumentalism was *Toward a Reasonable Society*, published in 1961. During the seventeen years in which these books came out, the United States had adjusted its pre-depression institutions with the New Deal, had defeated Nazi Germany and Imperial Japan, and had risen to levels of affluence never before experienced—and we were proud. Ayres explained in his books that while we were not perfect, our adaptations, our successes, and our affluence were envied by almost everyone; everyone that is, except for the cultural relativists. Ayres made all his major contributions during this age of American success.

### *The Age of Tool: Revolutionary Upsurge and Reactionary Malaise*

Tool, however, has been contributing (so far, he still is contributing) in a different sort of age. His *Discretionary Economy* appeared in 1979 and his *Essays in Social Value Theory* appeared in 1986. Tool's instrumentalism was reformed by the twin crucibles of revolutionary upsurge and reactionary response.

Tool has written during years of turmoil, of fundamental questioning and of angry reaction. During these years the pacifist nature of the American civil rights movement became much more militant and was met by fierce reaction from white Americans. The student free speech and peace movements were also met by fierce reaction from outside the academy. The women's movement rose and generated a backlash of its own. The Reverend Dr. Martin Luther King, Jr. and Malcolm X were murdered. Major cities erupted with urban riots and have simmered ever since with endemic violence. Students were shot dead by National Guardsmen at Kent State. Much later, women's health clinics and abortion facilities were bombed. Richard Nixon and Ronald Reagan were both elected president of a frightened nation by running reactionary campaigns against African Americans, women, and students. One of the few appropriate responses to the times came from Tool as he reformulated instrumentalism to meet the issues of his day. Tool explained in his books why we responded inappropriately with "ism-ideologies" to the revolutionary upsurges of our age and he explained how instrumentalism could provide us with more appropriate responses. So, revolutionary upsurge and reactionary response marked the age of Tool while the age of Ayres was marked by recovery from depression, victory in war, and rising affluence.

*Central Elements in Ayres's Instrumentalism*

Five elements were central in his thought: (1) *advancing science and technology*, driven by the cumulative dynamic of the tool-skill combination, meet (2) *institutional resistance* supported by past-binding tradition and superstition. (3) The resulting social problems need to be met with *institutional adjustment*. (4) The industrial revolution began in Western Europe because it was a *frontier region* with a full complement of science and technology but with a weak system of entrenched institutions. The advance of science and technology has gone farthest in the "the west" because it met the least resistance there. (5) *Cultural relativism* leads to moral agnosticism, a failure to understand and to promote the technological values pioneered by "the west."

Ayres (1952, p. 192) explained the technological advance—institutional resistance—institutional adjustment dynamic quite clearly:

> The progress of science and the industrial arts is continually altering the physical patterns of social life so as to produce situations contrary to the institutional practices of the community. [He continued:] The basic question is: at what point does our inherited institutional system inhibit economic progress? Where does the shoe pinch? This is a technological question. That is, adjusting the shape of a shoe to the shape of the foot is a matter of tool-skill, or instrumental efficiency; and raising such a question means the substitution of considerations of skill and efficiency for considerations of fashion and ceremonial adequacy.

Ayres built his instrumentalism to deal with the problems of his age and to overcome the moral agnosticism of cultural relativism. Ayres was particularly critical of the emotional conditioning of tribal cultures and of those who defended the "primitives" and their ceremonial traditions. Ayres (1961, pp. 140-41) stated:

> [I]t seems to me astonishing that social scientists should now appear as advocates of continued acceptance and practice of such traditions. What is most astonishing is the catholicity of these advocates of primitivism. They seem to argue that it makes little difference what people believe, what ceremonies they enact, or what mores they impose on their communities, so long as they believe something or other of a supernatural character and observe some regulations or other which are sufficiently arbitrary to be susceptible of no reasonable justification.

*Central Elements in Tool's Instrumentalism*

The frontier hypothesis and the particular form Ayres's critique of cultural relativism took are conspicuously absent from Tool's instrumentalism. Tool builds on much of Ayres as a foundation, but comes out with a different set of central elements to his instrumentalism. Those central elements are (1) the *human capacity* to think critically about experience and (2) "*the democratic quest*" to apply that capacity to the solution of social problems. But, (3) critical thought and participatory democracy have been met inappropriately by "*ism-ideologies*" that defend the hierarchical status and power embedded in the status quo of contemporary societies.

According to Tool, "The primary and dynamic element in social change is human beings' capacity to think critically and coherently over wide areas of their experience" (Tool 1986, p. 7; see also 1979, p. 165). This element, Tool argues, "has been the fundamental element subversive of *status quos* over the centuries" (1986, p. 7). This dynamic element is analogous to the dynamic element in Ayres. However, Tool's dynamic element emphasizes human capacity while Ayres's dynamic element emphasizes technological progress.

The retarding element, according to Tool, "consists of the propensity of people to retain and perpetuate the acquired habits of mind and behavior that provide for a delineation of hierarchical status or position, retention of power over others, and the like" (Ibid.). This retarding element is intellectually solidified in the form of "ism-ideologies," such as capitalism and communism. These ism-ideologies are systems of ideas and assumptions that support particular institutional forms. They come to determine the way problems are seen and their assumptions become "first principles" or "eternal truths" that lie beyond the realm of legitimate inquiry. Fully developed, they block inquiry (1979, pp. 26-29).

For both Ayres and Tool, the structure of their instrumentalism is strongly affected by their critique of mainstream, neoclassical economics. To Tool, neoclassical economics with its rigid assumptions easily becomes an ism-ideology that blocks inquiry (1986, pp. 104-25). To Ayres, neoclassical economics with its market obsession was a form of cultural relativism which leads neoclassical economists to completely misunderstand the nature of the modern economy. In neoclassical theory, the modern economy is guided by the market mechanism that merely reflects the exogenous preferences of individual market participants. Individual preferences are not to be disputed—this follows the dictates, not just of cultural but of individual relativism. Individuals have every right to want what they want. Economists should not "interfere" with that right but should merely study how the market organizes scarce resources to meet those subjective wants. Ayres disagreed. In a passage which has guided my research for the last fifteen years, Ayres (1952, p. 349) stated:

> The truth is that our economy is not organized by the market mechanism. The market is organized by the economy. The order which the market exhibits is derived from the organizational pattern of the economy and is an expression of such order as actually obtains in the economy.

Although they share a condemnation of neoclassical economics, the instrumentalisms of Ayres and Tool are structured differently; are critiques pointed in different directions. While Tool is no cultural relativist, his instrumentalism was not formulated as a critique of cultural relativism. It was formulated as a positive response to the revolutionary upsurges beginning in the 1960s, as an alternative to the reactionary response of the ism-ideologists. Ayres, on the other hand, formulated his instrumentalism as a critique of the moral agnosticism that resulted from the cultural relativism promoted by anthropologists. Those anthropologists, Ayres believed, were defending primitivism against the advances of the industrial way of life. The titles of two of his major books indicate very clearly what Ayres was trying to do: *The Industrial Economy: Its Technological Basis and Institutional Destiny* (1952) and *Toward a Reasonable Society: The Values of Industrial Civilization* (1961).

## The Frontier Hypothesis

Ayres argued that the industrial revolution began and had gone the farthest in Western Europe and her offshoots because Western Europe was a frontier region. It was "a frontier of ancient civilization. It was a frontier province in the same sense that the American colonies were much later" (Ayres 1952, p. 73). Western Europe was the heir to all of the technological advances of Rome, but with the fall of Rome, it lost the institutionalized structures of a culture that became "extraordinarily rigid and dogma-ridden" (Ibid. p. 74). Western Europe was spared this institutional rigidity, however, because it was partitioned by waves of barbarians. The cultures of these barbarians are given short shrift by Ayres, who argued that "their part was largely negative. They effected the partition. But they did not introduce another material culture" (Ibid. p. 75) Instead, they made Western Europe a frontier possessed of Roman technology but void of cultural baggage. The resulting frontier was uniquely open to new tools and skills and easily adapted ideas from the Arabs, Hindus, Chinese, and others. This superior flexibility and capacity for cultural borrowing of frontier Western Europe made it the spawning ground for the industrial revolution.

But the frontier hypothesis does not travel well. That is, the frontier hypothesis with its emphasis on superior flexibility and capacity for cultural borrowing in the West, does not convince many in the East to become instrumentalists. Furthermore, the frontier hypothesis has a major weakness. Many frontiers have existed and they are generally not places characterized by flexibility and openness to foreign cultural practices. Instead, many frontiers are places of intense conflict where Xenophobic rigidity and closed-mindedness are the rule. Many examples come to mind: The Iberian peninsula (modern Spain) was a frontier region for centuries between the people and culture of Christendom and the people and culture of Islam. Needless to say, the Spanish Inquisition was not a model of flexibility and openness to cultural borrowing. Nor did the expulsion of the Jews from Spain exemplify a friendly frontier spirit. Southeastern Europe was also a frontier region between Christendom and Islam. The hatred and closed-mindedness runs so deep that they are still conducting ethnic cleansing there. Then there is the current state of Israel as a frontier region where Jew and Arab rub elbows. Nor should we forget the Indian subcontinent where Hindu and Moslem have gone at each other for centuries in their frontier region. The American frontier in the seventeenth through the nineteenth century involved far more than a series of happy thanksgivings with the pilgrims and indians sharing turkey and pumpkin pie (See Loewen 1992). In sum, frontier regions are frequently not as Ayres depicted them.

Ayres was no cultural imperialist, no yahoo from Austin with a cowboy hat and an attitude. He searched for a universal criterion of judgment and made significant contributions. And yet, he was too bound by his own time and place. He has a quaint, dated quality when read in the 1990s, for a remarkable flow of human experience has taken place since he wrote. That experience has been humbling and enlightening to thoughtful Westerners, particularly to thoughtful citizens of the United States. Tool was wise to drop the frontier hypothesis. Without it, instrumentalism has brighter prospects for world wide influence. Tool states, "No nation, race, or group has a monopoly either on the generation of knowledge or upon its use." He continues, "Serious and extensive inquiry into the several aspects of the 'conventional wisdom,' East and West, North and South, is mandatory" (Tool 1979, p. 40).

## Resistance to Instrumental Knowledge

Instrumental knowledge, or reliable knowledge as Tool prefers, is matter of fact (Tool 1979, p. 296). It is opposed to ceremonial knowledge. Instrumental knowledge has to do with getting the job done, with solving social problems. Ceremonial knowledge has to do with getting credit (income or status) for the job, with acquiring social prestige. When ceremonial knowledge triumphs, a bitter adage is true: "It is not what you do, but who you know, that counts." Both Ayres and Tool explained that instrumental knowledge is opposed by ceremonial knowledge. Both agree that instrumental knowledge is not readily accepted and acted upon, but is resisted. Nevertheless, the two emphasize different types of resistance.

### *Resistance in Ayres: Past-Binding Myth*

Ayres argued that instrumental knowledge is resisted by past-binding myths that have their origins "in the folklore and mores of tribal tradition" (Ayres 1961, p. 114). These myths become solidified in institutions, systems of status based on habitual ways of thinking. "Every system of status is static precisely because it is oriented toward the past. Its keynote is authenticity, and authenticity derives only from the past, in which nothing can be changed" (Ayres 1961, p. 137). Entrenched habits of thought (institutions) become highly valued by the individuals who participate in them because of the emotional conditioning of the traditional community. Ayres explained: "What gives the typical institutions their solidity is the emotional conditioning the community has undergone by virtue of which people get emotional satisfaction from the continuance of the accustomed situation" (Ayres 1952, p. 46). Furthermore, past-binding myths are highly symbolic and take on the power of superstition and magic (Ayres 1961, p. 95). According to Ayres, "in the process of social change the institutional function plays a negative part. It resists change" (Ayres 1952, p. 49).

To Ayres, what instrumentalists have to work against, so to speak, is tradition, superstition, and magic. All these are anachronisms, holdovers from the tribal, primitive past—difficult adversaries, but not powerful enough to cause undue concern as to the outcome.

### *Resistance in Tool: Enabling Myth*

Tool would agree with Ayres that the past has endowed us with much unwanted baggage, but Tool would argue that the resistance to instrumental knowledge is far more powerful than Ayres imagined. While Ayres was steadfast in his opposition to tribal tradition and primitive superstition, Tool formulated his instrumentalism to do battle against far more powerful forms of resistance. Tool seeks "to provide a criterion of appraisal which will assist with the unmasking of power centers which remain unaccountable to those touched by such power" (Tool 1979, p. 299). Tool sees the major resistance to instrumental knowledge coming from elitism, not primitivism.

Tool also sees institutions differently from Ayres. To Ayres, institutions originate in past-binding myths and play a largely negative role in social change. Tool, however, views institutions more along the lines of John R. Commons than Clarence E. Ayres. Tool defines institutions as "the working rules, the codes, the laws, the customary ways which shape and pattern behavior and attitudes in a manner to accomplish some end-in-view or purpose" (Ibid., p. 74). Tool recognizes rational purpose and power in institutions when he states, "Institutions are the result of initiative behavior—of conscious, deliberate choice making on the part of people holding and using power to establish structure" (Ibid., p. 75). To Tool, institutions are not necessarily irrational holdovers from the past, but are products of rational choice and instruments of power. This allows Tool to ask a different kind of question of a particular institution. Does it provide for "continuity of human life and the noninvidious re-creation of community through the instrumental use of knowledge?" (Ibid., p. 293).

Furthermore, by introducing rational purpose and power into his treatment of institutions, Tool opens a different critical approach from Ayres. Rather than criticizing primitivism and tribalism, Tool's approach points toward a critique of the power of elites to impose invidious distinctions and cause disruptions of community re-creation through the use of ism-ideologies that block meaningful participation in the ongoing inquiry into how to further the good life. In vast areas of the third world, Ayres's instrumentalism is of little help to progressives, to what Tool refers to as "rational reformmongers." A critique of tribal tradition and primitive superstition is not needed by the indigenous people of Brazil, India, Indonesia, Zaire, or elsewhere. Their social problems involve far more than past-binding myths. The people of the Brazilian rain forests, for example, are not just defending their traditions and superstitions against the onslaught of our industrial way of life. They are defending themselves and their rain forests, along with their indigenous power and authority relations, against outside power and authority. Their indigenous power and authority relations may be shrouded in myth, but their indigenous power and authority relations are at least tenuously accountable to their own community. The outside power and authority they are fighting is not beholden to any such community constraints. It is in third world struggles such as this that Tool's instrumentalism is clearly superior to Ayres's, for it stresses accountability and participation and identifies elite power and irresponsibility as the "enemy," not tribal tradition and superstition.

Radical institutionalism's concept of enabling myth is a direct application of Tool's formulation (Dugger 1989, p. 6). An enabling myth is not a past-binding myth but a myth that enables an elite to exercise its power over an underlying population. The resistance provided by enabling myths or ism-ideologies is far more difficult to overcome when attempting to apply instrumental knowledge than is the resistance provided by past-binding myths. Belief in superstition and magic has been on the wane for centuries. Belief in the ultimate or absolute value of ism-ideologies or enabling myths is still strong. Once laid to rest, past-binding myths seldom re-emerge. But new enabling myths can spring up continually. Past-binding myths obviously originate in the past. Enabling myths, however, originate in the present, from the contemporary power of money and the contemporary influence of elite status.

## The Locus of Instrumental Value

Instrumentalists, Tool and Ayres included, look at value as a continuing process rather than an absolute state. This processual value of instrumentalism would appear to be rather vague, even nebulous, were it not for the fact that instrumental value is always given an objective locus or site in the social process. This is in contrast with neoclassical economics, which locates value in the subjective utility of individuals. While Ayres located instrumental value in the technological process; Tool locates instrumental value in the democratic process. The Ayresian locus is not necessarily contradictory with the Toolian. Instead, Tool's locus of value includes and extends Ayres's. Furthermore, both of them ground value in matters of fact, in terms of cause and effect; not in matters of taste, not in terms of individual utility and disutility. In this sense, both constructed an objective theory of value as opposed to a subjective one. That is, they each located their theory of value outside of the subjective pleasure or pain of consumers, which can be felt only by the consumers themselves.

### *The Locus of Value According to Ayres*

In making his instrumental value theory concrete, Ayres emphasized the technological process, or what he frequently referred to as the technological continuum. He stated, "It is the technological continuum which is, and always has been, the locus of value . . ." (Ayres 1944, p. 220). By this locus in the technological process, Ayres meant something very concrete about value: "Every decision intends to take account of facts, and every choice has as its prototype the mechanic's choice of the right tool" (Ibid., p. 219). Instrumental choice involves how to make a living. It is made in light of actual experience in living and has come to its highest level so far in the industrial way of life. As Ayres put it, instrumental value involves choosing between alternatives on the basis of which "will in fact contribute most to the continued efficient working of the technological system upon which all life depends." He continued, "The criterion of every economic judgment is 'keeping the machines running'" (Ibid., p. 223). Complemented by his deep understanding of the role played by effective demand in the capitalist system and by his equally deep understanding of the dangers of underconsumption, Ayres's instrumental valuations pointed squarely at the need to increase the flow of income to the poor. Doing so kept the machines running and furthered the industrial way of life (Ayres 1952, pp. 130-319). Furthermore, Ayres (1944, p. 231) argued: "If the technological process is the locus of value, the continuous development of the technological arts and crafts and the accompanying recession of superstition and ceremonially invested status is progress."

*The Locus of Value According to Tool*

Instrumental valuing, according to both Ayres and Tool, includes but goes beyond economic efficiency. Both support democratic economic planning and both agree that instrumental valuing involves the democratic harnessing, constraining, and directing of economic efficiency. But here is where Tool goes beyond Ayres in emphasizing the importance of democratic participation in valuing means and ends. Tool insists that those who are affected by valuations should participate in the valuations. As described above, Tool identifies elitism as the most serious resistance to progress in instrumental valuing. In keeping with this identification, Tool locates instrumental value itself in the democratic process. In the means and ends continuum, democracy is both. That is, the means for achieving progress must be democratic, and the ends-in-view must also be democratic. In explaining the means for achieving progress, Tool states, "Only 'evolutions from below' can succeed. Those whose behavior is to be revised must themselves understand the need for it, concur with it, and participate in it" (Tool 1979, p. 173). Turning his attention to the ends for progress, Tool states, "The *reason* for making changes in structure is to increase people's control over their own lives through the discovery of more instrumental solutions to economic and political problems" (Ibid., p. 175). For Tool, the democratic process and the process of instrumental valuing are almost the same. For Ayres, the technological process and the process of instrumental valuing are almost the same.

Tool's democratic emphasis allows him to be far more critical in evaluating the technological process itself. This is an important advance in instrumentalism. Tool understands and critiques the effects of new technologies on civil liberties, community interdependencies, individual participation, labor displacement, and power concentration (Tool 1986, pp. 62-70). Locating value in the democratic process allows Tool to formulate an instrumentalism that is a far more appropriate response to the revolutionary upsurge of women, people of color, and the wretched of the earth than the ism-ideologies offered by others. While the "technological Ayres" emphasized the need to keep the machines running, the "democratic Tool" emphasizes the need to keep the people growing. The contrast is brought out best by comparing Ayres's reason for increasing the flow of income to the poor with Tool's. Both argued that restricted income flow to the poor was inefficient. As described above, Ayres argued in favor of increasing the flow of income to the poor in order to keep effective demand increasing with industrial productivity, a perfectly valid argument and one with which Tool agrees. However, Tool (1979, p. 305) also states

> [A] paucity of income shrivels life's choices generally to the point where intellect, creativity, compassion, and commitment are stunted or destroyed for those denied. We then live in a layered or tiered community suffering from elitism and privation alike. This would appear to be inefficiency of monumental proportions.

## The Important Problems

Instrumentalists are problem solvers. Ayres and Tool are not exceptions. They both have directed their energies to identifying and solving the important social problems faced in their age. But since their ages were different, so too are the problems they faced. And this has made a significant difference in their thought.

### *The Problem According to Ayres*

The problem facing the United States, according to Ayres, was the need to keep the machines running, to make sure that effective demand kept pace with industrial productivity. Continued economic instability was the result of failing to do so, and economic instability itself caused even worse problems. Ayres followed John A. Hobson in blaming underconsumption for depression and for the imperialist struggle for markets. As Ayres saw it, "[T]he two greatest menaces to Western society as we have known it—depression and war—both are direct consequences of that instability by which our economy is afflicted" (Ayres 1952, p. 186). Ayres may have borrowed from Hobson, but Ayres's understanding of Keynesian economics was more profound and ahead of its time than one might suspect from his general contempt for the professional economics literature. In fact, he was a good Post Keynesian decades before that school even emerged. The Post Keynesians have improved upon a number of Keynes's original formulations, particularly upon his treatment of the marginal propensity to consume as largely subject to individual taste. The Post Keynesians now attribute changes in the aggregate MPC to changes in the distribution of income instead of changes in individual tastes. This is a significant advance over Keynes himself. Ayres anticipated the advance by many years when he concluded from his own analysis of the facts: "It follows from these facts that the proportion of the national income that is spent for consumers' goods and the proportion that is saved (that is, the community's propensity to consume and propensity to save) is determined by the income pattern . . ." (Ibid., p. 157).

*The Problem According to Tool*

Ayres, of course, was correct and the problem of economic instability remains. Nevertheless, another problem has evolved as well. The problem of the age, as Tool sees it, is how to respond positively to several revolutionary upsurges. Four specific revolutionary crises confront us: (1) a continuing and even widening income gap between the rich and the poor, both intra-nationally and internationally, (2) a continuing upsurge of women and minorities of a different color, (3) a continuing pressure for increased participation in economic and political decision making and (4) a worsening ecological crisis (Tool 1979, pp. 4-5).

Tool constructs four instrumentalist corollaries to apply to each of these four problem areas: (1) instrumental efficiency for the economy, (2) democracy for the polity, (3) noninvidiousness for human relations and (4) compatibility with the environment (Tool 1986, pp. 55-81). And, he tries to tie together his positive response to the revolutionary times with his instrumental value principle: "[T]hat direction is forward which provides for the continuity of human life and the noninvidious re-creation of community through the instrumental use of knowledge" (Tool 1979, p. 293). He constructed his instrumental value principle as a guide to appropriate responses to revolutionary upsurge. His instrumental value principle and the reformulated instrumentalism in which it is embedded place him considerably to the left of Ayresian instrumentalists (perhaps not of Ayres himself, however). His reformulated instrumentalism is not only a positive response to the revolutionary times, but it is also a response to a challenge made to liberals over half a century ago by John Dewey (1939a, p. 455):

> In short, liberalism must now become radical, meaning by "radical" perception of the necessity of thoroughgoing changes in the set-up of institutions and corresponding activity to bring the changes to pass. For the gulf between what the actual situation makes possible and the actual state itself is so great that it cannot be bridged by piecemeal policies undertaken *ad hoc*.

## Democracy

Central to Tool's emphasis on democracy and to his reformulation of instrumentalism is the community's need to find the truth and to correct mistakes, to exert its noninvidious discretion free from coercion. In his own democratic quest, Tool moved to the democratic left and even approvingly quoted from the Port Huron Statement of the Students for a Democratic Society (Tool

1979, p. 207). In fact, Tool shares much with radical institutionalism. (Compare with Dugger 1989). He may even be a radical institutionalist himself. For Tool understands full well that in inappropriately responding to the problems of his age, the elite leaders of the United States frequently have blocked inquiry and hidden their mistakes, particularly with respect to the U.S. involvement in the Vietnam War. Tool generalizes: "The propensity of elites caught in mistaken judgments seems to be to hide or distort the truth . . ." (Tool 1979, p. 209). Democratic participation is the needed antidote. Tool explains that judgments reached through the democratic process, "though obviously fallible, will, where discretion remains located with the community generally, look to the recasting of institutional structure which has become problematic . . ." (Ibid., p. 211).

Ayres argued that social progress occurred because new technology pushed against old tradition. Tool argues that social progress occurs because the "democratic quest" pushes against the elitist establishment. He identifies the "democratic quest" in terms of revolutionary upsurge: "[A]ll four of the separately identified areas of revolutionary unrest—productivity revolution, participatory revolution, racial and sexual revolutions, and the ecological crisis—are but facets or expressions of a common democratic quest" (Ibid., p 186). The democratic quest is resisted by oligarchy, not by tradition, although tradition plays a supportive role. Tool states: "Elitist power wielders impair the responsiveness of the political process. The Establishment, however defined and perceived, seeks to perpetuate the Establishment" (Ibid., p. 195). Tool argues that the democratic quest is blocked or distorted by a wide range of oligarchic processes and structures, including but not limited to bias in the mass media and bias in campaign financing. He emphasizes the power of money, not the power of tradition, in discussing these blockages and distortions (Ibid.).

To deal with the social unrest caused by the democratic quest pushing against the elitist establishment, Tool has reformulated the instrumentalism of Ayres into "a theory of participatory democracy as a conceptual vehicle of resolution" (Ibid., p. 197). Marc Tool has moved instrumentalism beyond technology to democracy. That is an impressive accomplishment.

## Notes

1. Warren J. Samuels and Marc R. Tool made helpful comments. This paper was presented at the January 1994 meetings of the Association for Social Economics, Boston. The University of Tulsa and DePaul University provided generous support.

# 13. MARC TOOL'S SOCIAL VALUE THEORY AND THE FAMILY

Jacqueline B. Stanfield and J.R. Stanfield

*Although authority and status have by no means disappeared from modern family life, it is certainly true that efficient teamwork plays a much larger part in the activities of the contemporary home.... There is less insistence ... upon status-determined rights and occupations and more concern for efficient cooperation.*

C.E. Ayres 1944

*I believe any economic policy must be judged by its effect on the family.*

Ronald Reagan 1985

*There are no fallen women; when women step out of place, they always step up.*

Florence King

The social value theory developed by Marc Tool is a useful perspective to bring to bear upon the manifold issues of family, gender, and nurturing of children at the close of the American Century (J.R. Stanfield 1992). Tool's theory, developed on the basis of the instrumental value theory tradition of Thorstein Veblen, John Dewey, C.E. Ayres, J.F. Foster, among others, suggests that the principle of institutional adjustment is capable of clarifying the issues posed by this dramatic social change, thereby indicating the way forward to a more effective meshing of institutional practice with current social valuations and individual development.

Gender and family relations have been steadily changing in the modern economic era. The commodity production economy has steadily shifted the function of integrating the division of labor out of the kinship or domestic economy into the market and by extension the state realms (J. R. Stanfield 1986, ch. 4). In the last half century in the USA, this steady change has accelerated to a tumultuous pace. The texture of social relationships is changing to a degree that leaves social roles and attitudes in the lurch. The resulting cultural confusion and functional lacunae are disruptive and wasteful.

## Social Value Theory

Social value theory is based upon the theory of instrumental valuation. Veblen provided the basis of instrumental value theory with his observation that "goods are produced and consumed as a means to the fuller unfolding of human life; and their utility consists, in the first instance, in their efficiency as means to this end. The end is, in the first instance, the fullness of life of the individual" (Veblen 1953, p. 11). Notwithstanding the subjective experience of individual development, its substance is instrumental or technological and social or relational. Human liberation consists of removing institutional barriers to individual participation in social processes.

Veblen clearly places the economy in human society as the process of social provisioning (Ayres 1963, p. 61). John Dewey developed this insight with more insistence about individual development and the inclusion of the context of meaning or experience. For Dewey, "progress means increase of present meaning." (Dewey 1957, p. 261; also Tool 1977) The economic effects of this release were secondary and unnecessary to legitimate the focus upon individual development for that development is the goal. Culture and social relations were to Dewey an essential aspect of development, superior to an expansion of output per se. Indeed, a large part of his diagnosis of the "crisis of liberalism" focused on the historically accidental preoccupation of liberalism with material wealth to the neglect of cultural quality (Dewey 1963, pp. 38-9).

Similar sentiments are readily available in C.E. Ayres's development of the ideas of Veblen and Dewey. The economy is the aspect of human life that sustains the "life process of mankind, in which values have meaning, . . . a process of doing and knowing" (Ayres 1961, p. 111). For Ayres the criterion of good and bad, right and wrong, is the advancement of the life process. This advancement consists in unleashing individual creativity. In one of his last essays Ayres lamented the tendency of the welfare state to overemphasize distribution and consumption and to neglect achievement and creativity (Ayres 1967, pp. 3-11).

Marc Tool's (1979) social value theory is a major reformulation of the instrumental conception of valuation that reflects the influence of Tool's mentor, J. Fagg Foster, the latter a powerful figure in the Ayresian oral tradition. Tool's social value principle for the making of social and individual decisions focuses has become the clarion call for instrumentalists: progress or the way forward is that "which provides for the *continuity of human life and the noninvidious recreation of community through the instrumental use of knowledge*" (Tool 1979, p. 293). Noninvidious continuity indicates the antagonism between invidious distinction and instrumental effectiveness. Distinguishing between people or comparing them in order to rank them according to merit or worth introduces an element of competitive emulation or gamesmanship into the economic process. Thus, the production and consumption of real output is not governed solely by the requirements of expanding the human capacity for knowing and doing but also by the logic of invidious competition. Invidious distinction induces serviceable output but it does so once removed since the objective is status competition not serviceability. This is of course the famous principle of unintended consequences expressed by Adam Smith's term, the invisible hand. But this development of the economic process also induces wastefulness, creates unnecessary inequality and deprivation, and distorts individual personalities.

A few implications of the instrumental definition of economy are important enough to make explicit at this point. The economy must clearly be ecologically sustainable. Economic institutions that lead to environmental disruption or rapid depletion of resources are eventually destabilizing and therefore fail the test of continuity.

Likewise cultural continuity is a factor in evaluating and shaping economic performance. The present meaning of the life experience must not be rended by excessively rapid or ill-designed economic change. The unfolding life process is shaped, defined, and interpreted by a context of patterned meanings, that is, culture. The purpose of the economy as instrumentally conceived is to provision and encourage, or at least not discourage, the development of individual personalities. The impacts of economic policy upon the family is important because the nurturing relationships of the family are important to individual development. Moreover, the most effective family operates in a milieu of close-knit community relations. The values and needs of workers as developing personalities are also important concerns of economic policy which should include collective action to structure the work process. Social policies with regard to family, community, and work relationships are an important part of the strategy for shaping economic development.

In short, the instrumental definition of the economy emphasizes lives and livelihood. The economy is evaluated on its ability to reproduce lives without disrupting them. The economy is not instrumentally valid if it destroys the natural habitat of human life, undermines vital relationships of community or family life, distorts personalities, or unnecessarily represses individual freedom and development.

The instrumental conception of the economy necessarily implies that the exchange economy should be subordinate to the development of individual human beings. Given its axial principle of capital accumulation by means of expanding commodity production, capitalism persistently threatens the social fabric of human interaction, necessitating artful intervention into economic relationships in the interest of social preservation. This is the thrust of Karl Polanyi's conception of the market capitalist economy as a disembedded economy (Polanyi 1957, chs. 3-6; J.R. Stanfield 1986; see also Marx 1964 and 1967, on alienation and commodity fetishism). The market capitalist economy, left to its own inner logic, tends to subordinate social and cultural life to pecuniary economic considerations. Hence, market capitalism conceived as a self-regulating process clearly fails the instrumental test (Ayres 1944, pp. 226-7; Tool 1979, pp. 305-6; and J.R. Stanfield 1979a, chs. 2, 9). Economic policy must be such as to subordinate the exchange economy to the necessity of reproducing society as an ongoing cultural process. A major focus of economic thought should be the continuous reform of the regulatory complex within which the market functions. This requires the characteristic institutionalist focus on institutional adjustment. "The crucial ingredient in instrumental value theory is the ongoing nature of the process" (Gordon 1980, p. 45). For the institutionalist, *the* economic problem is the continuous adjustment or reconstruction of economic institutions, in light of social change, to more perfectly serve human needs and development. The economic problem thus conceived is an adaptive process to secure continuity of existence as the basis for individual development. "The economic general theory must be the theory of institutional adjustment" (Foster quoted by Tool 1977, p. 837).

Technological and social changes disrupt the established ways and means, use and wont by which people make a living and order their existence. The key questions of the economic problem for institutionalists present themselves in terms of institutional failures and lacunae. Instrumental effectiveness lies in institutional adaptations to overcome these discontinuities. Such a focus cannot rely on the principle that the market process effectively monitors all relevant social preferences. There are important social costs and benefits not expressed in the market's pecuniary calculus and the extant power structure is reflected in market prices (J.R. Stanfield 1979b).

The process of identifying and implementing progressive institutional adjustment faces severe obstacles. Such change is costly in itself in that human beings are creatures of habit who evidence considerable inertia to revamping their comfortable modes of use and wont. Institutional adjustment means redistribution of power which is inevitably resisted by those who are currently well-served by the institutional configuration. It is to be expected that considerable institutional or cultural lag will always exist in human society so that a menu of ideological re-viewing and practical reform is a permanent feature of the social landscape. For this reason institutionalists insist upon the principle of institutional adjustment as the fundamental focus of social economic theory.

## The Changing American Family

The American family as a social institution is in a constant state of change (Levitan and Belous 1981), and this change is a major concern because the definition of family continues to broaden and include more than the traditional nuclear family (Zimmerman 1988). The changing family has been studied since the latter part of the nineteenth century after the impacts of the Industrial Revolution on the family became obvious (Yorburg 1983, p. 8). The social functions of the family shifted and the role of women in the family and society began to change in a manner that has continued to the present.

Many of the traditional functions of the family have been shifted to specialized social institutions (McNall and McNall 1983, here and throughout this section). The early American frontier family produced most of its own food, fashioned its own clothing, and built its own housing, largely from "scratch." The family had to locate or raise the raw materials needed to produce the goods it needed. For the most part, education was home-centered and vocationally oriented; children were taught by parents the skills needed to function in the frontier economy. The sharp definition of gender roles in domestic production was reflected in gender-differentiated education. Religious instruction as well was home-centered to a much greater extent than in the more differentiated world to come. Home security and defense were also major concerns for the isolated frontier families.

With the rise to dominance of the commodity production economy, industrialization, and urbanization, these functions and other functions were in large part shifted to specialized social institutions. To some extent this is not surprising. Intensified division of labor leaves less time for home-based instruction and renders such instruction inadequate in the nature of the case. Although some controversy exists concerning the causes and implications of these changes, there is agreement that the family's functions have shifted to a significant degree to other social institutions and that this shift has significant consequences.

Early in the twentieth century, the evolutionary study of the family developed into the study of the problems presented by social change and to the advocacy of social reform (Hutter 1981, p. 35). This meant the study of the family in the context of such social problems as illegitimacy, prostitution, and child abuse that were concomitant to rapid commodification, industrialization, and urbanization. The social reform focus was the core of the sociological functionalists at the Chicago School. Led by William F. Ogburn, this school developed the loss of family functions argument into a relatively coherent theory of social change and reform (Yorburg 1983, p. 17). In a manner reminiscent of Veblen's (1953) theory of institutional lag, Ogburn (1964) examined the effects of social change on the family in terms of cultural lag. For Ogburn, family was an adaptive culture that lagged behind the material culture. That is, technology increased more rapidly than the family could adjust to it, resulting in a social maladjustment between the adaptive culture and the material culture.

These changes affected the internal character of family life. The family evolved from an extended kinship system for instituting a wide range of vital socio-economic functions to a more restricted or nuclear family with reduced socio-economic functions. With this evolution to the modern companionate family (Burgess 1926; Burgess and Locke 1945), intimate contact and nurturing rise in proportion to the totality of family functions. In the companionate family, although they remain significant, socio-economic functions have fallen dramatically in proportion to procreation and affection functions.

As the social functions of the family evolved, the way opened for increased participation of women in the paid labor force. Engels argued that capitalism would eventually undermine patriarchy by drawing women into the labor force, thereby reducing women's dependency on men and dissolving gender into class as a category of oppression (Wheatley-Mann 1986). Veblen's cultural examination (1953) of patriarchal culture was much less sanguine about this prospect, and unfortunately, more accurate (Wheatley-Mann). Nonetheless, the role of women in the family and the wider society has certainly changed at an accelerating pace over the last century (Levitan and Belous 1981, p. viii; McNall and McNall 1983, Ch. 11; Yorburg 1983, pp. 25-27; Huber 1973, pp. 1-4; J.B. Stanfield 1985). As evolving functions within the family opened up opportunities for women to acquire education and skills and enter the paid labor force, women became less economically dependent on men and gender relations within the marriage bond became somewhat more egalitarian (Yorburg 1983, p. 25). This opened the way for an increase in single adults living alone who are either divorced or never married.

Cultural change abetted these functional trends. The women's movement became a more or less permanent force in the social landscape. Wartime employment led to an increasing number of women who questioned traditional gender roles (Deckard 1983) and thereby felt some affinity to the movement for eradication of social barriers to women's participation in political economic processes. Not surprisingly, increasing numbers of women began to enter colleges, universities, and trade schools to acquire the skills necessary to compete for better jobs. Technological changes such as more reliable contraceptive devices and labor-saving household appliances and processed goods also increased the capacity of women to participate in the paid labor force.

Postwar economic trends contributed to the dramatic increase in women's participation in the paid labor force. The quarter of a century boom to 1970 increased demand in the pink collar occupations dominated by women and generated labor shortages in other fields that were not the traditional parvenu of women. Along with the changing social relations between the genders, which increased women's responsibilities for supporting themselves and their children, the stagnant real wage in the American economy since the 1970s has added considerable economic stress and induced more intensive recourse of women to the paid labor force (Abelda 1992; Schor 1991). The above changes have been mixed blessings for women who have all too frequently worked the double day or "second shift" (Hochschild 1989) in that their spouses were slow to begin sharing the domestic labor as paid labor force participation became more equalized. And of course increasing numbers of women are raising children without assistance in domestic labor and all too often with little financial support from absent fathers.

## Cultural Lag and Family Policy

For all progressives, *ceteris paribus*, it is desirable to remove socially structured inequality that limits the full participation of individuals within a social group. In light of Veblen's view that women possess relatively greater cultural residuals of the parental bent, institutionalists are especially sanguine about the prospects of a society in which women exercise greater influence. Recent feminist literature on the greater nurturing propensity of women supports Veblen's view (Wheatley-Mann). Institutionalists of course do not expect this progress to be spontaneous nor to occur without significant refashioning of habitual attitudes and practices. In this there is to be expected considerable resistance.

Having witnessed the nativistic reaction of the last twenty years one needs little reminder of the phenomenon of cultural lag. Principles once considered settled insofar as the necessary public role in a mature capitalist economy have been forgotten before a mind-numbing recrudescence of nineteenth century ideology. In America, the recent atavism of some elements of the Republican Party and its intellectual crowd has been especially nauseating. The most committed devotee of waxing irrelevantly in order to protect wealth and privilege must have found unsettling the GOP convention in 1992.

The deadlock of governments in the industrial democracies is further compelling evidence of cultural lag (J.R. Stanfield 1979a, ch. 5 and 1983). Nowhere is this more apparent than in America where the deteriorating social landscape and decaying infrastructure has long been evident. The logic of reform (Gruchy 1947, pp. 620-1; J.R. Stanfield 1986, ch. 5) is no less persistent and its neglect by those in power steadily exacerbates an urgently precarious social economic situation. The Galbraithian (1958) institution of cultural lag, social imbalance, becomes all the more evident in this era of gridlocked government. Along with growing social imbalance such a stalemate of political economic forces raises the specter of authoritative resolution as described by Hayek (1944) and Polanyi (1957) with respect to interwar Europe.

The existence of cultural lag is particularly evident in the area of gender and family relations. Even the common definition of the family is an ideological holdover cast in terms of the patriarchal past. This definition emphasizes a particular family structure—husband/father, wife/mother, and children—to the exclusion of other living arrangements that fulfill the companionate nurturing function (McNall and McNall 1992). This definition ties the functionalist sociological perspective to a specific, traditional patriarchic definition of the family in which each adult in the family fulfills a traditional role oriented toward the birth and rearing of children (Parsons and Bales 1955). The Bureau of the Census (1989, p. 3) continues this traditional practice by defining the family "as a householder and one or more other persons living in the same household who are related to the householder by birth, marriage, or adoption." Although this does not preclude a single parent household, so long as same sex marriage is not legally recognized, it does require heterosexual marriage given the presence of two adults. Moreover, any structurally-oriented definition is likely to lag behind social change and therefore exclude many arrangements by which people seek to fulfill the nurturing function of the family (*USA Today* 1987). Hence these exclusionary definitions limit the analytical and political discourse on family policy.

For example the recent family values discussion, habitually focused upon the traditional family, has neglected the most basic question of whether families lack values or time and resources. Poverty is degrading and economic insecurity undermines family cohesion. The facts seem to suggest that no fundamental change in family values has occurred that matches the rising level of economic stress of the last twenty years (Abelda 1992; Schor 1991; Stanfield and Stanfield 1980). The social safety net for the maintenance of family functions has not been kept abreast of the times.

This is another instance of Galbraithian social imbalance. In the area of gender and family relations, profit opportunity leads to accommodation in food processing, service industries, catalog sales, and household technological changes but the public goods response has been slow. As a result, poverty becomes feminized and its incidence accelerates at its most tragic and destructive locus, children (Peterson 1987; Northrup 1990; J.B. Stanfield 1992). Much of this is not only the traditional ideological lag of the anti-government mentality but also of the patriarchal culture. Indeed even those whose political persuasions may be considered modern liberal contribute to the feminization of poverty if they operate upon the traditional family assumption. Measures designed to protect the income of male breadwinners —unemployment compensation, workers's compensation, social security payments, and mandated union representation—do not necessarily augment the income of women and children not living with a male. These policies, and especially their costs in an era of restricted budgets, tend to deflect attention from family policy aimed at *all* families and the need for policies focused upon specific employment and income constraints faced by women such as child care needs and occupational discrimination.

State income support payments for women and children continue to be structured by the mores of a patriarchal culture. Only the concept of patriarchy can account for the curiously dualized welfare system that the US has evolved (Peterson 1992, pp. 184-8; Petersen and Felder 1992; and Peterson and Petersen 1993). Women and children who have lost the income provided by the death, disability, or retirement of a male earner receive higher income and benefits than those who are without a male earner because of desertion, divorce, or single parenthood. Yet women in both categories face the same obstacles to earning income in the market; women and children in both categories have similar economic needs. Nothing distinguishes the two types of women and children except their prior relationship to men. The determination of the life chances of women and children on the basis of moral judgments of their relations to men is patriarchal culture at its most insidious.

## Toward Institutional Adjustment

Progress in the implementation of family policy requires a more dynamic, process-oriented definition of the family that is more inclusionary with respect to family structure because it is focused upon the function rather than the structure of family life (Zimmerman 1988; Lanciaux 1992). The modern family must be viewed as having wider functions than regulating sexual behavior and producing children. The companionate, nurturing function is inherent in adult relationships as well and important production of goods and services for direct household consumption occurs in the household. The concept of *leisure* needs to be relieved of its passive connotation lest we sacrifice socially vital activities in the interest of increasing pecuniarily measured productivity and income (Schor 1991; Waring 1990).

The family policy discourse needs to be informed by an inclusionary, process-oriented conception of the family as an on-going social arrangement composed of people who are committed to meeting each other's psychological, social, and physical needs (J. B. Stanfield 1992; Zimmermann 1988). This process-oriented definition addresses the many things that families do and includes all of the varieties of family life that might exist. Policymakers using this definition can direct their energies toward developing policy relevant to social problems rather than debating platitudes about the morality of family structure. This should allow clarification of the problems and alternatives involved in the family policy area and reduce the tendency toward endless debate on differing definitions of the family and family policy (Steiner 1981, p. 17; Moen and Schorr 1987). It is particularly important to separate the views of those who want to design family policy to finance a family income floor and those who seek morally-oriented regulation of behavior (Aldous and Dumon 1991). The moral regulation tactic is further evidence of the heldover patriarchal culture that generates the dualized income support system.

The process-oriented view of family policy encompasses both implicit and explicit family policy. The difference between explicit and implicit policies that affect families is related to their policy goals and objectives. Explicit family policies are those in which the goals or objectives for families are deliberately included (Zimmerman 1988, p. 20). Implicit family policies are those which are not intended directly to impact upon families but which do. Policy primarily aimed at areas other than family are likely to have implicit impacts upon the family. A more concerted focus upon family in the policy area should include careful audits of these impacts alongside the explicit goals and measures of family policy per se.

Viewed inclusively, family policy is the examination of social policy in terms of its impacts on families. This inclusionary focus introduces a multicultural family perspective into the policy arena, taking into account the impact that policy has on all varieties of families. One specific aim of incorporating a family perspective into policy would be to finance the empowerment of women and children. A concerted multicultural family policy would have to directly confront socially-structured gender inequality. The patriarchal society continues to allocate resources and life chances differentially by gender. Financing the empowerment of women and children will require more adequately funded, better constructed programs to aid families with dependent children. Programs are needed to abet women in the acquisition of marketable skills, in securing employment and compensation commensurate with these skills, and in balancing the demands of child care and employment. Parental leave, family allowances, expanded earned income and child care tax credits, subsidized high quality child care, national health insurance, and flex time work arrangements are examples of the policies that should be highly placed on the policy agenda.

## Conclusion

For the American social economy at the present time the most pressing issue is the adjustment of political economic institutions to the reality of changing family and gender relations. The deterioration in the life chances of children is an ominous harbinger of future social decay and lagging productivity. The increased dualization of individual life chances between those reared in families with and without a male present is a cause for concern not only in its own right, given the wasted potential and avoidable misery endured, but also because of the everpresent reality of violence and social unrest it breeds. As James O'Connor has suggested to the authors in personal communication, it is plausible that the observed downward stickiness of long term interest rates in the US economy is indicative of the failure to address the problems of urban decay and dualized life chances. A society that is not investing in much of the new generation that must become its labor force and that is allowing its urban centers to decay into quagmires of poverty, idleness, underground economic activity, and violence is not notably creditworthy. The Clinton surprise in the long bond market may have as much to do with the sort of spending advocated as with the prospects of reduced budget deficits. The prospect of reversal of over two decades of neglect of the collective action needed to reverse urban and economic decline should be reassuring to the long term financial markets.

The argument here is that the institutional adjustment needed to reverse this decline needs to have as one of its key foci the empowerment of women and children without regard for their relationships to males. This empowerment must be financial since finance is the power system of the commodity production economy. The family values debate is a red herring. Families likely do not lack values but resources (Abelda 1992). The atavistic moralizing about the decline of the traditional family is a lamentable waste of time in the face of the increasing urgency of instituting an effective response to the economic and social challenges at the close of the American Century (J.R Stanfield 1992).

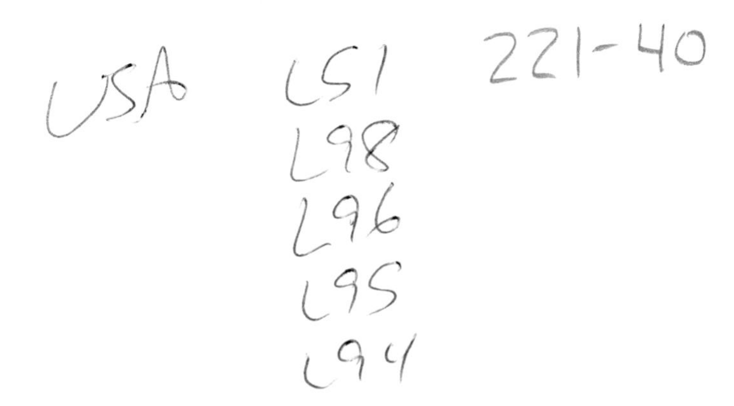


# 14. MARKET FAILURE AND REGULATORY REFORM: ENERGY AND TELECOMMUNICATION NETWORKS AS A CASE STUDY

Harry M. Trebing

The deregulation of public utilities continues to be a source of controversy and debate. Economic regulation has traditionally been justified on the grounds that the provision of necessary services for all sectors of society at just and reasonable rates requires control of the firm's ability to set exploitative prices and restrict or denigrate basic service. Proponents of deregulation argue that such regulatory intervention constitutes a barrier to innovation, protectionism for special interests, and a disincentive to minimize the cost of service. Furthermore, they insist that replacing regulation with free markets will force prices toward costs, control excess profits, and sweep aside residual pockets of monopoly power in a grand Schumpeterian manner. However, experience over the past decade has shown that these arguments are seriously flawed. This paper will examine these defects and point to institutionalist oriented reforms.

## The Neoclassical Critique

Much of the intellectual support for the deregulation movement has come from neoclassical economists who believe that utility industries are inherently competitive and cases of market failure are either isolated phenomena or incidental spillover effects associated with an otherwise smoothly functioning system of markets. In those instances where market failures exist, neoclassical analysis relies on Pigouvian or post-Pigouvian models of market failure to correct the problem. Externalities, high information and transaction costs, and free rider problems can be reconciled, it is argued, within a free market framework through devices such as marketable pollution rights, formalized incentives and penalties, and new markets for information and data. Where monopoly focal points exist because of scale economies, mandatory interconnection and simple price caps will negate any potential for abuse. Even the existence of high degrees of market concentration need not serve as an excuse for widespread regulatory intervention since the market power of the dominant firm will be nullified through the action of potential entrants—assuming that one accepts the theory of contestable markets.[1]

On balance, there appears to be a consensus among neoclassical economists and proponents of the interest-group theory of government that markets are superior to political forums in allocating resources and promoting efficiency. They admit that markets may not always function perfectly, but they argue that failures associated with the retention of regulation or the adoption of a political approach to allocation will have far more serious consequences and will constitute a far greater threat to economic efficiency and individual freedom. This type of rationalization for a retreat from traditional regulation is evident in recent public policy actions in electricity, natural gas, and telecommunications.

In electricity supply, vertical integration from generation through transmission to local distribution within a single firm has been seriously challenged in the Energy Policy Act of 1992. EPAct defines as a major goal the promotion of direct competition in wholesale power markets and the encouragement of new entrants into generation. Furthermore, new entrants such as independent power producers, cogenerators, and affiliated power producers are promised virtual exemption from regulation if they enter this phase of the production of electricity.[2] Power generation as a source of pollution would likewise be handled in a quasi-market fashion through the sale and trading of pollution rights as sanctioned by the 1990 Amendments to the Clean Air Act.

In natural gas supply, the old regulatory regime under which pipelines acted as purchasing agents for local gas distribution companies (LDCs) was completely upset by Federal Energy Regulatory Commission Order 636 (1992). This order required that pipelines provide only transportation for LDCs, large industrial customers, and gas producers so that these buyers and sellers could negotiate directly. At the same time, natural gas was completely deregulated as a commodity and its price, whether spot or long-term, was allowed to fluctuate according to changing market conditions. Other deregulated markets were established for trading pipeline capacity and storage. Arguments have also been made that interpipeline rivalry could serve as a constraint on extortionist pricing for gas transmission if one considers so-called marketing centers which are served by more than a single pipeline as a point of reference.[3]

In telecommunications, the most comprehensive public policy change culminated in the divestiture in 1984 of the old Bell system and the creation of AT&T as a long distance carrier and the seven regional Bell holding companies (RBHCs) as providers of local exchange and short-haul toll service. The assumption was that competition would take place in the long distance market and that the local exchange would continue to be a natural monopoly that would remain under regulation. In the intervening years, however, the threat of bypass of the local exchange and the prospect of rivalry from cable networks, cellular phone carriers, and personal communications systems have been cited as evidence that even the local exchange is subject to competitive pressures. Over all, new technology has been described as the major determinant of change, creating new services, new markets, and new systems of supply. The incumbent firms (whether RBHCs or independent carriers) have been quick to seize upon this line of argument and press for abandonment of traditional rate-base/rate-of-return regulation.

Yet the case for reevaluating options for reforming rather than abandoning regulation has not received equal treatment from most neoclassical economists or from public policy makers. Instead, idealized markets are typically compared to flawed regulatory institutions despite widespread evidence of market failure, exploitative pricing, and the shifting of risk and costs to captive customers. A detailed examination of these abuses will be set forth later in this paper, but at this point it is sufficient to note that more attention should be given to reforming regulation and determining the role of markets within a larger regulatory framework. Setting forth this rationale is a task for institutional economists.

## Institutional Economics and "Progressive Regulation"

American institutionalists represent a long tradition of promoting social reform. Accordingly, they are inclined to take a much broader view of market fallibility and the need for government intervention to protect captive markets and limit the social costs to be borne by the community as a whole. Further, they seek policies that will promote higher levels of societal efficiency that both include and transcend the much narrower concept of market efficiency. Marc Tool has sought to integrate this form of public interest regulation into his concept of instrumental value.

Tool notes that ". . . instrumental value theory, as developed by institutionalists in the Dewey tradition, provides guidance for the formulation of judgments in the regulation of economic activity and power in the public interest" (Tool 1990c, p. 535).[4] Continuing, Tool states that regulation may be ". . . deemed progressive . . . when it contribute(s) to the resolution, at least for a time, of actual problems encountered. Other sorts of criteria have generated regressive regulation and have failed significantly to contribute to a public interest view of problem solving" (Ibid., p. 536). He recognizes that regulation *per se* will ". . . advantage some and . . . disadvantage others. At issue is whose interests or advantages *ought* to be served" (Ibid.). To handle this question Tool turns to social value theory to guide regulatory adjustments. Social value theory, in turn, involves those measures that provide "for the continuity of human life and non-invidious re-creation of community through the instrumental use of knowledge" (Ibid., p. 539). He argues that the attainment of social value requires democratic control over the creation and employment of regulation, which means that all participants in the process must have access to all relevant knowledge as well as the power and opportunity to act on that knowledge politically.

In addition to the concern over social values, institutionalists have pointed to the shortcomings of the Pigouvian and post-Pigouvian market failure models. They argue that by focusing on the resolution of social costs within a market context, neoclassical analysis fails to adequately determine the source of the problem and explore the full range of solutions because it denies direct controls as a potential option. Further, neoclassical efforts to integrate individual actions into a set of incentives and penalties embodying a structure of property rights will involve all participants in a tangle of litigation and damage suits far greater than that which would prevail under more direct forms of economic regulation. Moreover, it cannot be assumed that secondary, supporting, or ancillary markets will perform in a fashion that will consistently reconcile financial self-interest and the negation of social costs. The weak performance of the market for pollution rights in the electric utility field is a case in point. Efforts at collaborative action, such as class action suits, have likewise proven to be a poor and largely ineffectual remedy for handling cases of market failure and discriminatory behavior. Direct regulatory action must be considered as a potentially more effective method for achieving overall social efficiency and controlling unacceptable behavior, even after the costs of regulatory administration and compliance are considered.

Institutionalists also point out that the neoclassical and public choice schools ignore the fact that the initial distribution of wealth, power, and property rights will adversely affect the outcome of deregulation. Expressed somewhat differently, one of the original justifications for economic regulation by government was recognition of the need to redress the imbalance between the wealth and power of the corporation on the one hand, and a large number of unorganized and dispersed consumers on the other. Indeed, much of the movement toward deregulation can be interpreted as the exercise of political and economic power by incumbent firms fearing a loss of market dominance if they are handicapped by governmental constraints in responding to new markets and potential rivals. This is particularly evident in the case of the seven regional Bell holding companies as they seek to establish major positions in both the new multimedia industries and the new markets created by the interaction of computer and communications technologies. As a demonstration of the exercise of this power, over the period 1984-1992, 44 of the 50 state commissions significantly relaxed traditional regulatory constraints over telecommunications earnings, prices, and selected services (Communications Workers of America 1992, p. 10-13). Concurrently, state governments have severely circumscribed or limited public funding for consumer intervention before regulatory and judicial bodies. Much of this assault on publicly funded consumer intervention undoubtedly reflects successful political activity on the part of firms desiring greater freedom from regulation. Indeed, it is not too much of an exaggeration to argue that the simultaneous weakening of control over earnings and prices and the diminished funding of public intervention serve as a clear testimonial to the exercise of political and economic power rather than the public acceptance of deregulated markets.

An examination of the emerging structure of public utility industries and the strategies of the major players will serve to reveal the comparative contribution of the neoclassical and institutional models as guidelines for public policy. Such an examination will also disclose the complexity of the issues involved, the barriers to competition, and a broader range of options for reform than those afforded by the simple deregulation model.

## Public Utilities as Infrastructure

Electricity, natural gas, and telecommunications have always been readily differentiated from the manufacturing and service sectors on the basis of their heavy capital investment per unit of output, but it has only recently been noted that these utilities play a significant role as a part of the nation's infrastructure. Public utilities provide a comprehensive network linking a wide variety of consumers with either centralized or diverse sources of supply. For example, 25 major interstate natural gas transmission companies provide over 216,000 miles of installed, wide-diameter, high-pressure pipeline. They therefore constitute a private infrastructure every bit as significant as schools, highways, and health care facilities.

The relationship between infrastructure, productivity, and real income has been well documented (Peterson 1994). It is also clear that society benefits whenever that infrastructure is designed and utilized in a responsive and efficient fashion. Insofar as utility networks are concerned, there are at least ten significant characteristics that must be considered in achieving this goal. First, networks require a heavy minimum threshold investment because of the need to interconnect with all customers in the service territory. Second, significant common and joint costs will yield important economies of joint service or joint product development. Networks permit the development of multiple services at a lower cost than if each service were to pay its stand-alone cost. Third, there will be significant economies of scale from building capacity in advance of demand as long as that demand is properly forecasted. Fourth, adding a segment to a network typically increases traffic on all other segments of that network. Fifth, networks provide inexpensive backup and increased reliability through routing alternatives, pooled reserves, and spreading outages. Sixth, the more comprehensive the network, the greater the potential for reducing the level of capacity to meet individual peaks. Seventh, advances in software and modernization improve network functionality and flexibility. However, associated software costs will increase both the overhead costs of the network and attendant economies of scale and joint production. Eighth, network size and new technology interact to permit new methods of packaging and transmitting service—particularly in telecommunications, as evidenced in the shift from packet switching to the transmission of data by asynchronous transfer mode (ATM). ATM reinforces scope and joint production economies for telecommunications networks offering voice, video, and data services. It also creates opportunities for cross subsidization between these services—especially for the firm moving from voice to video service. Ninth, the incremental cost of adding a specific service decreases as the size of the network increases. Tenth, networks produce significant positive externalities. To note two examples: (1) networks increase the size of the market thereby permitting users to achieve a greater division of labor and higher productivity, and (2) networks can also diminish the market power of an individual user.

With or without regulation, the success of a capital intensive network requires maintaining a careful balance between usage patterns and inherent cost characteristics. Failure to achieve this balance will result in poor plant utilization, rising unit costs, and a drastic fall in earnings. For management, achieving this balance provides a strong incentive to exploit the demand characteristics of each market through price discrimination and, whenever possible, cross subsidization. The task for progressive regulation will be to achieve high levels of utilization and network optimization without recourse to undue price discrimination, cross subsidization, or risk shifting. Imperfect competition will be a highly flawed constraint on such practices in the absence of direct regulation.

There is another consequence of achieving an efficient utilization of the networks as infrastructure. An increase in network efficiency will typically be achieved at the expense of greater market concentration in that utility industry. Accordingly, there is a potential conflict between attaining network efficiency and maintaining across-the-board intraindustry competition. To a large degree this difficult tradeoff arises because the effective planning and operation of a network constitutes a barrier to entry and competition. For example, the incumbent firm has a substantial advantage in terms of established market coverage.[5] Furthermore, the new entrant will encounter a long gestation period before it can achieve financial viability.[6] The large sunk investment needed to establish a network will also serve as a barrier to potential entry and negate the theory of contestable markets. Finally, realization of the network economies previously described requires that a firm achieve a minimum efficient market share (MEMS). If MEMS is greater than 50 percent of the total market, then only one supplier or a dominant firm will survive. In this setting, other firms will exist at the sufferance of the dominant firm and will constitute an ineffectual force for competition over time.

## The Failure of Pervasive Competition to Emerge

There are at least five significant effects associated with the failure of pervasive competition to emerge in the wake of partial deregulation. The first is the persistence of high levels of concentration. Assuming that market dominance exists when one firm has 40 percent or more of a market, all of the major public utility markets still display this characteristic. In no sense can the major segments of the electric and gas industries be characterized as highly competitive if concentration is the test. In the interexchange /interLATA market, concentration still persists ten years after AT&T divestiture. While AT&T's share has declined, it still retains about 60-65 percent of the domestic long distance market. Similarly, its share of all overseas telecommunications revenues has remained remarkably stable, with 69.6 percent of the overseas market in 1980 and 68.7 percent in 1992. It is also important to note that the rate of decline in AT&T's share of the total domestic long distance market has flattened out in the last several years. At the local exchange level, dominance is still much in evidence despite the appearance of competitive access providers (CAPs) such as Teleport which link big business customers to long distance carriers.

A second outcome is the persistence of consistently high levels of profitability. Effective competition would normally tend to limit profits over time, but this has not been the case. The traditional measure of an acceptable level of profits under regulation was a market-to-book ratio of 1.05-1.10. AT&T's market-to-book averaged 1.05 between 1969 and 1978. For the twelve months ending December 1993 it had increased to 5.02. For the twelve months ending December 1993, the market-to-book ratio for the electric utilities was 1.44; for combination electric and gas utilities, 1.45; for natural gas distribution companies, 1.79; for natural gas pipelines, 1.93; and for telecommunication companies, 2.66 (C.A. Turner Utility Reports, March 1994). These high levels of profitability would have activated rate case proceedings had traditional rate-base/rate-of-return regulation been followed.

A third outcome is the persistence of price discrimination, cross subsidization and risk/cost shifting. Energy and telecommunications utilities serve markets that are clearly differentiated along the lines of (1) large business customers, (2) public sector customers, (3) commercial customers, and (4) residential/small business customers. Each market has distinctive demand characteristics, and the greater the inelasticity of demand, the more vulnerable that market will be to arbitrary cost allocations, the assignment of write-offs or accelerated depreciation charges, and different target levels of profit. It can be argued that arbitrage serves as a check on discrimination between different markets, but independent brokers, resellers, and enhanced service providers offer only a very limited check on such abuses. They are vulnerable to a vertical squeeze by the underlying utility or facility-based carrier, or to the restructuring of bulk and retail tariffs by the vertically integrated utility. There are numerous recent examples of cost shifting and cross subsidization in the utility industries. In telecommunications, these include the incentive to shift accelerated cost recovery to basic/core service customers, the shifting of non-traffic sensitive costs to subscriber line charges (especially as minimum bills for basic telephone service), the recovery of local transport charges through a residual interconnection charge and the implicit assignment of video dial tone costs to telephone users. In natural gas, examples include the partial assessment of take-or-pay charges and the complete assessment of transition costs (arising from restructuring) against residential, commercial, and small business customers. Yet these customers were neither the principal cause for incurring these costs nor the principal beneficiaries of the change. In electricity, proposals to assess the cost of stranded plant against users of the transmission grid represent comparable behavior.

A fourth outcome is the emergence of substantial market power exercised by monopsonist buyers in energy and telecommunications. Monopsonists depress the prices that they pay, thereby shifting costs to other classes of users. Large users typically introduce the threat of bypass to extract concessions from the supplying utility. The utility, in turn, makes rate concessions to this class of user while raising prices to basic service customers to recover any revenue shortfall. Numerous examples of this behavior are evident in electricity, gas, and telecommunications. In fact, the situation has grown to a point in telecommunications where much of the demand for modernization appears to be driven by big users rather than by the public as a whole.

A fifth outcome is the emerging pattern of pricing for core/basic service sales on the one hand, and large industrial sales on the other. For example, in telecommunications, patterns of conscious parallelism and price leadership appear for basic message toll service, while price rivalry appears in custom network offerings for large users. This reflects three-firm oligopoly rather than high levels of workable competition.[7] In other utility industries, where tight oligopoly or, in some cases, duopoly prevails similar pricing patterns can be expected.

A sixth outcome is the potential impairment of the network as an integrated, fully functioning entity. This could come about through an absence of appropriate competitive-market constraints on behavior coupled with substantial deregulation. It would appear in the form of network fragmentation, duplication, disinvestment, reduced operating efficiency, or a failure to achieve optimum scale *vis a vis* the relevant market. It could also arise because the network was manipulated to exploit those consumers or users most dependent upon it. In either case, the contribution of the network to both public and private welfare would be proportionately diminished. FERC Order 636, which mandated unbundling and open access, serves to illustrate three areas of possible impairment. First, efficient use of the network requires centralized control over gas swaps, trades, flow routing and storage scheduling to permit balancing receipts and deliveries for diverse points over time. Order 636, on the other hand, grants shippers a share of pipeline capacity and storage through contracting and ownership of the gas to be transported. This could be a significant barrier to centralized dispatch and operation which, in turn, would increase transaction costs and lower overall performance. Attempting to correct this problem through Pigou-type pricing incentives and penalties or so-called operational flow orders would complicate matters even more and raise transaction costs for all users. Second, the introduction of market-based, deregulated prices for storage capacity would create an incentive for the regulated pipeline to sell off storage or transfer it to an unregulated affiliate. This affiliate could then raise the price of storage capacity to a point where it captured all of the savings to consumers from reducing peak capacity costs. Furthermore, capturing these savings would not be constrained by market forces since new storage capacity is typically being built by joint ventures of pipelines and producers. Third, open access and unbundling means that each LDC must now reserve pipeline/storage capacity and gas supply to meet the highest anticipated winter space-heating peak. The collective cost of meeting this demand for each LDC could significantly exceed the cost of having the pipeline meet it since the pipeline would have the advantage of balancing different peaks and transferring capacity and gas supply as needed, thereby reducing the total reserve requirement.[8]

## Changing Corporate Strategies

In the 1990s it has become apparent that a basic shift has taken place in the values of public utility management. Concern over reliability and adequacy of service has given way to greater emphasis on "the bottom line." To some degree this reflects a lack of confidence in regulation as a source of protection, but it also reflects the perceived attractiveness of unregulated and overseas markets. The attractiveness of these markets, in turn, has been reinforced by a relaxation of traditional regulatory constraints and the easy adaptability of the holding company format to permit simultaneous operation in regulated and nonregulated markets.

The new strategies of AT&T and the regional Bell holding companies demonstrate this change in management perspective. AT&T appears to have developed three essential lines of attack to retain a position of market dominance. The first is to tie customers to the network. By employing network economies to maximum advantage, it can offer customized or special services to big users at low incremental cost. The second is to aggressively pursue diversification, both domestically and overseas. Through the acquisition of McCaw Cellular, AT&T will be in a position to bypass the local exchange and avoid payment of access charges to local phone companies while providing comprehensive end-to-end services for its premiere class of users. In effect, AT&T will have rid itself of the restrictions of the 1956 Consent Decree, which limited it to tariff services, while at the same time bypassing the market shares policy implicit in the Modified Final Judgment that broke up the Bell System in 1982. Overseas expansion also plays an important role in AT&T's strategy. AT&T has announced that 50 percent of its revenue will come from overseas markets by the year 2000. To achieve this goal it has purchased substantial interests in Canadian, Venezuelan, and other overseas telephone properties; it has aggressively promoted equipment and service sales in Eastern Europe, the Middle East, and the Far East; and it has negotiated collaborative alliances with national telecommunications systems in Hong Kong, Singapore, Japan, Sweden, Switzerland, and Holland. These alliances, which AT&T calls "World Partners," essentially provides bundled one-stop offerings to the large multinational corporations in the European Common Market and the Pacific rim. A third feature of AT&T's strategy has been aggressive cost reductions. Its work force has been reduced by 100,000 persons since divestiture, suggesting that expense padding may have been a legitimate criticism of the old regulatory process. Of course, some of this reduction would have come about in any event because of new technology.

The regional Bell holding companies fear becoming the supplier of last resort; hence they have moved aggressively into cable TV, both domestically and internationally, while seeking removal of the MFJ restrictions that preclude them from entering interstate long distance markets, telecommunications equipment manufacturing, and selected enhanced services. The most obvious examples are US West's acquisition of 25 percent of Time-Warner, Southwestern Bell's joint venture to acquire Telmex (Mexico's telecommunications system), Pacific Bell's proposed entry into video dial tone, and the Bell Atlantic/Ameritech acquisition of the New Zealand phone company. In addition there are numerous examples of joint ventures between RBHCs and cable operators in Europe and elsewhere. What appears to be emerging is a complex system of alliances between telephone companies and firms in the multimedia industry which will involve integrated participation in computers, communications, consumer electronics, entertainment, and publishing. Market dominance will therefore have been shifted from traditional voice communications to control over the content, delivery, and manipulation of all forms of information.[9]

Foreign diversification programs appear to be particularly attractive when promoted through joint ventures, contracts, acquisitions, and consortium arrangements. Excluding AT&T and MCI, nine large telephone carriers have 265 programs in 52 different foreign countries. In passing it should be noted that the energy utilities have also discovered the attractiveness of overseas diversification. Twenty companies (including electric, gas distribution, pipelines, and parent holding companies) have 73 programs in 32 foreign countries. All these data apply to overseas diversification primarily in the period covered by the late 1980s to 1993 (Wasden 1993).

If deregulation allows these programs of domestic and overseas diversification to continue, the only constraint will be antitrust action. However, antitrust has not been a dynamic force since 1980, and there is little reason to assume that it will become an effective constraint on either domestic diversification or overseas expansion. Furthermore, once these programs have been put in place, it will be virtually impossible for state commissions to exercise authority and gather the necessary data to review pricing practices and earnings for the new multiproduct firm. But if national programs transcend state authority, global expansion of the type taking place in telecommunications may transcend national control. AT&T's World Partners, the British Telecom-MCI joint venture to provide global service, and the proposed joint venture between Sprint, France Telecom, and German Telekom could transcend the ability of any one nation to monitor or regulate their performance. It also follows that once these alliances and joint ventures are in place, the potential for future entry would be minimal.

Overseas diversification by American companies is closely related to the growing popularity of the privatization of government-owned utility enterprises in other nations. An examination of privatization is needed to determine whether it simply replicates much of the U.S. experience, or whether it contains the potential answer for successfully combining market forces and the attainment of social policy goals.

## The Growth of Global Privatization

The movement toward deregulation in the United States has been matched by a parallel movement toward privatization in both developing and industrialized nations. Some pressures for privatization are similar to those underlying deregulation, notably a greater emphasis on economic efficiency rather than on equity, a desire to improve infrastructure as a platform for growth, and a belief that privatization would make these industries more responsive to consumer needs. However, other pressures are less immediately evident. There has been strong support for privatization from those who see the transfer of ownership as a means of attracting foreign capital for new plant, thereby reducing government deficit financing. Similarly, privatization has been endorsed as a method for improving cost control and the elimination of subsidized services for residential customers. Multinational corporations also see privatization as an opportunity to exercise their bargaining power to extract price concessions from a privatized supplier rather than from a public enterprise obligated to provide basic service at low rates as a matter of public policy. At the same time, privatization has been supported by the state-owned enterprises themselves as an important opportunity to both expand the scope of their activities and open up new sources for raising capital. The entry of British Telecom and British Gas into global markets after privatization serves as an example. Conversely, privatization has been supported by U.S. utilities seeking entry into overseas markets that had previously been closed to them.

A special impetus for privatization has come from the change in lending policies of the World Bank. In the 1960s and '70s the Bank focused primarily on lending programs to fund modernization and organizational improvements for state-owned enterprises. Disenchantment with the results led the Bank to shift its emphasis in the late 1980s to support privatization. However, in sharp contrast to much of the deregulation literature in the U.S., the Bank has taken a strong stand against privatization without appropriate regulation. It endorsed a concurrent move to both privatize utility properties and install a regulatory authority. The preferred form of regulation appears to follow a model designed to encourage (1) transparency and openness, (2) greater managerial autonomy, (3) free entry for private power producers, (4) interconnection and competition, (5) constraints on cross subsidization, and (6) price caps rather than rate-base/rate-of-return regulation. By 1993, the Bank did not appear to have been satisfied with the results, and a Bank discussion paper concluded that "the single most troubling issue in recent reforms is slow progress in developing regulatory capabilities" (World Bank Telecommunications Experience 1993, p. 10). It fears that in the absence of regulation and procompetitive policies, prices will be high, innovation will be slow, monopoly will become entrenched, and privatized firms will only be interested in serving highly profitable niche markets rather than making long-term investments in core markets. Regrettably, the Bank has not come to grips with the strengths and weaknesses of a regulatory model that is set up primarily to encourage competition. Nor did it consider the shortcomings of new tools such as price caps or the potential conflict between attempts to promote market efficiency and the need to recognize the importance of societal efficiency.

**Information Superhighway vs. Institutional Value Theory**

In contrast to U.S. deregulation programs and the World Bank's effort to employ regulation to promote competition, the Clinton Administration's proposal to create a national information superhighway would appear to mark a radical change in the approach to telecommunications infrastructure. The goal would be to integrate government policies and private sector initiative to exploit new telecommunications and computer technology in a fashion that would ensure that the benefits of the information revolution would be made available to everyone. Accordingly, this proposal would appear to involve government planning to integrate social values and market forces. The question can then be raised whether this promises to be a significant step toward the realization of Marc Tool's concept of social value in the form of some type of progressive regulation.

According to the National Telecommunications and Information Administration (NTIA 1993), the superhighway proposal consists of four main features: (1) promotion of universal access to the superhighway for all classes of consumers and communities; (2) establishment of a broadband capability for the interactive delivery of all forms of information; (3) prevention of private monopoly control; and (4) removal of regulations that restrict corporate initiative.

However, there are serious shortcomings that must be addressed. For example, how will universal access be funded? A telephone carrier will be extremely reluctant to invest in thin markets or provide discounts to marginal users when the alternative is to enhance the return on equity by domestic and overseas diversification. Second, how will alternative delivery systems be integrated to enhance consumer choice? If these systems are supplied by independent firms, it would not be in the financial self-interest of a firm to voluntarily interconnect with potential rivals. Merger and acquisition are more attractive options. Mandatory interconnection would be required to achieve a network of independent networks. Third, how will the cost of broadband investment be recovered? One suspects that imperfect markets will allocate overhead costs on the basis of the relative demand elasticity of each market. Finally, there is an inherent contradiction between preventing monopoly control and removing regulatory restrictions that impinge upon corporate initiative. Any compromise such as "light" incentive regulation and simple price caps will enhance the latter at the expense of the former. In fact, some telecommunications carriers have used implementation of the superhighway as a rationale for weakening regulatory control of earnings or as an argument for entry into multimedia activities. On balance, the superhighway is a far cry from the progressive regulation embodied in institutional value theory.

## Toward Progressive Regulation

Marc Tool has defined progressive regulation as the resolution of problems through the regulation of economic activity and power in the public interest. Tool believes that social value theory can contribute criteria for judging whether the quality of life and the welfare of the community have been enhanced by such intervention.

Without question, the pattern of flawed markets combined with flawed public policies described in this paper will diminish net social gains, but a public policy that recognizes the inherent structural features of these industries and the limitations of markets should be able to enhance them. An institutionalist approach to regulatory reform must face the challenge of defining and identifying social benefits and social costs, negating the adverse effects of the exercise of political and economic power, and working to emancipate government from political coercion while improving its ability to engage in industry-specific planning. Toward these ends, institutionalism will emphasize a holistic approach to problems, a recognition that reform is an evolutionary process, and a willingness to treat theoretical constructs (whether neoclassical, Chicago School, or other) in a postmodernist fashion that "holds that there is no neutral, objective, scientific language" (Hoksbergen 1994, p. 685).

Elements of social value will undoubtedly differ between developing and industrialized nations. This paper will set forth a general framework and key tasks that must be considered in any effort to rekindle progressive regulation in the United States or comparable advanced industrialized societies. Six major tasks will be examined.

The first task of progressive regulation will be to determine the proper size and scope of the network relative to the market to be covered. For electricity, this will include the transmission and distribution grid together with power generation. The current move to segregate generation from transmission is counterproductive since generation and transmission are substitutes under certain conditions. In addition, efficient employment of generation capacity requires centralized dispatch of power plants by the managers of the overall grid. For natural gas, this will include production, gathering lines, pipeline transport, storage, and the local distribution network. Since production is an integral part of this process, factors such as the presence or absence of competition among producers must be addressed directly, and a dismissal of gas as a deregulated, competitive commodity, without supporting evidence, is unacceptable. For telecommunications, networks would be defined to cover all major systems of supply, including public switched, cable, wireless, Internet, private, CAP, and LEC networks.

In each industry it is important to determine the parameters within which networks can be optimized. For example, expansion of the network will match gains from enhanced network economies against the losses associated with greater size. The results of such studies could form a portion of the basis for establishing market structure guidelines to evaluate acquisitions, mergers, and proposals for diversification. These guidelines would differ from the merger guidelines developed by the U.S. Department of Justice Antitrust Division and the Federal Trade Commission. The DOJ-FTC guidelines apply only to horizontal mergers and acquisitions, while the goal of these network guidelines would be to balance gains in network efficiency against the negative effects of greater market concentration. While these studies can be particularly straightforward in electricity and gas, they will be much more difficult in telecommunications because each discrete network will have both a competitive and a complementary relationship to other networks. If there is a strong complementary relationship between, for example, landline and wireless networks, then public policy makers will have to decide whether concentrating both networks through merger and acquisition or mandatory interconnection is the preferred option in the face of rapid technological change. If interconnection is chosen, then monopoly focal points must be identified and cost-based access pricing put in place.

The second task involves greater surveillance of network accessibility and adequacy of service. In electricity and natural gas, both access and transmission pricing will become crucial. At the same time there will be a need to strike a balance between the desire of the individual user to employ the network for personal advantage versus the requirements for central dispatch and overall planning to make sure that all inherent network efficiencies are exhausted and social needs are met. Fulfilling these requirements will give regulatory oversight an entirely new dimension of responsibility—unless one wants to entrust the final decision to tight oligopoly and the corporate conscience.

In telecommunications, the growing importance of network functionality will enhance the ability of the individual subscriber to utilize the network for his own specific needs. Whether the subscriber is a bank, a hospital, a business firm, government, or a private individual, functionality will permit the user to select or exclude services, thereby providing what for all practical purposes can become a customized offering. The economics of functionality has yet to be explored, but it appears that 60-80 percent of the cost of a modern switch is software, reflecting the developmental costs of engineering and design. The incremental software cost that is tied to a specific function appears to be quite small. In effect, the emergence of software could create new, significant economies of scale and opportunities for promotional pricing. In the future, questions of accessibility and adequacy of service will focus more on the responsiveness of network functionality than on universal service or open access. Open network architecture will become little more than a given. Achieving accessibility and reliability will depend upon full interconnection between disparate networks, the introduction of cost-based prices for access and transmission, maximum use of competitive pressures whenever feasible, and nondiscriminatory access to all types of information and content resellers and brokers. To the extent that collective action through regulation can enhance network functionality, it will serve to significantly empower the individual subscriber. In effect, collective action would serve to strengthen individual action and enhance subscriber freedom of choice.

The third task involves regulatory oversight of modernization and maintenance of the network. Given the perceived attractiveness of utility-related investments overseas which may be subject to little or no foreign government oversight, it is inappropriate to argue that the solution to the problem of network maintenance is to pay progressively higher prices so that carriers will earn a rate of return sufficiently high to deter disinvestment in the domestic network. This type of neoclassical argument represents a distortion of the concept of opportunity cost because it makes domestic rates of return a function of the vulnerability of foreign governments to corruption. Similarly, domestic investments in nonregulated activities may be more attractive than warranted when the network is under the control of a holding company. The financial synergism inherent in combining the stable income of the utility or carrier with the more volatile income of the nonregulated activity could give the parent holding company a lower composite cost of capital than that of the nonutility firm in the nonregulated activity. This would give the holding company a special incentive to diversify into nonregulated activities.

What will be needed for oversight is a system of direct monitoring that sets standards and imposes penalties for poor network service. There are recent data which suggest that some disinvestment in portions of the domestic telecommunications network may already have taken place when annual depreciation charges exceed net new investment.[10] These studies must be used with caution because software is often treated as an expense rather than as new plant investment. Nevertheless, they do suggest a cause for regulatory concern.

Attention must also be given to the impact of monopsony buyers on network investment patterns. Robin Mansell has summarized the misallocation inherent in designing networks and making concessions to multinationals in the field of telecommunications (Mansell 1993). To a lesser degree this problem may also exist in electricity and natural gas.

A fourth task is the need to look at the distributional consequences of regulatory intervention and imperfect markets. It is not sufficient to assume that efficient markets will eventually prevail and that distributional consequences are trivial. The difficulty is that market imperfections will be magnified by public policies designed to protect a transition to deregulation. This is evident in FERC's assignment of 100 percent of transition costs to LDCs; FERC's attempt to assign stranded electric utility plant to users of the transmission network in the Cajun case;[11] and the FCC's willingness to permit the assignment of accelerated depreciation charges to traditional telephone service. The last point deserves elaboration. Given the rapid rate of technological advance in telecommunications, it is important to determine who will get the technological dividend. This dividend is measured by the difference between the average embedded cost of existing plant and the incremental or stand-alone cost of new plant utilizing the most modern technology. If the burden of obsolescence is to be assigned to residential customers when that class of user derives little or none of the technological dividend, then this should be a decision for public policy makers to justify rather than a decision for corporate strategy to disguise. A more appropriate action would be to assign obsolescence in proportion to the extent that a specific group of customers places demands on the network for modernization and accordingly becomes the principal beneficiary of that modernization.

The fifth task is the continuing challenge of developing adequate guidelines for constraining various forms of exploitative pricing. The neoclassical standard holds that the maximum price should not exceed the stand-alone cost of providing a specific service, while the minimum price should not fall below the incremental cost of providing that service. Aside from measurement problems, the difficulty with this argument is that it would prevent the gains from the joint development of services from accruing to consumers in monopoly markets (assuming that maximum price is set on the basis of stand-alone cost). Yet the joint production economies inherent in a network typically mean that the cost of an individual service will be less than if it were produced on a stand-alone basis.

Popular acceptance of price caps to protect monopoly markets also suffers from serious handicaps. As currently practiced, price caps adjust rates upward to reflect the general level of inflation, but they contain a productivity offset which is applied against the price increase. For example, if the inflation rate was 5 percent and the productivity offset was 3 percent, the firm would be able to raise rates in monopoly markets by 2 percent. This approach suffers from a number of serious deficiencies. There is no incentive to experiment with lower prices in monopoly markets; index-driven prices will tend to grow at a compound rate that eventually becomes totally divorced from any cost-of-service standard; and an average price cap applied to both monopolistic and competitive services will not constrain cross subsidization. In addition, it makes no sense to base an inflation adjustment on the general price level for industries such as telecommunications where rapid technological advance has reduced the cost of inputs. A more appropriate basis would involve actual input costs for adjusting prices upward minus an imputed rate of productivity gain that could reasonably be expected to take place in telecommunications.

Given the inherent multiple/joint product nature of a network together with its significant overhead costs, there appear to be only two workable solutions for controlling exploitative pricing while still giving management the flexibility to achieve high capacity utilization.

The first involves a fully allocated costing methodology that takes into account the relative benefit from joint development in making an assignment of overhead costs. An example of this approach was developed by Martin Glaeser for the Tennessee Valley Authority in the 1930s (Glaeser 1939; Trebing 1989). Each class of service would pay its direct (or avoided) costs plus a share of the overhead cost based on the benefits derived by that service from joint use of the network. This would be measured by the difference between the stand-alone cost for the service and its direct cost. The resulting fully allocated cost would serve to establish a relative revenue contribution which an individual service would have to make to avoid cross subsidization. Application of the Glaeser model would also prevent uneconomic bypass.

The second approach would involve the structural separation of the network from a marketing subsidiary that would package and sell services in competition with independent marketers, brokers, resellers, and enhanced service providers. The network would remain under regulation and be compelled to sell its output to everyone on equal terms for comparable service. The separate marketing subsidiary would be deregulated and free to compete in any market. Consumers would have the benefits of choice while the network would remain obligated to provide adequate service at cost-based prices. If holding company control were to be retained over both the network and the unregulated subsidiary, then the network should have its own set of directors and its own ability to engage in outside financing to prevent risk shifting. If the network were to provide basic service to all those requesting it, a universal service access charge levied against all classes of users would be appropriate to cover the high cost of serving thin markets. This would be necessary because nonregulated brokers and marketers, as well as the separate subsidiary, would be free to build their own plant if the network were no longer the least-cost source of supply.[12]

## Conclusion

If government is to explore public policies that hold the promise of enhancing the general welfare, then it must explore options for regulatory reform that incorporate both regulatory control and market forces. By a process of institutional experimentation, progress can be made toward an authentic form of progressive regulation. However, it is necessary to keep in mind that this involves, as Marc Tool has noted, both public planning and democratic participation on the part of all parties involved. This may be one of the biggest obstacles to overcome, but at least the outcome, if successful, will be infinitely more rewarding than a blind reliance on deregulation and an implicit faith in the performance of inherently flawed markets.

## Notes

1. An overview of neoclassical pricing integrated into an acceptance of the theory of contestable markets is supplied by Baumol and Sidak (1994). A comprehensive criticism of contestability is provided by Shepherd (1984).

2. The move toward pluralism in electricity generation stems from a search for alternatives to the cost overruns, redundancy, and poor reliability associated with large-scale nuclear and coal fired plants built in the late 1960s and 1970s. Proponents of regulation would argue that strict enforcement of the prudence/used-and-useful standards would have resulted in disallowance of such plant and the avoidance of attendant rate increases.

3. FERC Order 636 was designed as a remedy for a period of gas shortage and curtailment in the 1970s, followed by gas oversupply and patterns of discriminatory pricing in the 1980s. Proponents of regulation would argue that FERC capitulation to producers through acceptance of take-or-pay, indefinite escalators, and most favored nation clauses in supply contracts permitted gas prices to increase in the face of falling demand. They would argue that strict enforcement of producer regulation at both the interstate and intrastate levels could have corrected the problem.

4. Edythe Miller's work in public utility regulation represents an application of instrumental value theory. See Miller (1993 and 1994). The institutionalist debate between proponents of Tool's social value concept and proponents of relativism is summarized in Hoksbergen (1994, p. 691-96).

5. This advantage applies to facility-based utilities and carriers with comprehensive networks reaching ultimate customers. Mandatory leasing of capacity would give independent marketers, brokers, and resellers access to these customers; however, such entrants would be vulnerable to the price charged for capacity and the incumbents' pricing strategies in retail markets. This type of "bounded contestability" would be a feeble constraint on price discrimination, monopoly earnings, or predatory behavior on the part of the incumbent. The deregulated marketing affiliates of major pipelines would have the ability to pursue such practices in periods of constrained supply.

6. It took MCI at least ten years to achieve minimum levels of profitability. When combined with excess capacity in the long distance markets, this would constitute a major barrier to the creation of new network carriers.

7. The incentive for price leadership comes from the desire to avoid price competition in basic service markets, thereby maximizing the contribution of these markets to overall profits. In addition, aggressive price cutting by the dominant firm could bring demands for reregulation or antitrust action by rivals. For evidence of price leadership in telecommunications, see Virginia State Corporation Commission (1994); also, Bolter (1994, Exhibit 10). No data are reported for discounting in custom network offerings.

8. It can be argued that individual LDCs could meet winter peaks by buying gas on the spot market. Assuming that gas was actually available, it would command a very high price during a period of short supply, as would no-notice transport. These penalty payments would, of course, be passed forward to consumers.

9. Confrontations between AT&T and the RBHCs have erupted--particularly after secret talks to reconcile differences collapsed. The Wall Street Journal reported, "In 1991, outside the oversight of regulators, AT&T and the seven regional Bell companies held a year of secret talks aimed at crafting terms for urging the federal court to dissolve the (consent) decree. The plan was code-named Acorn. ... Talks collapsed over how soon the Bells should be allowed into the long-distance business ..." (*Wall Street Journal*, 7/22/94).

10. Several studies have been undertaken by commission staff, but the most comprehensive review was contained in the Economics and Technology Research Report, *Patterns of Investment by the Regional Bell Holding Companies*, Boston, May 1993.

11. In Cajun Electric Power Cooperative v. FERC, No. 92-146, decided July 12, 1994, the U.S. Court of Appeals for the District of Columbia Circuit held that permitting Entergy (the incumbent electric utility) to recover its stranded investment in generation through charges against those using Entergy's transmission grid would constitute an anticompetitive tying arrangement. It would permit Entergy to compete for generating sales outside of its grid without concern for a stranded investment charge, but Entergy's competitors could not compete for customers in Entergy's territory using its transmission system on the same basis.

12. This approach to structural separations is based on the proposal submitted by Rochester Telephone to the New York Commission (see New York Public Service Commission, Petition of Rochester Telephone for Approval of Proposed Restructuring Plan - Joint Stipulation and Agreement, Case No. 93-C-0/03, May 13, 1994). It would separate the regulated network from the deregulated marketing function, but both would be under a parent holding company. The deregulated affiliate would compete with AT&T, RBHCs, CAPs, etc. The network would be under pressure to be innovative and efficient. The basic service customer would have the option of buying from the network on a cost-of-service basis or from a deregulated entity as part of a bundled offering. The Commission could also review and disallow payments from the network to the parent holding company if it suspected any abuses or disinvestment. Finally, the Glaeser model could be applied to pricing various network offerings.

## 15. THORSTEIN VEBLEN: SCIENCE, REVOLUTION AND THE PERSISTENCE OF ATAVISTIC CONTINUITIES

Rick Tilman[1]

### Introduction

Those familiar with Marc Tool recognize both how important an influence Thorstein Veblen (1857-1929) is on his life work and Veblen's significance in the formation of Tool's own optimistic social value theory. It must be recognized, however, that the political and economic radicalism of Veblen should be counterbalanced against his cultural and institutional pessimism; he certainly viewed science and its handmaiden technology as massive determinators and indicators of progressive change, yet he remained cognizant of the retardant and even atavistic effects of politics, culture and society. It is arguable, in fact, both that, on the one hand, he did some of the most advanced theorizing in left and progressive circles as did Tool at a later date, but that, on the other, he also falls in certain respects into the camp of the cultural pessimists and the conservative futilitarians who believe humanity is trapped by "imbecile institutions." Nevertheless, Veblen's (1) view of scientific progress is (2) linked with his political theory which, in turn, is related to (3) his analysis of the possibilities of change, of both a progressive and atavistic nature. His view of science is a modest one; its capacity as a form of predictive inquiry is unassuming, its claims tentative and provisional at best. Yet there is no superior alternative to science as a social change process for politics, the main alternative at hand, is mostly an expression of the values and power of business enterprise and commercial civilization, while the likelihood of political revolt against capitalist culture and institutions is indeterminant in what Veblen calls the "calculable future."

**Veblen on Science and Political Theory**

The classic text for analyzing Veblen's interpretation of the nature and function of science, is, of course, "The Place of Science in Modern Civilization" first published in 1906 (Veblen 1930). In it he lays out his most detailed interpretation starting with a simple yet penetrating definition of it as "impersonal, dispassionate insight into the material facts with which mankind has to deal" (Veblen 1991, p. 1). It is this which gives Western industrial societies an advantage over the less developed countries. As he put it "a civilization which is dominated by this matter-of-fact insight must prevail against any cultural scheme that lacks this element" (Ibid., p. 2).

However, Veblen does not accept the exaggerated claims made for science by scientistic cultists, for his own claims for science are more modest and he does not extend them to what passed for political theory in his day. Indeed, he differentiates between the use of science on the one hand and more "pragmatic"[2] forms of inquiry on the other hand, and it is in this latter category that political theory falls.

> Its habitual terms of standardisation and validity are terms of human nature, of human preference, prejudice, aspiration, endeavor, and disability, and the habit of mind that goes with it is such as is consonant with these terms . . . In the modern scheme of knowledge it holds true . . . that training in divinity, in law, and in the related branches of diplomacy, business tactics, military affairs, and political theory, is alien to the skeptical scientific spirit and subversive of it (Ibid., p. 20).

Indeed, Veblen's skepticism regarding political theory as it existed in his own day is, perhaps, more extreme than his rejection of the received economic theoretical wisdom of his time for it is at best merely a form of pragmatic knowledge, not a kind of scientific inquiry. As he (Ibid., p. 19) put it:

> Pragmatism creates nothing but maxims of expedient conduct. Science creates nothing but theories. It knows nothing of policy or utility, of better or worse. None of all that is comprised in what is to-day accounted scientific knowledge. Wisdom and proficiency of the pragmatic sort does not contribute to the advance of a knowledge of fact. It has only an incidental bearing on scientific research, and its bearing is chiefly that of inhibition and misdirection. Wherever canons of expediency are intruded into or are attempted to be incorporated in the inquiry, the consequence is an unhappy one for science, however happy it may be for some other purpose extraneous to science. The mental attitude of worldly wisdom is at cross-purposes with the disinterested scientific spirit, and the pursuit of it induces an intellectual bias that is incompatible with scientific insight. Its intellectual output is a body of shrewd rules of conduct, in great part designed to take advantage of human infirmity.

Veblen (Ibid., p. 21) continues his analysis of those disciplines which in his day still resisted the blandishments of science:

> The reasoning in these fields turns about questions of personal advantage of one kind or another, and the merits of the claims canvassed in these discussions are decided on grounds of authenticity. Personal claims make up the subject of the inquiry, and these claims are construed and decided in terms of precedent and choice, use and wont, prescriptive authority, and the like. The higher reaches of generalization in these pragmatic inquiries are of the nature of deductions from authentic tradition and the training in this class of reasoning gives discrimination in respect of authenticity and expediency. The resulting habit of mind is a bias for substituting dialectical distinctions and decisions *de jure* in the place of explanations *de facto*. The so-called "sciences" associated with these pragmatic disciplines, such as jurisprudence, political science, and the like, are a taxonomy of credenda.

Veblen's objections to the political theory of his day are either that it is infected with Hegelianism with its emphasis on the fulfillment of reason in history, or that it is contaminated with the crudely pragmatic and utilitarian aims of vested interests, or that it contains heavy residues of natural law with its focus on final cause guiding the development of both individuals and groups toward their appointed *telos* or end. All these, in Veblen's view, are manifestations of the non-scientific status, that is, predarwinian state of political science as a discipline. All but the most arbitrary reading of his essay on the place of science in modern civilization indicates that until the study of politics becomes a genuine political science, it will have little predictive or explanatory power.[3] One need only look at the failure of specialists in Soviet politics, kremlinology and strategic studies to anticipate recent changes in Eastern Europe to recognize that Veblen's skepticism regarding the "scientific" status of political inquiry was warranted then and now.

This is not to suggest, however, that he thought it impossible to predict the course of future political events including revolution itself; rather, it was that he viewed science as having made only slight inroads into the study of politics. His view of the future of the politics of industrial societies was, therefore, several-sided and, in the final analysis, open-ended.

## The Future of Industrial Society

What follows is a projection of his views on the future course of events in the West for there are four alternative paths which can be derived from his basic mode of analysis.[4] First, the industrial system will be controlled by a Soviet of engineers and technicians through the strategy of the general strike. This strike might succeed if it were supported by the labor force whose favor would be gathered through persuasion, publicity, and a growing realization that the institutions of business enterprise are incompatible with the welfare of the common man. This course of action and its outcome seemed unlikely to Veblen. It was atypical of his projection and was discussed at length in only one of his basic works. Therefore, it should play a secondary role in any balanced analysis of his social and political ideas.[5]

A second view of the future he held is one in which the cumulative impact of science and technology has "technologized" the values of the masses, the system of business enterprise has decayed, and an "industrial republic" with utopian features has become the new order.[6] If and when this industrial republic emerges, it will be one in which the present institutions of the political economy wither away and are replaced by organizational structures whose mechanisms of control are essentially industrial, although Veblen was not specific about this.

Veblen never closely defined his "industrial republic" which suggests that it had vaguely utopian structures; nevertheless, his occasional references to the desirability of "an ungraded commonwealth of masterless men" lead to the conclusion that even though the Darwinian evolutionary process can arrive at no predesignated end, this is what Veblen would enact if he were sovereign. In Veblen's view such ends are inextricably bound up with the mass fostering and achievement of "idle curiosity" (critical intelligence), the "parental bent" (altruism), and the "instinct of workmanship" (industrial proficiency). What thus lies ahead in this industrial republic is the large scale realization of the values and ethos of science, community and craftsmanship.

Third, although Veblen did not quite project his analysis in this way, his mode of analysis could be used to emphasize the cumulative impact of science and technology on the values and behavior of the middle class. Part of the middle class could become infected with the spirit of scientific inquiry, or could achieve the "rationality" fostered by interaction with the machine process. The direction the middle class could take would depend upon occupational discipline, whether scientific or technological in nature. The fostering of these values in the psyche of the middle class would create skepticism about the virtues of the system of business enterprise. This might usher in an era of piecemeal change which could erode the more cumbersome institutional restraints which inhibit industrial productivity. Consequently, part of the middle class might join with the industrial working class in demanding structural change which would result in some redistribution of power and wealth. It must be kept in mind that this course of development is never explicitly stated for Veblen was skeptical about incremental political and economic reform carried out under the auspices of the middle class.

Finally, in dynastic States such as Imperial Germany and Japan, which were characterized by conservative, authoritarian, and militaristic institutions and values, the recently introduced machine culture would, in the long run, prove incompatible with both the system of business enterprise and autocratic dynasticism. Veblen thus predicted a future German and Japanese State fusing the advantages of science and technology with the autocratic and militaristic institutions of the old order into something resembling the corporate States of Hitler and Tojo. In the long run the industrial economy was incompatible with both business enterprise and the predatory dynastic State. In the short run, however, the machine process could exist in a system in which the "feudalistic animus of fealty and subservience" has been rejuvenated.

In *The Theory of Business Enterprise* (1904) Veblen argued that human values resulting from interaction with the machine process lead to skepticism or even contempt for the ceremonial values of the predatory or "kept" class. In short, machine technology in the industrial process generates its own value system in the minds of those who work around it. This value system is characterized by secularism, equalitarianism, reasoning in a matter-of-fact way from cause to effect, and rejection of the more traditional forms of authority and its privileges. In Veblen's scheme, it is the technological values generated by the machine process which eat like a corrosive acid into the institutional vitals of the present order. As he (Veblen 1964b, p. 201) put it:

> There is, indeed, a curiously pervasive concomitance, in point of time, place and race, between the modern machine technology, the material sciences, religious skepticism and the spirit of insubordination that makes the substance of what are called free or popular institutions.

The values resulting from the conditioning of the machine process are to be found in purest form among industrial workers whose occupations demand constant interaction with machine technology. But Veblen believed that these technological values and the ethos of science could spread to other social strata in the calculable future. The question that remained to be answered was, how far and how fast since this involved the degree of institutional resistance to the spread of such values? Also, a major variable in calculating the future was the degree of likelihood of the resurgence of atavistic traits among the masses such as superpatriotism and status emulation as well as the infusion of new life into the predatory elements in American business culture.

The long range perspective Veblen held in his more optimistic moods was that of movement toward the industrial republic as a consequence of the progression of science and technology and the technological value system this process generates among the masses. But the triumph of the New Order would long remain in doubt due to the power of the vested interests, the rigidity of established institutions, and the ambivalence of human nature. These kept open the possibility of a reversion to barbarism, or an era of conservative economic stagnation, perhaps like the one through which we passed in the last years of the Reagan-Bush era. Thus, any balanced view of Veblen's political ideas would emphasize his dislike of traditional and modern authoritarianism, but it would also include his realization that "imbecile" institutions are capable of revival if new life is breathed into them during periods of social stress and tension.

In short, Veblen's ideal society, the industrial republic, was one possibility but so was the reversion to authoritarian militarism and barbarism which Veblen predicted might occur in totalitarian Germany and Japan long before it actually did. The industrial republic was one possible future course of social and political development but so was the Corporate State of Hitler and Tojo. Particularly was this true in those countries that lacked experience with representative government and whose socio-political institutions had not yet adjusted to the logic of science and the machine process.

While it was conceivable that the spread of the scientific ethos and the machine process would change middle class values to the point where the middle class would demand economic reform through political action, Veblen knew that leisure class values and aspirations were shared by the rest of society including industrial workers most under the influence of the machine process. In short, the reservoir from which most of capitalist society drew its values was the system of property relations and the practices of pecuniary and status emulation. Thus the rest of society looked to the leisure class and its ethic for the derivation and legitimation of their values. Although interaction with the machine process made industrial workers partially immune to leisure class values, this was less true among small property owners and white collar workers who were often far removed from machine technology and scientific inquiry. So leisure class values still prevailed in the middle class making it relatively satisfied with the status quo, and unlikely to undertake political reform aimed against the existing system of business enterprise. Veblen was particularly critical in his last writings about the success of salesmanship, advertising, and sharp business practice in polluting the values of those groups in society about whom he had once been more optimistic. He believed that the American Federation of Labor, for example, was almost indistinguishable from the corporate vested interests because of its commercial values and pecuniary behavior (Veblen 1967, chapter 13).

## Conclusion

The corpus of Veblen's work can be broken into empirical, normative and prudential components, that is, the *is*, the *ought* and the what *can be*, the usual epistemological divisions found in the realm of political theory. Veblen, of course, has been faulted in all three areas by his critics, but from my perspective, and probably Tool's, the weakest point of his analysis is the prudential. This is, of course, in the Deweyan sense the means—ends relationship writ large; and it compels Veblen's interpreters to ask how, or if, he really intended to pursue implementation of his larger vision for social transformation and political reconstruction? More specifically, did he have a genuine sense of political praxis in wanting to influence events through his writing and activism, or was he a detached cynic with no real sense of commitment to progressive change?

Depending on the prevailing mood of his work and the domestic and international situation, Veblen can thus be interpreted as 1) a radical conservative who doubts that society will ever rid itself in the calculable future of the ruling elites and ceremonialism that cause society to stagnate; 2) a leftist proponent of a utopian political economy that will effectively serve the life process of mankind by abolishing the institutional restraints that inhibit maximum use of the industrial economy;[7] 3) an occasional but faltering proponent of incrementalism who was aware of the possibility of a middle way between reaction and radical change.

Why, in the Veblenian analysis, is change not progressive in a linear sense and what are his reasons for predicting the reversibility, or at least retardation, of even what appear to be successful instrumentally adaptive adjustments on the part of the community? Veblen's belief was that the human species had ceremonially encrusted minds in that the predatory traits such as force, exploit and cunning, although seemingly submerged, might undergo an institutional resurgence.

But the concept and, indeed, the possibility of "revolution" indicates not merely an intellectual cleansing of nostrils, but a fundamental change in social relationships, a liquidation of existing cultural values and a basic reorganization of the present political economy. To what extent, then, did Veblen actually share the ideals and the illusions of contemporary utopians like Edward Bellamy (Tilman 1985) and, later, political revolutionaries such as Lenin and Trotsky? The corpus of his writing suggests ambiguity on his part. His "generic ends of life" would be better served if the existing cultural and institutional straitjacket shed its skin. But as both a historian and cultural anthropologist he knew of too many instances in which the "peaceful" traits had become contaminated by their opposite, the "predatory" traits, to be uncritical of the possibilities for success of schemes for social reconstruction which rested on the creation of a new humankind. Also, Veblen believed that the permeation of Western culture with the ethos of science was a slow and apparently reversible process, a fact which many of his contemporaries failed to grasp. Indeed, the potential of science for its own contamination, subordination, emulation and mystification did not escape his attention.

Some of Veblen's interpreters have understood him as a "radical conservative", that is, as an intellectual who favored large-scale structural changes in Western societies and political economies, yet believed these changes were unlikely to occur and would fail to achieve desirable results even if they did. The view that atavistic continuities will resurface, even when they appear to have been eradicated, is a plausible reading of parts of Veblen's work. The indeterminacy of his projections of the future thus make it possible to link him both with cultural pessimists like Hanna Arendt and those of a more optimistic bent such as Erich Fromm and John Dewey. Veblen, like Marc Tool, was not Oscar Wilde's cynic who knows the price of everything and the value of nothing, but neither was he a pollyanna who expects to enter the land of milk and honey.

## Notes

1. The author thanks Paul Goldstene, Ruth Porter-Tilman and Cathy Peterson for commenting on earlier drafts of the manuscript. The usual disclaimers hold. He also thanks Frank Genovese, Editor of the *American Journal of Economics and Sociology* for permission to reprint part of "Thorstein Veblen: Incrementalist and Utopian," (Tilman 1973).

2. Veblen's use of the terms "pragmatic" and "pragmatism" in this context means essentially "self-interested," "expedient" or having to do with "worldly wisdom" and should not be confused with his one-time colleague John Dewey's philosophy of "instrumentalism."

3. Although Veblen suggests that scientific method is more likely to produce desirable results in the social sciences than other approaches, he also recognizes its moral and cultural limitations.

> But while the scientist's spirit and his achievements stir an unqualified admiration in modern men, and while his discoveries carry conviction as nothing else does, it does not follow that the manner of man which this quest of knowledges produces or requires comes near answering to the current ideal of manhood, or that his conclusions are felt to be as good and beautiful as they are true. The ideal man, and the ideal of human life, even in the apprehension of those who most rejoice in the advances of science is neither the finikin skeptic in the laboratory nor the animated slide-rule. The quest of science is relatively new . . . . The normal man, such as his inheritance has made him, has therefore good cause to be restive under its dominion (Veblen 1991, p. 30).

4. What follows is treated is more detail in Rick Tilman, "Veblen's Ideal Political Economy and Its Critics," (1972) and "Thorstein Veblen: Incrementalist or Utopian," (1973). Also, see the author's *Thorstein Veblen and His Critics, 1891-1963: Conservative, Liberal and Radical Perspectives* (1992).

5. "Technocratic elitism" or "Technocratic managerialism" is a substantial part of the mistaken interpretation offered by Daniel Bell (1963, p. 638); David Riesman, *Thorstein Veblen: A Critical Interpretation* (1953) p. 7; Suzanne Keller, *Beyond the Ruling Class* (1963) p. 124; Lev Dobriansky, *Veblenism A New Critique* (1957) p. 389. For a more recent critique of the technocratic elitist perspective and its critics as well as a new interpretation of Veblen on this subject see Malcolm Rutherford, "Veblen and the Problem of Engineers," (1992).

6. In Veblen's scheme, machine technology fosters an environment in which the spirit of scientific inquiry can flourish; thus technological and scientific values are roughly identical in terms of their impact on the individual. Both the industrial worker and the scientist may acquire a skeptical, matter-of-fact, materialist perspective. The core of Veblen's theory of social and economic change is contained in his belief that technology is an important locus of value and that it is a primary determinant of institutional adaptation and change. The human material involved has persisting qualities which are predatory (the "sporting" instinct and the propensity toward gain) or peaceful (the instinct of workmanship and the parental bent). What causes human behavior to differ in various societies depends, therefore, on the dynamism of its technology, the rigidity of its institutional fabric, and, thus, the adaptability of its population. On these points, see Clarence Ayres, *The Industrial Economy* (1952) pp. 305-315, and Marc Tool, *The Discretionary Economy* (1979).

7. Glimpses of Veblen's utopia are contained in the following of his writings; "Some Neglected Points in the Theory of Socialism," *Annals of the American Academy of Political and Social Science*, 2 (1892) pp. 387-408. "Christian Morals and the Competitive System" in *Essays in Our Changing Order* (1930) pp. 200-218. *An Inquiry into the Nature of Peace* (1964b), *The Engineers and the Price System* (1963). *The Theory of Business Enterprise* (1995) chs 9 & 10.

## REFERENCES

Albelda, R. 1992. "Whose Values, Which Families?" *Dollars and Sense* No. 182 (December):6-9.

Adams, John. 1980. *Institutional Economics: Essays in Honor of Allan G. Gruchy* (Boston: Martinus Nijhoff Publishing).

Aldous, J., and Dumond. W. 1991. "Family Policy in the 1980s: Controversy and Consensus," in A. Booth, ed. *Contemporary Families: Looking Forward, Looking Back* (Minneapolis, MN: National Council on Family Relations).

Appadurai, Arjun. 1986. "Introduction: Commodities and the Politics of Value," in *The Social Life of Things* edited by Arjun Appadurai (Cambridge: Cambridge University Press).

Appleby, Joyce. 1979. *Economic Theory and Ideology in the Seventeenth Century* (Princeton: Princeton University Press).

Atkinson, Glen. 1990. "Book Review," *Journal of Economic Issues* 24 (March):271-275.

Atkinson, Glen. 1987. "Instrumentalism and Economic Policy: The Quest for Reasonable Value," *Journal of Economic Issues* 21 (March):189-202.

Atkinson, Glen. 1983. "Political Economy: Public Choice or Collective Action?" *Journal of Economic Issues* 17 (December):1057-65.

Atkinson, Glen, and Mike Reed. 1991. "Rejoinder," *Journal of Economic Issues* 25 (December):1136-1140.

Atkinson, Glen, and Mike Reed. 1990. "Institutional Adjustment, Instrumental Efficiency, and Reasonable Value," *Journal of Economic Issues* 24 (December):1095-1107.

Averitt, Robert T. 1968. *The Dual Economy* (New York: W. W. Norton).

Ayres, Clarence E. 1967. "Ideological Responsibility," *Journal of Economic Issues* 1 (June):3-11.

Ayres, Clarence E. 1964. "The Legacy of Thorstein Veblen," in *Institutional Economics: Veblen, Commons, and Mitchell Reconsidered* (Berkeley: University of California Press).

Ayres, Clarence E. 1961. *Toward a Reasonable Society* (Austin: University of Texas Press).

Ayres, Clarence E. 1952. *The Industrial Economy* (Boston: Houghton Mifflin).

Ayres, Clarence E. 1950. "Value and Welfare," Class notes taken by Gladys Foster at The University of Texas, Spring 1950.

Ayres, Clarence E. 1949. "Instrumental Economics," *The New Republic* 121 (17 October):18-20.

Ayres, Clarence E. 1944. *The Theory of Economic Progress* (Chapel Hill: The University of North Carolina Press). Reprint 1978 (Kalamazoo, Michigan: New Issues Press).

Battista, Clare and Matthew Allison. 1994. "The Political Economy of Literary Production and Professional Authorship," unpublished working paper.

Baumol, W.J. and J.G. Sidak. 1994. *Toward Competition in Local Telephony* (Cambridge MA and Washington DC. MIT Press and American Enterprise Institute).

Becker, Carl. 1932. *The Heavenly City of the Eighteenth Century Philosophers* (New Haven: Yale University Press).

Bell, Daniel. 1963. "Veblen and the New Class," *American Scholar*, 32 (Autumn):616-638.

Best, Steven, and Douglas Kellner. 1991. *Postmodern Theory: Critical Interrogations* (New York: Guilford Publications).

Bhaskar, Roy. 1989. *Reclaiming Reality* (London: Verso).

Blecker, Robert A. 1992. *Beyond the Twin Deficits* (Armonk, NY: M.E. Sharpe).

Block, Fred. 1990. *Postindustrial Possibilities: A Critique of Economic Discourse* (Berkeley: University of California Press).

Bluestone, Barry and Bennett Harrison. 1982. *The Deindustrialization of America* (New York: Basic Books).

Bolter, W.G. 1994. "Assessing Facilities Competition in Telecommunications: A Perspective of Major Issues from U.S. Experience." Paper presented at Workshop on Telecommunications Infrastructure Competition: Issues and Policies, OECD, Athens, Greece, Sept. 20, 1994.

Bordo, Susan. 1987. *The Flight to Objectivity: Essays on Cartesianism and Culture* (Albany: State University of New York Press).

Bordo, Susan. 1990. "Feminism, Postmodernism, and Gender-Scepticism," in *Feminism/Postmodernism*, edited by Linda Nicholson (New York: Routledge).

Boulding, Kenneth E. 1981. *Evolutionary Economics* (Beverly Hills: Sage Publications).

Bowles, Samuel, David M. Gordon, and Thomas E. Weisskopf. 1990. *After the Waste Land* (Armonk, NY: M.E. Sharpe).

Breit, William, and William P. Culberston, Jr. 1976. *Science and Ceremony: The Institutional Economics of C. E. Ayres* (Austin: University of Texas Press).

Bronowski, Jacob. 1965. *Science and Human Values* (New York: Harper and Row).

Brown, Douglas. 1994. "Radical Institutionalism and Postmodern Feminist

Theory," in *The Economic Status of Women Under Capitalism* edited by Douglas Brown and Janice Peterson (Aldershot: Edward Elgar Publishing, Ltd).

Brown, Douglas. 1993. "The Production of Social Heterogeneity in Postmodern Capitalism," paper presented at the annual meeting of the Association for Social Economics, Anaheim, CA.

Brown, Douglas. 1992. "Doing Social Economics in a Postmodern World," *Review of Social Economy* 50 (Winter):383-403.

Brown, Douglas. 1991. "An Institutionalist Look at Postmodernism," *Journal of Economic Issues* 25 (December):1089-1104.

Bruchey, Stuart. 1990. *Enterprise* (Cambridge, MA: Harvard University Press).

Burgess, E., and H.J. Locke. 1945. *The Family From Institution to Companionship* (New York: American Book).

Burgess, E. 1926. "The Family as a Unity of Interacting Personalities," *The Family* VII:1.

Bush, Paul D. 1993. "The Methodology of Institutional Economics: A Pragmatic Instrumentalist Perspective," in *Institutional Economics: Theory, Method, Policy* edited by Marc R. Tool (Boston: Kluwer Academic Publishers).

Bush, Paul D. 1991. "Reflections on the Twenty-fifth Anniversary of AFEE: Philosophical and Methodological Issues in Institutional Economics," *Journal of Economic Issues* 25 (June):321-346.

Bush, Paul D. 1989. "The Concept of 'Progressive' Institutional Change and Its Implications for Economic Policy Formation," *Journal of Economic Issues* 23 (June):455-464.

Bush, Paul D. 1987. "The Theory of Institutional Change," *Journal of Economic Issues* 21 (September):1075-1116.

Bush, Paul D. 1986. "On the Concept of Ceremonial Encapsulation," *The Review of Institutional Thought* 3 (December):25-45.

Bush, Paul D., William M. Dugger, F. Gregory Hayden, Baldwin Ranson, and Rick Tilman. 1980. "Five Reviews of Marc R. Tool's *Discretionary Economy*," *Journal of Economic Issues* 14 (September):759-73.

Caldwell, Bruce. 1984. *Appraisal and Criticism in Economics* (Boston: Allen and Unwin).

Caldwell, Bruce. 1982. *Beyond Positivism* (London: George Allen & Unwin).

Clark, Charles M. A. 1993. "Spontaneous Order Versus Instituted Process: The Market as Cause and Effect," *Journal of Economic Issues* 27 (June):373-85.

Clark, Charles M. A. 1992b. "An Institutionalist Critique of Sraffian Economics" *Journal of Economic Issues* 26 (June):457-468.

Clark, Charles M. A. 1992a. *Economic Theory and Natural Philosophy* (Aldershot, U.K.: Edward Elgar).
Clark, Charles M. A. 1991. "Naturalism in Economic Theory: The Use of 'State of Nature' Explanations in the History of Economic Thought" in *Perspectives on the History of Economic Thought Vol. VI*, edited by William J Barber. (Aldershot, U.K.: Edward Elgar).
Coats, A. W., R. A. Gonce, James D. Shaffer, and Gary E. Francis. 1974. "Four Reviews of Allan G. Gruchy's *Contemporary Economic Thought: The Contribution of Neo-Institutional Economics*," *Journal of Economic Issues* 7 (September):597-615.
Commission on the Skills of the American Workforce. 1990. *America's Choice: High Skills or Low Wages* (Rochester, NY: National Center on Education and the Economy).
Committee on New American Realities. 1990. *Preparing for Change: Workforce Excellence in a Turbulent Economy* (Washington, DC: National Planning Association).
Commons, John R. 1961 [1934]. *Institutional Economics: Its Place in Political Economy* (Madison, Wisconsin: The University of Wisconsin Press).
Commons, John R. 1950. *The Economics of Collective Action* (Madison: The University of Wisconsin Press).
Communications Workers of America. 1992. "State Telephone Regulatory Report," *Information Industry Report*, Washington DC, Jan. 30, 1992.
Competitiveness Policy Council. 1992a. *Building a Competitive America* (Washington, DC: U.S. Government Printing Office).
Competitiveness Policy Council. 1992b. News Release, March 1.
Competitiveness Policy Council. 1992c. News Release, April 20.
Copleston, Frederick. 1979. *On the History of Philosophy and Other Essays* (New York: Barnes and Noble Books).
Council on Competitiveness. 1987. *America's Competitive Crisis: Confronting The New Reality* (Washington, DC: Council on Competitiveness).
Cuomo Commission on Competitiveness. 1992. *America's Agenda: Rebuilding Economic Strength* (Armonk, NY: M.E. Sharpe).
Cuomo Commission on Competitiveness. 1988. *The Cuomo Commission Report* (New York: Simon and Schuster).
Davis, John B. 1989. "Axiomatic General Equilibrium Theory and Referentiality," *Journal of Post Keynesian Economics* 11 (Spring):424-38.
Deckard, B.S. 1983. *The Women's Movement* (New York: Harper & Row).
Dertouzos, Michael L., Richard K. Lester, Robert M. Solow, and the MIT Commission on Industrial Productivity. 1989. *Made in America* (Cambridge, MA: MIT Press).
Dewey, John. 1963. *Liberalism and Social Action* (New York: Capricorn

Press).
Dewey, John. 1958. *Experience and Nature* (New York: Dover Publications).
Dewey, John. 1957. *Human Nature and Conduct* (New York: Modern Library).
Dewey, John. 1950. *Reconstruction in Philosophy* (New York: New American Library, A Mentor Book).
Dewey, John. 1946. *The Problems of Men* (New York: Philosophical Library).
Dewey, John. 1939a. *Intelligence in the Modern World* edited by Joseph Ratner (New York: Random House).
Dewey, John. 1939b. *Theory of Valuation* (Chicago: University of Chicago Press).
Dewey, John. 1938. *Logic: The Theory of Inquiry* (New York: Henry Holt); alternatively, John Dewey. 1986. *The Later Works: 1925-53*, Vol. 12: 1938, Jo Ann Boydston, ed., (Carbondale: Southern Illinois University Press).
Dewey, John. 1929. *The Quest for Certainty* (New York: G.P. Putnam's Sons); alternatively, John Dewey. 1984. *The Later Works, 1925-1953: Vol. 4: 1929*, Jo Ann Boydston, ed., (Carbondale: Southern Illinois University Press).
Dicken, Peter. 1992. *Global Shift: The Internationalization of Economic Activity* Second Edition (New York: Guilford Publications).
Diesing, Paul. 1991. *How Does Social Science Work? Reflections on Practice* (Pittsburg: University of Pittsburg Press).
Dobriansky, Lev. 1957. *Veblenism: A New Critique* (Washington, D.C.: Public Affairs Press).
Dorfman, Joseph, et al., ed. 1963. *Institutional Economics* (Berkeley: University of California Press).
Dorfman, Joseph. 1934. *Thorstein Veblen and His America* (New York: The Viking Press).
Douglas, Mary. 1986. *How Institutions Think* (Syracuse, NY: Syracuse University Press).
Dowd, Douglas F., ed. 1958. *Thorstein Veblen: A Critical Reappraisal* (Ithaca: Cornell University Press).
Dugger, William M. 1993. "Beyond Technology to Democracy: The Tool Legacy in Institutionalism." Manuscript.
Dugger, William. 1990. "The New Institutionalism: New But Not Institutionalist," *Journal of Economic Issues* 24 (June):423-31.
Dugger, William M. 1989a. *Corporate Hegemony* (Westport CT: Greenwood Press).
Dugger, William M. Ed. 1989b. *Radical Institutionalism*. (New York: Greenwood Press).

Dugger, William M. 1989c. "Radical Institutionalism: Basic Concepts," in *Radical Institutionalism: Contemporary Voices*, edited by William Dugger, (New York: Greenwood Press).

Dugger, William M. 1989d. "Instituted Process and Enabling Myth: The Two Faces of the Market," *Journal of Economic Issues* 23 (June):607-16.

Dugger, William M. 1988. "A Research Agenda for Institutional Economics." *Journal of Economic Issues* 22 (December):983-1002.

Dugger, William M. 1984. *An Alternative to Economic Retrenchment* (New York: Petrocelli Books).

Dugger, William M. 1983. "The Transactional Cost Analysis of Oliver E. Williamson: A New Synthesis?" *Journal of Economic Issues* 17 (March):95-114.

Dugger, William M. 1980. "Power: An Institutional Framework of Analysis," *Journal of Economic Issues* 14 (December):897-907.

Dugger, William M. and William Waller, editors. 1992. *The Stratified State: Radical Institutionalist Theories of Participation and Duality* (Armonk, NY: M.E. Sharpe, Inc).

Economic Strategy Institute. 1992. *An Economic Strategy for America* (Washington, DC: Economic Strategy Institute).

Economic Strategy Institute. 1990. *Looking to the Twenty-first Century* (Washington, DC: Economic Strategy Institute).

Edgell, Stephen, and Jules Townshend. 1991. "John Hobson, Thorstein Veblen and the Phenomenon of Imperialism," A Paper Presented at the WSSA Conference, April 25-27, Reno, Nevada.

Eggertsson, Thrainn. 1990. *Economic Behavior and Institutions* (Cambridge: Cambridge University Press).

Feher, Ferenc, and Agnes Heller. 1988. *The Postmodern Political Condition* (New York: Columbia University Press).

Ferguson, Thomas. 1984. "From Normalcy to New Deal," *Industrial Organization* 38 (Winter):41-94.

Feynman, Richard P. 1985. *Surely You're Joking Mr. Feynman: Adventures of a Curious Character* (New York: W. W. Norton).

Field, Alexander J. 1979. "On the Explanation of Rules Using Rational Choice Models," *Journal of Economic Issues* 13 (March):49-72.

Flower, Elizabeth, and Murray G. Murphey. 1977. *A History of Philosophy in America* (New York: Capricorn Books).

Foster, Gladys P. 1994. "The Obsession with Deficits in the US in the 1990s," *Economies et Societies*, edited by Alain Parguez. Series *Money and Production* 9 (Janvier-Février):189-206.

Foster, Gladys P. 1991a. "The Compatibility of Keynes's Ideas With Institutionalist Philosophy," *Journal of Economic Issues* 25 (June):561-68.

Foster, Gladys P. 1991b. "Cultural Relativism and the Theory of Value,"

*American Journal of Economics and Sociology* 50 (July):257-67.
Foster, J. Fagg. 1981. "The Papers of J. Fagg Foster," *Journal of Economic Issues* 15 (December):857-1012.
Foster, J. Fagg. 1948. "Value and Its Determinants," Transcript of lectures taped at the University of Denver, 1948. In archives, Penrose Library, University of Denver.
Foucault, Michel. 1986. "Of Other Spaces," *Diacritics* 16 (Spring):22-26.
Foucault, Michel. 1980. *Power/Knowledge*, edited by Colin Gordon (New York: Pantheon).
Foucault, Michel. 1971. *The Order of Things: An Archaeology of the Human Sciences* (New York: Pantheon Books).
Fox-Genovese, Elizabeth. 1991. *Feminism Without Illusions: A Critique of Individualism* (Chapel Hill: The University of North Carolina Press).
Fraser, Nancy, and Linda Nicholson. 1988. "Social Criticism without Philosophy: An Encounter between Feminism and Postmodernism," in *Universal Abandon: The Politics of Postmodernism*, edited by Andrew Ross, (Minneapolis: University of Minnesota Press).
Friedman, Milton. 1953. "The Methodology of Positive Economics," in *Essays in Positive Economics* (Chicago: University of Chicago Press).
Galbraith, John Kenneth. 1987. *Economics in Perspective* (Boston: Houghton Mifflin Company).
Galbraith, John Kenneth. 1958. *The Affluent Society* (Boston: Houghton Mifflin Company).
Gambs, John. 1980. "Allan Gruchy and the Association for Evolutionary Economics," in *Institutional Economics: Essays in Honor of Allan G. Gruchy* edited by John Adams (Boston: Martinus Nijhoff Publishing).
Glaeser, M.G. 1939. "Those TVA Joint Costs," *Public Utilities Fortnightly* 24:259-733.
Gordon, Wendell. 1992. "The Implication of 'Process,'" *Journal of Economic Issues* 26 (September):891-899.
Gordon, Wendell. 1990. "The Role of Tool's Social Value Principle," *Journal of Economic Issues* 24 (September):879-86.
Gordon, Wendell. 1984. "The Role of Institutional Economics," *Journal of Economic Issues* 18 (June):369-81.
Gordon, Wendell. 1980. *Institutional Economics* (Austin: University of Texas Press).
Gordon, Wendell, and John Adams. 1989. *Economics as Social Science: An Evolutionary Approach* (Riverdale, Maryland: The Riverdale Company).
Graham, Otis L. 1992. *Losing Time: The Industrial Policy Debate* (Cambridge, MA: Harvard University Press).
Gruchy, Allan G. 1987. *The Reconstruction of Economics: An Analysis of the Fundamentals of Institutional Analysis* (New York: Greenwood Press).

Gruchy, Allan G. 1972. *Contemporary Economic Thought: The Contributions of Neo-Institutional Economics* (Clifton, N.J.: Augustus M. Kelley).

Gruchy, Allan G. 1969. "Neoinstitutionalism and the Economics of Dissent," *Journal of Economic Issues* 3 (March):3-17.

Gruchy, Allan G. 1947. *Modern Economic Thought: The American Contribution* (New York: Prentice-Hall).

Hahn, Frank. 1991. "The Next Hundred Years," *The Economic Journal* 101 (January):47-50.

Hamilton, David. 1991a. "Is Institutional Economics Really 'Root and Branch' Economics?" *Journal of Economic Issues* 25 (March):179-86.

Hamilton David. 1991b. "Ceremonialism as the Dramatization of Prosaic Technology: Who Did Invent the Coup de Poing?" *Journal of Economic Issues* 25 (June):551-60.

Hamilton, David. 1986. "Technology and Institutions are Neither," *Journal of Economic Issues* 20 (June):525-532.

Hamilton, David. 1973. *Evolutionary Economics* (Albuquerque: University of New Mexico Press).

Hamilton, David. 1953. *Newtonian Classicism and Darwinian Institutionalism* (Albuquerque: University of New Mexico Press).

Harding, Sandra. 1986. *The Science Question in Feminism* (Ithaca: Cornell University Press).

Harrison, Bennett and Barry Bluestone. 1988. *The Great U-Turn* (New York: Basic Books).

Hartsock, Nancy. 1990. "Foucault on Power: A Theory for Women?" in *Feminism/Postmodernism*, edited by Linda Nicholson (New York: Routledge).

Harvey, David. 1991. "Flexibility: Threat or Opportunity," *Socialist Review* 21 (January):65-78.

Harvey, David. 1989. *The Condition of Postmodernity: An Enquiry into the Origins of Cultural Change* (Cambridge, Mass: Basil Blackwell).

Hassan, Ihab. 1987. *The Postmodern Turn: Essays in Postmodern Theory and Culture* (Columbus: Ohio State University Press).

Hayden, F. Gregory. 1989. "Institutionalism for What: To Understand Inevitable Progress or for Policy Relevance?" *Journal of Economic Issues* 23 (June):633-45.

Hayek, F.A. 1944. *The Road To Serfdom* (Chicago: University of Chicago).

Hayes, Robert H. and William J. Abernathy. 1980. "Managing Our Way to Economic Decline," *Harvard Business Review* 58 (July-August):67-77.

Heckscher, Charles C. 1988. *The New Unionism* (New York: Basic Books).

Heilbroner, Robert L. 1988. *Behind the Veil of Economics* (New York: Norton).

Heilbroner, Robert L. 1970. *The Worldly Philosophers* (New York: Simon and Schuster).

Hickerson, Steven R. 1987. "Instrumental Valuation: The Normative Compass of Institutional Economics," *Journal of Economic Issues* 21 (September):1117-1143.

Hill, Lewis E. and Donald W. Owen. 1984. "The Instrumental Philosophy of History and the Institutionalist Theory of Normative Value," *Journal of Economic Issues* 18 (June):581-587.

Hirsch, Abraham, and Neil di Marchi. 1990. *Milton Friedman: Economics in Theory and Practice* (Ann Arbor: The University of Michigan Press).

Hobson, John A. 1938. *Imperialism* (London: Allen and Unwin).

Hochschild, A. R., and A. Machung. 1989. *The Second Shift: Working Parents and the Revolution at Home* (New York: Viking).

Hodgson, Geoffrey M., Warren J. Samuels, and Marc R. Tool. 1994. *Elgar Companion to Institutional and Evolutionary Economics* (Aldershot: Edward Elgar).

Hoksbergen, Roland. 1994. "Postmodernism and Institutionalism: Toward a Resolution of the Debate on Relativism," *Journal of Economic Issues* 28 (September):679-713.

Horowitz, Irving L. 1961. *Philosophy, Science and the Sociology of Knowledge* (Westport, Conn.: Greenwood Press Publishers).

Huber, J., ed. 1973. *Changing Women in a Changing Society* (Chicago: University of Chicago Press).

Hutter, M. 1981. *The Changing Family: Comparative Perspectives* (New York: John Wiley & Sons).

James, William. 1908. *Pragmatism: A New Name for Some Old Ways of Thinking* (New York: Longmans Green).

Jameson, Fredric. 1991. *Postmodernism: Or the Cultural Logic of Late Capitalism* (Durham, N.C.: Duke University Press).

Jameson, Fredric. 1988. "Regarding Postmodernism—A Conversation with Fredric Jameson," in *Universal Abandon: The Politics of Postmodernism*, edited by Andrew Ross (Minneapolis: University of Minnesota Press).

Jennings, Ann. 1993a. "Feminism," in *Companion to Institutional and Evolutionary Economics* edited by Geoffery Hodgson, Warren Samuels and Marc Tool (Aldershot: Edwin Elgar Publishing, Ltd).

Jennings, Ann. 1993b. "Public of Private? Institutional Economics and Feminism," in *Beyond "Economic Man": Feminist Theory and Economics* edited by Marianne A. Ferber and Julia A. Nelson (Chicago: University of Chicago Press).

Jennings, Ann. 1992. "Not the Economy: Feminist Theory, Institutional Change, and the State," in *The Stratified State: Radical Institutionalist Theories of Participation and Duality* edited by William Dugger and William Waller (Armonk, NY: M.E. Sharpe Inc).

Jennings, Ann and William Waller. 1994. "Evolutionary Economics and Cultural Hermeneutics: Veblen, Cultural Relativism and Blind Drift," *Journal of Economic Issues* 28 (December):997-1030.

Jennings, Ann and William Waller. 1990a. "Constructions of Social Hierarchy: The Family, Gender and Power," *Journal of Economic Issues* 24 (June):623-631.

Jennings, Ann and William Waller. 1990b. "Rethinking Class and Social Stratification: Towards a Coherent Feminist Economics." A paper presented at the 1990 annual meeting of the Southern Economics Association, New Orleans, November.

Jonas, Norman. 1986. "The Hollowing of America," *Business Week* (March 3):56-58.

Junker, Louis J. 1968. "Theoretical Foundations of Neo-Institutionalism," *American Journal of Economics and Sociology* 27 (April):197-213.

Junker, Louis J. 1967. "Capital Accumulation, Savings-centered Theory and Economic Development," *Journal of Economics Issues* 1 (June):25-43.

Kalen, Horace M. 1933. "Pragmatism," in *Encyclopedia of the Social Sciences* (New York: The MacMillan Company).

Kanne, Marvin E. 1988. "John Dewey's Conception of Moral Good," *Journal of Economic Issues* 22 (December):1213-23.

Keller, Suzanne. 1963. *Beyond the Ruling Class* (New York: Random House).

Keynes, John Maynard. 1964 [1936]. *The General Theory of Employment, Interest and Money* (New York: Harcourt Brace Jovanovich).

Keynes, John Maynard. 1921. *A Treatise on Probability* (New York: Harper and Row).

Klamer, Arjo, Donald McCloskey, and Robert Solow (editors). 1988. *The Consequences of Economic Rhetoric*. (New York: Cambridge University Press).

Klein, Phillip A. 1992. "Was Ayres Overly Optimistic?" Paper presented at the Southwestern Social Science Association Annual Meeting, Austin, Texas, March 1992.

Klein, Phillip A. 1984. "Institutionalist Reflections on the Role of the Public Sector," *Journal of Economic Issues* 8 (March):45-68.

Klein, Philip A. 1983. "Reagan's Economic Policies," *Journal of Economic Issues* 17 (June):463-74.

Klein, Philip A. and Edythe S. Miller. Forthcoming. "Concepts of Value, Efficiency, and Democracy in Institutional Economics," *Journal of Economic Issues*.

Koch, Don. 1992. "Instrumentalism as a Replacement for Traditional Methods of Inquiry: Six Aspects of Dewey's Moral Philosophy." Manuscript. Department of Philosophy, Michigan State University.

Kochan, Thomas A. and Michael J. Piore. 1984. "Will the New Industrial Relations Last?" *Annals of the American Academy of Political and Social Science* 473 (May):177-189.

Kochan, Thomas A., Harry C. Katz, and Robert B. McKersie. 1986. *The Transformation of American Industrial Relations* (New York: Basic Books).

Krugman, Paul. 1990. *The Age of Diminished Expectations* (Cambridge, MA: MIT Press).

Kuhn, Thomas. 1964. *The Structure of Scientific Revolutions* (Chicago: University of Chicago Press).

Kuttner, Robert. 1991. *The End of Laissez-Faire* (New York: Alfred A. Knopf).

Kuttner, Robert. 1985. "The Poverty of Economics," *The Atlantic Monthly* 225 (February):74-84.

Lanciaux, Bernadette. 1992. "The Role of the State in the Family" in Dugger and Waller 1992.

Lash, Scott, and John Urry. 1987. *The End of Organized Capitalism* (Madison, Wisconsin: University of Wisconsin Press).

Lawrence, Robert Z. 1984. *Can America Compete?* (Washington, DC: The Brookings Institution).

Leontief, Wassily. 1982. "Letter to the Editor," *Science* 217 (July 9):104-105.

Lepley, Ray, ed. 1949. *Value: A Cooperative Inquiry* (New York: Columbia University Press).

Levitan, S.A. and R. Belous. 1981. *What's Happening to the American Family* (Baltimore: John's Hopkins University Press).

Lewis, Margaret and David Sebberson. undated. "The Rhetoric of the Rhetoric of Economics." unpublished manuscript.

Lewis, Margaret and David Sebberson. 1992. "Why McCloskey's Rhetoric is Not Feminist," A paper presented at the International Association for Feminist Economics, Washington, D.C., July.

Liebhafsky, E.E. 1993. "The Influence of Charles Sanders Peirce on Institutional Economics," *Journal of Economic Issues* 27 (September):741-754.

Livingston, John C. 1981. "Private Vice, Public Virtues," *The Review of Institutional Thought* I (December):9-16.

Livingston, John C. 1979. *Fair Game? Inequality and Affirmative Action* (San Francisco: W. H. Freeman and Company).

Livingston, John C. and Robert G. Thompson. 1963. *The Consent of the Governed* (New York: Macmillan).

Loader, Colin, Vernon Mattson, and Jeffrey Waddoups. 1991. "Thorstein Veblen and Werner Sombart on the Jews," A Paper Presented at the WSSA Conference, April 25-27, 1991, Reno, Nevada.

Loewen, James W. 1992. "The Truth about the First Thanksgiving," *Monthly*

*Review* 44 (November):12-32.

Lowe, Adolph. 1988. *Has Freedom A Future?* (New York: Praeger).

Lowe, Adolph. 1981. "Is Value Still a Problem?" in *Essays in Political Economics: Public Control in a Democratic Society* by Adolph Lowe, edited by Allen Oakley (Washington Square, New York: New York University Press).

Lowe, Adolph. 1967. "The Normative Roots of Economic Value" in *Human Values and Economic Policy* edited by S. Hook (New York: New York University Press).

Lower, Milton D. 1987. "The Concept of Technology Within the Institutionalist Perspective," *Journal of Economic Issues* 21 (September):1147-76.

Lutz, Mark A. 1985. "Pragmatism, Instrumental Value Theory and Social Economics," *Review of Social Economy* 43(2):140-172.

Lyotard, Jean-Francois. 1984. *The Postmodern Condition: A Report on Knowledge* (Minneapolis: University of Wisconsin Press).

Magaziner, Ira C. and Robert B. Reich. 1982. *Minding America's Business* (New York: Vintage Books).

Maki, Uskali. 1993. "Two Philosophies of the Rhetoric of Economics," in *Economics and Language* edited by Willie Henderson, Tony Dudley-Evans and Roger Backhouse (London: Routledge).

Mansell, R. 1993. "From Telecommunications Infrastructure to the Network Economy: Realigning the Control Structure," *Illuminating the Blindspots: Essays Honoring Dallas Smythe* edited by J. Wasko, V. Mosko, and M. Pendakur (Norwood, NJ: Ablex Publishing).

Marshall, Ray. 1993. "Commons, Veblen and Other Economists: Remarks Upon the Receipt of the Veblen-Commons Award," *Journal of Economic Issues* 27 (June):301-322.

Marshall, Ray. 1987. *Unheard Voices* (New York: Basic Books).

Marshall, Ray. 1983. *Some Trends Influencing the US Industrial Relations System* (Austin, TX: LBJ School of Public Affairs).

Marshall, Ray and Marc Tucker. 1992. *Thinking for a Living: Education and the Wealth of Nations* (New York: Basic Books).

Marx, Karl. 1967 [1867]. *Capital, Volume 1* (New York: International Publishers).

Marx, Karl. 1977. *Capital, Volume I* translated by David Fernbach, (New York: Vintage Books).

Marx, Karl. 1964. *The Economic and Philosophic Manuscripts of 1844* (New York: International Publishers).

Mayhew Anne. 1990. "Waller on Radical Institutionalism: A Comment," *Journal of Economic Issues* 24 (September):890-96.

Mayhew, Anne. 1987a. "A Critical Analysis of Tool's *Essays in Social Value*

*Theory*," a paper read at the Annual Meetings of the Association for Institutional Thought, El Paso, Texas, April.
Mayhew, Anne. 1987b. "Culture: Core Concept Under Attack," *Journal of Economics Issues* 21 (June):587-603.
Mayhew, Anne. 1981. "Ayresian Technology, Technological Reasoning, and Doomsday," *Journal of Economic Issues* 15 (June):513-20.
McCloskey, Donald N. 1990. *If Your So Smart: The Narrative of Economic Expertise* (Chicago: University of Chicago Press).
McCloskey, Donald N. 1989. "Why I Am No Longer a Positivist," *Review of Social Economy* 47 (Fall):225-38.
McCloskey, Donald N. 1985. *The Rhetoric of Economics* (Madison: University of Wisconsin Press).
McNall, S., and S.A. McNall. 1992. *Sociology* (Prentice Hall: Englewood Cliffs, New Jersey).
McNall, S., and S. A. McNall. 1983. *Plains Families: Exploring Sociology through Social History* (New York: St. Martin's Press).
Mill, John Stuart. 1848. *Principles of Political Economy, with some their applications to Social Philosophy* (London: John W. Parker).
Miller, Edythe S. 1994. "Economic Regulation and Social Contract" *Journal of Economic Issues* 28 (September):799-818.
Miller, Edythe S. 1993a. "Some Market Structure and Regulatory Implications of the Brave New World of Telecommunications," *Journal of Economic Issues* 27, (March):19-39.
Miller, Edythe S. 1993b. "A Consideration of Contracting and Competitive Bidding as Alternatives to Direct Economic Regulation in Imperfect Markets" *Utilities Policy* 3 (October):323-332.
Miller, Edythe S. 1992. "The Economics of Progress," *Journal of Economic Issues* 26 (March):115-24.
Miller, Edythe S. 1991. "Of Economic Paradigms, Puzzles, Problems and Policies; or, Is the Economy Too Important to be Entrusted to the Economists?" *Journal of Economic Issues* 25, (December):993-1004.
Miller, Edythe S. 1990. "Book Review," *Journal of Economic Issues* 24 (March):275-278.
Miller, Edythe S. 1989. "Economic Folklore and Social Realities," *Journal of Economic Issues* 23 (June):339-356.
Minsky, Hyman P. 1986. *Stabilizing an Unstable Economy* (New Haven: Yale University Press).
Mirowski, Philip. 1991. "Postmodernism and the Social Theory of Value" *Journal of Post Keynesian Economics* 13 (Summer):565-582.
Mirowski, Phillip. 1989. *More Heat than Light* (New York: Cambridge University Press).
Mirowski, Phillip. 1988a. "The Philosophical Basis for Institutional

Economics," in *Evolutionary Economics: Volume I Foundations of Institutional Thought* edited by Marc Tool (Armonk NY: M.E. Sharpe, Inc) also in *Journal of Economic Issues* 21 (September 1987):1001-38.

Mirowski, Phillip. 1988b. *Against Mechanism: Protecting Economics from Science* (Totowa, NJ: Rowman and Littlefield).

Misselden, Edward. 1971 [1623] *The Circle of Commerce* (New York: Augustus M. Kelley).

Moen, P. and A.L. Schorr. 1987. "Families and Social Policy," in *Handbook of Marriage and the Family* edited by M.B. Sussman and S.K. Steinmetz (New York: Plenum Press).

Morse, Chandler, ed. 1958. *Fact and Theory in Economics: The Testament of an Institutionalist, Collected Papers of Morris A. Copeland* (Ithaca: Cornell University Press).

Mufson, Steven. 1990. "Missing the Broad Side of the Barn," *Washington Post Weekly Edition* (May 28-June 3):13.

Munkirs, John R. 1988. "The Dichotomy: Views of a Fifth Generation Institutionalist," *Journal of Economic Issues* 22 (December):1035-1044.

Murphy, John P. 1990. *Pragmatism: From Peirce to Davidson* (Boulder, Colo.: Westview Press).

Myers, Francis M. 1956. *The Warfare of Democratic Ideals* (Yellow Springs, Ohio: The Antioch Press).

Myrdal, Gunnar. 1944. *An American Dilemma* (New York: Harper and Brothers).

National Telecommunications and Information Administration. 1993. *The National Information Infrastructure: Agenda for Action* (Washington, DC: NTIA).

Neale, Walter C. 1990. "Absolute Cultural Relativism: Firm Foundation for Valuing and Policy," *Journal of Economic Issues* 24, (June):333-44.

Neale, Walter C. 1982. "Language and Economics," *Journal of Economic Issues* 16 (June):355-369.

Nell, Edward. 1981. "Value and Capital in Marxian Economics" in *The Crisis in Economic Theory* edited by Daniel Bell and Irving Kristol (New York: Basic Books).

Nelson, Julie. 1992. "Gender and Metaphor, and the Definition of Economics," *Economics and Philosophy* 8 (April):103-125.

Nichols, Alan. 1969. "On Savings and Neo Institutionalism," *Journal of Economic Issues* 3 (September):63-66.

North, Douglass. 1990. *Institutions, Institutional Change and Economic Performance*. (New York: Cambridge University Press).

North, Douglass. 1978. "Structure and Performance: The Task of Economic History," *Journal of Economic Literature* 16 (September):963-78.

Northrup, E.M. 1990. "The Feminization of Poverty: The Demographic

Factor and the Composition of Economic Growth," *Journal of Economic Issues* 24 (March):145-60.

Office of Technology Assessment. 1981. *U.S. Industrial Competitiveness: A Comparison of Steel, Electronics, and Automobiles* (Washington, DC: U.S. Government Printing Office).

Olson, Paulette. 1991. "Reconceptualizing Gender: Insights from the Margins," in *The Economic Status of Women Under Capitalism* (Aldershot: Edward Elgar Publishing, Ltd).

Ostrom, Elinor, Larry Schroeder, and Susan Wynne. 1993. *Institutional Incentives and Sustainable Development: Infrastructure Policies in Perspective* (Boulder: Westview Press).

Parsons, T., and R.F. Bales. 1955. *Family Socialization and Interaction Process* (New York: The Free Press).

Peirce, Charles S. 1958a [1877]. "The Fixation of Belief," in *Values in a Universe of Change: Selected Writings of Charles S. Peirce* edited by Philip P. Weiner. (New York: Doubleday & Company, Inc.).

Peirce, Charles S. 1958b. "How to Make Our Ideas Clear," *Values in a Universe of Chance: Selected Writings of Charles S. Peirce.* Philip P. Wiener editor, Stanford: Stanford University Press.

Perlman, Selig. 1952. "Perlman on Commons," in *The Development of Economic Thought* edited by Henry W. Spiegel (New York: Wiley).

Petersen, C.D. and H.E. Felder. 1992. "Disparate Treatment of Needy Children Across the Federal and State Income Support Programs: Or, Should Deadbeat Dads Be Dead," presented to the Association for Institutional Thought, Denver, CO, April.

Peterson, Janice. 1992. "Women and the State," In Dugger and Waller 1992.

Peterson, Janice. 1987. "The Feminization of Poverty," *Journal of Economic Issues* 21 (March):329-37.

Peterson, J.L. and C.D. Petersen. 1993. "Social Welfare Ideology and the Instituting of Inequality Among Women and Children," presented to the Association for Social Economics, Anaheim, Ca, January.

Peterson, Wallace C. 1994. *Silent Depression* (New York: W.W. Norton).

Peterson, Wallace C. 1991. "The Silent Depression," *Challenge* (July-August): 29-34.

Petr, Jerry. 1984. "Fundamentals of an Institutionalist Perspective on Economic Policy," in *An Institutionalist Guide to Economics and Public Policy* edited by Marc R. Tool (Armonk, N.Y.: M. E. Sharpe).

Petr, Jerry L. 1983. "Creationism versus Evolutionism in Economics: Societal Consequences of Economic Doctrine," *Journal of Economic Issues* 17 (June):475-83.

Piore, Michael J. 1982a. "Can the American Labor Movement Survive Re-Gomperization?" *Proceedings of the Thirty-Fifth Annual [Industrial*

*Relations Research Association] Meeting* (December):30-45.
Piore, Michael J. 1982b. "American Labor and the Industrial Crisis," *Challenge* 35 (March-April):5-11.
Piore, Michael J. and Charles F. Sabel. 1984. *The Second Industrial Divide* (New York: Basic Books).
Polanyi, Karl. 1957 [1944]. *The Great Transformation: The Political and Economic Origins of Our Time* (Boston: Beacon Press).
President's Commission on Industrial Competitiveness. 1985. *Global Competition: The New Reality, Volume I* (Washington, DC: U.S. Government Printing Office).
Radzicki, Michael J. 1990. "Institutional Dynamics, Deterministic Chaos, and Self-Organizing Systems," *Journal of Economic Issues* 24 (March):57-102.
Ramstad, Yngve. 1989. "'Reasonable Value' Versus'Instrumental Value': Competing Paradigms in Institutional Economics," *Journal of Economic Issues* 23 (September):761-77.
Ramstad, Yngve. 1986. "A Pragmatist's Quest for Holistic Knowledge: The Scientific Methodology of John R. Commons," *Journal of Economic Issues* 20 (December):1067-1106.
Ramstad, Yngve. 1985. "Comments on Adams and Brock Paper," *Journal of Economic Issues* 19 (June):507-511.
Randall, John Herman, Jr. 1926. *The Making of the Modern Mind* (Boston: Houghton Mifflin).
Ranson, Baldwin. 1991a. "Warren Samuels: The Absolute Relativist," *Journal of Economic Issues* 25 (September):842-46.
Ranson, Baldwin. 1991b. "A Relativist is an Agnostic Who Can't Understand Continuity: A Comment on Neale," *Journal of Economic Issues* 25 (December):1141-47.
Ranson, Baldwin. 1981. "John Fagg Foster," *Journal of Economic Issues* 15 (December):853-56.
Ranson, Baldwin. 1980. "Review of *The Discretionary Economy,*" *Journal of Economic Issues* 14 (September):764.
Rasmussen, Charles T., and Rick Tilman. 1991. "Mechanistic Physiology, and Institutional Economics: Jacques Loeb and Thorstein Veblen," A Paper Presented at the Western Social Science Associtien Conference, April 25-27, Reno, Nevada.
Reich, Robert A. 1983. *The Next American Frontier* (New York: Times Books).
Renteln, Alison Dundes. 1988. "Relativism and the Search for Human Rights," *American Anthropologist* 90 (March):56-72.
Riesman, David. 1953. *Thorstein Veblen: A Critical Interpretation* (New York: Charles Scribner's Sons).
Robertson, Linda. 1993. "Social Circles: Being a Report on J. Hillis Miller's

Campus Visitiation," in *The Intimate Critique: Autobiographical Literary Criticism* edited by Deane P. Freedman, Oliver Frey, and Francis Murphy Zauhrr (Durham, N.C.: Duke University Press).

Rorty, Richard. 1990. "Pragmatism as Anti-Representationalism," in *Pragmatism: From Peirce to Davidson*, edited by John P. Murphy (Boulder, Colo.: Westview Press).

Rorty, Richard. 1982. *Consequences of Pragmatism* (Minneapolis: University of Minnesota Press).

Rorty, Richard. 1979. *Philosophy and the Mirror of Nature* (Princeton: Princeton University Press).

Rosenau, Pauline Marie. 1992. *Post-Modernism and the Social Sciences: Insights, Inroads, and Intrusions* (Princeton: Princeton University Press).

Rosenthal, Michael. 1992. "What Was Postmodernism?" *Socialist Review* 22 (July):83-106.

Rosenthal, Pam. 1991. "Jacked In: Fordism, Cyberpunk, Marxism" *Socialist Review* 21 (January):79-103.

Ross, Robert, and Kent Trachte. 1990. *Global Capitalism: The New Leviathan* (Albany, N.Y.: State University of New York Press).

Rowen, Hobart. 1992. "Regaining the Competitive Edge," *The Washington Post* (March 5).

Ruccio, David F. 1991. "Postmodernism and Economics" *Journal of Post Keynesian Economics* 13 (Summer):495-510.

Rutherford, Malcolm. 1992. "Veblen and the Problem of the Engineers," *International Review of Sociology*, New Series No. 3:182-204.

Samuels, Warren J. 1993a. "In (Limited but Affirmative) Defence of Nihilism," *Review of Political Economy* 5 (April):236-44.

Samuels, Warren J. 1993b. "Instrumental Valuation" (manuscript).

Samuels, Warren J. 1991a. "'Truth' and 'Discourse' in the Social Construction of Economic Reality: An Essay on the Relation of Knowledge to Socioeconomic Policy," *Journal of Post-Keynsian Economics* 13 (Summer):511-24.

Samuels, Warren J. 1991b. "Veblen and Self-Referentiability: Reply to Baldwin Ranson," *Journal of Economic Issues* 25 (September):847-50.

Samuels, Warren J. 1990a. "The Self-Referentiability of Thorstein Veblen's Theory of the Preconception of Economic Science," *Journal of Economic Issues* 24 (September):695-718.

Samuels, Warren J., editor. 1990b. *Economics as Discourse* (Boston: Kluwer Academic Publishers).

Schmid, A. Allan. 1987. *Property, Power and Public Choice: An Inquiry Into Law and Economics* (New York: Praeger Publishers).

Schor, J.B. 1991. *The Overworked American: The Unexpected Decline of Leisure* (New York: Basic Books).

Schorr, A.L. 1962. "A Family Policy in the United States," *International Social Science Journal* 14:452-467.

Schultze, Charles L. 1983. "Industrial Policy: A Dissent," *The Brookings Review* (Fall):3-12.

Screpanti, Ernesto, and Geoffrey M. Hodgson, eds. 1991. *Rethinking Economics* (Aldershot: Edward Elgar).

Sebberson, David. 1990. "The Rhetoric of Inquriy or The Sophistry of the Status Quo? Exploring the Common Ground Between Critical Rhetoric and Institutional Economics," *Journal of Economic Issues* 24 (December):1017-1026.

Seligman, Ben B. 1962. *Main Currents in Modern Economics* (Glencoe: The Free Press).

Seung, T. K. 1982. *Structuralism and Hermeneutics* (New York: Columbia University Press).

Sheehan, Michael F. and Rick Tilman. 1992. "A Clarification of the Concept of 'Instrumental Valuation' in Institutional Economics," *Journal of Economic Issues* 26 (March):197-208.

Shepherd, W.G. 1984. "Contestability vs. Competition," *American Economic Review* 74 (September):572-587.

Silverman, Hugh J., and Donn Welton, ed. 1988. *Postmodernism and Continental Philosophy* (Albany: State University of New York Press).

Simon, Herbert A. 1991. "Organizations and Markets," *Journal of Economic Perspectives* 5 (Spring):25-44.

Smith, Adam. 1976 [1776]. *An Inquiry into the Nature and Causes of the Wealth of Nations* Edited by R.H Campbell and A.S. Skinner (Oxford: Clarendon Press).

Soper, Kate. 1991. "Postmodernism, Subjectivity and the Question of Value" *New Left Review* no.186 (March):120-128.

Stanfield, J. B. 1992a. "Family Policy in America: A Continuing Controversy," *Review of Social Economy* 50 (December):420-31.

Stanfield, J. B. 1985. "Research on Wife/Mother Role Strain in Dual-career Families," *American Journal of Economics and Sociology* 44 (3):355-63.

Stanfield, J. Ron. 1992. "Economy and Society at the Close of the American Century," *Review of Social Economy.* 50 (December):366-73.

Stanfield, J. Ron. 1986. *The Economic Thought of Karl Polanyi* (London: Macmillan Press and New York: St. Martin's Press).

Stanfield, J. Ron. 1984. "Social Reform and Economic Policy," *Journal of Economic Issues* 18 (March):19-44.

Stanfield, J. Ron. 1983. "The Institutional Crisis of the Corporate-Welfare State," *International Journal of Social Economics* 10 (6-7):45-66.

Stanfield, J. Ron. 1979a. *Economic Thought and Social Change* (Carbondale, IL: Southern Illinois University Press).

Stanfield, J. Ron. 1979b. "Phenomena and Epiphenomena in Economics," *Journal of Economic Issues* 18 (December):885-898.

Stanfield, J. Ron, and J. B. Stanfield. 1980. "Consumption in Contemporary Capitalism: The Backward Art of Living," *Journal of Economic Issues* 14 (June):437-450.

Stark, Werner. 1994. *History and Historians of Political Economy* edited by Charles M. A. Clark (New Brunswick, N.J.: Transaction Publishers).

Stark, Werner. 1991 [1958]. *The Sociology of Knowledge* (New Brunswick, N.J.: Transaction Publishers).

Stark, Werner. 1976 [1943]. *The Ideal Foundations of Economic Thought* (Fairfield, N.J.: Augustus M. Kelley).

Steiner, G. 1981. *The Futility of Family Policy* (The Brookings Institution: Washington, D.C.).

Steiner, George. 1989. *Real Presences* (Chicago: University of Chicago Press).

Stigler, George J. 1984. "Economics—The Imperial Science?" *Scandanavian Journal of Economics* 86 (3):301-313.

Stockman, David A. 1987. *The Triumph of Politics* (New York: Avon Books).

Sturgeon, James I. 1992. "Nature, Hammers, and Picasso," *Journal of Economic Issues* 26 (June):351-64.

Sturgeon, James I. 1986. "In Memoriam: W. Nelson Peach," *The Review of Institutional Thought* 3 (December):9-12.

Sturgeon, James I. 1981. "The History of the Association for Institutional Thought," *The Review of Institutional Thought* 1 (December):40-53.

Swaney, James A. 1989. "Our Obsolete Technology Mentality," *Journal of Economic Issues* 23 (June):569-78.

Thompson, Carey C., ed. 1967. *Institutional Adjustment* (Austin: University of Texas Press).

Thurow, Lester C. 1992. *Head to Head* (New York: Morrow).

Thurow, Lester C. 1985. *The Zero-Sum Solution* (New York: Simon and Schuster).

Tilman, Rick. 1992. *Thorstein Veblen and His Critics, 1891-1963: Conservative, Liberal and Radical Perspectives* (Princeton, N.J. Princeton University Press).

Tilman, Rick. 1990a. "Darwinism and Institutional Economics: Recent Criticism of Veblen and Ayres," *Journal of Economic Issues* 24 (March):263-69.

Tilman, Rick. 1990b. "New Light on John Dewey, Clarence Ayres, and the Development of Evolutionary Economics," *Journal of Economic Issues* (December):963-79.

Tilman, Rick. 1987a. "Some Recent Interpretations of Thorstein Veblen's

Theory of Institutional Change," *Journal of Economic Issues* 21 (June):683-90

Tilman, Rick. 1987b. "The Neoinstrumental Theory of Democracy," *Journal of Economic Issues* 21 (September):1379-1401.

Tilman, Rick. 1973. "Thorstein Veblen: Incrementalist or Utopian," *American Journal of Economics and Sociology* 32 (April):155-170.

Tilman, Rick. 1972. "Veblen's Ideal Political Economy and Its Critics," *American Journal of Economics and Sociology* 31 (July):307-317.

Tool, Marc R. 1995. *Pricing, Valuation, and Systems: Essays in Neoinstitutional Economics* (Aldershot: Edward Elgar).

Tool, Marc R. 1993a. "The Theory of Instrumental Value: Extensions and Clarifications," in Tool, ed. *Institutional Economics: Theory, Method, Policy* (Boston: Kluwer Academic Publishers).

Tool, Marc R., ed. 1993b. *Institutional Economics: Theory, Method, Policy* Boston: Kluwer Academic Publishers).

Tool, Marc R. 1993c. "Pricing and Valuation," Presidential Address, Association for Evolutionary Economics.

Tool, Marc R. 1992. "Marc R. Tool, 1921-," in *The Biographical Dictionary of Dissenting Economists* edited by Philip Arestis and Malcolm C. Sawyer (Aldershot: Edward Elgar).

Tool, Marc R. 1991. "Contributions to an Institutional Theory of Price Determination," in *Rethinking Economics* edited by Ernesto Screpanti and Geoffrey M. Hodgson (Aldershot: Edward Elgar).

Tool, Marc R. 1990a. "Instrumental Value an Eternal Verity? A Reply to Wendell Gordon," *Journal of Economic Issues* 24 (December):1109-1122.

Tool, Marc R. 1990b. "Culture Versus Social Value? A Response to Mayhew," *Journal of Economic Issues* 24 (December):1122-33.

Tool, Marc R. 1990c. "Social Value Theory and Regulation," *Journal of Economic Issues* 24 (June):535-544.

Tool, Marc R. 1989. "An Institutionalist Legacy," *Journal of Economic Issues* 23 (June):327-36.

Tool, Marc R. 1988a. "Editor's Report on European-North American Workshop on Institutional Economics, The Mansion House at Grim's Dyke (London), 26-29 June 1988," *Journal of Economic Issues* 22 (December):1035-1252.

Tool, Marc R., ed. 1988b. *Evolutionary Economics* (Armonk, N.Y.: M. E. Sharpe).

Tool, Marc R. 1986. *Essays in Social Value Theory: A Neoinstitutionalist Contribution* (Armonk, New York: M.E. Sharpe).

Tool, Marc R., ed. 1984. *An Institutionalist Guide to Economics and Public Policy* (Armonk, N.Y.: M. E. Sharpe).

Tool, Marc R. 1983. "Equational Justice and Social Value," *Journal of*

*Economic Issues*, 17(June):335-344.

Tool, Marc R. 1982. "The Veblen-Commons Awards: J. Fagg Foster," *Journal of Economic Issues* 16 (June):351-352.

Tool, Marc R. 1981a. "The Compulsive Shift to Institutional Analysis," *Journal of Economic Issues* 15 (September):569-92.

Tool, Marc R. 1981b. "The Compulsive Shift to Institutional Analysis," *The Review of Institutional Thought* 1 (December):17-39.

Tool, Marc R. 1981c. "In Memoriam—John C. Livingston," *Review of Institutional Thought* 1 (December):6.

Tool, Marc R. 1980a. "Economics, Politics, and Social Change: A Neoinstitutionalist Perspective," *The Forum* (North Texas State University, Spring).

Tool, Marc R. 1980b. "The Social Value Theory of Orthodoxy: Review and Critique," *Journal of Economic Issues* 14 (June):309-26.

Tool, Marc R. 1979. *The Discretionary Economy: A Normative Theory of Political Economy* (Santa Monica, Calif: Goodyear Publishing Company, Inc.).

Tool, Marc R. 1978. "Constructs of Value, Freedom, and Equality in Institutional Economics," *Social Science Journal* (January):27-38.

Tool, Marc R. 1977. "A Social Value Theory in Neoinstitutional Economics," *Journal of Economic Issues* 11 (December):823-846; reprinted in Tool (1986).

Tool, Marc R. 1966. *The California State Colleges Under the Master Plan* (San Diego: Aztec Press).

Tool, Marc R. 1953. "The Philosophy of Neo-Institutionalism: Veblen, Dewey, and Ayres" (PhD. diss., Boulder: University of Colorado).

Tool, Marc R., and Warren Samuels, eds. 1989a. *The Methodology of Economic Thought*, 2nd ed., rev., (New Brunswick: Transactions Publishers).

Tool, Marc R., and Warren Samuels, eds. 1989b. *The Economy as a System of Power*, 2nd ed., rev., (New Brunswick: Transactions Publishers).

Tool, Marc R., and Warren Samuels, eds. 1989c. *State, Society, and Corporate Power*, 2nd ed., rev., (New Brunswick: Transactions Publishers).

Trebing, Harry M. 1989. "Telecommunications Regulation—The Continuing Dilemma," in *Public Utility Regulation* edited by K. Nowotny, D. Smith, and H. Trebing (Boston: Kluwer Academic Publishers).

Trebing, Harry M. 1986. "Apologetics of Deregulation in Energy and Telecommunications: An Institutionalist Assessment," *Journal of Economic Issues* 20 (September):613-32.

Turner, C.A. 1994. *Utility Reports* (Moorestown, NJ).

U.S. Bureau of the Census. 1989. Current Population Reports,

Series P-60, No. 165, *Earnings of Married Couple Families: 1987* (Washington, D.C.: U. S. Government Printing Office).
*USA Today*. 1987. "The Family Changes Shape," April 13.
Veblen, Thorstein. 1995 [1904]. *The Theory of Business Enterprise* (New York: Augustus Kelley).
Veblen, Thorstein. 1991 [1919]. *The Place of Science in Modern Civilization and Other Essays* (New Brunswick: Transaction Publishers).
Veblen, Thorstein. 1975 [1899]. *The Theory of the Leisure Class* (New York: Augustus M. Kelley).
Veblen, Thorstein. 1967 [1923]. *Absentee Ownership* (Boston: Beacon Press).
Veblen, Thorstein. 1964a. *The Vested Interests and the Common Man* (New York: Augustus M. Kelley).
Veblen, Thorstein. 1964b. *An Inquiry into the Nature of Peace* (New York: Augustus M. Kelley).
Veblen, Thorstein. 1963. *The Engineers and the Price System* (New York: Harcourt, Brace and World).
Veblen, Thorstein. 1941 [1914]. *The Instinct of Workmanship and the State of the Industrial Arts* (New York: W.W. Norton & Company, Inc.).
Veblen, Thorstein. 1930. "Christian Morals and the Competitive System" in *Essays in Our Changing Order* (New York: Viking Press).
Veblen, Thorstein. 1898. "Why is Economics Not An Evolutionary Science?" In Veblen 1991.
Veblen, Thorstein. 1892. "Some Neglected Points in the Theory of Socialism," *Annals of the American Academy of Political and Social Science* 2:387-408.
Virginia State Corporation Commission. 1994. *The InterLATA Market in Virginia, 4th Quarter, 1993.* Division of Economics and Finance Report.
Wachterhauser, Brice R., ed. 1986. *Hermeneutics and Modern Philosophy* (Albany: State University of New York Press).
Wall Street Journal. 1994. "Telecom Showdown: Battle Lines Harden as Baby Bells Fight to Kill Restrictions," L. Cauley, J. Keller, D. Kneale. July 22, 1994, Sec. A:1.
Waller, William T. 1990. "Avoiding the Cartesian Vice in Radical Institutionalism: A Reply to Mayhew," *Journal of Economic Issues* 24 (September):897-901.
Waller, William T. 1988. "Radical Institutionalism: Methodological Aspects of the Radical Tradition," *Journal of Economic Issues*, 22 (September):667-674.
Waller, William T. 1982. "The Evolution of the Veblenian Dichotomy: Veblen, Hamilton, Ayres, and Foster," 16 *Journal of Economic Issues* (September):757-72.
Waller, William T. and Ann Jennings. 1991. "A Feminist Institutionalist Reconsideration of Karl Polanyi," *Journal of Economic Issues*, 25

(June):485-497.

Waller, William T. and Ann Jennings. 1990. "On the Possibility of a Feminist Economics: The Convergence of Institutional and Feminist Methodology," *Journal of Economic Issues*, 24 (June):613-622.

Waller, William, and Linda R. Robertson. 1993. "A Comment on Marc Tool's 'The Theory of Instrumental Value: Extensions, Clarifications.'" In *Institutional Economics: Theory, Method, Policy* edited by Marc R. Tool (Boston: Kluwer Academic Publishers).

Waller, William T. and Linda R. Robertson. 1991. "Valuation as Discourse and Process: Or, How We Got Out of a Methodological Quagmire On Our Way to Purposeful Institutional Analysis," *Journal of Economic Issues* 25 (December):1029-48.

Waller, William T. and Linda Robertson. 1990. "Why Johnny (Ph.D., Economics) Can't Read" *Journal of Economic Issues* 24 (December):1027-1044.

Walras, Léon. 1954. *Elements of Pure Economics* (New York: Augustus M. Kelley).

Walras, Léon. 1909. "Économiques et Mécanique" *Bullentin De La Societe Vaudoise Des Sciences Naturalles* 45:313-25.

Walras, Léon. 1860. "Philosophie des Sciences Économiques," *Journal Des Economistes*:196-206.

Waring, M. 1990. *If Women Counted* (New York: Harper Collins).

Warsh, David. 1993. "Economic Principals: What has eight schools and nine opinions?" *The Boston Sunday Globe*, 15 August, Business Section.

Wasden, C.D. 1993. *A descriptive compendium of the international activities of major US-based utility holding companies* (Columbus: Ohio State University/National Regulatory Research Institute).

Weinel, Ivan, and Philip D. Crossland. 1989. "The Scientific Foundations of Technological Progress," *Journal of Economic Issues* 23 (September):795-808.

West, Cornel. 1988. "Interview with Cornel West," In *Universal Abandon: The Politics of Postmodernism*, edited by Andrew Ross (Minneapolis: University of Minnesota Press).

Whalen, Charles J. 1993a. "Institutional Labor Economics: Reports of Its Death are Greatly Exaggerated," presented at the *Western Social Science Association* Annual Meeting, 1993.

Whalen, Charles J. 1993b. "Taking the First Step: Confronting Structural Economic Change," presented at the *Allied Social Science Associations* Annual Meeting, 1993.

Whalen, Charles J. 1992. "Schools of Thought and Theories of the State," in Dugger and William Waller 1992.

Wheatley-Mann, K. 1986. "Engels and Veblen on the Oppression of

Women," M.A. Technical Paper. Colorado State University.

Wibble, James R. 1984. "The Instrumentalisms of Dewey and Friedman," *Journal of Economic Issues* 18 (December):1049-70.

Wilber, Charles K. and Robert S. Harrison. 1978. "The Methodological Basis of Institutional Economics: Pattern Model, Storytelling and Holism," *Journal of Economic Issues* 12, (March):61-89.

Williamson Oliver E. 1985. *The Economic Institutions of Capitalism: Firms, Markets, Relational Contracting* (New York: The Free Press).

Wisman, Jon D., and Joseph Rozansky. 1991. "The Methodology of Institutionalism Revisited," *Journal of Economic Issues* 25 (September):709-37.

Wittgenstein, Ludwig. 1965. *Philosophical Investigations* (New York: Macmillan).

Wolfson, Martin. 1990. "The Causes of Financial Instability," *Journal of Post Keynesian Economics* 12 (Spring):333-355.

Wootton, Barbara. 1950. *Testament for Social Science: An Essay in the Application of Scientific Method to Human Problems* (London: George Allen and Unwin, Ltd).

World Bank Discussion Papers. 1993. *Telecommunications World Bank Experience and Strategy*, No. 192. (Washington D.C.: World Bank).

Yorburg, B. 1983. *Families and Societies: Survival or Extinction* (New York: Columbia University Press).

Zimmerman, S. 1988. *Understanding Family Policy: Theoretical Approaches* (Newbury Park, California: Sage Publications, Inc).

# About the Authors

**Glen Atkinson** earned his Ph.D. in economics at the University of Oklahoma and is currently Professor of Economics at the University of Nevada. His work has been published in the *Journal of Economic Issues*, *The American Journal of Economics and Sociology*, *Inter-American Economic Affairs* and *The Social Science Journal*. Currently his teaching and research is directed to intergovernmental fiscal relations and the economics of integration and common markets. He is engaged as a consultant with several government jurisdictions regarding intergovernmental fiscal issues.

**Doug Brown** is Associate Professor of Economics at Northern Arizona University where he has been teaching since 1985. His research and publication areas are primarily in the fields of political economy and comparative economic systems, and he has most recently co-edited a volume with Janice Peterson entitled *The Economic Status of Women Under Capitalism: Institutional Economics and Feminist Theory* (London: Edward Elgar, 1994). Other publications include: *Towards A Radical Democracy* (London: Unwin Hyman, 1988) and articles in the *Journal of Economic Issues* and the *Review of Social Economy*. His current research areas concern postmodernism, globalization of capitalism, and the problem of global sustainability.

**Paul D. Bush** is Professor of Economics at California State University, Fresno. He is a past president of the Association For Evolutionary Economics and a former member of the Editorial Board of the *Journal of Economic Issues*. A founding member and past president of the Association For Institutionalist Thought, he served as the editor of its journal, the *Review of Institutional Thought*. He is also a founding member of the European Association for Evolutionary Political Economy. His publications in institutional economics have focused on institutionalist methodology and the theory of institutional change.

**Charles M. A. Clark** is Associate Professor of Economics at St. John's University, New York and recently held the position of Visiting Professor of Economics at University College Cork, Cork, Ireland. His publications include: *Economic Theory and Natural Philosophy* (1992) and *History and Historians of Political Economy* (editor) (1994) and articles in the *Journal of Economic Issues*, *Journal of Post Keynesian Economics*, and *History of Economic Ideas*. He is a member of the Board of Directors for the Association For Evolutionary Economics and the Editorial Board for the *Journal of Economic Issues*, as well as being the Book Review Editor (English Language) for the *History of Economic Ideas*. His current research interest include: income distribution and basic income.

**William M. Dugger** is Professor of Economics at the University of Tulsa. His publications include: *Alternative to Economic Retrenchment; Corporate Hegemony; Underground Economics; Radical Institutionalism* (editor); and *The Stratified State* (co-editor). He has published widely in scholarly journals and has served as President of the Association for Social Economics and as President of the Association for Institutional Thought.

**Gladys Parker Foster** received her Ph. D. in Economics from the University of Colorado at Boulder (at the age of sixty-four) where she is currently Adjunct Professor of Economics. She attended the University of Texas at Austin, The University of Paris and the University of Denver. She is a member of the Board of Directors of the Association for Evolutionary Economics, the Association for Institutionalist Thought, and the Gray Panthers of Denver, as well as the Advisory Board of the Institute for Women's Studies and Services at Metropolitan State College of Denver. In 1990 she was awarded an honorary Doctorate of Public Service from Metropolitan State College of Denver.

**Lewis Hill** earned his B.A., M.A. and Ph.D. degrees from the University of Texas at Austin. He has served as President of the Association for Social Economics, and he was awarded the Ludwig Mai Service award from that association. He is currently serving as Professor and Chair of the Department of Economics at Texas Tech University, Lubbock, Texas.

**Philip A. Klein** is Professor of Economics at Pennsylvania State University. He is author of *The Management of Market-Oriented Economies* (1973) and *Essays in Institutional Economics* (1994); co-author of *Monitoring Growth Cycles in Market-Oriented Economies* (1985); and editor of *Analyzing Modern Business Cycles* (1990) and *The Role of Economic Theory* (forthcoming). He is widely published in journals on business cycle, public sector, and institutional economics. He is the recipient of three Fulbright Fellowships and was consultant to the United Nations, European Economic Community, and World Bank. He is past-president of the Association for Evolutionary Economics and the recipient of its Veblen-Common Award in 1991.

**Edythe S. Miller** is an unaffiliated economist. Past associations include service as commissioner and chairwoman of the Colorado Public Utilities Commission, and professor and chairwoman of the economics department at Metropolitan State College in Denver. She has been president or chairwoman of the Association for Evolutionary Economics, the Transportation and Public Utilities Group of the American Economic Association, and the Board of the National Regulatory Utility Commissioners. She is a frequent contributor to and has served on the board of editors of the Journal of Economic Issues. Her research centers on topics in institutional theory and methodology and regulatory and public utility economics.

**Warren J. Samuels** is Professor of Economics at Michigan State University, specializing in the history of economic thought, law and economics, and methodology. He is the author of *The Classical Theory of Economic Policy* and *Pareto on Policy* and co-editor of *Research in the History of Economic Thought and Methodology* and *The Elgar Companion to Institutional and Evolutionary Economics*. He is a recipient of the Veblen-Commons award. His principle current research is on the use of the concept of the invisible hand in economics.

**Jacqueline B. Stanfield** is Associate Professor and Chair of Sociology at the University of Northern Colorado. She has published several contributions on family and gender relations including "Radical Institutionalism, Sociology, and the Dual Career Family" in *The Economic Status of Women Under Capitalism* edited by Doug Brown and Janice Peterson. She is presently continuing her research on the social economics of gender and family relations.

**J. R. Stanfield** is Professor o Economics at Colorado State University. He is a past president of the Association for Social Economics and the president-designee of the Association for Institutionalist Thought. He is the author of *The Economic Surplus and Neo-Marxism, Economic Thought and Social Change, The Economic Thought of Karl Polanyi*, and *Economics, Power, and Culture: Essays in the Development of Radical Institutionalism*. He is presently writing an intellectual portrait of J.K Galbraith and continuing research on reciprocity and gender and family relations in late capitalist society.

**Rick Tilman** is Chairman of the Department of Public Administration at the University of Nevada, Las Vegas. He works in the areas of political economy, modern social theory, and American intellectual history. He is the author of *C.*

*Wright Mills* and *Thorstein Veblen and His Critics, 1891-1963* and is writing a trilogy on Veblen. Currently, he is the Director of the International Thorstein Veblen Association.

**Roger Traub** is Professor of Economics at Texas Tech University. Pursues a long-term research program focusing on socio-economic system change particularly with regard to global economic development and international economic relations. He has produced over 80 papers and publications (including ones in the *Journal of Economic Issues*) which deal in one fashion or another with that program.

**Harry Trebing** is Professor of Economics, Emeritus, and former Director, Institute of Public Utilities, Michigan State University. Past positions include Chief Economist, U.S. Postal Rate Commission and Chief, Economic Studies Division, Federal Communications Commission. He is a past president of the Association For Evolutionary Economics and a recipient of the Veblen-Commons award. He has served on various advisory panels for Congressional Office of Technology Assessment; the Comptroller General's Panel on Regulatory Accounting and the National Research Council Panel on Statistics on Natural Gas. He is the author and editor of numerous articles and books dealing with public utility regulation.

**William Waller** is Professor of Economics at Hobart and William Smith Colleges, Geneva, New York. His research has focused on economic methodology, critical rhetoric and economics, and institutional economic theory. His work in these areas appears frequently in the *Journal of Economic Issues* and in numerous recent volumes on institutional and heterodox economics. He is co-editor of *Alternatives to Economic Orthodoxy* (1987) and *The Stratified State* (1992).

**Charles J. Whalen** is Resident Scholar, The Jerome Levy Economics Institute of Bard College. He has served on the faculty of both Cornell University and Hobart and William Smith Colleges, and his contributions to institutional economics have appeared in a number of academic journals and research volumes. He is editor of *Political Economy for the Next Century* (M.E. Sharpe, forthcoming).

# Author Index

# Subject Index